FOR EXECUTIVES ONLY

An Anthology of the
Best Management
Thought

DARTNELL

Chicago and London

---PERMISSIONS---

The following acknowledgements are made:

Chapter 1, "What Is Management," from *Freedom's Faith*, copyright 1953 by Clarence B. Randall, and *A Creed for Free Enterprise*, copyright 1952 by Clarence B. Randall, by permission of Atlantic-Little, Brown and Company.

Chapter 7, "Resistance to Change," by William B. Given, Jr., from *How to Manage People*, copyright 1967 by Prentice-Hall, Inc., Englewood Cliffs, N. J.

Chapter 9, "Creative Thinking," reprinted with the permission of Charles Scribner's Sons from Chapters 1, 2, 10, and 21 of *Applied Imagination*, revised edition, by Alex F. Osborn. Copyright 1953 and 1957 by Charles Scribner's Sons.

Chapter 10, "Chain of Command," by Burleigh B. Gardner and David G. Moore, from *Human Relations in Industry*, copyright 1945, 1950, 1955, and 1964 by Richard D. Irwin, Inc. Used by permission.

FOREWORD

The awesome responsibilities of a chief executive probably can be understood thoroughly only by those who now occupy the driver's seat of a modern company or one of its divisions or departments.

Some of the problems and the opportunities facing the top man in any enterprise undoubtedly are partially realized by the men who have lately been on their way up, and now come face to face with the prospect of taking the helm of a company.

It is for this elite group—those who have assumed command or those who are on their way up through the ranks—that these pages of learned counsel and inspiration are devoted. The many faces of leadership are revealed sharply in the more than 30 chapters of *For Executives Only*, written by men whose knowledge comes from long experience and introspective study of the executive command.

As the business world moves into the closing years of the 20th century, it becomes startlingly clear that the modern business executive needs to know a lot more and to *be* a lot more than his predecessors.

His personal power is no longer so absolute—he must exercise leadership within a constricting aura of powers and countervailing pressures from stockholders, directors, governments, publics, and an executive staff and employees whose collective strengths and professional disciplines are quite different from the generally malleable work force of the past. Also, the increased emphasis on the marketing and sales of products and services requires more skill from the modern executive than the production-oriented business world of the past.

Today's executive must know precisely when a problem requires his personal attention and intervention and when it is best that he turn his back and walk away to let specialists handle it. More and more the chief executive is concerned with creating the environment in which the right things can be done to create profits and generate long-range expansion for the company. Less and less is he concerned with immediate day-to-day routine.

To the typical executive of a hundred or so years ago, people were largely formless, faceless figures who produced, transported, or sold the company's products. People were minor figures—sub-totals on the production tally or the company balance sheet. If there was any humanism in an executive's approach to business, it lay in the generous nature of the man himself.

Today, so complex and interrelated has the business world become, that the study of people is a necessity for any executive whose company is to survive and grow in a briskly competitive climate.

Human relations, public relations, labor relations, customer relations . . . all these have precise meanings and disciplines for the modern business executive. They are no longer mere words, but practical subject areas in which problems must be solved with knowledge.

At the same time, technical progress in all aspects of business continues at bewildering speed. And it is not enough simply to keep on top of the new techniques. The successful executive must know *when* his company is ready for automation, and for what *kind* and to what *degree*. He must know when to change methods, incentives, and policies, and how to select the best for his particular company from a number of alternatives. And he must have the skill to get his people to accept change and innovations.

Needless to say, such demands call for constant self-improvement on the part of the executive himself. He must continually improve his reading, writing, speaking, and discussion skills. The important area of communication is not neglected by the authors of *For Executives Only*.

The contributors to this volume are of two sorts. They have either commanded important business enterprises themselves and led them to great accomplishment, or they have acted as top consultants to major business enterprises. Their names and impressive backgrounds are listed on the next page. Following that are the chapters in which they leave legacies of wisdom for today's executives—wisdom gleaned on the firing line of some of the most exciting episodes in modern business history.

This is a book which the thoughtful executive or potential executive will want to keep on his desk for years to come. There is inspiration and know-how which can help in almost any career crisis. It is recommended not only for rewarding original reading, but also as a constant reference companion.

William Harrison Fetridge
President, THE DARTNELL CORPORATION

CONTRIBUTORS TO
FOR EXECUTIVES ONLY

Stanley Arnold, *president,*
Stanley Arnold & Associates, marketing consultants.

John Cameron Aspley, *chairman emeritus,*
The Dartnell Corporation.

Eugene J. Benge, *management and marketing consultant.*

William T. Brady, *former chairman,*
Corn Products Company.

Ray E. Brown, *director, graduate program in hospital administration,*
Duke University.

Harry A. Bullis, *former chairman,*
General Mills, Inc.

George Champion, *chairman,*
Chase Manhattan Bank.

Raymond Dreyfack, *professional business writer;*
former lecturer, New York University Management Institute.

Peter F. Drucker, *economist and management consultant.*

Walter E. Elliott, *director,*
Walter E. Elliott Associates, management consultants.

William Harrison Fetridge, *president,*
The Dartnell Corporation.

Clarence Francis, *former chairman,*
General Foods Corporation and The Studebaker Corporation.

Bruno Furst, *founder,*
School of Memory and Concentration.

Burleigh B. Gardner, *president,*
Social Research, Inc.

William B. Given, Jr., *former chairman,*
American Brake Shoe Company.

Theodore V. Houser, *former chairman,*
Bell & Howell Company and Sears, Roebuck and Company.

Robert Wood Johnson, *chairman,*
Johnson & Johnson.

Ray Josephs, *public relations consultant.*

Harold J. Leavitt, *professor,*
graduate school of industrial administration, Carnegie Institute
of Technology.

James F. Lincoln, *chairman,*
Lincoln Electric Company.

Douglas McGregor, *professor of industrial management,*
Massachusetts Institute of Technology.

Robert N. McMurry, *psychologist and personnel consultant.*

David G. Moore, *dean,*
New York State School of Industrial and Labor Relations.

Murray Morison, *former educator,*
authority on tension.

Ralph G. Nichols, *chairman,*
department of rhetoric, University of Minnesota.

Alex F. Osborn, *co-founder,*
Batten, Barton, Durstine and Osborn, advertising agency.

James Cash Penney, *founder,*
J. C. Penney Company.

Clarence B. Randall, *former chairman,*
Inland Steel Company.

Robert C. Sampson, *president,*
Sampson Associates, management counselors.

John R. Sargent, *partner,*
Cresap, McCormick and Paget, management consultants.

Ralph C. Smedley, *founder,*
Toastmasters International.

Thomas G. Spates, *professor emeritus,*
Yale University; former vice-president, General Foods Corporation.

Herman W. Steinkraus, *chairman,*
Bridgeport Brass Company.

Howard Stephenson, *public relations consultant;*
educational consultant, United States Air Force.

Leonard A. Stevens, consultant in industrial communications.

E. J. Thomas, *chairman of the board,*
Goodyear Tire & Rubber Company.

E. F. Wells, management training consultant.

Jesse Werner, *president,*
General Aniline and Film Corporation.

Howard Wilson, *executive director,*
Management Conferences.

Hilda Whitener Yoder, *director,*
Yoder Center for Reading Improvement.

CONTENTS

x

CHAPTER 1

WHAT IS MANAGEMENT?

By Clarence B. Randall

A hundred years ago, when the foundations of our way of life in modern industry were being laid, a man began an enterprise and ran it himself. The handy man around horses became a harness maker, and the carpenter began to build wagon boxes. As the business grew, he grew with it. Always it was his money that was being risked. His customers were his neighbors and he saw to it that they paid their bills. If he changed the set of a collar for a horse or lengthened the wagon box, he did it because he knew exactly what the farmers in his village wanted. If they liked his work they told their cousins down the road, and after a while he had to hire a man to help him.

As the years passed he realized he had a good thing, and began to take chances because he hoped to make big money. Eventually, the harness maker went into the leather business, and the wagon maker founded an automobile company.

Such times bred strong men, but the emphasis was on self. The hired man was there in those days, but always in a secondary spot. He did not aspire to the boss's job because he knew that this was reserved for the founder's son, his only resource being to leave and set up his own ship if he became too restive.

The legacies from that generation to ours, and the evolutionary process that lay between, are fairly easy to see.

To the extent that the emphasis on self persevered, it helped to bring about the New Deal and the revulsion against businessmen. The public rebelled when told that the force of self-interest was not governed by self-restraint.

The sense of having a strong personal stake in the enterprise is still found in our country in small business, and that is a vital thing which we must at all costs preserve. To the extent that in big business important decisions are made by men who have little or no personal stake in the outcome, our economy has unfortunately lost some of the toughness and virility that characterized those earlier days.

The hired man had to come into his own, however. Great corporations came into being which no man, however gifted, could direct all by himself. Family considerations gave way to merit as a basis of selection for positions of responsibility. The pace grew hot and the American tradition of equal opportunity fulfilled itself.

*　　*　　*

The secret of free enterprise is that we harness the natural instinct of each man to serve himself, and rely on other natural forces to see that as he serves himself he serves society.

*　　*　　*

Today management is a profession. As such, it is rapidly progressing toward the establishment of standards of conduct comparable to those of the learned professions, such as law, medicine, and the ministry. Although management is selected by the owners, its overriding obligation is to the public; and in preservation of free enterprise in a democracy there might be times when management's first duty would be to stand between the stockholders on the one hand, and the employees or the customers on the other.

So far as I know, those standards have not yet by common consent been reduced to writing. There are no formal canons of ethics for this new profession, but an outline is already discernible.

The practical, first requirement of good management is to make a profit for the enterprise, so that those who made the capital available may be rewarded and thus encouraged to

14

provide more through further saving, and so that the worth and dignity of profit as the source of progress and improvement may be continuously established.

This financial return to the owners must be reasonable and competitive with that of other enterprises, when tested both by the immediate situation and the requirements of the future. Keen, discriminating judgment is needed to determine what proportion of earnings should be utilized in a self-generative way for the expansion and further development of the business, and what distributed for present enjoyment.

To the customers, good management must at all times provide a product or a service that is equal to the best in the market, and superior if possible. The article sold must in every respect be what it purports to be, for integrity knows no substitute. The harness maker's collar must still fit the horse.

To the employees is due remuneration that is fully competitive with that obtainable elsewhere, and an atmosphere of employment which discovers and fosters individual initiative and growth. The wagon maker knew whether his hired man liked his job, because they played in the village band together.

Toward competitors there must be fairness, but aggressive and rugged competition based on deep-seated conviction that such a relationship is essential not only for the welfare of society, but for the progress of the company itself. When a new blacksmith shop was opened in my town when I was a boy, I never heard that the territory was divided up. Each man tried to shoe all the horses he could.

But the highest call to duty for management today lies in the subordination of the interest of self to that of the institution which the man serves, just as the welfare of the company itself is subordinated to the well-being of the community.

The American people today are highly sensitive to abuses of power and neglect of duty wherever found, and the good name of the free enterprise system is occasionally jeopardized by behavior on the part of corporate officers which suggests that they are exploiting rather than leading their companies. Because of the wide diffusion of stock ownership in even the moderate-size institutions, such over-reaching can go far before it is curbed if the governing group does not impose upon itself the rule of reason. When the curb has to be applied by an aroused public, the repercussions damage seriously the system as a whole.

Obligations of Conscience

The lavish use of expense accounts is a sign to watch in testing a man's understanding of his responsibility as a part of management, and such use has not been helped by long years of the subjection of business to heavy taxation. The best of consciences have been dulled by the thought that, after all, the government was paying the major part of the bill.

The rapid and in many cases highly desirable increase in the number of airplanes for executive use has brought temptations for a man who wouldn't think of having his company buy his railroad and Pullman tickets for a duck-hunting trip, but who now so easily slips into the habit of flying up to Minnesota or down to Arkansas. And there are the private dining rooms that approximate the club atmosphere more than the conference table, the elaborate suites of offices, the company hunting and fishing lodges, the yachts for the entertainment of customers, and other perquisites which suggest softness and special privilege.

Oftentimes the criticism made of executive conduct is grossly unfair. The carrying of heavy responsibility in management is physically and emotionally exhausting, in addition to which it can be a very lonely job. Whatever tends to relieve unnecessary strain and improve physical comfort is urgently desirable. It is bad economy to bring a man through a quarter of a century of training, and then when his chance comes have him added to the casualties listed in the next Heart Fund campaign merely because he was not given working conditions suited to his responsibility.

But that does not discharge him from the obligations of conscience.

16

The main source of criticism is executive compensation, and there again a few widely advertised abuses have damaged the good name of our business system. Actually there come many times in the lives of those who bear large management responsibility when the money they receive, expressed in terms of what they have left after paying income taxes, is too small to make them want to go on.

The grief they have to take can't be paid for in money, and they would stop gladly if they did not feel a compelling sense of going on just for the sake of doing the job well, and not being a quitter.

Nevertheless, they create a problem for businessmen everywhere when they cause their companies to pay them and the

*   *   *

In the management of a business the sharp bite of honest, aggressive competition is the automatic corrective that safeguards the public from extortion. No man can be said to be making too much profit if many others are trying to beat him at his own game and none can succeed. The larger his profit, the greater will be the number of those who will try and the greater the chance that they will succeed . . . How could there be a better formula than that for bringing about continuously the maximum of effort by all of the people?

*   *   *

inner executive circle salaries and bonuses that are excessive. I have no rule to suggest to determine what is reasonable and what is not in the matter of executive compensation, having in mind on the one hand the importance of preserving incentive, and on the other an awareness of social responsibility, but there do seem to be two possible guideposts.

The first is comparison with companies in the same industry, regardless of size, to establish a norm on some unit of production, and comparison with companies of similar size in other industries. The second is preserving reasonable intervals between salaries within the company. I am always suspicious when I see in a proxy statement that the top man's compensation far exceeds that of the second and third men. When the chairman takes twice what the president is paid, and the salary of the executive vice-president is far below that of the president, something is wrong.

But there can be no fixed rule; good judgment and a clear conscience are the only ultimate standards.

Because professional-management men are now compelled to rely more upon pensions than savings for security for themselves and their families, a new rigidity has been introduced into corporate administration that is not fully recognized. A quarter of a century ago it was taken for granted that a company which was suddenly deprived of its chief officer by death or resignation before the replacement was ready would hire away the Number two man of a competitor. That seldom happens any more, for the reason that at middle life a man who is participating in a pension plan cannot afford to separate himself from it. There is no way the new employer can give him equivalent protection, since pension payments are a function of years of service, and no increase in pay can offset the loss in security, because the income tax collector takes most of it. We would have more lively competition for talent, and more frequent cross-fertilization of ideas in administration if this inflexibility which our tax laws have brought on could be overcome.

The modern executive has at hand one complete answer to those who criticize his compensation and other emoluments, and that is the amount of stock he himself buys. Little though it may be, if he puts his entire lifetime savings into the enterprise, no stockholder can be bigger, because none can have made a greater proportionate commitment.

When he risks all that he has, he puts the final stamp of integrity on his own conduct.

The Executive's Dilemma

I believe that the most important attribute of management is that of making decisions. The outstanding characteristic of the good executive is his capacity for making up his mind and then translating thought into action. His constant dilemma is how to make choices that reflect wisdom and still make them promptly.

Some very able and conscientious men never make effective executives because their approach to difficult problems is judicial in its quality, rather than dynamic. They concentrate so exclusively on the necessity for doing the best thing, that they do nothing. They lack the sense of urgency which is required in the fast-moving routine of modern administration.

Wise as counselors, they perform an important function in cautioning their impetuous associates against pitfalls that otherwise might have been overlooked, but left to themselves they will never come up affirmatively with a positive program of action. Actually, in most business situations there are half a dozen possible plans proposed, any one of which would work reasonably well, and it is far more important to select one and get on with the job than it is to prolong the debate until the last shred of doubt as to which is the perfect best can be removed.

Then there are some men who fail as executives because making up their minds is torture to them. They have something close to physical fear as the time for that final tough choice approaches, and will twist and turn and accept any temporary expedient that will give them a little more postponement. When they can no longer escape, such men are apt instinctively to hedge the risk of failure by communicating their decision to their subordinates in such equivocal language that they can later claim they were right no matter what the outcome.

Over against these must be set the men who decide too quickly and too easily. There is no self-satisfaction in the world like that of little men when they make breathtaking decisions with the utmost calm. All that their associates can do is to shudder, and go quietly back to their desks, shaking their heads. Happily, by the law of chance, such men are occasionally right.

Little has been written that I know of on the art of deciding, but I should guess there would be consensus on the following points. Each phase of the problem must first be explored so far as time permits. This involves talking with as many others who have knowledge of the problem as one can, to make sure that the various points which bear upon it have been brought out and properly evaluated. You cannot weigh the pro and con without finding out what they are.

After this there must be time for reflection. This is very difficult to obtain amidst the pressure under which we all must live, since so often the man who decides must shoot from the hip. Putting a matter on the back of the stove for a bit when we can does wonders for the ultimate quality of the conclusion. What seem to be insoluble conflicts have a way of arranging themselves into an orderly whole if given an opportunity.

But reflection must not degenerate into weakness or cowardice; it must yield to crispness. When the time is ripe there is no way to decide but to decide.

And once decided, the matter should stay that way. I consider it a sound rule of administration never to reopen a matter once the decision is made, unless it can be shown that the circumstances have changed or that new evidence has been discovered which was not previously taken into account. Nothing slows down action in a company more than the belief that what is decided today may be reversed tomorrow. The prudent fellows then wait and see.

Communicating the decision is as important as making it. Those who are to carry it into effect must not be left in doubt as to what their instructions are, and all who need to know must be told.

A common method for making decisions known is the group conference, and some courageous men who are stalwart in deciding do this part badly. This phase of management requires not only the articulate quality that flows from a clear brain, so that the words convey what the speaker means, but an emotional impact that subtly conveys confidence in the rightness of the conclusion reached.

Such conferences must of course be distinguished from those where the executive is exploring the subject and seeking guidance. There he must listen, and talk no more than is necessary to provoke decision, for it is the flow of ideas toward him that is important.

How to Delegate Authority

Once policy has been established, the executive must look to others for its fulfillment, and his effectiveness lies in the skill with which he directs the activities of others. This requires the establishment of clear lines of authority and responsibility in the echelons below him. The two must go together, for no man should be held accountable unless he has been given power.

This capacity for the delegation of authority and responsibility with just the right touch is a rather rare quality. Many men pride themselves upon possessing it who in fact do it badly.

I know a man who honestly believes that this is one of his strong points, but this is the situation as I have it from one of his associates. On Monday he calls in a subordinate, explains the problem, and tells him to get into it at once; on Tuesday he delegates it to another; on Wednesday he does the job himself and tells neither of the others that he has acted.

I know another executive who delegates all right—he never does anything himself if it can be avoided—but never in accordance with any discernible pattern; it is usually the first man he meets as he walks down the hall to whom he hands the file.

Often a corporate officer delegates eagerly the things he dislikes, no matter how important, and keeps those that interest him, no matter how trivial. If a man likes purchasing he is apt not to trust his buyer, if he is a chemist by profession he clears his desk of financial matters but keeps his hand on research, if he was once a lawyer he isn't sure the company is employing the right counsel, but would put trust at once in an engineer whom he knows little about.

There is one final test, however, in my opinion by which it can be determined whether an executive is objective and consistent in the practice of delegating authority, and that is this: If he can turn a job over to a junior and then support him in carrying it out in a manner quite different from that which he himself would have chosen, then he understands.

The fine art of delegating isn't as easy as just drawing a chart with vertical and horizontal lines that tie either jobs or people together, or even drafting a precise and detailed description of duties, for as often as not it works out that such documents serve to limit initiative rather than promote it. When too much emphasis is placed upon job definition, a junior is apt to think more about the limits of his authority than upon his opportunity, and hold back in fear of trans-

*   *   *

Any leader worth following gives credit easily where credit is due. He does not take someone's idea, dress it up and offer it as his own. He offers it as theirs. Otherwise, ideas will soon cease to flow his way. He plays fair with everyone and recognizes the strong points in people as well as the weak ones. He never takes advantage for his own selfish purposes.

—Franklin J. Lunding, chairman, Jewel Tea Co.

*   *   *

gressing instead of plunging ahead with a bold course of action.

Since the object of management is to draw out the best that is in each member of the group, the emphasis must be on the encouragement of creative impulses, rather than upon restraint.

Where it is felt that a formal job description is desirable, it is helpful to require the man to make the first draft himself, to see the extent to which he displays an instinct for sensing his own suitable place on the team. No written statement of duties can ever be more than a guide, for the variety in the simplest responsibility will baffle description, and what is applicable today may be rendered obsolete tomorrow by unpredictable circumstances.

There is no substitute for the give and take of experience under a wise leader.

Delegation implies control, and that likewise calls for deft skill. The organization must be kept on the beam, and the effort of all must be directed toward a common end, yet the widest latitude which will not defeat that purpose must be permitted for the play of individual deviation in order that the drive that comes from enthusiasm may be maintained. "Doin' what comes naturally" is an important thing to foster in team play, for the man who does it his own way may do it better and faster than if he does it the way that would appeal to the boss. On rare occasions control must be absolute, and then the executive must be firm.

A good administrator not only learns to delegate authority, but he also seeks to share his thinking with as many others as possible. This is not an easy habit for some men to acquire, however. Strong characters, in particular, tend to regard thinking as their prerogative only.

The top executive shares his thinking on the company's problems first of all with his board of directors. If he is wise he makes the latter a real working group, before whom tough questions actually are threshed out to decision, instead of letting it degenerate into the mumbling of incoherent affirmatives on a few formal resolutions, with prompt adjournment for an excellent luncheon.

The board, to be effective, should be a good mixture of "inside" and "outside" men, in my opinion. Some senior officers should be elected directors in order that the board may have the benefit of their intimate knowledge of the business. But a board constituted exclusively from that group either tends to reflect the opinion of one man only, or else puts officers in the unpleasant position of having to lead opposition to the boss.

Directors chosen from other fields not only bring the richness of their own diverse experience to the board, but also the courage and objectivity imperatively required for controversial questions, including that of executive compensation, and the succession in the senior offices.

But at every level of responsibility management men need to both share and delegate thinking. People won't remain long where they are forbidden to think.

Developing Your People

The role of modern management begins and ends with an effort to discover and bring forth the utmost of capacity residing in the working and supervisory forces of the company. How does the manager do this?

He begins, of course, by taking inventory. He must find out what skills and talents are available, yet simple as that statement sounds it is disconcerting how inadequately it is done in industry. I have known men who could draw you to scale, from memory, an accurate sketch of a machine entrusted to their care, but who couldn't with confidence tell you even the name of the man who was running it, let alone give you a statement of his education, training, or degree of emotional stability.

Yet hidden away in the minds and hearts of those men beside the machines or behind the desks may be a great wealth of undisclosed abilities if the boss would only make it his business to dig them out.

He finds out by being warm and human himself, by having a genuine interest in all that concerns each person, by cultivating his subordinates off the job as well as on, and by setting up cross bearings through taking the judgments of others than himself about particular individuals.

Once this inventory of human resources has been carefully taken, the alert supervisor reexamines his tables of organization with new interest and a sharply critical eye. He will become as conscious of human waste as he is of material waste. Where it is clear that a subordinate possesses talent or skills not finding full outlet in the job presently assigned to him, he will watch for a chance to give such a man responsibility more suited to his capacity.

Often this has to be done without change in earnings or promotional status, but the man can be made much happier, and the effectiveness of the group enhanced. And if no such opportunity occurs in his own group, the supervisor seeks opportunity elsewhere for such a man by talking with associates of parallel responsibility. He thus demonstrates that the worker is, in his eyes, a person and not a number.

The inventory of human resources will disclose not only proven abilities that are unemployed, but will also bring to light new abilities in men that otherwise have been passed over. There again is the real pay dirt in a searching study into the capabilities of a group, and the one which should rouse the keenest sense of challenge in the supervisor.

What can be more satisfying than to be the medium by which some other person is brought to glimpse new possibilities for his own achievement?

There are many tools with which the supervisor may go quietly to work to develop the latent abilities of a subordinate. The facilities of adult education, which are now so abundantly available throughout the country are, of course, high on the list. The young man who has had general education only, and who feels at a competitive disadvantage with his technically trained associates, can overcome that handicap somewhat by night courses in chemistry or electrical engineering; the metallurgist who feels tongue-tied when it comes to making verbal or written reports can study speaking or writing; and the accountant who has worked with statistics but not with people can plunge into the subject of labor relations.

The thoughtful boss can suggest all these things and then watch carefully the impact of new intellectual adventures upon those involved. He can in particular thus determine whether they have the courage to tackle something for which they were not trained, and the perseverance to see a tough assignment through.

But over and above further formal education, there is available the important working tool of change in duties and responsibilities. The utility of learning by doing is obvious, as is the complementary advantage to the supervisor of testing character and ability under varying circumstances. To take a man out of one sequence and jump him into another where the duties are different, and the risk of failure substantial, takes executive courage and insight, but it is a marvelous technique for developing those who seem to have promise. I call it horizontal promotion. The man himself cannot bring it about, wistful though he may be to have a chance at something different.

A boss with daring and imagination attempts it; one without those qualities lets seniority and accident govern placement, takes no risks for the sake of development, and upon his own retirement bequeaths his successor nothing but a miscellany of assorted specialists, no one of whom is capable of assuming broad responsibility.

Your Most Valuable Tool

Management's most important incentive, of course, is promotion. Clearly this must always be done on merit, and merit alone. Among men of equal ability, length and loyalty of service should be given great consideration, but they must never govern absolutely. In a system of free enterprise each organization must at all times give its utmost to the service of the public, and if this is to come to pass there must never be any compromising on the question of ability. The best man available must always be given the job. With his inventory of human resources before him, and his program of individual development kept up to date, the supervisor must give the promotion unqualifiedly to the person most likely to bring out the best joint effort from those entrusted to his charge.

If wise, he will plan his promotional steps long in advance, having alternate solutions in mind to suit the contingencies which the accidents of life may bring about. This means planning in depth, with two or three steps ahead in his mind for a man of promise, who should not get shunted off into a dead-end sequence.

Such planning in depth, moreover, requires skill in appraising human capacity, and firmness in judging when each subordinate has reached his ceiling of achievement. There seem to be promotional limits for each one of us. Wise indeed is the man who recognizes this both as to others, and as to himself.

Much unhappiness can be caused, and tension created, within an organization by the hearty back-slapping boss who promotes a man because he likes him, without adequate insight into his capacity, and then has to back away from his decision after a period of dismal trial and error.

Another too-common case is in underestimating the capacity of youth, and yielding reluctantly to the claims of seniority. The only safe guide is promotion strictly on merit every time, based on searching inquiry into the qualifications of all eligible candidates.

Promotion presents the further question of whether each new opportunity should be given, without exception, to some person present in the organization, or whether a company should occasionally "go outside." Again a sense of balance is required. Certainly the company which always fills an important post by enticing a man from a competitor reveals itself bankrupt in personnel policy, and indifferent to its social responsibilities. The development of our human resources is a task which all should share.

On the other hand, we all know of companies that have become inbred. It doesn't seem altogether sound to me to boast, as some companies do, that "when the chairman retires, we hire an office boy." The crossbreeding that comes from introducing occasionally a man with a fresh point of view and a sharply contrasted set of traditions can be very salutary.

No program of development, though well conceived and executed, can be altogether satisfactory, however, if the group itself was not well selected. Intelligent hiring is the bedrock upon which all sound personnel programs must be built; by which, of course, I mean hiring plus initial placement. Brains will not come out at the top of an organization unless they are put in at the bottom.

This is now universally recognized in the leading companies, and the search for brains and character is becoming a highly significant aspect of the times.

Such prospects must be actively sought out, and must be recruited on the basis of the general reputation of the company.

Placement is equal in importance to selection, however, and if each new employee is discerningly assigned to the task best suited to his apparent ability, there will be less human wastage. The exceptional person will be given the continuing challenge that his inner drive requires, and at the same time the skills of those of more moderate ability will find full usefulness.

In this entire range of problems one quality seems to be required for the development of the full power of any group, be it a business or an army. Whether we are the supervisor or the supervised, we need a sensitive awareness of the impact of the words and actions of each person upon the conduct of others.

This begins, of course, with ourselves. To the extent that we can observe, objectively and critically, the influence our own actions have on those about us, we can set out consciously to eliminate the harmful and strengthen the good. Having acquired some proficiency in this respect in our own conduct, we may then hope to bring improvement to the lives of those others for whose welfare we are responsible.

CHAPTER 2

THE ART OF ADMINISTRATION

By Ray E. Brown

A great deal of effort has been made to describe the characteristics of the effective administrator. One is impressed by the similarity of the list of characteristics of the effective administrator and those ascribed to the average good citizen.

Certainly the effective administrator must be honest, loyal, trustworthy, and love his fellow men if he is going to be allowed to run loose in society and not be avoided by his own secretary. It is very doubtful, however, that he can parlay those virtues alone into a successful career as an administrator. Neither does a knowledge of the science of administration seem to assure success in the use of the science. Knowledge of the theories and principles of administration provide important tools for the administrator, but the value of these tools, like that of all tools, depends upon the manner in which they are used.

It is what the administrator does, or does not do, that produces an effect on the organization. Administration is practiced, and it is the practices of the administrator that determine his effectiveness. But any attempt to define good administrative practices ends up pretty much in the same situation as attempts to describe the good administrator. Perhaps a more fruitful approach would be to study ineffective administration and attempt to isolate its causes first.

Here are seven causes of ineffective administration that were observed in a study undertaken for such a purpose. These causes represent very human tendencies shared by all administrators and perhaps can never be completely eliminated. Effective administration seems dependent, however, on successfully modifying their effect on administrative conduct.

An awareness that these tendencies do exist, and the ability to recognize them in one's own behavior, is the first and most important step toward neutralizing them.

Fault No. 1: The Black-or-White Complex

High among the causes of ineffective administration is the tendency to classify everything as black or white—as good or bad. This tendency denies the fact that it is the executive's task to discriminate between acceptable alternatives more often than between right and wrong.

Situations are rarely ever black or white; they are usually varying shades of gray. At least if the administrator is fulfilling his proper function, only the gray decisions will reach his desk. The easy ones will be settled down the ladder, where the facts are more abundant and better understood.

The urge to use the black-or-white technique in administration is a strong one and can develop from several directions. The deficit of time that always plagues the administrator doubtless causes him to seek quick answers. The housekeeper instinct to get things settled and the file off the desk can also lead to quick, off-the-cuff decisions.

In other instances, emotional factors can cause the administrator to pick sides and thus eliminate the bother of looking at "the other side."

The proven advantage of decisiveness in administration may also be a strong factor.

Problems that reach the top level of the organization usually carry with them the troubled ponderings of those involved along the line of ascent. Whether the need is for a choice between conflicting views, or reassurance as to proper direction, questions properly reaching the top level must be treated with respect.

This may call for a meeting with the individual or individuals involved. It not only demonstrates interest and concern on the part of the administrator but can also uncover the facts and the feelings that produced the problem. Feelings often give more weight to a problem than do the facts. When a person is disturbed, fancy can be easily confused with the facts, and the two must be carefully unraveled before a solution will be fully accepted by the individual concerned.

Fault No. 2: Making Mountains Out of Molehills

Somewhat related to the black-or-white tendency is the failure to recognize the necessity of proportion in administration. This fault manifests itself in several ways in administrative behavior.

One of these is best described by the old expression "making a mountain out of a molehill." This results in overemphasizing incidents and problems that have little consequence to the organization. It not only wastes the energies and attention of the administrator, but it diminishes his influence in matters that are important. Subordinates easily develop organizational calluses, and for this reason both the whip and the sugar should be given only when circumstances warrant.

This fault is also exhibited by administrators who are unhappy unless they "skin an elephant" every day. They find it difficult to properly distribute their enthusiasm and energies, and are interested only in big projects and big deals. With such individuals, even the interest in the big deal usually isn't sustained, and it soon suffers from inattention.

The demands on the time and the energies of the administrator make it mandatory that he learn to put *first things first*. Administration is always a matter of selective attention—of recognizing the *significant*. This is so important that every administrator should preview his activities each day and allocate his time and interest to those problems and matters requiring top priority. If he does not, he cannot avoid practicing administration by random instead of by plan. He pretty soon becomes a troubleshooter who aims from the hip at the first problems that come into view each day.

This is likely to be the same kind of executive who boasts of an open-door policy and doesn't recognize that the open latchstring is an administrative snare. Doors were invented for the simple purpose of permitting *discriminate* entry. The administrator must exercise discrimination as to *who* gains entry, or else his time and attention will be devoted to the problems of the more verbose and forward members of the organization rather than to those with more important and timely problems.

Unless the executive establishes priorities for the things he is to do himself, he will not be able to delegate responsibility properly, because he will never know what to delegate.

This may demonstrate he is able to carry a heavy load, but it also proves he is not smart enough to share it. The insecurity that is bound to result from failure to exercise selective attention may be the reason that some of us never quit worrying—even about problems that are already solved or that never even existed.

It can be argued that the habitual practice of administration by reflex rather than by an orderly plan is evidence of insecurity on the part of the administrator. Direct involvement is a way of demonstrating one's importance to the affairs of the enterprise. The person who isn't sure of his grip on the organization has to keep proving, to himself and the organization, that he *is* important by personally tackling every problem that pops into sight.

Even the best of executives must constantly fight the urge to become involved in the problems of the day to the exclusion of those of tomorrow. There is both excitement and satisfaction in tangling with the tangible. Long-term problems are generally vague and offer frustratingly few exposed surfaces in which to sink one's teeth.

Another violation of "proportion" in administration occurs in the use of the "crisis" technique by some executives to obscure more serious problems and situations within the organization. Certain problems are blown up far out of proportion to their significance to the company, or to their difficulty of solution, in order to draw attention away from the more basic problems whose solution has eluded the administrator. Such "decoy" administration may go so far as to create situations for the purpose of *concealing* inadequacies of the administrator.

But whether created or overly magnified, the effect is to divert the attention and resources of the organization away from the more significant and meaningful problems.

Basic problems do not fade away when unattended but thrive best when ignored and obscured. When allowed to go unattended, basic problems ultimately become so crucial that they start erupting, and the executive is permanently wedded, if he survives, to his role of firefighter.

Fault No. 3: The Perfectionist Approach

One of the most common characteristics of ineffective administration is the tendency to attempt *only perfect* solutions instead of the *accomplishable*. This can be described as the all-or-none complex.

Administratively, this all-or-none complex can lead to either of two extremes—both of which are harmful to the organization.

On the one extreme it may mean that improvements are never undertaken because the ideal solution isn't currently available or possible. In such instances, necessary changes are never started because the opportunity for perfect solution rarely comes along. Major changes are always difficult to accomplish, and even the bravest and most energetic executives are sometimes tempted to rationalize their distaste for facing up to those difficulties by holding out for the perfect solution.

On the other extreme it may mean that the action undertaken is too radical, and the organization is subjected to turmoil and violent upheaval. Under these circumstances the changes attempted may be ultimately correct but currently just not accomplishable. Such moves ignore the necessity for administrative timing.

The successful administrator must, on occasions, tolerate conditions of inefficiency rather than court failure by attempting to clear all the obstacles with one big jump. He must determine his goals and evaluate the opposition to them. This permits him to maintain constant pressure toward the desired ends without allowing the pressure to explode into an open break.

It also enables him to accept, and attempt, alternatives if they lead toward the ultimate objective. Among his repertory

*   *   *

Only the most adept and agile of quick-change artists could qualify for a role that calls for so many different faces as some critics would have the administrator present simultaneously:

The executive is exhorted to serve as a leader but to let the group command; to serve as a social worker but to abhor paternalism; to play Freud but respect the privacy and dignity of the individual; to eliminate stress within the organization but to encourage and nurture the nonconformist and the misfit; and to have convictions but be so broadminded he does not know the difference between right and wrong. The overtones imply that high efficiency is somehow equivalent to low morality.

If we want to improve the practice of administration we must first establish what administration is and what it is supposed to do. If we want to prevent its gullibility to each new fad, we need to understand the role of administration sufficiently to determine the relevancy and utility of the new ideas and tools that become available.

*   *   *

of virtues, the effective administrator needs a high frustration level.

Somewhere between the extremes of procrastination and those of abortive change the effective executive finds the path of consistent progress. By proceeding along that path step by step, the administrator can ultimately achieve his long-range plans and at the same time find the personal stimulation—so necessary to his own morale—which derives from immediate accomplishments. It will help him if he keeps the fact constantly in mind that apparently ideal solutions are themselves only estimates at a given time, and therefore are subject to the errors inherent in predicting results of human activity.

Fault No. 4: Yielding to Pressures of the Moment

Before someone interprets the above as an argument that the good administrator is afraid of his own shadow, an opposite characteristic that is equally conducive to ineffective administration should be pointed out.

This is the urge to act from expediency—the attempt to buy one's way out of problems by yielding to immediate pressures and ignoring the long-run effects of the solution.

Side-stepping an important issue is just as bad as stiff-arming it. In some ways it may be worse, because it permanently weakens the administrator's influence in the organization. Yielding to the pressures of the moment is an open invitation for a raid by the most aggressive and most vocal members of the organization. It is a sort of "cafeteria" administration, in which everyone strong enough picks out his own policies. It is properly interpreted by other members of the organization as evidence of indecision and uncertainty and, organizationally speaking, the only thing worse than a bad decision is indecision.

It demonstrates a lack of conviction as to long-run goals, or else an unwillingness to stand up and be counted on issues important to the welfare of the organization. Either situation results in administration by default. A policy of peace at any price has seldom produced peace, but it can be counted on to always raise the price.

In this connection it should be pointed out that administration is not a popularity contest and that many administrative decisions, of necessity, represent choices between opposing views within the organization. While all members of an organization may have the same long-term interests, their ideas as to how to achieve those goals are not always unified.

Under such circumstances it isn't possible to have all sides like all administration decisions, but it is possible and important that they respect them.

The failure, or inability, to see the implications to the organization of decisions based on expediency may produce two unfavorable results. As in all cases where the treatment is aimed at the symptoms, rather than the cause, it may (1) mask the basic cause of the problem and thus prevent the solution at the time the solution is most easily accomplished.

Administration is not a game of solitaire that can ignore the rights that individuals develop in precedent and in established practices within an organization. The results of expedient decisions may not come to a head until long after strong organizational habits have been developed, and strong claims staked out, on the basis of those decisions. Corrective meas-

* * *

Obeisance to form has been particularly noticeable in administration in recent years and accounts, among other things, for the rapid growth in red tape. Valuable new ideas often prove to be hindrances because of the emphasis given to form over substance.

For instance, much study has been given in the last two decades to communications in administration, and now communications is a much-improved tool for administration. But some organizations have developed elaborate means for communicating but do not seem to realize that the quality of the communication counts far more than the form.

* * *

ures will usually take an even longer time to implement unless upheaval is to result. The trauma to the organization is bound to be greater when circumstances are not corrected and encouraged to grow into situations.

A second unfavorable result from decision-making on a first-come-first-served basis is the damage to continuity of policy.

Perhaps no requisite is as important to an organization as that of predictability of administrative reaction. It is the only way the administration can influence the hundreds of decisions made at all levels in even the smallest of organizations. It is tough enough to develop an organization that wants to do what the administration wants done, but it is impossible to accomplish the administration's wishes unless those wishes can be predicted.

Without consistency in decision-making at the top level, there is no basis for predicting administrative wishes at other levels in the organization. Broken-field decision-making imposes an intolerable burden on those who have the task of keeping in step with the leader. *Ad-libbed policies for the sake of pleasing the critics can cause the rest of the cast to lose their place in the administrative script.*

Fault No. 5: The Victory Complex

The obsession to win represents another serious handicap of some executives. This is often demonstrated in the attempt to win a "moral victory," even after decisions have been clearly discredited. Too much emphasis is given in administration to the necessity of saving face and not enough thought paid to the problem of saving respect.

The administrator may silence, but he cannot fool, those responsible for carrying out an impractical decision. If face-saving is really important, it would seem better strategy for the administrator to sweep his errors under the carpet as quickly as possible rather than give them the prominence that results from the disgruntlement and ill will of those compelled to operate with them.

As every child knows, the best thing to do with a lemon is to make lemonade out of it. It is surprising how many improvements can come out of things that go wrong, and it is very possible that individuals *learn more from their failures than from their successes.* Mishaps that are admitted generally cause one to review events and correct his swing.

The administrator should consciously develop the ability to lose a point gracefully. In too many instances we not only finally lose the point, but we succeed in losing the good will of those involved. The effort to perpetuate an error can sometimes eat heavily on the time and energy of the administrator. But more important is the way it chews on his disposition.

This is demonstrated by the feeling of relief and even pride one experiences on those occasions when one is big enough to admit he was wrong.

Admission of error is also one of the best means of taking the fight out of the opposition. No one wants to be guilty of jumping all over the loser.

The obsession to win at all costs is one of the biggest deterrents to full participation by colleagues and subordinates. There can be no battle of ideas within the organization if the reward is disfavor and ill will from the boss. The willingness and the ability to permit decisions to be discussed and pulled apart before committing the organization to follow them, represents about the only method available for pretesting of administrative ideas. The executive or administrator deals in ideas and these, unlike objects and goods, cannot be tested in the model stage before placing them on the market.

Permitting colleagues to participate in decision-making is not so much a favor to the participants as it is to the executive. It not only permits pretesting of decisions and ideas by exposing them to the scrutiny of those who will have to use them, but it most often assures support instead of sabotage.

Human nature being what it is, there is no better way to insure support, as well as defense, than to involve others. To coin a phrase, this represents conspired leadership, and such leadership is probably the most adhesive of all.

The compulsion to dominate often affects the judgment of the administrator. This can perhaps best be described as an unwillingness to share the spotlight. It is not the same as the obsession to win. Actually, the desire for attention at times may be better satisfied by defeat if the issue is one that gives the loser a sort of martyr's role. Such dramatic opportunities are not too frequent, however, and usually this complex is demonstrated in connection with success situations. It represents a serious handicap to effective administration in several ways.

In its most common manifestation, it means the administrator takes personal credit for the ideas and accomplishments of his subordinates. Instead of acknowledging the contributions of his staff, he takes over their ideas as his own. In the long run he is, of course, not fooling anyone, but he is stifling initiative and building up resentment against himself.

Some executives recognize this fact so strongly that they give credit down the line for ideas that actually originated in the mind of the executive himself.

Another consequence of this drive to be the center of attention is its effects on communications. Unless held in check, it results in the administrator's becoming a master of the monologue. He feels compelled to do all the talking, regardless of the situation, and this extends even to casual and social conversations.

Even when he isn't talking, he is so occupied in looking for an opening to take over the conversation that he does not listen. This fact is demonstrated by the way he breaks into a discussion if the speaker pauses for a second, even though it is obvious to those who were listening that the speaker is in the middle of a point.

Fault No. 6: Getting Too Close to His People

The failure to maintain an impersonal status in the organization often proves to be a serious handicap to the administrator. He must keep a sufficient air of aloofness to permit administrative action without its being taken personally.

Admittedly, he must be responsive and friendly so that his colleagues will not hesitate to approach him. But he must recognize the difference between liking his associates, and liking everything they do. Personal relationships that inhibit detached evaluation and frank criticism represent a disservice to all concerned.

Criticism is fundamental to improvement, and every member of the organization has a right to expect that he will be told when his performance needs improvement. Nothing shakes the morale of an organization as much as the sudden lowering of the boom on an individual without prior notice to improve his deficiencies.

The rules of fair play are applied more strictly to the executive than to anyone else, and these rules require that a person be told *where* he stands and *why*.

The necessity for fair criticism might seem at variance with the "sweetness and light" doctrine one hears preached so often today. If that doctrine means the administrator or executive has no right to show and express irritation, it is indeed at variance with proper administrative conduct.

Just as the administrator should demonstrate approval for a job well done, so should he demonstrate disapproval for faulty performance. It's the only way the organization can determine the level of performance expected by the administration.

The important thing is that the executive be able to demonstrate irritation without demonstrating hostility and without creating antagonisms. Only by reserving a margin of impersonal relationship can he hope to appear emotionally casual as he carries out his task of modifying human conduct.

Fault No. 7: Believing That People Act Logically

This matter of human conduct brings us to another cause of ineffective administration. This is the mistaken assumption that people act logically. Individuals do not usually act either logically or illogically when they are personally involved. In such instances they are most apt to act nonlogically.

This is because they are human beings and bring to every situation their own personal experiences, biases, desires, and needs. Situations are seen from each individual's uniquely personal perspective. This requires that the administrator must, at times, temper his decisions so as to allow for the personal equation, and work toward the modification of preconceived notions of those affected by his decisions.

The fact that individuals have changing patterns of values and motivations—and that these may change more rapidly than we think—makes such modification both necessary and possible. It also requires that the executive learn about those with whom he works without stereotyping them. It means that his own outlook also is subject to change as he has new experiences.

To whatever extent possible, he needs to be cognizant of his personal biases and to allow for these in his evaluations of people and situations. At the same time, it is highly important that he maintain respect and confidence in his own judgment. He simply cannot command any more respect from others than he has in himself.

The high degree of "inference proneness" with which executives are necessarily afflicted often seriously inhibits their

* * *

Those who argue that the organizational requirement for conformance is stifling creativity are placing blame on the wrong factor. Such stifling of ideas is the fault of the manner in which the organization is being administered rather than an inherent defect in the concept of organization.

An effective administration designs the organizational structures so as to encourage creativeness and the transmission of ideas. It attempts to create a climate in which the enterprise has the greatest possible gain from the ideas generated at all levels within the organization.

The organization needs the obedient rebel who thinks on his own, but it cannot function efficiently and tolerate the rebels who have no sense of the responsibilities to which they must be obedient.

* * *

work. Jumping to conclusions is an occupational hazard of the administrator, because he is destined to make most of his decisions from obscure and incomplete data. Most problems are problems only because the full facts are not known—and most often not available.

The administrator is compelled to spend much of his time reading between the lines and in making projections from his experience and from his knowledge of the environment in which he is working. His skill in inference-drawing is indeed a highly valuable asset, but it must be used properly and with caution.

Here, then, are seven causes of ineffective management as turned up in one special study. There are other causes, of course. But the ones I have mentioned are quite common— too common, in fact—and are clearly serious obstacles to sound and effective administration.

Fortunately, however, they can be controlled if the manager or administrator will work at controlling them hard enough and consistently enough.

The only basis for administration is the assumption that it causes human behavior. Unless this assumption is true, there is no justification for administration. Unless desired behavior results, there is no point in having administration. The purpose of administration is to influence human behavior, both internal and external to the organization, through modifying the causes by some system of inducements so as to accomplish the objectives and ends of the particular organization.

Stated more precisely, it means the interference with human behavior that does not conform with the pattern adopted for the organization. If people always did naturally what was best for the enterprise, then there would be no need for the administration.

Administration affects human behavior, then, by modifying the causes of it through some system of inducements. No matter what else we might like to call these inducements, they are simply a matter of rewards and penalties, and administration must always regard them as such.

Must Consider Workers' Rights

Too much has been written of leadership as if it were a sort of confidence game. For some reason it has become necessary to appeal to the subconscious, rather than the conscious, to act covertly rather than overtly, when seeking desired behavior from personnel.

This administration by seduction is somehow expected to maintain the dignity and self-esteem of the worker. Actually nothing could possible degrade the individual more than this sort of attitude toward him.

The rights of individual decision and personal responsibility are basic to human dignity. These imply a rational choice between options, each of which should be expected to produce different consequences so far as the individual making the choice is concerned. The individual attempts to maximize the satisfaction of his needs and drives through his conduct, and the administration attempts to maximize the control of the individual's conduct through the satisfaction of those needs and drives. The aims of both should be explicit and open.

Administration cannot be expected to utilize the resources of the enterprise in behalf of those needs and drives that are not job-related or do not affect job behavior. Neither does administration have any right to involve itself in the affairs of individuals except for the purpose of influencing job behavior. *Anything else places administration in the position of playing God.*

Mission of Administration

The mission of administration is obviously to accomplish the purposes of the enterprise.

Its sole purpose is to secure the ends of the enterprise through influencing the behavior of all concerned in achieving those ends.

The sorts of behavior that administration may seek are dictated by the ends the enterprise is intended to serve. Administration is a process and, like all processes, it works within a set of dimensions. The weight exercised by each dimension varies with the ends sought by the particular enterprise.

At least four such dimensions of administration can be identified. One is the efficiency dimension, best defined as *performance-oriented*. It is based on the concept that the purpose of the organization is to produce the best possible product or service at the least possible cost.

This one must be tempered by the second, which can be classified as the human dimension. It is *personnel-oriented* and is based on the concept that the purpose of the organization is to provide the greatest possible benefits to the members of the organization. This is the dimension to which unions attach almost complete attention.

Both of these dimensions must in turn be compromised with the public dimension. This dimension is *community-oriented* and represents the concept that the welfare of the public is paramount. Our public-regulated enterprises, such as the utilities, are examples of enterprises where this dimension has been highly emphasized.

Finally, there is the *institutional dimension,* which is concerned with strengthening and enlarging the enterprise itself. There is a sharp difference between the goals of the enterprise and the goal of maintaining and perpetuating the enterprise. This is best illustrated in the nonprofit and noncompetitive enterprises that fight to survive long after the purposes for which they were established have been fulfilled.

Four Functions of Administration

In the long run, no enterprise can be effectively administered unless the major functions of administration are carefully watched and adequately performed. There are four such functions that are unique to the administrative process and are both the prerogatives and responsibilities of the administration.

The first of these functions is *representation.* This means giving the enterprise a voice so as to make it articulate. Somebody must speak for the enterprise since it cannot speak for itself. The administration may employ a mouthpiece, as they say in Hollywood, but the administration must remain ultimately responsible for representing the enterprise internally and externally.

The second function is that of *direction.* This is the function of choice—of decision-making. Administration is continuously confronted with alternatives, and it is the choice between these alternatives that permits it to impose its ideas and thinking upon the enterprise. The fact that decisions are made in the face of incomplete and inadequate data makes it necessary that the administration have a philosophy to bridge the gap of incomplete information.

A third function is that of *organization*. This is the function of arrangement. It is a matter of establishing relationships and of deploying the resources of the enterprise—both human and material. This function permits the administration to departmentalize the operations, to set up the organizational hierarchy, and to establish the lines of communication within the enterprise.

The fourth function is one of *evaluation*. This can be described as the judicial function. It is a matter of assessing and reviewing performance at all levels of the organization. Unless this function is fully accepted by administration, it cannot know where the enterprise is going, or even where it has been. It is undoubtedly the most difficult function of administration because it is the least exciting.

It is difficult also because it requires that administration pass judgment on its own accomplishments and performance. To pass judgment on its own work, administration needs to keep in mind what it is supposed to be doing.

It must understand that it is a process, a means, and that it has as its task the securing of appropriate behavior in behalf of the goals of the enterprise.

CHAPTER 3

BUILDING CORPORATE CHARACTER

By Clarence Francis

Sometimes I am asked to look back over my years in business management, then look ahead, and offer a few thoughts which may be helpful to the executives of today and tomorrow. If I had to boil my conclusions down to three points, I would say:

1. Procedures have changed enormously; the principles remain the same.
2. We need a full understanding of the new significance, the real meaning, of management's mission in the complex world of today.
3. We must define, reaffirm, and constantly uphold the basic beliefs which have formed our national character and guided our country to a worldwide position of leadership—economic, political, and moral.

For the moment I won't go into the subject of management methods, techniques, or the personal characteristics, abilities, and training which make for executive success. Important as these things are, I am much more interested in finding a definition of what really constitutes "success." The dimensions of management's task have grown so dramatically that the old yardsticks simply won't do.

It was quite enough to say, at one time, that the objective of management was to operate at a profit—period. That is still management's absolutely essential first purpose, of course. Profits are the lifeblood of our free economic system, the true source of freedom itself. But profitability today is just the beginning, not the end, of managerial success.

Ours is a business civilization, the first in history. Two great forces, government and business, have come into balance as the dominant factors in American life, overshadowing all others. This balance must be preserved and the two forces—equally indispensable—must operate harmoniously if peace is to prevail and freedom is to survive in the world of the future.

Does this sound like the sort of inspirational message one hears at graduation time? Perhaps, but I am in dead earnest when I say that the most practical, down-to-earth, operating problem of management today is that of maintaining and strengthening the system of competitive enterprise which is the foundation of our national greatness. Technical proficiency is only half the battle. The need is for leadership in public affairs.

Consider the contrast between the world of today and the world as it was when I entered business some 50 years ago. America even then was a young industrial giant, glorying in its achievements in the age of steam and steel. Since then we have rushed headlong into the age of atomic energy, the age of the supermarket and the superhighway, air conditioning and refrigeration, technicolor and television, jet travel, electronic computation, and cosmology.

Meanwhile our population has more than doubled. The number of our business enterprises has quadrupled, and the gross national product—after due allowance for the change in dollar values—has multiplied sixfold.

Conditions Are Reversed

What has this meant to the people of our country and the way in which they live? Fifty years ago there were two farmers for every businessman in the land; today there are four businessmen for every farmer. White-collar workers now outnumber blue-collar workers, and there are more people engaged in distribution than production. The work-week has shortened incredibly, and recreation has become a major industry. College education, then the exception, is now becoming the rule.

Now here is another great contrast. Fifty years ago there was little talk of war, except for border skirmishes and occasional distant rumblings from Europe. Our military establishment was tiny. Government was a relatively minor factor in the economic scheme of things. In fact, the cost of the whole federal government was $715 million in 1913. We now spend more than that to run just one governmental unit, the Federal Aviation Agency.

Today ours is a nation perpetually at war. We have entered the age of "Big Government," like it or not. We devote 55 percent of our federal budget to cold-war purposes, and 15 percent of our labor force to governmental operations. As a matter of fact, government (federal, state, local, and the military) employs more people than our 500 largest industrial corporations combined.

In the days when I went to work in industry, little or nothing was known of scientific management, time-and-motion study, sales and marketing methods, research, cost control, production control, industrial design, modern purchasing and distribution techniques, or records management —much less of incentives, profit-sharing, decentralization, operations research, electronics, and automation. Advertising was a strange, new thing. There was no word for public relations. Stockholder and employee communications were virtually unknown, and personnel administration was largely limited to the crude procedures which took place at the plant hiring gate.

That is just one list of the things management didn't have to know about in those earlier days. Here is another: federal income taxes, state income taxes, unemployment insurance, Social Security, Selective Service, antidiscrimination laws, pension plans, stock options, the latest rulings of the Internal Revenue Service, the Securities and Exchange Commission, the Federal Trade Commission, the National Labor Relations Board, and many other federal regulatory bodies (not to mention the state and local)—plus the European Common Market, the gold flow, the General Agreement on Tariffs and Trade, and the Agency for International Development.

Likewise, largely unknown to the management vocabulary of 50 years ago were the United Fund, the corporate contributions committee, regional development and urban redevelopment, smoke-and-noise abatement, air-and water-pollution control, civil defense, community relations, and educational relations. All in all, the management man of today, whatever his technical qualifications, needs an understanding of history, economics, and political science just to keep up with the trends, forces, and factors which affect the operation of his business at every turn.

All this adds up, I admit, to a pretty tall order. I said before that the procedures of modern management have become enormously complex. I also said, and I now insist, that the principles remain the same. Further to illustrate, let me review: (a) the evolution of management thought, (b) the growing realization of industry's new responsibilities in recent decades, and (c) the personal qualities which—in my observation—will make a man successful in management under the exacting conditions of today as well as they ever did at any time in American life.

New Set of Responsibilities

The 20th century's swift advance in management methods and techniques, dating from about 1910, had its origins in a drive for greater efficiency, productivity, and profitability. Little was said at the outset about "responsibility." Then, under the stress of war, depression, government expansion, more war and cold war, we moved further in our thinking. A good deal of soul-searching went on as we contemplated the changing nature of the corporation in a changing society.

In addition to the financial balance sheet, a new set of accountabilities, social and human, confronted us. We concluded that management had a definite obligation to see that the gains of industry's growing productivity and invention were properly allocated to their several claimants—consumers, employees, investors, government, and the community. And we acknowledged responsibility for keeping the interests of all these elements in balance—not just as something good to do when we felt like it, but as part of our jobs.

This position, once considered quite enlightened and progressive, is today becoming an accepted premise of management philosophy. Yet, as we have seen, it is only a premise— just the first chapter, so to speak—in the modern catalog of management's expanded responsibilities.

The execution of those responsibilities, it follows, will require certain special capacities and qualities. These have been enumerated, analyzed, cataloged, stated, and restated in a hundred ways by many men of wisdom and experience. For some years I have been setting down my own choice of the traits that make for managerial success as these six:

Imagination
Initiative
Decision
Judgment
Integrity
Human understanding

Today I am no longer quite satisfied with my own list. To it I would now add one more quality—*Character*.

The character of our corporations and the character of the men who manage them will provide the real key to the destiny of our whole system of enterprise today and in the critical years just ahead. Corporate character, by the way, is quite a different thing from the "corporate image" of which we have heard so much—too much, I think—in late years. To me, "image" seems vague, illusory, and contrived. Character is a reality. Good, bad, or indifferent, it exists.

Henry David Thoreau once said, "It is truly enough said that a corporation has no conscience; but a corporation of conscientious men is a corporation with a conscience." When I speak of the need for a reaffirmation of American principles, a revitalization of our basic beliefs, I am simply saying that our national future will be as great as our past—if we have the character to make it so. And these principles, to repeat,

50

are just as clear, just as sound, and just as simple as they were when our forefathers conceived them.

One homely example will help illustrate those principles. Going back to Thoreau's day, we had Longfellow's village blacksmith "under the spreading chestnut tree." Countless schoolboys have since declaimed, "The smith, a mighty man is he." Actually he may have been more than that. Perhaps he was a classic case study in successful management.

To begin with, the blacksmith had the *imagination* to see the need for a forge. He had the *initiative* and *decision* to build it, the *judgment* and *integrity* to operate it successfully, and the *human understanding* and *character* to make him a

*   *   *

Every great institution, as Emerson once pointed out, is the lengthened shadow of a single man. His character determines the character of his organization.

In the same way every department, every section, every unit within that organization is the lengthened shadow of the executive, manager, or supervisor who heads that particular group. The kind of person he is determines the kind of ideals and goals his people will adhere to. It's that simple, that important, that fundamental for the success of the entire organization.

*   *   *

respected member of his community. All the myriad functions of modern management were lodged in that one man. He was the chief executive officer of his enterprise, responsible for policy and operations. His policy was to provide useful goods and services to the public at a profit that was honest and fair, no more and no less. This he did for good, sound, selfish reasons. He was not the only blacksmith in the county; he knew it and the people knew it. He wanted steady patronage and he was willing to compete for it.

He took pride in his work. As engineering executive, therefore, he designed, and, as production manager, built good, sturdy horseshoes, which he mounted with skill and care. As sales manager, he solicited business and, as advertising manager, hung out a sign. He may have engaged in a bit of market research, too, to the extent of observing, "Guess there'll be a lot of folks in town for the county fair—I'd better get ready for it." Then, as personnel director, he may have put on extra help. We can suppose that he chose his apprentices carefully; trained them well; treated them with fairness, firmness, and *human understanding;* and imbued them by example with his own philosophy.

As treasurer, our blacksmith kept his books straight and put money away for capital improvements, maintenance, and contingencies. As purchasing director, he negotiated and, as controller, approved the procurement of materials and supplies. As head of his own legal and tax department, he may have applied to the village council for certain permits, or, on occasion, argued a point with the tax assessor. Perhaps his public-relations instincts prompted him to shoe the horses of the volunteer fire company without charge. In any case, he was not behindhand in his contributions to church and charity.

As a citizen, he willingly did jury duty, served in the militia, was perhaps a member of the school board, and regularly attended town meetings. Because he was a thoughtful man who kept himself informed on public questions, his opinions were respected by his neighbors and weighed into the balance when community decisions were made.

As an American, the blacksmith believed that government was meant to be the servant of the people, not their master. The principles of Jefferson, Madison, and Lincoln were living things to him. He identified his own liberty with the right of free men to create, to invent, to own, to invest, and otherwise better their condition. He was therefore opposed to governmental intervention in matters which citizens could handle for themselves.

He may have thought (and probably did) that the railroads were due for a bit of government regulation. But he would have fought at the drop of a hat against any form of regimentation, collectivism, or totalitarianism. These would have been strange words to him, of course, but he would have recognized and opposed their substance wherever he encountered it.

In the end the village blacksmith was deeply honored by his fellow citizens as a man who left the world a little better than he found it. He had a sense of responsibility, leadership, and character, and he exemplified the principles of individual enterprise and independence for which he stood. He was thus a prime example of truly successful management—and so is any business leader who adheres to his principles today.

Perhaps I have somewhat idealized our friend the blacksmith because I wanted to underscore the positive qualities of his character. Doubtless there were inferior blacksmiths, dishonest blacksmiths, and capable but mediocre blacksmiths who were negative as individuals and indifferent as citizens, like the Miller of Dee who sang, "I care for nobody, no, not I—and nobody cares for me."

My point is that the man I have described was a real man— one of many—who lived and breathed the ideals and attitudes which shaped a great nation and lifted it high above the commonplace. Had there been no such men, the world would not be turning toward America for leadership today.

Now the character of corporations can differ just as much as the character of blacksmiths. There are companies today which produce shoddy goods, companies which fall into the hands of schemers and fast-buck promoters, and companies whose executives suffer serious ethical or moral lapses. Instances of this sort are really more conspicuous than numerous. Bear in mind, when you read of some disturbing scandal, that more than $2 billion worth of business is transacted every working day in this country on the basis of confidence, credit, and trust.

Nevertheless ethical failures do occur. And when they do, the unhappy companies concerned either perish or undergo drastic changes in management.

Then there are the companies which simply "rock along," making and selling acceptable products at reasonable profits, paying their taxes, meeting the going rate as employers, and even giving modest support to charitable, educational, and community activities. These companies thus operate with due regard for the balanced interests of consumers, employees, investors, and the community. By yesterday's standards they would be considered "successful." Measured against the real responsibilities of today and tomorrow, they are negative, dull, and lacking in leadership.

Real success in business today can only be defined as success in life itself. To innovate, to build, to compete, to win— these have always been the great satisfactions of good management. But business life offers so much more now. It offers the opportunity to help shape the course of human events,

* * *

A piece of metal is what it is because of the tiny molecules that hold it together. It cannot be made any stronger, any better than it is except by changing those molecules that compose it.

And so with a company. Its corporate personality or character reflects, and is the sum total of, all the individual personalities that make up its management. Each person who is a member of this group is an indispensable link in forming, for better or worse, the character of the corporation as a whole.

* * *

to preserve the peace, to hasten human progress, to participate in the final triumph of freedom over tyranny and plenty over poverty in the world. A career in modern management should only be viewed as one of life's most meaningful adventures.

There are those who consider business dull, monotonous, and unrewarding. Many of our young people give a low rating to business as a career. Yet I look back on my business life with a mixture of wonder, amounting almost to disbelief, and gratitude for my good fortune.

There is a story you have no doubt heard before about a man who watched two masons working on a building. One frowned, groaned, and cursed over his labors. Asked what he was doing, he replied, "Just piling one stone on top of another all day long until my back is about to break." The other mason whistled at his work. His movements were swift and sure, and his face wore a glow of satisfaction. Asked what he was doing, he replied, "Sir, I'm not just making a stone wall— I'm helping to build a cathedral."

That's imagination! And it is my belief that those who regard business as mere monotonous money-grubbing are themselves lacking in imagination. Good management is, first of all, creative. Some years ago, the chief executive of an industrial company came to one of my associates for advice. He had a very serious problem which he identified as labor trouble. He was nervous, haggard, obsessed with the state of conflict which existed between him and his employees. Naturally he wanted the best technical advice he could get from an expert on human relations.

But he didn't get technical advice. Instead he got questions. What were his plans for the development of his company? What were his goals in terms of production, marketing, and research? How would he finance expansion? What was his policy on prices, profits, dividends, incentives, pensions, and so forth—and did he have a written statement of policy that everybody from the office boy to the chairman of the board could understand? In short, how did he view his responsibilities? Why was he in business anyway?

The result of this interview was a transformation in the attitude of the man himself. His imagination was stirred. He met the challenge, called his staff together, and worked night and day to hammer out a comprehensive plan and a policy for the long-range development of the company. In turning toward the main goal he forgot labor trouble, and the labor trouble presently disappeared. He was creating a new atmosphere of hope, opportunity, and confidence which pervaded the whole organization. He was using his imagination.

Now it follows almost automatically that a good manager with an active imagination will take the initiative in putting his plans into effect. Real leaders not only start things and make them go; they encourage others to innovate, experiment, and grow. Yet I have known instances in which men with good ideas have been slowed down or halted by the more cautious men around them. I have seen top-management men meet with discouragement from members of their board of directors when they proposed new capital investment or expansion. But where, the ultracautious ones will say, is your market? How do you know you can sell more? (This is such an easy attitude to take. Yet it runs counter to the philosophy which has made competitive enterprise great.)

My own answer to the counsels of the ultracautious (assuming a proposal to be soundly conceived and sensible) is a rather simple one, and I have used it often: "Production must push sales." I have seen it work again and again.

In order to test any such proposition, of course, someone has to make a decision. One of the biggest decisions I ever had to make came in connection with the marketing of a national product which was largely regarded as a luxury item, although it had a high volume of sales. For many years a fixed margin of profit had been maintained—which was fine as long as the volume held up. But eventually sales began to fall off and, to maintain the margin, prices were raised again —with, ultimately, a further decrease in volume.

How long this exercise in the law of diminishing returns might have gone on, or where it would have ended, I will never know. The time had come for a decision. We discarded the arbitrary profit margin, cut prices sharply, and watched the volume go up nearly 50 percent in a very short time with a corresponding increase in gross profits.

Looking back, this sounds like a simple decision to have made, although it was a hard one at the time because of the millions of dollars involved. But I mention it to illustrate two points which we are all too likely to forget: (1) Never hold up a price umbrella for the shelter and convenience of your competitors, and (2) in the economy of today, you can easily make the mistake of assuming that a product is a "luxury" when, in reality, it is ready for the mass market.

Such decisions, of course, are a matter of judgment. And good judgment, it seems to me, consists of a number of elements. It is partly instinctive, it is partly a matter of experience. But there is one important part of it which is a matter of attitude and can be cultivated.

One Error Can Be Fatal

If I had to make a rule about this, I would say: Be sure your premises are correct. A whole train of perfectly logical actions, running according to a plan that is sound in all its details, can go right off the track because of one wrong premise. It is really necessary in these days to keep challenging and testing every premise on which a business decision is based. A premise can be factually incorrect. Be sure you're smart enough to know when you don't know—and then get the facts. The grounds on which a premise stands can change —as witness the assumption regarding a "luxury" product, to which I have already referred.

Finally, there is the danger of the incomplete premise. I thought I had learned my lesson about that until one day in a management meeting I ordered a change, which seemed to me minor, in the design of a major product. This was accepted respectfully and I was pleased—pleased, that is, until one member of the management group took me aside and told me how many million dollars my "minor" change would add to manufacturing expense.

My premise, complete as to everything but cost, might have changed the profit picture of the company substantially—and not for the better. My hasty decision, I assure you, was even more hastily reversed. (I have often said that I am glad no one person knows of all my mistakes—and I'd hate to see a convention of all the people who know of some of my mistakes.)

But there is one area of decision and judgment in which self-reversal is unthinkable. When a question of principle, of integrity, is involved, there is no turning back. The premises of a moral decision are never hard to define. When integrity is at stake, judgment is hardly required to determine the one right course of action. The biggest mistake a man in management can make, I believe, is to back down on a matter of principle. Early in my days as a salesman, I was confronted by an important customer who demanded a discount to which, according to my knowledge of company policy, he had no claim. He insisted that he had been receiving preferential treatment not only from my predecessor on the job but from higher-ups in the company.

I stood my ground under considerable pressure. Then, suddenly, the customer's attitude changed completely. He smiled, patted me on the shoulder and said:

"You'll do. I was just making sure I could rely on you."

I've often thought about that. Had I acted differently I would, and should, have been fired. That isn't fatal. Many young men get fired and recover. But I would also have had to overcome the knowledge—in the minds of others and, worse still, in my own heart—that I had failed in a test of integrity.

Years later, on a matter of principle, I found myself opposed to one of the nation's most powerful labor leaders in a battle of wills that affected thousands of employees in many plants and communities. It was an out-and-out power play. Wages, hours, and working conditions were not involved. The issue was the closed shop—or else! We stood toe to toe, alone, and slugged it out. And finally I was able to convince this man that my determination was greater than his own, that I was ready to risk more than he was—on a matter of principle.

On another occasion I was literally ordered to "get into line" politically or face all sorts of disasters, the least of which would be the loss of my job. An intermediary warned me confidentially that my company would be investigated, regulated, prosecuted, persecuted, and harassed to the limit if I failed to comply.

"If this is the kind of country I think it is, you're wrong," I said. "And if you're right, it's time we both found it out."

That was the end of it. None of the threats materialized. It was a wise man who said, "Prepare for the worst and be equal to it." This inner conviction provides one with a very special sort of armor against men who fear the worst or are willing to back down on principle to avoid the worst.

In trying times, I have always been grateful to the business associates who stood by me in moments of decision. Some of them didn't always agree when I decided to take a stand. But once the decision was made, they closed ranks and saw me through. They had the quality of human understanding, the spirit of teamwork without which there can be no leadership.

If now I were to try to set forth my beliefs concerning personnel administration, I would have to write a book. Instead, let me recommend a book, *Human Values Where People Work*, by my friend and long-time associate Thomas G. Spates, perhaps the wisest and most stimulating single volume in the whole literature of human relations.

It is easy to hire and fire people, of course. The problem is to find and keep the right people. There is a fine line to be drawn between supervision that is so exacting that you lose good men and so lenient that you keep poor ones. One of my rules has been to give a good man a second chance after he makes a mistake, even a big mistake, if there has been no sign of dishonesty, weakness, or premeditation. One should also make it a rule never to ask a man to do anything that you yourself would not try or could not do. In recruiting a winning team, there are these main steps: (1) Define the job; (2) Find the right man; (3) Give him the authority and freedom to do the job as well as the responsibility; and (4) Back him up.

The spirit of leadership is something which one man detects in another almost instinctively. There is the quality of being a "good boss" which cannot easily be defined in words, yet it transcends all methods, all techniques, and all theories. Once, during a period when labor strife was prevalent throughout the country, I was asked to give a talk on "The Causes of Industrial Peace." Instead of going into the problems of legislation and regulation which were currently being debated, I looked for fundamental principles. I cited the case of two almost identical industrial operations, in different locations, in which the productivity of one exceeded the other by 25 percent, and I pointed out that:

"This and many similar examples indicate that employee attitudes are a vital factor in positive industrial peace. Can we go one step further and conclude that employee attitudes are conditioned by management attitudes toward employees? I believe we can, for it has always seemed to me that:

"You can buy a man's time.

"You can buy a man's physical presence in a given place.

"You can even buy a measured number of skilled muscular motions per hour or day.

"But you cannot buy enthusiasm . . . you cannot buy initiative . . . you cannot buy the devotion of hearts, minds, and souls.

"You have to earn those things!"

The Meaning of Character

In one way and another, I have touched on the qualities of management leadership that constitute the ingredients of character. The real leader of today and tomorrow, I believe, will be marked by the magnitude of his comprehensions and the view he takes of his own mission. "Make no little plans," we have said; "think big!"

And this reminds me of a conversation I had with a prime minister of France, with whom I was working on a problem of concern to both our nations.

"If you are doing big things, you attract big men," he observed. "If you are doing little things, you attract little men. Little men usually cause trouble." Then he paused, shook his head sadly and added:

"We are having an awful lot of trouble."

We have reviewed the human qualities which make for business leadership. Let us go back now to the new significance of management's task. What did I mean, really, when I said our biggest practical problem is that of maintaining and strengthening our system of competitive enterprise?

For one thing I meant that the "private sector" of our economy is the mainspring of our national wealth, strength, and security—and hence the fundamental bulwark of freedom in the world. It is the duty of management to make the competitive system work with constantly increasing dynamism, efficiency, effectiveness—and validity.

But I also said that technical proficiency was only half the battle. And by that I meant that management must be prepared to fight for better understanding of the importance of competition and the vitality of the profit system. Further encroachments of government upon the private sector must be resisted. Further restraints on the sources of growth must be checked. The air must be cleared of hostility. Positive incentives and sensible ground rules of operation must be established.

It is, to me, madness to talk about "government versus business" as though the two were locked in some sort of life-and-death struggle, in which one or the other must finally prevail. In a free country you can't have one without the other. Government can't create schools, highways, hospitals, social benefits, and a strong defense establishment. Government can only do these things with the taxes derived from the profits of industry. And industry can't operate in a vacuum. It is the generator, not the arbiter, of the national wealth. Our economy is a partnership in which business must insist on reasonable freedom.

Yet management cannot hope to advocate our economic system effectively unless it stands on the firm ground of its own good citizenship. That is why I also said, "The need is for leadership in public affairs."

It is the plain duty of management to make a definite policy of better understanding between the company and government—legislative and executive—at every level. Long ago most companies recognized the need to become better acquainted with consumers, dealers, and stockholders—realizing that understanding comes from knowing the other fellow's problems, giving him a hand when you can, and anticipating frictions by removing their causes. Why, then, should an artificial barrier block two-way communications between business and government?

In the spirit of the town meeting and the cracker barrel, management must join all good citizens in working for better, more efficient, more economical government—see that our citizens get the best for their money in the town, the city, the state, and the nation; in education, public services, health, and defense. The Constitution under which our freedom has flourished is not an eternal guarantee of freedom; it is simply a working franchise which must be renewed by the thought, devotion, and hard work of each generation.

I therefore repeat: The procedures have changed enormously; the principles remain the same. No supermen will be required to meet the challenges of today and tomorrow. What we need is management leadership—men of intelligence, vision, character, determination, and faith in our basic traditions. With such men at the helm, our national principles will prevail.

CHAPTER 4

THE ART OF LEADERSHIP

By John R. Sargent

Defining or characterizing leadership is a very difficult task. There are many quotable definitions of leadership by men who apparently fall into the leadership category, and each tends to stress somewhat different qualities or attributes. As GE's former chairman, Ralph Cordiner, stated: "The hallmark of leadership is the ability to anticipate the reasonably foreseeable needs of tomorrow and beyond tomorrow with at least some clarity and confidence."

Former President Eisenhower is quoted as saying that leadership is "The art of getting someone else to do something you want done because he *wants* to do it." We could go on indefinitely with quotes from leading people and still not be close to providing a basis for a practical program of leadership development.

Philosophers, psychologists, educators, sociologists, all sorts of people have tried to see if there can be a simple definition for leadership. Actually, it appears that 50 years of study have failed to produce one personality trait or simple formula which can be used to discriminate between leaders and non-leaders. In essence, leadership is complex—it is not definable by one or a few traits, *but it is definable.*

In dissecting leadership into its numerous components, and analyzing each of these, we find two somewhat startling and reassuring things:

First, each of the traits or elements of leadership can be developed. The statement that "leaders are made, not born" seems clearly proved by a study of the components. It explodes the myth that leadership is based on some God-given trait or traits.

Second, practically everyone has within him some of the basic traits or elements of leadership. The real difference is in the degree of development of each trait, and their proportions, one to another.

Thus, in reality, no one can separate all of us into two groups and say, "These are leaders and these are followers." There are all degrees of leaders, based on the permutation and combination of the individual component leadership factors within each of us. Of course, we all have a threshold in mind, and when an individual shows unusual leadership qualities, especially as regards a given situation, we tend to say, "This is a leader."

The "given situation" is a new factor which may possibly complicate, but will also test and clarify, our concept of leadership—the applicability of the individual "package" of leadership qualities to any one or more situations presented.

We have all seen military men who were leaders in their particular area but somewhat less, for example, in the political area—or businessmen who were leaders in their particular businesses but far from it when they ventured into social or government areas. This helps explain why there is so much confusion and why there are such differing definitions of leadership.

It explains why a relatively obscure person may rise suddenly to prominence, based on the unusual development of one leadership trait which is peculiarly attuned to the situation at hand.

It explains, also, why that individual can drop from prominence if the situation changes and if his "package" of leadership qualities is not strong and balanced. Of course, there are individuals with unusual development of each of the component leadership qualities, which provides them with versatility in coping with almost all kinds of situations.

These are the rare men who are balanced leaders.

With that introduction to the subject of leadership, and remembering that we are discussing durable rather than "flash in the pan" leaders, we believe there are eight key traits or qualities possessed by a leader.

1. Desire for achievement
2. Mental energy
3. Decisiveness
4. Persistence
5. Confidence
6. Integrity
7. Persuasiveness
8. Ability to handle people

It is impossible to rate these as to their relative importance, although we know that profound weakness in any one, such as integrity or confidence, can interfere with the achievement of leadership by a man who is relatively strong in the others. Their relative importance can substantially depend upon the specific situation being faced, and the balanced leader can draw upon strength in each area according to the immediate need.

As they are reviewed one by one, you will recognize that, although each is separately definable, there are interrelationships among them.

1. Desire for Achievement

The desire for achievement appears to be a key common-denominator trait in leaders. Practically never are there leaders who don't want to be leaders—but it's more than that. The real leader has a strong will for achievement; in the popular, somewhat overworked term, "He is highly motivated." His drive may be based on a desire for power or wealth, but very often that is only a part of it—if it is a factor at all. He has a built-in "want" to get things done, to overcome obstacles, to achieve for achievement's sake. Some psychologists ascribe it to a "fear of failure," which may be part of the picture, but there seems to be a good deal more than this in most outstanding leaders.

It may be this element that causes some of the confusion about "born leaders." Certainly it is true that some individuals have, or develop, a much greater drive to become leaders, but this is vastly different from saying that they were born with the requisite traits or qualities.

2. Mental Energy

A second key characteristic trait of leadership is a mental energy or drive which far exceeds the average. Of course, mental energy by itself doesn't make a leader, but conversely, it's fairly certain that a leader can't be mentally lazy.

Sometimes it is stated that leaders have ideas and imagination—both of which are true—but this can come from continued mental activity rather than from any special spark of genius. Imagination, like invention, seems to be a matter of about 90 percent perspiration and 10 percent inspiration—mental perspiration, of course. When leaders are described as restless, dissatisfied individuals, it is meant in mental terms, for some leaders have been notoriously lazy physically—apparently applying mental energy to save physical energy.

The true, durable leader, especially in the field of business, is characterized by constant thinking—and particularly, thinking before he acts.

3. Decisiveness

The third key trait is related to the preceding one, mental energy, but it deserves separate consideration. We all seem to know people who give evidence of great mental activity, but it doesn't lead anywhere—it isn't well harnessed. The term "decisiveness," as applied to leadership here, means mental organization and self-discipline in channeling the thinking process toward solving specific problems, and then making a decision.

Of course, this means sound decisiveness, not snap-judgment decisions, although some leaders, through practice, are able to make soundly based decisions with a speed which may be thought of by many as "snap judgment."

It is surprising how often serious business problems can be traced back to indecision on the part of a participating executive. No wonder, then, that decisiveness is usually one of the major traits looked for in determining the qualifications of an individual for a top executive position.

In discussions of business leadership, it is frequently brought out that planning ability is felt to be a key element of the leader. Of course, planning ability is a valuable asset but, important as it is, it is included under this category of decisiveness because planning really is a preamble to action. The leader must comprehend both the preliminary work—the planning—and then the action phase.

Much planning and preparatory work can be done by someone other than the leader. Leadership is exhibited in "wrapping up the package"—taking the program, hammering out a cold, feasible plan of action, and then coming to a decision and making it work!

4. Persistence

The fourth key leadership trait, persistence, can be described and illustrated in a number of ways. Some of our intellectual leadership analysts talk of a "strong survival orientation" or a "high frustration tolerance." It can be referred to as "determination to win" or, even more simply, as just "guts."

Stories of our great leaders, such as Washington or Lincoln, almost always relate to the obstacles they faced—sometimes almost insuperable odds—where weaker men would have backed down or compromised. Their persistence or determination was a large element in their leadership.

However, it is obvious that the line between persistence and stubbornness is not a clear one. Other leadership factors, such as decisiveness, must play an important part in determining a course of action. Washington retreated more than once; obviously, persistence must be tempered by good judgment.

5. Confidence

This fifth element or trait also is a recognized common denominator among leaders. It is generally agreed that you must have confidence in yourself before you can engender the confidence of others. In other words, confidence breeds confidence; it is contagious.

A leader can give people courage they otherwise would not have had. Certainly, men who have attained high levels of authority, such as Churchill and Roosevelt, possessed an abnormal amount of confidence.

Confidence and enthusiasm are, of course, not synonymous, but they belong together in this category. They are both contagious and their differential importance relates somewhat to the nature of the situation involved. There are some types of undertakings where confidence is more important than enthusiasm—for instance, you couldn't say Eisenhower was enthusiastic over the invasion of Europe, but he was confident that it would succeed.

On the other hand, in many types of business situations, both confidence and enthusiasm must be at a high level and closely linked.

Obviously, inspiring confidence in yourself and in others is no easy task. It can't be built on hollow promises or bluff. It requires a competent knowledge of the subject or situation involved, a sense of purpose and direction, and firmness in dealing with other people involved in the matter.

6. Integrity

The importance of integrity cannot be overlooked in analyzing the basis of lasting, constructive leadership. We are not thinking of the leader as being a paragon of virtue, but as basically honest with himself and honest with other people. He must have a well-developed sense of responsibility and a reputation for keeping his word. People at all levels want to put full trust in their leaders—and many are the men with other desirable leadership qualities whose ascendancy to truly top positions has been cut off by some action on their part which reduced people's faith in their integrity.

7. Persuasiveness

This is a trait which some people think of as the essence of leadership. President Eisenhower's definition of leadership gives much credit to the persuasion factor. The business author Ordway Tead defines leadership as "the activity of influencing people to cooperate toward some goal which they come to find desirable." Influencing, persuading, convincing are all very closely related. No one can expect to get ahead in the business world unless he can express his ideas to other people in a convincing manner.

Actually, clarity of expression seems fairly basic to achieving success in almost any field of endeavor.

The leader must have, then, among his other traits, the highly developed ability to communicate persuasively. In the past, men were accepted as leaders who could write brilliantly but were dull speakers. Today, with the emphasis on oral communications, effective leadership generally calls for the ability to speak logically and forcefully.

Depending upon the situation, effective communications can also benefit from a sense of the theatrical—from humor, or possibly from other touches which make an appropriate impression. During World War II, General MacArthur's statement "I shall return" was not only confidence-building, it was tremendously effective, persuasive communications. It had a theatrical impact (and this isn't meant negatively in any sense), just as did Winston Churchill's calling for "blood, sweat and tears."

Franklin Roosevelt had both the manner and the sense of the theatrical to persuade his friends, and disarm or distract his foes. Logic and reason may be enough to do the necessary job of convincing, but most leaders put something extra into their communications to be certain of persuading their audience.

8. Ability to Handle People

Last, but by far not least, is a leadership trait—a quality which is almost an art—that, for want of a better title, can be called the "ability to handle people." This is another element which is frequently thought of as the keynote to leadership, and there is no doubt about its importance—but it requires melding with the other factors to represent true, durable leadership.

"Handling people," of course, requires an understanding of people and a genuine interest in them; it is almost impossible to "fake" in this area for any length of time. The facets of the subject are too numerous to cover briefly; sizable books have been written on it. It embraces a knowledge of psychology and the motivating factors in people; the delegation and assigning of responsibility for work without losing control; the application of consideration and tact; the complimenting of people, developing their sense of importance, and

*　　*　　*

The true function of the leader is to take the average individual and broaden his concept of his potential capacities.

　　　　　　　—Helen G. Hurd, National Business Woman

*　　*　　*

backing them up; the handling of discipline, and a host of other matters.

Included in this area, because it relies so heavily on a knowledge of people, is the ability to select, judge and train people for positions of responsibility. The business leader is not a "Pied Piper of Hamlin"—one leader with a mass of low-level followers; he is a man with a carefully selected organization of assistant leaders—department heads, section and group heads, and so on.

The effective business leader cannot for any length of time expect to dominate a situation without being sure of his strength in terms of personnel; in short, he cannot afford to tolerate an ineffective supporting staff.

Yet this is an area in which many an otherwise promising leader has failed, either through fear of potential competition or through the false sense that he could do the entire job himself. So common and serious a problem deserves repetition in somewhat different words—through failing to select strong individuals for their supporting team, many men miss the fulfillment of the leadership position which they had hoped to attain.

Those, then, are the eight key traits or qualities which together represent balanced leadership. No two individuals are the same regarding what might be called the "combined package" of traits or qualities; each has a somewhat different degree of development of the component factors.

Perhaps you are satisfied with your present package of leadership factors, and it may happen to be a sufficient combination for the leadership challenges you will face. What's

*　　*　　*

A leader must realize that he is in a position to set an example and must deny himself, therefore, many of the privileges of a follower. Further, he must realize that, as he progresses to positions of increasing leadership, he must continue to study, train and practice. His efforts to develop himself must be unceasing if he is to meet the challenge of leadership.

—*Gordon Ellis in the* Optimist

*　　*　　*

more, further development of some of the traits or qualities can represent a great deal of effort.

On the other hand, developing a greater strength and balance in each of the factors represents something of an insurance policy—it should enable you to cope with a broader range of situations requiring leadership, whatever comes. In some of the elements, it is impossible to be too good.

Understanding the leadership factors, recognizing that each is capable of development, and wanting to do enough about your development to consciously lay out a program, represent the starting point. Before you can go much farther, however, you need a fairly careful assessment of where you stand at the moment; that is, your relative strengths and weaknesses in each factor.

Can you do this yourself? Yes, for the most part. If you have the ability to be brutally honest with yourself, you can do a self-analysis job—a sort of mental leadership inventory.

Of course, if you have close personal friends of the kind who will lay it on the line, they can help in the process. Some people feel they get a better perspective on their strengths and weaknesses from their enemies. Based on experience, however, you may be tougher on yourself than others would be. In any case, nothing is a substitute for the healthy process of introspection and self-analysis. Leadership can be elusive un-

*   *   *

A good leader takes a little more than his share of blame, a little less than his share of credit.
                                        —*Arnold H. Glasow*

*   *   *

less you can reasonably, thoroughly and coldly evaluate your assets and liabilities as a preamble to self-development.

How about comparing yourself with others as a part of the self-assessment process? There is nothing wrong in comparing yourself with some "leader" and learning from observation, but be sure that such comparisons don't discourage you to the point of being a major hindrance to your self-development program.

Everyone has been in the position of seeing some outstanding individual in action and wondering whether he could ever do a comparable job. Although you may not be able to develop a comparable strength in the area of say, persuasiveness, don't overlook the fact that combined strengths in the other factors can often offset brilliant strength in one.

Benjamin Franklin was no match for many of the brilliant statesmen of his day in oratory or a few other attributes, but his versatility—the balance of his leadership qualities—was such as to put him high in the hall of fame. Franklin made a statement which seems quite appropriate: "Every man I meet is in some way my superior, and in that I learn from him."

It is not feasible to review here all the things that can be done to develop each of the key leadership elements; usually the process of self-evaluation relative to these traits suggests to a person logical steps he can take to improve his own leadership capabilities. I shall make only a few remarks relative to the development process for each trait.

1. Desire for Achievement

It is frequently said that the desire to achieve cannot be developed, which is tantamount to saying that a man has no control over himself or his destiny. Yet we have all known people whose desire for achievement increased, and we have all seen some in whom it decreased. It is capable of being controlled and developed.

The key seems to be how high an individual sets his goals, and how easily satisfied he is. There have been many salesmen, for instance, who had never made more than $8,000 or $9,000 and then, through some stroke of good fortune, increased their income to $15,000—and then stopped. It was much more than they had ever expected to make, and they were satisfied. Ordway Tead sums it up this way: "Dissatisfaction with oneself and one's performance is essential to improvement."

Dissatisfaction is often credited with being a key basis of the dynamics of the American economy. It would follow that, if and when ours comes to be a nation of satisfied people, our progress will be extremely slow—and our generating of leaders will be almost nil.

2. Mental Energy

The psychologists seem to feel that intelligence cannot be controlled or developed, but mental activity—application of the thinking process—is another matter, and one that can be controlled.

Intellectual brilliance is wonderful, and brilliance plus a high rate of applied mental energy is a terrific combination.

Many intellectually brilliant people tend to be lazy, however, and some of us who fall in the less-than-brilliant category can outpace them by the application of discipline to our output of mental energy. When I was in college, out of six Phi Beta Kappas in our class, only one could be put into the really "mentally brilliant" category. The others achieved it by the application of mental energy—hard work!

Certainly, as life becomes more complex there are growing demands on our time, and many of these tend to be diversions to the thinking process. Probably today there are more opportunities to be mentally lazy than ever before, and a large share of TV—or, for children, comic books—represents such diversion.

Thinking—consciously setting aside time to sweat out problems and ideas—takes mental discipline, but who can deny that this ability can be developed if a person is determined to do so. A very disturbing thing that we observe as consultants is the small amount of time set aside by most managers and executives for "just thinking."

A surprisingly large share of executives are "loaded to the gills" with day-to-day details which allow very little time for the creative thinking process. Sometimes this is the result of a company's deliberate policy of limiting the size of its executive and supporting staff, under the mistaken notion that there is economy in keeping the personnel loaded with regular duties.

In other cases it can be attributed to the unwillingness of the person in charge to delegate responsibility, or to his mistaken conviction that, in handling certain routine tasks personally, he is of substantial value to the company. Sometimes it's just mental laziness.

Whatever the reason, it is a tremendous barrier to leadership development.

3. Decisiveness

Some time ago, when I was visiting a client, the president had to excuse himself from our meeting, for a couple of hours, to meet an important customer who was dissatisfied with the equipment he had bought and wanted a rather substantial adjustment. The vice-president and the marketing and sales managers had filled the president in on the supporting facts, but had made no recommendation as to what the company should do specifically. In other words, the hammering out of the final decision was left completely to the president.

This is not uncommon; we see it all the time. Nonleaders don't offer "finished staff work" and some top executives don't demand it—"finished staff work" meaning the providing not only of facts and supporting data, but a specific recommendation as to what the person thinks should be done.

The development of skill in decision-making requires practice. If you are not asked for decisions, you should probably decide what you would do in any case. Very importantly, you can't develop decisiveness without "sticking your neck out"; if you are unwilling to do this, don't bother any further about your development in this area—and, parenthetically, you might as well forget about becoming a leader.

4. Persistence

It is obvious that some persons have a greater natural persistence than others but, as in the case of the other traits, this quality is capable of substantial development. What is required seems to be a combination of attitudes and experience—the mental resolve not to become discouraged—plus experience in overcoming obstacles. The man who has successfully met a major challenge has a stronger backbone for the next problem to be faced—but he must be willing to venture into difficult situations in order to get much experience.

5. Confidence

This is about the most difficult trait of all to discuss in connection with its development. Some individuals seem to develop it gradually as they grow in experience and stature, whereas others have to cross some major threshold or go through some crisis or crucible to attain it.

Confidence is a complex quality and is probably more closely interrelated with the other leadership factors than any other;

most certainly, decisiveness, persistence, persuasiveness and the ability to handle people all contribute to the development of confidence. As with the other traits, careful self-appraisal should suggest ways for its further development.

6. Integrity

Is integrity controllable and, therefore, open to development? Most certainly it is, assuming a man has a conscience, and apparently we are all supposed to have one. Breaking habits—what the psychologists refer to as "behavior patterns"—is difficult, but a person can do it if he wants to; he can be honest with other people, and brutally honest with himself.

7. Persuasiveness

This and the next trait, the ability to handle people, represent major development opportunities for most persons; it is almost impossible to be too good in these.

We regularly see men, possibly rightly convinced of their merit as sound thinkers, who feel they have been passed by—yet who admit weakness in communications. In this day and age, there is no excuse for any executive to be deficient in expressing himself, either privately or publicly, unless he has some physical impairment. It is possible to get help in effective speaking through schools, clubs, associations and private agencies—and many larger companies make special courses directly available to their personnel.

Many men participate in community activities such as the PTA, dramatic groups, and so on, as part of their own development program in this trait, as well as for development of some other qualities. Beyond a certain point, it is impossible to build skill in this area from knowledge alone; it requires observation and practice, and the opportunities for these are everywhere.

8. Ability to Handle People

Although this trait is so fundamental that many people consider it alone as the key to leadership, possibly the discussion thus far has convinced you that there is more to leadership than this, important as it is.

For someone who has no interest in—or basically doesn't like—people, perhaps the only starting place is a psychiatrist. This is not a common problem, but most people simply haven't taken the time to plan their development in this complex art. Fortunately there is no dearth of helpful material available to someone who is not satisfied with his present abilities— and no leader or potential leader ever seems to be.

Of course, a basic knowledge of psychology is helpful. Beyond this, there are many good books on the subject, courses

* * *

I believe that a business's greatest assets are its human assets, and that the improvement of their value is both a matter of material advantage and moral obligation; I believe that employees must be treated as honorable individuals, justly rewarded, encouraged in their progress, fully informed, and properly assigned, and that their lives and work must be given meaning and dignity, on and off the job . . . If I have the supervision of so much as one other person, I will strive to honor these principles in practice.

—Clarence Francis, Hippocratic Oath for Executives

* * *

available both at schools and through associations—such as the American Management Association—and articles in almost every other issue of business management publications. Working with a man who is a master strategist in this area can be a tremendous experience, but it is also possible to learn from observing the mistakes of others.

As in the case of persuasiveness, knowledge will take you only part of the way in developing your skill in handling people; the rest lies in practice. It is something everyone must attempt to do all his life, so why not work on doing it well?

I hope this analysis of leadership takes some of the mystery out of it. Defining the components makes it possible to get some idea of where we stand personally—and recognizing that each trait is capable of development is both reassuring and stimulating.

I don't believe much needs to be said as to why it is worthwhile to make the effort to develop and balance these leadership qualities. The material benefits to the individual, his associates and his company can be tremendous; beyond this, the personal satisfaction and gratification which come from the exercise of true leadership are immeasurable.

CHAPTER 5

WORKING WITH PEOPLE

By J. C. Penney

Ask any group of executives what it takes to be successful in management and you'll get a score of different answers. No one has yet hit upon a simple one-two-three count that will give you the magic touchstone of executive success.

And probably there is no such "critter." How could there be? Management of business—whether it is a factory or retail store, the presidency of a huge corporation, or the supervision of just one of its departments—is a highly complicated affair. It calls for every trait you can find in the book, and then some.

My definition of an executive's job is brief and to the point. It is simply this: Getting things done through other people.

Obviously, then, you've got to know how to handle people, how to motivate them. How to get them, so far as possible, to do the things you want them to do because they want to do them.

Hard? I should say so. That's why John D. Rockefeller once said, "I will pay more for the ability to deal with people than for any other ability under the sun."

Since people are different from each other in hundreds of ways, this poses problems—any number of problems. And the larger your share of human understanding, the farther you will go in this highly important and highly exacting job of managing people—which is another term for the executive function.

I am reminded of a piece I read some time ago by F. F. Beirne. It was a parody of the attitude held by so many employees that an executive has nothing to do. It went like this:

"As everybody knows, an executive has practically nothing to do—except—

"To decide what is to be done; to tell somebody to do it; to listen to reasons why it should not be done, why it should be done by somebody else, or why it should be done in a different way, and to prepare arguments in rebuttal—

"To follow up to see if the thing has been done; to discover that it has not been done; to listen to excuses from the person who should have done it—

"To follow up a second time to see if the thing has been done; to discover that it has been done but done incorrectly; to point out how it should have been done; to conclude as long as it has been done, it may as well be left as it is; to wonder if it is not time to get rid of a person who cannot do a thing correctly, but to reflect, then, that the person at fault has a wife and seven children, and that certainly no other executive in the world would put up with him for a moment, and that any successor would undoubtedly be just as bad—

"To consider how much simpler and better the thing would have been done had he done it himself in the first place; to reflect sadly that if he had done it himself, he would have been able to do it right in 20 minutes but that, as things turned out, he himself spent two days trying to find out why it was that it had taken somebody else three weeks to do it wrong; yet to realize that such an idea would strike at the very foundation of the belief of all employees that an executive 'has nothing to do.' "

Is it any wonder, then, that so many executives sprout gray hair and grow old before their time? It's working with people, God bless them—human beings, not machines—that does it.

The higher up the executive ladder you go, the more heavily these human problems will weigh upon you. Oh, there are plenty of others, too, but these will certainly be among your knottiest. It will often take the wisdom of Solomon, the patience of Job, and the expert insight and knowledge of a Freud or Adler to solve them.

How does one go about solving them? That's a long and difficult story, and no one has a monopoly on the answers. But as good a short answer as any other I have come across can be found in these words of Clarence B. Randall, retired board chairman of Inland Steel Company:

"Leadership, like everything else in life that is vital, finds its source in understanding. To be worthy of management responsibility today, a man must have insight into the human heart, for unless he has an awareness of human problems, a sensitivity toward the hopes and aspirations of those whom he supervises, and a capacity for analysis of the emotional forces that motivate their conduct, the projects entrusted to him will not get ahead—no matter how often wages are raised."

8 Rules for Success

An understanding, then, of people—of why they are what they are, of why they behave the way they do—is one of the most vital attributes to executive success I know of. People are the principal asset of any company, whether it makes things to sell, sells things made by other people, or supplies intangible services. *Nothing moves until your people can make it move.*

A. H. Smith, a former president of one of our leading railroads, once defined his business this way: "A railroad is 95 percent men and 5 percent iron."

The same principle holds true for every other kind of business organization, including your own. How well do you get along with people?

So far as I am concerned, I have never yet found a better guide to human relations than the Bible, particularly the Sermon on the Mount. Study these valuable words and you will grow in management stature. They're just as much needed today as they ever were.

If you want me to spell this whole matter out in a little more detail, let me quote eight rules for executive success as given by Dr. Lydia Giberson, noted medical consultant. You will observe that, with the exception of one of them, they all have to do with improving human relations:

1. Acquire the art of kindliness and persuasion. Kindliness is an attribute of the strong.
2. Put consideration of human dignity above pay, promotion, or environment.
3. Get rid of double standards of behavior: one for workers, and another for management.
4. Start a request to subordinates with "please." Proper words and actions inspire confidence.
5. Give credit where credit is due. Praise fearlessly. If you must tell somebody off, never do it in front of others. Most people's self-esteem can't take it.
6. Don't be afraid to make changes. If something has been done in a particular way for 20 years, that alone is often a sign that it is being done wrong.
7. In handling grievances, let the employee tell his full story without interruption. A kind word will help.
8. Learn to listen. The occupational disease of a poor executive is inability to listen.

How do *you* stack up as an executive under these rules?

There are many other traits an executive must have if he is to be highly successful. Some of those most commonly mentioned are character, integrity, loyalty, good judgment, and industriousness—no rule for success will ever work if you don't.

Others are a positive mental attitude, willingness to accept responsibility, decisiveness, thorough knowledge of one's work, sound health, cooperativeness, emotional stability, faith, enthusiasm, and perseverance.

Now I don't plan to give a play-by-play description of how each of these will contribute to management success. To do so might place me in the position of belaboring the obvious. What I do want to do, however, is dwell upon a few traits I have found from my own experience to be particularly valuable to the embryonic and the "case-hardened" executive alike.

82

Need for Courage, Creativity

One is the quality of courage—the willingness to "stick your neck out," to innovate, to make changes (and occasionally mistakes)—in a word, to be progressive. Call it what you will, it marks the mature executive from the immature executive, the man who is on top of his job from the man whose job is on top of him.

Too many would-be executives are slaves of routine. They don't seem to realize, as Dr. Giberson points out, that the mere fact that something has been done the same way for 20 years is often a sign it is being done wrong. These people remind me of the old army sergeant who was put in charge of a plot of grass in front of administrative headquarters in a camp in Michigan.

The sergeant promptly delegated the job to a buck private and told him to water the grass every day at 5 o'clock.

This the private did conscientiously.

One day, however, when there was a terrific thunderstorm, the sergeant walked into the barracks and saw the private doing bunk fatigue.

"What's the matter with you?" the sergeant bellowed. "It's 5 o'clock and you're supposed to be out watering the grass!"

"But sergeant," the private said, looking confused, "it's raining. Look at that thunderstorm."

"So what!" yelled the sergeant. "You've got a raincoat, haven't you?"

Rain or shine, some people go about their jobs the same way every day of the week, every week of the month, every month of the year, with never a single new idea to contribute to their company that might prove in the least worthwhile. And then they sometimes wonder why younger, less-talented men (or so they seem to think) go sailing past them into positions higher up the executive ladder that they had been hoping to get themselves.

The reason may well have been that the "less-talented" men had a few suggestions now and then that helped cut costs, increase profits, improve efficiency, facilitate distribution, or otherwise enable the company to enlarge its scope of operations.

Progress is the law of the universe; it is the law of economic life. The minute a company ceases to progress, it starts to fall back. Competition is so keen today that if a company stands still for one year—changeless in a changing world—it may never again be able to catch up with its competition.

New products, new services, new methods of making current products, new ways of performing current services are being developed almost every day. No company can afford not to move forward. It may be at the top of the heap today but at the bottom of the heap tomorrow, if it doesn't.

Take the chemical field, for instance. In any given year, 30 to 40 percent of the sales are of products that weren't even in existence 10 years earlier. In the course of just one year, not long ago, chemical firms brought out 500 brand-new products that had never been available before.

Bell and Howell estimates that more than 80 percent of its current sales are from products that were not in existence even five years ago, and only 2 percent of its sales from products available 10 years ago.

A controls manufacturer with approximately 3,000 lines states that 65 percent of its current products are less than five years old, and 99 percent less than 10.

Executives of giant General Dynamics estimate that 95 percent of its sales did not exist in their present form—or, in many cases, in any form at all—a decade ago.

Corning Glass Company received three-fourths of its income in a recent year from new products.

Du Pont estimates that more than half of its current sales are from products developed during the past 20 years or so.

And it can certainly be said that, for business as a whole, more than one-fifth of this year's sales come from products practically no one heard of 25 years before.

"Creative destruction," you might call it. That's the phrase coined by the late Professor Joseph A. Schumpeter of Harvard to characterize "the incessant change both in the structure and in the product of our economy."

I cite these figures merely to show what a dynamic business world we are living in today. More than ever before, the health of our economy rests upon a constantly changing foundation of new products. What was good enough for our fathers is no longer good enough for us, and the product that is king of the market today may be obsolete tomorrow. Obviously, then, no company will be any more successful than the state of its planning for tomorrow.

And no executive will be any more valuable to his company's success than his ability to help his company move forward and progress. He must be willing to make changes, he must be able to contribute new ideas, he must be creative and know how to sell his ideas to his superiors and subordinates alike. To content himself with being a "slave to routine" is merely to court disaster.

The Secret of Achievement

There is another important trait that makes for management success—in fact, any kind of success. And that is the plain old habit of industriousness. I have yet to find a better prescription for getting ahead in this world. Marrying the boss's daughter may still be the shortest route to the top, but few men stay there very long unless they are willing to put in long hours—hard hours—to stay there. Business has no place for part-time executives. Let's look at the matter this way for a moment.

What makes geniuses tick? Why have they been able to accomplish such prodigious feats?

According to some authorities, it is not necessarily because they were gifted with phenomenal intelligence or mental powers. In fact, Dr. George Stoddard of New York University, an expert in the field, has asserted that many children with near-genius I.Q. scores are actually of mediocre intelligence. And according to a Stanford University study, many famous geniuses have not had unusually high I.Q.s.

What is the secret of their accomplishments, then?

No one knows for sure, but you will notice that industriousness—the capacity for grueling work plus the ability to immerse himself in whatever he is doing—is a common thread that is woven into the fabric of each and every top producer I have ever heard of.

Geniuses themselves don't talk about the gift of genius; they just talk about hard work and long hours. As Edison said:

"Genius is 1 percent inspiration and 99 percent perspiration."

Others have said much the same thing in different words.

Michelangelo: "If people knew how hard I work to get my mastery, it wouldn't seem so wonderful after all."

Carlyle: "Genius is the capacity for taking infinite pains."

Paderewski: "A genius? Perhaps, but before I was a genius I was a drudge."

Alexander Hamilton (considered a financial wizard): "All the genius I may have is merely the fruit of labor and thought."

Well, there you have it, laid right on the line—the value of hard work. While hard work alone won't necessarily make a genius any more than it will make a successful executive, it is clearly the sine qua non (the "without which not") of success —any success. And I would like to warn any embryonic executives right now that unless they are willing to drench themselves in their work beyond the capacity of the average man, they are just not cut out for positions at the top.

Getting Along With People

Then there's cooperativeness—the ability to work as a loyal member of the team. This is a quality that I rate almost as important as the "capacity for taking infinite pains." There is no room in management for the lone-wolf executive—the self-centered type of person who thinks of No. 1 first, last, and all the time. He may flash brilliantly for a while, but his star will not be in the ascendant for long.

Working With People

All business is a group enterprise, and it demands the best efforts of every one of its members working in unison, like an orchestra, if it is to stay ahead and reach its goals.

Someone rather aptly described cooperativeness as "not so much learning how to get along with others as taking the kinks out of yourself so that others can get along with you."

You'll undoubtedly come across lots of people in the business world whom you may not particularly like—perhaps some whom you may even cordially dislike. You may possibly find them in your own company ranks; we nearly all do!

But if we allow ourselves to base our cooperativeness upon our likes and dislikes, we are putting ourselves first and our company's interests second. No loyal executive can afford to do this, because so far as his work for his company is concerned, his company's interests must transcend his own.

There's no reason why we need to mingle in our off-hours with persons we don't care for; but so long as we are on the job, it's a part of that job to be a willing and cooperative teamworker.

In business, as in sports, it takes teamwork to reach goals. And other people won't help us reach our goals unless we help them reach theirs.

Company success is a matter of how well all members of the team work in harmony to help their company reach its goals. Obviously no company can be fully successful if there is internal dissension and bickering; too much energy that should go into constructive purposes is wasted on negative or destructive activities. It is like a man who is at war with himself; he is drained of his energy before he has had a chance to devote it to its proper purpose.

Perhaps we can all profit by the advice of one business consultant, who has cautioned: "No rewards are handed out for cooperating merely with the people we like. It's cooperating with the stinkers that counts."

I'm afraid you'll come across more than one "stinker" in your executive life. You'll just have to remind yourself that if the world were made up of people with the dispositions of angels, there would be no problems—and it's the problems in life that make it challenging and so keep it interesting.

Knute Rockne, sometimes called the greatest football coach who ever lived, said: "A football team is like a fine watch—all precisioned. If one small part is not working in harmony, the watch fails to function properly."

The same holds true of a modern business team. Like the coach of a football team or the maker of a watch, the executive has the responsibility for making his group—as well as himself—function in harmony with the rest of the organization.

Ability to Delegate Essential

What are some of the other qualities I would look for in an executive?

One certainly is whether he knows how to delegate properly. The inability to do this is, in my opinion (and in that of others I have talked with on this subject), one of the chief reasons executives fail. Another is their inability to make decisions effectively. These two personality lacks have contributed more to executive failure than any amount of know-how lacks.

There are a number of reasons why an executive must analyze his workload and delegate as much of it as he can, thus allowing himself more time for the planning and creative aspects of his job.

Delegation gives you an opportunity to take on additional work yourself; to expand your department or division.

Delegation relieves you of petty, routine details that are not part of your executive job and which can probably be done just as efficiently by someone else (perhaps with a little further training).

Delegation helps keep your department from becoming a bottleneck, which is very apt to happen when the executive insists on doing everything himself, "because that is the one sure way it will be done right."

Delegation improves the morale of your employees by giving them a feeling of sharing responsibility.

While it is true that many employees shirk responsibility, it is equally true that the best way to cure an associate of this unreasonable fear is to give him a greater share of the responsibility for his department's work. The one great enemy of employee morale is boredom—monotonous, humdrum work that is just being done because "I am told to do it."

A little more responsibility, a little more authority that will put the employee more "on his own," is often the answer.

Proper delegation of work also keeps you from becoming one of those harassed individuals whose desks are always overloaded with unfinished (or even unopened) business, whose briefcases are jammed at night with work that they didn't have time for during the day, and whom their families never see in the evening because they are busily poring over office "musts."

Such an executive immediately gives me the impression that the higher up he goes, the more the entire company business will fail to get done—or at least done properly and efficiently and on time. He would hardly be presidential timber, because no man can run a company successfully by himself. I have seen some presidents try to do this, and the results have always been disastrous.

The surest way for an executive to kill himself is to refuse to learn how, and when, and to whom to delegate work.

Facing Up to Decisions

Equally fundamental to executive performance is the ability to make sound decisions and stick by them until proved wrong. This trait is one that is often hard to come by because the average person bitterly dreads being proved wrong. It's a severe blow to his ego—to his pride and self-esteem—and he will squirm to avoid the responsibility.

This is certainly human behavior but it is not rational executive behavior, and one always respects a person far more who is willing to admit his mistakes than one who always tries to alibi his way out. I never trust an executive who tends to pass the buck. Nor would I want to deal with him as a customer or supplier.

Besides, what is so terrible about making a mistake? It is from our mistakes that we learn. Without mistakes there can be no progress. As Lawrence A. Appley, president of the American Management Association for many years, has said:

"It is hard to realize why almost paralyzing fear of error curbs the initiative of so many men in management. This fear of error is one of the main reasons for costly red tape and controls that are established to insure against errors which,

*   *   *

Mr. Penney's original rule-of-thumb practices which have been adopted throughout his nationwide chain of stores:

1. *To serve the public, as nearly as we can, to its complete satisfaction.*

2. *To offer the best possible dollar's worth of quality and value.*

3. *To strive constantly for a high level of intelligent and helpful service.*

4. *To charge a fair profit for what we offer—and not all the traffic will bear.*

5. *To apply this test to everything we do: "Does it square with what is right and just?"*

*   *   *

if made, *could not cost anywhere near as much as the controls do.* It is this intolerance of mistakes that curbs decentralization of responsibility and authority. It is unreasonableness of this kind that causes able men to 'keep their noses clean and their mouths shut.' "

Better to own up and face the music when you've made a wrong decision than to play the mealymouthed innocent. It may help under these circumstances to recall a story about Samuel Johnson, the famous man of letters, who, almost single-handed, compiled the first "scholarly" dictionary of the English language.

Like all great works, this book contained some mistakes, and occasionally these were brought to Johnson's attention in no flattering way.

On one occasion a pompous dowager cornered him and in a rather malicious way asked how he could have defined pastern as the knee of a horse when it was obviously part of the horse's foot.

Taking a firm grip upon his mental faculties and looking the woman firmly in the eye, Johnson replied:

"Ignorance, madam; pure ignorance!"

I wonder how many executives would have the courage and self-confidence to reply in such a forthright way if they were asked why they had made a mistake in judgment.

If vacillation is the result of the fear of making a wrong decision, then it might almost be desirable to make a wrong decision once in a while, since any degree of action is better than none at all. However, as a guide to better decision-making in general, you might find these rules helpful. Here they are, as developed by a group of executives at a workshop sponsored by the New York Adult Education Council:

Decide what the problem or opportunity is.

Evaluate the situation in terms of its scope, your individual responsibility, the other people involved, and company policy.

Analyze the situation in terms of available facts, information sources, precedent, your empirical knowledge, competitive factors, possible alternatives, and creativity.

Consider the emotional climate and physical environment involved and the problems of status, skill, competency, coordination, and communication.

Do not fear responsibility for what you decide.

Never default; make the decision!

Remember, if at least 51 percent of your decisions are right, you are batting with the best decision-makers in anybody's league. The only man who never makes a mistake is the man who does nothing—the vacillator. Indecision is one of the greatest occupational hazards of the executive function.

Can You Take Criticism?

There is another trait I would like to cite that seems to me of particular importance to management success: the ability to capitalize upon criticism. It's one of the hardest things in the world to accept criticism, especially when it's not presented in a constructive way, and turn it to your advantage.

If you can do this, though, you possess a rare quality because, like mistakes, criticism can prove a most valued teacher. I think it was Marshall Field who said:

"Those who enter to buy, support me. Those who come to flatter, please me. Those who complain, teach me how I may please others so that more will come. Only those hurt me who are displeased but do not complain. They refuse me permission to correct my errors and thus improve my service."

As Marshall Field, one of the country's great merchants, discovered early in life—like many others who have taken the same common-sense approach to criticism—praise is a wonderful "pick-me-up," but it is only through criticism that we are enabled to know what we have been doing wrong and thereby correct our failures and shortcomings.

No one really *enjoys* criticism; there would be something wrong with him if he did. But it is always the mark of a mature, well-adjusted executive to be able to accept criticism— at least, constructive criticism—in the spirit in which it is offered, without feeling embittered by it.

You have plenty to gain if the criticism may in any way be justified.

The Rewards of Listening

Some time back it was mentioned that the executive should learn to listen.

Most of us think we are pretty good listeners. I know when I started out in life I thought I was a good listener. But the longer I live, the more I realize that listening is not something that comes naturally; it is an acquired art. For most of us, listening, whether in a social conversation or around the table at a conference, is just a pause we feel obliged to grant a speaker until we again have a chance to air our own opinions.

This is not real listening, in any sense of the word. Listening is not a passive activity during which we let our own thoughts intrude upon what someone else is saying. To actively listen to another person requires willpower, concentration, and great mental effort. Its rewards are great, because only then do we really learn something about the other person—his feelings, his ambitions, his hopes, his aspirations, what kind of person he really is, what his gripes are, what his needs are.

You'll be surprised how much more you can learn from others by listening in this way once you set your mind to it, and how much it can help you in your work—whether with subordinates or superiors.

There will be far fewer misunderstandings, senseless arguments, and emotional outbursts. You will be much better equipped to appraise and evaluate the drives and needs of other people—subordinates, superiors, and fellow associates —from *their* point of view, rather than from your own.

All this makes for freer and calmer exchange of ideas, opinions, and information. As a result, people's minds become receptive instead of hostile. Progress and improvement follow as "closed-mind-itis" disappears.

The art of effective listening is essential to clear communication, and clear communication is necessary to management success. Since the biggest part of your job as an executive consists in getting things done through people, it will pay you to learn how to become a good listener, if you aren't one already.

What makes a good executive, then? He's what we have discussed—and more.

He can work feverishly for long-range goals and yet not "blow up" or sulk if things go wrong, or he temporarily fails.

He doesn't demand that others accept his ideas; he welcomes discussions with others.

He can "win without exulting and lose without moping," and can keep his impulses to "get even" under control.

He is a loyal member of his company team; indeed, he regards loyalty as an absolute essential of executive success.

He is a fighter, but he fights clean because he realizes that the way of business is a competitive one—to see what company can be of the greatest service to our economic well-being.

Above all, the executive respects the rights of other people and treats them with consideration. For he knows that only through their cooperative efforts can he hope to reach his goal of leadership.

CHAPTER 6

INNOVATION IN MANAGEMENT

By William T. Brady

The renowned jurist Oliver Wendell Holmes was on a train once and unable to find his ticket. After watching him fumble through his pockets in growing dismay, the conductor said politely: "That's all right, Mr. Holmes; I'm sure you have your ticket somewhere. If you don't find it until you have gotten off, just mail it in to the railroad. We'll certainly trust you to do that."

Looking the conductor straight in the eye in a way that betrayed his concern, Holmes replied: "Young man, that isn't my problem at all. My problem is not to find my ticket. It's to find out where in the blazes I am going!"

Executives have a lot in common with the distinguished Supreme Court Justice in that particular moment of tribulation he went through. Not that they make it a custom to overlook or forget their train or plane tickets (most of us have pretty efficient secretaries to take care of that for us), but that too often some of us haven't the foggiest idea of where we are going. Or where our companies are going.

In a fast-moving world like today's that is beset with changes of every kind—economic, political, sociological, technological, and educational—this unawareness can be almost catastrophic for the executive and his company. It is no mere coincidence that a Dun & Bradstreet survey of 170 of the country's largest corporations disclosed that many of the presidents felt that intensive planning for the future—knowing where they were going—was an indispensable attribute of effective management.

New products, new ways of doing things, new ways of making things are the order of the day. How can any company's crown be tacked on securely enough to withstand these winds of constant and incessant change? Most of the companies that rate among the top 100 today have reached their position within the last 20 years—perhaps even the last 10. They are the companies that have started entirely new industries or else transformed old ones to meet modern customer preferences, some of which they themselves nourished into being.

In a word, they have developed and grown to meet changing conditions. Somehow they have kept themselves alert enough to recognize—and flexible and adaptable enough to adjust their thinking to—the world-wide flux that envelops us on every hand.

I submit, therefore, that management of change—management of innovation—is probably the most critical and pervasive task facing business and industry today. Indeed, it is my firm conviction that innovation has always been the basic function of management, whether in the field of business, politics, science, or the arts, and that it is up to management to coax and coddle it into being as best it can.

Just as energy is the basis of life itself, and ideas the source of innovation, so is innovation the vital spark of all man-made change, improvement, and progress. If we believe our capacities are still unfulfilled, our business still unfinished, we must then accept that our future—and that of mankind itself —depends first, last, and always upon innovation—on rearranging the known to create something new, something of even greater value than ever before.

This is my thesis.

And what new forms, new procedures, new products, new technologies, new ways of living emerge will be shaped, at least in part, by our skills and knowledge of the process of innovation, and by our ingenuity in managing change.

The task is both awesome and challenging; awesome in the sense that its scope is so wide and varied and the responsibility so great; challenging in the sense that a huge potential is yet undeveloped. We must accept that challenge with vigor and confidence.

Some years ago a friend of mine was taking his small daughter on a cruise around Manhattan Island. It was one of those beautifully clear days. Suddenly the little girl exclaimed, "Daddy, I can look farther than my eyes can see!"

Think about that. "I can look farther than my eyes can see!" What a wonderfully perceptive child.

The plain, unhappy truth is that too few of us have that ability to look any farther than our eyes can see. We might have had it once, as that child did. But for too many of us it has been lost. Lost in the petty routines, the confusions, smugness, and pigheadedness that start closing in on us as we set out in this world. Yet, somehow, if we are to be effective managers of change—successful innovators—we have to regain that lost ability. We have to be able once again to "look" beyond the horizon. More important, to want to look beyond the horizon and into tomorrow.

For the great majority of us this is not easy, and for some of us it is exceptionally difficult, in fact. Most of us desperately seek an order and pattern to life—one that will leave us with a feeling of constancy, not change. Too few of us are, consequently, receptive to rearrangements. When they are suggested to us, we become disturbed, upset, and even hostile.

Must we accept meekly that nothing can be done, then? Must we surrender to our own weakness? I don't think so.

Operation Survival

Not only is innovation the basic function of management, it is essential to every company's survival.

It follows that in any organization the manager can never be the sole source of innovation, no matter how great his genius. How, then, can he draw from his colleagues the wealth of their creative thinking except by stimulating the spirit of innovation among them?

We know painfully little about the process of innovation. We occasionally mine and refine previous innovation, but we often bungle the job of creating new sources or even conserving those available to us. The answers seem to have escaped even the greatest of our enterprises.

I don't mean to give the impression that only a few companies are really innovating. From what I see and read, many are. But no one who can hear the clock ticking away on America's precious time lead, who feels the urgency of human need, can be satisfied with our degree of progress.

Nor do I want to give the impression that there are only a handful of persons who are innovating. From what I see and hear, there is no shortage of ideas, big and little, in all our

* * *

Obsolescence is a fact and not a theory . . . Old communities will modernize or die. So will old industries.

—*Bernard Kilgore, president,* The Wall Street Journal

* * *

organizations. But no one who has seen the way big ideas shrink into old familiar forms as they pass through established channels can be satisfied that our organizations are innovating as much as they can or should.

Not only is the search for innovation a significant one today; it is also urgent.

What time we have left need not be spent identifying and analyzing innovation or creative thinking. We know it when we see it. However, we do have to identify those things which stifle it, and root them out. Let me try, then, to put my finger on a few of the inhibitors to genuine creative thinking.

First, in our society there seems to be a basic cultural distaste for innovation. Years ago, we admired and rewarded innovation and creativity. We were continuously in search of new frontiers. The innovator was a hero, not a nuisance.

98

Today, however, in sharp contrast to the past, innovation goes frequently unrewarded. We appear to have developed a critical disapproval, a kind of snobbishness that looks down on anything new. We are fearful—and so resent those who upset apple carts. Security is the slogan of our society.

Reacting against innovation, we lionize the sensible man, the man of facts, the practical realistic man, the man who "gets things done." The man of ideas is too often thought of as "out of this world." And too often we leave him there.

Perhaps our society has overstructured its systems and locked its people in. Perhaps we have insisted too much on getting everything regimented. In our efforts to be efficient, we have created systems which wear out but which we are loathe to change or drop completely.

All this is characteristic of a society in retreat. These are dangerous and demoralizing attitudes for a nation on a new frontier.

Further, any company operating within a climate that is at best only lukewarm toward innovation produces some obstacles of its own to this process. Here are a few:

There is the tendency, for instance, in too many organizations to hold power and decision at the top. It is based on the mistaken notion that the only competent, intelligent, thinking individuals are those at the top.

Petty Empire-Building

These people monopolize the power of decision. They coordinate, they direct, they do what little innovating they have time for—they work hard. In fact, their work becomes so consuming that they have little time for anything but their day-to-day tasks.

But the man whose eyes are focused only on today is not planning for the future. The long-term perspective is missing, or woefully inadequate.

With this clustering of power comes the building of empires. Little cliques of "yes men" spring up. Innovation—

takes only the direction the leaders want it to take. And in the struggles for prerogatives and status, the creative thoughts of people all along the line are stifled.

More particularly—and, unhappily, often too—the objectives of the company, its purposes, are subordinated to the aims and goals of its most aggressive and colorful personalities. The real business of the company, as a whole, is either poorly defined or forgotten. Each division or functional unit develops its own narrow aim and perspective. Decisions, unfortunately, are made in terms of their parochial interests.

Moreover, in such an unhealthy environment, fear and anxiety all too frequently foul the atmosphere. Caught in the pull-and-tug of the top leaders, many people are never certain where they stand. In such a climate it is difficult for them to identify with the larger organization or to feel any sense of participation.

Rather, they must, if they are to have any measure of security at all, find it within one of these cliques. And if, like most people, they wish for advancement and bigger rewards, they soon realize they must play along with its ritual. Oftentimes the advice given to newcomers in a department is to "find out what the boss wants and likes—and do it."

In such a sterile system, lines of communication are a one-way street. Information flows from the top and usually never reaches the bottom. Even that information is often screened by the top, and only what they think is fitting gets through.

Here, then, are some of the organizational factors that inhibit innovation:

1. Overcentralization of power and control
2. Lack of planning
3. Building of little empires
4. Spreading of fear and anxiety
5. Limited loyalties
6. Poor communications

A third barrier to innovation centers in the *individual himself*.

100

We generally live far below our creative limits. Most people possess creative power they never use.

Too many people in business are bored stiff. They are apt to characterize all their work by the amount of routine it includes—and all our jobs include a good bit of it. Going through the motions, shuffling papers, their workday takes on the character of deadening monotony.

It is almost as if men were being paid by the pound for their work. Their effort is measured in terms of volume of work, none of which may be really productive or lasting. And far too often none of the work is truly innovative.

All too frequently when the individual in business gets completely wrapped up in himself, he loses sight of greater goals and is content to just coast by. There are those who resist change because they are unwilling to risk whatever amount of social status they've achieved where they are. They have little ambition, and jealously guard their own job against any change whatsoever.

Under these patterns, in many of our large organizations, there is a tendency to develop organization men—men who are concerned primarily with following a pattern that others lay down. Highly sensitive to what others think of them, anxious to please, dependent, their own individuality is submerged. They are afraid to take responsibility for their own ideas. They hew too closely to the line, and until they find out what the line is, they don't hew at all.

Barriers to Innovation

Although some measure of conformity is essential in any large enterprise, I for one believe the balance between individuality and conformity has swung too far away from individuality. Creative thinking has suffered or disappeared altogether, and we are all the poorer for its loss.

The barriers, therefore, to innovation and creativity lie in these areas:

1. Within our society
2. Within the organization itself
3. Within the individual

If we are to liberate our creative forces, we must eliminate these inhibitors, substituting a climate that facilitates innovation and growth. Let's look at what can be done, first for the individual

For one thing, we can provide an atmosphere in which the individual's sensitivity can flourish rather than wither away. Creativity or innovation comes from awareness of a need or a problem. The problem or need may exist within the individual himself, or it may be present in the organization, or in the public it serves. To solve it requires an openness of mind—a capacity for being receptive to new ideas.

We must also enlarge a man's knowledge about what's going on around him and encourage and help him to learn more about his own field.

We can give him the opportunity to develop and improve the techniques and skills of his work. He should also get the basic fundamentals of his job. For while the novice may generate insight on his own, he usually is in no position to use it to his or his organization's advantage. He does not possess the skills and techniques required to follow through on ideas.

This is important. For an idea to be a good one, it must be carried through to its ultimate conclusions. Otherwise it is a passing fancy—a wish, a dream.

It must be communicated, it must be implemented, it must be put into effect. And here's the rub.

Some people can come up with great ideas, but they cannot implement them. They are "idea men" and either cannot or will not carry them through to completion. However, we need these people. It's pretty hard to bench a .400 hitter who can't field.

We must develop, then, their ability to implement, or put others alongside them who have abilities in these fields. In short, create teams capable of supplementing thought with action.

We must also provide enough time for the innovator to create. He needs time for preparation, time for the incubation of ideas, time for evaluation and redefinition, and time for complete double-checking.

Let Him Speak Out

We must give the innovator a forum for his ideas. He must be part of a "community of creativity." Such a community of interaction stimulates; it serves as a catalyst to others. And in this forum there must be free exchange of ideas, constructive criticism, and disagreement without penalty.

Further, we must give the innovator a sense of belonging to management. For only if he participates in the formulation of goals, and only if he is part of the broad creative effort of the entire organization, can his contributions be real. And don't forget, *"People support what they help create."*

We must recognize the dignity of every person at every level, in every department, at every type of work.

As I have pointed out, every man has within him the potential for innovation, no matter how little formal education he may have, no matter how humble his background. We must use every resource of every man, for his sake and for the sake of society. We must be careful that we do not put people in strait jackets—that we do not try to make them over in our own image and likeness. For when we try, the individual becomes only the caricature of himself, a pathetic "me-too-er."

These keen and sensitive words of Thoreau have long been a favorite of mine and are particularly appropriate here:

"If a man does not keep pace with his companions, perhaps it is because he hears a different drummer. Let him step to the music which he hears, however measured or far away."

Now, the world's work must be done. Yet we must strive to permit differences and indeed to preserve them—well within the framework of constructive policy and direction. We can take no other course.

This is not a one-way street. The individual must give something in return. I refer to responsibility and a sense of dedication. Responsibility is primarily personal. It implies a sense of obligation for benefits received and a willingness to justify them by his own best efforts. Responsibility cannot be imposed. Rather, it must come from within the individual.

And, most importantly, every individual must find his own sense of purpose, his area of dedication. He must develop a strong sense of what needs to be done, a constructive discontent. He must be concerned by what does exist and be excited about what could exist. Creativity comes only to those who are intensely committed—from men with a burning desire that every tomorrow be better than today.

These are the conditions that tend to stimulate the natural growth of creativity in the individual—an environment of freedom and participation on the one hand, and the prepared, responsible individual on the other.

Now let me try to distinguish between what we can or must do for individuals, and what I call "innovation in management." This, in effect, translates a number of these principles concerning the treatment of individuals into organizational terms.

First, there is the relationship of supervisor to subordinate, of associate to associate.

It's probably quite true that a person's activity is geared in large measure to what his boss wants or expects him to do. The manager sets the stage, creates the role. And although one's associates are also important in setting expectations, in the end it is the boss who has the greatest influence.

Therefore, what the supervisor does or does not do in fostering innovation is crucial. He can crush it, stifle it, condemn it, or he can cultivate and encourage it. But, all too often, he resists any creative effort by a subordinate, because for him change is disturbing. It may require more work on his part.

The answer is that management must reward the supervisor who encourages innovation in himself, in his line, and staff. The individual who innovates must be rewarded. So also, greater recognition must be given the supervisor under whom it takes place. *Both are necessary.*

104

Coupled with this is the need for a strong program in long-range corporate planning. This involves establishing long-range objectives, the continued examination of what lines of business a company should be in, intensive studies of the emerging economy, and the formulation of plans well into the future.

Further, our system of communication must be open. And when I say "open" I don't mean "loose."

Communications have to be organized and properly channeled. But having done this, having taken care of the formal

*   *   *

It is hard to realize why almost paralyzing fear of error curbs the initiative of so many men in management. This fear of error is one of the main reasons for costly red tape and controls that are established to insure against errors which, if made, could not cost anywhere near as much as the controls do. It is this intolerance of mistakes that curbs decentralization of responsibility and authority. It is unreasonableness of this kind that causes able men to "keep their noses clean and their mouths shut."

—Lawrence A. Appley, president, American Management Assn.

*   *   *

requirements, it is highly desirable to get people in close touch with one another and keep them in close touch.

The creative act thrives in an environment of mutual stimulation, feedback, and constructive criticism—in a community of creativity. Defensiveness and critical attack restrict and inhibit. There is no place for either in an organization that is growing. Rather, the order of the day must be constructive and cooperative.

Organizationally we must provide for a system of sequential controls, which will make certain that ideas are brought forward, evaluated, and carried through. As managers of innovation we must have a logical, orderly approach to new ideas. We cannot allow ourselves to become so infatuated with the idea of change that we are blindly uncritical of the merit and consequences of suggested changes.

What we must also try to do is instill in our people the knowledge that we recognize the necessity of new ideas, of experimentation, the different approach, the unconventional solution to the conventional problem—the breakthrough.

Now, the man who attempts the new, the different, the man who seeks innovation, is likely to make some mistakes. But, isn't it infinitely more desirable to assure a man of some reasonable measure of freedom to perhaps spark some fresh, imaginative thinking, than to slap him down when he commits his first error—and perhaps stifle him forevermore?

Let's be practical about it. We have no choice but to pin our faith in people. No matter how brilliant, how energetic we imagine ourselves to be, we cannot do it all. How much better it is, then, to let your key people know that, once having made the team, they have been given a bank account of confidence against which they can draw without our countersignature.

Should this strike you as a rather lax way to run a business, let me point out that in return for this deposit of confidence there has to be a requirement on our part for strict accountability. There is a point somewhere along the line at which a man can overdraw his account if his errors in judgment prove him unworthy of this trust.

What Price Mistakes?

But it seems to me that too many of our companies today overpenalize the mistake and undercredit the fresh and new. I can't think of anything that annoys me more than the man who says, "Here's the way we handled it last year, and the year before, and we'd better handle it the same way this year." What he's actually saying is, "It's the old safe way, and therefore it's the only right way."

There is one thing he's got to learn—and if he doesn't, we've got to show him—that things are changing every day, and they'll continue to change, so we've got to change with them. If we continue to apply yesterday's solutions to tomorrow's problems, we're going to find out pretty soon that they just aren't getting solved.

Sometimes we forget how eager we were to try out our new ideas. All our people, I'm sure, have new ideas, too. They're itching to take a crack at putting them into practice, to swim in a little deeper water and justify their membership on the team.

Good. You give them the chance. But, maybe the idea doesn't work out quite so well. If there's a reprimand, what happens? Every time that enterprising spirit is broken down even a little, every time that little spark of originality is snuffed out, we are choking off the very tap roots of our organization's precious fund of creativity.

One of my neighbors is the head of a thriving electronics firm. When I asked him the other day whether or not he permitted the freedom to make mistakes in his organization, he replied with a perfectly straight face, "My people don't make mistakes."

I asked for more on this bit of dogma.

"No, my people don't make mistakes," he repeated. "They may come up with some pretty harebrained ideas—some of them simply not workable. But when they do, we most certainly do not dampen their creative ardor by telling them that they have made a mistake. Rather, they are advised most tactfully to try again and use a little different approach. No, my people don't make mistakes.

"And it's a funny thing," he added in afterthought, "some of those ideas we thought at one time were a little far out in left field have now become a part of our standard operating procedure. Certainly our people have the freedom to make mistakes—how else would we progress?"

I do not believe for a moment that this man underemphasizes the value of discipline in his training and supervision—that he condones or encourages haphazard disregard for corporate law and order. That would invite disaster. People are expected to do their jobs within the framework of the requirements and demands of their jobs, never overlooking their ultimate goals and obligations.

But, in some way, we must also put the point across that the greatest milestones in our nation's industrial and scientific history were achieved by men who did not shy away from the unconventional, who were not intimidated by fear, whose pride did not rule out the trial-and-error method. I shudder to think of our status among nations today if this had not been the case. It is the great paradox of our time that the fruit of their efforts may well be an overprosperous, overindulged economy, placid and unconcerned in a changing world.

But if our innate pioneering spirit, our national creativity, is encouraged to grow and flourish, there is no limit to the goals we can achieve.

The freedom to make mistakes, I submit then, is another essential factor of an environment in which creativity is to flourish, and growth is to be vigorous and dynamic.

And lastly, I would set this goal: *"Keep the path open to talent."*

Key positions within an organization must not all be filled with persons who have gradually risen by mere seniority, who plow the same worn-out acreage, year after year. If this happens, no fresh talent is brought to light, and much is plowed under.

There must be enough open positions filled with people on the move to provide the necessary on-the-job training spots.

For instance, an assistant department head should never be chosen who does not have the capacity to move into the top job. We must exert the strongest effort to bring individuals of ability to the fore, men possessing energy, clarity of thinking, and strong will.

We need people to carry the mail—and we need people to be looking for new routes!

But talent does not always stand up for the world to see. It is frequently a shy thing. It must be developed and groomed. Therefore it is imperative that we initiate long-range programs and plans for development, that we employ accurate methods for evaluating individuals, and that these programs and plans be pursued vigorously and continuously.

I've just about spoken my piece. It's a quick excursion through a vastly complicated area, one full of gaps, unexplored subjects, unanswered questions—such as:

The nature of creativity in the individual.

The conditions that lead to its development—the environment of creativity, the stages of the creative process, and how this can be managed.

Further, we must learn how to develop more know-how and insight into the task of blending in the new without shaking established foundations. This is a very real and significant problem. For innovation means more than developing something new. It means dropping the old, the useless. How do we determine what should be dropped? What criteria do we use?

These are difficult questions. We need to know the answers.

We need to learn how to fuse creative talent to an organization, mobilize it in a given direction—in a word, achieve creativity within an organization which will serve organizational and social needs.

Make no mistake about it. The most important job ahead of all of us in management ranks is to manage innovation. How well each one of us does this—our greatest responsibility—will determine how well our world survives the convulsions of change.

In the final analysis, all responsibility is personal. Every organization is built upon these many individual responsibilities. No matter how they may be allocated, shared, blended, or merged, they rest on men, and not on something as abstract as an organization.

It is to those men who earnestly assume these responsibilities that we may confidently entrust the future of the world's people and their problems.

It is top management that must assume responsibility for providing these people with opportunity, stimulation, climate, incentive, and recognition.

CHAPTER 7

RESISTANCE TO CHANGE

By William B. Given, Jr.

There is much talk and writing these days about resistance to change. This is an important topic in an age of fast-moving markets and technologies. However, the problem has not, in my opinion, been analyzed correctly in many discussions. The real pitfalls lie not in inability to master the technical aspects of new products and processes, nor in some inherent unwillingness to change one's ways of doing things. Rather, the pitfalls lie in the field of human relations, especially in the manager's relationships with his subordinates, his colleagues, and his boss.

The more skillfully and sensitively he can handle these relationships, the more successfully he can manage change in his organization.

Let us, then, examine seven of the most difficult problems that arise and see how the manager can deal with them. The problems are:

1. Resistance to change in an organization because of loyalty to a former boss and his ways of doing things (an especially vexing problem when you are taking over a new job).

2. Resistance to change because of preoccupation with present products and processes.

3. Overly slow progress in changing over to new practices and products.

4. Resistance to being "unspecialized"; i.e., to being asked to work or think in an area outside one's habitual specialty.

5. Obstructiveness apparently due to laziness, lack of imagination, uncooperativeness, and so forth.

6. Resistance stirred up among manufacturing people because of irritation at a staff expert's approach.

7. Difficulty on the part of subordinate supervisors in catching on to new management ways.

Problem 1: Loyalty to the Old Boss

In modern management you cannot avoid this problem no matter how hard you try, and the better you are as a manager, the more often you will face it. This is because a capable executive can expect a succession of new assignments and responsibilities, and many of these will find him taking over for a man who had the job before him. Stepping into the shoes of a predecessor is an interesting but often challenging experience.

The former boss may have been strong or weak, friendly or remote, a bear for detail or a great idea man. Whatever his style, his subordinates are used to it and have adjusted to it. They'll make comparisons and, at the start, the comparisons are not likely to favor the new executive. But no one can imitate another man's pattern effectively, no matter how admirable it is. You will soon be in trouble if you try.

Yet it is only normal if your own ways are at first resisted. Your predecessor formed a team around him, in all probability. If he ruled with a strong hand, his subordinates are not accustomed to responsibility and will not find it easy to field a lot of the new assignments you want to throw at them.

You may feel that, ideally, your new men should behave like a group of Boy Scouts eager to help a new arrival. Some may actually be eager to help, but others may feel differently, for reasons that make good sense to them. One man may feel resentful because he or his nominee didn't get the job. A second may suspect that you're just a flash in the pan. A third man may fear you as a rival. Is it any wonder that they seem to resist some of the changes you want to introduce?

Solution A: Accept the Men's Feelings

In dealing with such problems, the first step is to accept these loyalties to the old boss and his pattern as perfectly natural and human. Who would want people working for him who are incapable of loyalty? As the new boss you can earn loyalty, too, not by aping your predecessor but by giving the best you have to give.

If the former pattern is wrong for you and the needs you face, you have the right and responsibility to change it. But remember that it takes time to change habits, attitudes, and ways of operating that have been formed over a period of years. Unless the organization is in a state of collapse, it will probably function as before, certainly long enough for you to decide what changes you need to make.

Does a subordinate seem ineffective? He may be, but there may also be reasons that he was more effective under your predecessor. You might try to work with him differently or find another spot where he can do better.

Solution B: Use Your Advantages

Remember in all this that you have at least one great advantage: A change of administration offers many an opportunity for improvement. A leading cause of mediocre performance is the boredom that springs from routine. The old ways may have been sound and sensible but grown tiresome. In other words, while there will be a certain amount of resistance to change, there will also be a certain *welcoming* of a new pattern—a "freshening up" in people's outlook and thinking as a result of a new boss's coming onto the scene. If you handle it right, you won't disappoint those who have this feeling.

Remember, too, that most of these men don't know much about you. Unlike your new boss, they probably didn't review your qualifications or pass on your hiring. There will be an interest in your outlook and reasoning, as a result. Eyes will be on you to see if you want to earn your place. If you answer their questions affirmatively, you can turn a psychological disadvantage into an advantage.

Of course, this situation is basically the same one you have encountered every time you moved into a new group of equals —at school, socially, or on the job. Only this time you're stepping in at a higher level, and more will be expected of you.

Problem 2: Preoccupation With Old Ways

When production men have become expert in a certain process, it is not easy to convince them that a new one might be better. When purchasing agents have been trained in a certain approach to price negotiation, they are naturally likely to think it is as good as any new one. When a salesman is selling all his division can make of a particular grade of alloy to a large customer, it is not easy to convince him that you want to let the customer try a new material which you hope, but are not sure, may be better. He thinks you are jeopardizing his account. In his opinion, you are introducing another chance for competitors to take business away from him.

Illustrations of this kind abound in business. They represent one of the most common, most significant, and most baffling-to-deal-with sources of resistance to innovation. Whether you are a veteran or newcomer in a certain administrative post, you will surely have to deal with this problem repeatedly. Let me offer some observations and suggestions.

Solution: Check for Human-Relations Troubles

Quite often our efforts to introduce change fail because we get so engrossed with the technology or methodology of the idea that we fail to see its effect on worker satisfactions. In one case, for instance, a change in production methods resulted in the conveyance of work produced by each operator out of his view. Now, it was important to the operators' satisfaction that they be able to see the units they produced, and they were unhappy that the output was now taken out of their sight by mechanical means. Therefore they resisted the change in methods even though it was a sound one technically.

Unfortunately, the production experts were so immersed in the mechanics of the change that they could not understand the operators' discontent. If they had, they could easily have arranged for the units produced to be left in sight of the workmen without sacrificing the technical innovation. Since they didn't see this, however, a chronic restriction in production output resulted.

By contrast, there have been many other instances where changes in production technique have been made without creating such resistance. Here management was careful to listen for signs that the relationships between operators or between groups of operators might be disturbed by the innovation. If it heard such signals, it would talk the situation over with the men and work out some way of making the methods change in a satisfactory way from a human-relations standpoint.

In other words, by working *with* the "society" of the plant instead of against it, they were able to have technical progress and good morale, too.

Problem 3: Overly Slow Progress

One of the most common sources of irritation reported by executives is that a pet project seems to be going too slow. Perhaps a department's data processing is being changed over from punched cards to more highly automatic machines. Or perhaps a new packaging method is being attempted. "The people here resist change," a frustrated executive says. "It's a small project but it's new and people don't like to change to new ways."

Solution A: Be Realistic About Schedules

Many of us, I am afraid, haven't learned yet that it takes time to put a new system or procedure into successful operation. This is true no matter how carefully we have planned the project. And it is true even when there is no resistance at all to the changeover itself.

Sometimes managers pay lip service to this principle. "Sure, I know that," they say. But they have not taken into account that their personal enthusiasm and responsibility give them an unrealistically compressed view of what is reasonable. For instance, they overlook that operators must often develop special skills to use new methods and equipment efficiently. Also, there are usually bugs to be taken out of a new method or system, no matter how well planned and engineered.

Solution B: Maintain Strong Relationships

What, therefore, should you and should you not do when this kind of "resistance" seems to be developing?

You should *not:*

—Lose your patience with the amount of time that the new steps are taking, for the people you are working with will then feel that you are unfairly pushing them.

—Accuse the operators of resisting change, for if they are trying to learn a new procedure or approach, there is nothing they hate more than being blamed for resisting change!

On the other hand, you *should:*

—Do your best to understand any obstacles causing a slow-down. Try to see these obstacles as the men and women on the job themselves see them.

—Maintain your customary work relationships when discussing the rate of progress on the project or what can be done to speed up development. Don't abruptly start "bulling" your way or barking orders if (as I hope) that is not the way you ordinarily work with your people on problems.

Problem 4: Resistance to Being Unspecialized

A fourth kind of resistance to change that it is important to deal with results from specialization. Actually, it is not so much specialization by itself that causes the trouble, as the narrow thinking that specialized occupations may lead to. We get into the habit of objecting to anything that doesn't follow from what we are already doing.

As we all know, specialization begins to influence us long before we get into business. When a boy gets his first football, he wants to excel in running, passing, tackling, catching, kicking—even remaking the rules, if he doesn't take to them. But then he goes to high school where, because of his speed and rugged physique, the coach decides to make him into an end. Unusually adept at catching passes, he soon finds himself on the offensive platoon only.

Eventually, in his senior year, he may be in the game only on certain series of plays; e.g., long passes. The extreme, of course, is the point-after-touchdown specialist who only has a chance to perform after the team has produced a touchdown.

It is no wonder, therefore, that specialization of skills and attitudes occurs swiftly in a business career. The young salesman finds himself becoming a soloist, and not just that but a particular kind of soloist, as in the selling of abrasive-resistant materials or door-to-door items. And the man with a statistical bent finds himself narrowing more and more into some aspect of quality control or forecasting. In American Brake Shoe Company, as in other corporations, we have found that it takes much hard management effort to counteract these tendencies and induce people to enlarge their horizons.

What makes the situation tough for the individual manager is that in his department, specialists are probably necessary— specialists in engineering, maintenance, safety, market research, communications, and other fields. Company after company has them and finds it difficult to do without them. This does *not* mean, however, that you must reconcile yourself to narrow, rigid points of view that resist any and all efforts to be imaginative. What can you do?

Solution A: Assign Varied Tasks

One useful step is to start right off with a new man by giving him an ever-changing variety of tasks. You can't do this so successfully with the old-timers, of course, but it's effective with the younger men and women who do not yet have too much to "unlearn." They have not yet lived with the same operating load so long that they are in ruts. They have not yet grown oblivious to the possibilities of a specialized operation. Hence you can do them a real favor by putting them on jobs that keep them stretching, reaching out, turning in fresh directions.

Solution B: Keep Your Contacts Alive

A second useful step with employees at all levels is to keep your lines of contact, communication, and understanding especially sensitive during the period of transition. You want to find out what ideas and relationships will be supported or endangered by the new system. Bear in mind that countless changes in business occur without any resistance at all. When people are working closely with each other and continually swapping ideas, variations are introduced constantly into their work patterns.

But because they are working closely with each other, they don't see any reason for obstructing change; they accept it. It is when managers come in from outside the work group and prescribe a new routine that they object. Then they are *being* changed.

If, therefore, you can keep men from drifting into specialized operations where they are out of contact with you and your assistants, you will not be in the position of having to "butt in" all of a sudden when a new project looms. Nor will you have to call the men in to attend some carefully contrived "participation" session. You will have been in contact with them all the time, asking questions and talking things over, and the new project can be discussed in the same manner as everything else has been.

Problem 5: Lack of Interest and Motivation

Another common reason given for resistance to change is lack of interest, lack of motivation, and "poor attitudes."

Sometimes, of course, these reactions are inevitable. But at least part of the time the trouble is due, I believe, to the tactlessness of the manager himself in working with the man on the job. The manager's approach is such that resistance to his idea is only human and natural.

Solution A: A Give-and-Take Basis

To illustrate the right and wrong ways, let me cite a study by Paul Lawrence and Harriet Ronken called *Administering Changes*. One engineer in this study was quite successful in keeping things moving in his department. Quite frequently he suggested ideas for change to the operators (mostly women), and quite often, too, they passed suggestions on to him.

For example, he was likely to come up to the operator some day and say: "I got to thinking last night about that difficulty we've been having on assembling this part. Maybe we could get around the trouble by washing the part in a cleaning solution just before assembling it." The operator would respond with interest—"Sounds like it's worth trying." The engineer might then promise to get the right cleaning solution and suggest trying it on 50 or so parts to see what happened. The operator would promise to keep track of the results and notify the engineer.

In contrast to this boss, who was so effective, there was another who approached the operators in quite a different way. For example, one day he decided to make a change in one of the parts of the product where there had been problems. He walked up to the operator with some new parts he had prepared, and indicated with a gesture that he wanted her to try using them in a few assemblies of the product. The operator picked up the new parts dutifully but did not handle them with her usual care.

After she had assembled the product, she tested it and it failed to pass inspection. She turned to the boss and said triumphantly, "It doesn't work." He indicated she should try some of the other new parts; she did (but, again, not with her usual care), and none of them worked out, either. He walked away without satisfaction.

Now, in these cases the technical aspects of the change were almost identical; the operator was asked to make a modification in the procedure for assembly. But in the first case, the engineering supervisor treated the operator as a person with valuable knowledge and skills, whereas in the second

118

case the supervisor came up brusquely with instructions and showed no interest in the operator as a person having ability and a sense of responsibility (qualities that were ordinarily recognized in her by employees). It should not be surprising that in one case there was no "resistance to change" while in the other there was.

Solution B: Look for Indirect "Messages"

In managing changes in a business organization you will also profit greatly from an awareness of the signs employees are always passing back and forth which indicate their feelings about the human problems. Obviously you don't want to discuss human-relations problems to the exclusion of other matters; that would be a mistake. You must go on discussing job assignments, technical difficulties, and programming problems as usual.

But when you are discussing these matters, keep your ears open for messages going out in the form of seemingly casual remarks, questions, an extra word, tones of voice—messages indicating that the person on the job is worried about whether or not he can really be frank, or whether or not the technical change will affect his job status, or whether or not the change will result in his having to work with people he doesn't like.

If you can stay tuned to these messages, you can proceed more discerningly to the questions and problems that affect workers' attitudes under the surface. Much of the time these problems can be resolved simply and directly once you know they exist and are willing to talk about them. But if you don't deal with them, you may well end up as just another manager who is frustrated by lack of cooperation.

Problem 6: Irritation at Staff Experts

Many fine ideas for improvements in products and processes come from staff specialists. If management can coordinate their work effectively, the company can profit in many ways— not only with improvements in products and facilities, but also in the form of a more stimulating atmosphere for operating personnel. For the specialist, being more a "professional" than most of us are, draws on the thinking of a whole field of experts outside the company, much as a lawyer or doctor does.

Yet staff specialists are often the cause of resistance to change. They can be one of the severest headaches the manager has. This is because they work so hard on their proposals for change that an idea becomes their "baby"—for no one else to tamper with. They lose interest in the reactions and suggestions of the operator on the job.

If the operator doesn't see the change just as the staff specialist does, that is because the operator is backward (or so the staff man thinks). Is it any surprise, therefore, that the operators become balky after a while and that the staff expert goes around saying that they "resist change"?

Solution: Stimulate Flexible Thinking

If the staff experts under your wing have the rigid attitudes described, you cannot hope to change them overnight. To a certain extent a staff man is likely to feel this special identification with his ideas because he is a staff man, and to change him completely you would have to take him out of staff work.

Nevertheless, there are certain steps you can take which will help, if you are patient. You will still find operators getting irritated and balky sometimes, but the benefits that the expert brings will outweigh the disadvantages. You can:

(1) Prod the staff expert to see the operators' point of view a little better. Kid him along a little bit, if he can take it. Ask him questions every so often about where operator Joe Doakes lives, or how long Doakes has been on the job, or what he was out sick with last week. It may well be that you can stimulate the staff man to see the operators (or salesmen, clerks, production-control men, and so forth) as human beings with feelings much like he might have if he were in their place.

(2) Educate the staff expert to see that by trying to force his ideas unchanged on the operators, he denies them a chance to be creative. To staff men, the satisfaction of being productive and creative is highly important. They are in sympathy—

in principle, at least—with the desire of others to obtain similar satisfaction. Often their trouble is simply that they don't see themselves as the operators do. You can help them toward that understanding.

(3) Keep the staff man moving around from project to project so that he doesn't get too firmly wedded in his mind to any single one. If he has been working on just one "baby" for a long time, he is more likely to develop rigid, inflexible attitudes about it than he would if he rotated among a variety of assignments.

Problem 7: Difficulty in "Catching On"

Finally, I want to discuss resistance to change among supervisors. It is not unlikely, for instance, that you will some day face the problem of getting supervisors to adopt a different pattern of operations. Some may find it easy enough to change over, but others may stubbornly cling to their old ways, offering no end of excuses why they can't or shouldn't operate differently.

In *The Changing of Organizational Behavior Patterns*, Paul R. Lawrence reports on the efforts of a supermarket chain to decentralize management responsibility. These efforts produced conflict in the thinking of the district managers, who had been used to keeping a tight rein on the store managers and were now being asked to turn more responsibility over to the stores, and to keep guiding and helping the store managers but not running their operations for them.

Some of the district managers made the transition well (although even for them, Lawrence reports, there was some agony), but others did not. One district manager, for instance, went on telling his store managers what to do, and expecting them to do it just as he told them. "I thought the old way was much better," he said. "I had a team operating in my territory that you just couldn't beat." Yet—and this was the frustrating thing—at the same time he went on believing that he was a loyal manager. He *thought* he was complying with top management's new philosophy even though he wasn't.

121

Solution: Help Develop Self-Awareness

Here again there is no easy answer to the boss's problem. But there is a very useful approach to it, and following this will help you become more effective.

Almost every person, like you, has ideas of what kind of person he is and of what he wants to do and become. He tries to keep these ideas reasonably consistent. For example, if he thinks of himself as a good, reliable company man, he will try to do things and learn things that make sense in view of this concept. (Not everything he does will check with this, of course, but that is only human.) If, say, he thinks of himself as a top maintenance expert, he will keep himself well read on technical developments, work industriously, come to work sober, and do other things that are consistent with this view of himself.

On the other hand, if he thinks of himself as a "Robin Hood" or as a character who can always get a good laugh from the boys, he is the kind who—no matter what great potentials he may possess—can probably be counted on to throw a monkey wrench into a new departmental project. Sometimes he may do wonderful work on a job, but you can count on him to "cut up" every so often or make trouble in some ingenious way.

Everyone's ideas of himself tend to change with time, psychologists tell us. However, some people grow much faster than others because they understand themselves better and hence can respond more quickly and intelligently to the need to change. Their efforts to grow and progress are especially likely to be successful if they feel "accepted"; that is, if they feel that their associates understand what they want to be and are in tune with them. When this is the case, they find it easier to see what they are doing that needs changing, and to take constructive criticism. If, on the other hand, they don't feel that anyone understands them or wants to understand them, they can be exceedingly stubborn in their ineffective ways. Sometimes the man that a boss thinks is an obstructionist is behaving that way simply because he thinks everyone is against him or doesn't have sympathy for him.

In the case of the troublesome district manager in Lawrence's study, note that the man thought of himself as loyal and faithful to top management. He didn't think of himself as an obstructionist at all. What he failed to see was that his stubbornness to follow in the new path was not consistent with being a loyal, effective manager. If someone could have patiently, sympathetically, understandingly helped him to see that inconsistency, he would have made the change more effectively.

In the case of the district managers who did make the transition well, Lawrence found that they had in fact become aware of the gap between what they were doing and the kind of managers they wanted to be.

When you have supervisors or assistant supervisors who don't seem to be catching on to a new system, therefore, don't just assume that the men are dumb or unwilling. It may be that they are basically poor men for the job, but it may also be that they could progress if helped in the right way. Make it a point, first, to understand the man's concept or image of himself. If he's a good manager in spirit, then you can help him by tactfully indicating that by doing this or that he's not really meeting the standards of the new system.

Don't expect to accomplish much in one conversation, of course; you'll probably have to work on him for some time. But when you succeed you cannot only show better departmental results to your boss, but also you will have a happier, better adjusted supervisor working under you. One of the principal conditions of emotional health, psychologists report, is the feeling that we are developing in the general ways that are important to us.

Summary

We have seen that resistance to change takes many forms. In all cases, however, the problem may be quite different in actuality from what it appears to be on the surface. What managers call "resistance to change" may really be resistance to the people who are trying to do the changing, or lack of understanding of how the person's actions are inconsistent with what he believes.

Some of the most effective ways of coping with apparent resistance to change are:

1. Accepting the men's feelings as natural and human (this is helpful when, for instance, the resistance is to you as a new boss with a new pattern, and comes from people who are loyal to the old boss and his ways).

2. Looking to see if worker relationships on the job are being disturbed (helpful when a technical change upsets the way the operators on the job have been working with each other).

3. Being realistic about the time needed to make a change-over (helpful when whole new skills and work patterns must be learned).

4. Maintaining wide open lines of communication (especially important in keeping individuals and groups from getting too specialized and out of phase with the rest of the department).

5. Practicing a give-and-take attitude (helpful when the operator whose job is being changed has strong feelings of his own about what needs to be done).

6. Keeping staff experts flexible in their views (helpful when the operators are irritated over too much interference from the specialists).

7. Developing increased self-awareness (helpful when the man asked to change doesn't see the inconsistency between his actual behavior and the behavior he wants to achieve).

CHAPTER 8

MAKING DECISIONS

By Harry A. Bullis

This is truly an age of technological progress. Virtually every morning's newspaper reports advances in human knowledge. Scientists probe farther into space and deeper into matter. Engineers harness the new knowledge to production. Everywhere, new ways are found to shift the heaviest and dreariest tasks from human shoulders to the tireless nerves and muscles of computers and machines.

Machine power levels old buildings and moves mountains of earth; the unskilled laborer with his pick and shovel is rapidly disappearing. In factories and stores, fewer workers are found. On farms, the "hired man" is becoming extinct. In offices, whirring wheels and flashing lights do in moments tasks which only yesterday would have required armies of clerical workers for days on end.

The pace of change shows no signs of slowing.

One can understand why this headlong rush of progress should cause some uneasiness. If so much work which once filled human lives is now to be done by machines, what role remains in the future for us? In the past, we have been taught that it would take our hands, feet, brains, and hearts to master all the difficulties and to get what we needed and wanted.

The answer, of course, is as obvious as it is challenging. With every new discovery, there opens a new world for man to conquer. With more and more machines at our disposal for doing things, human fulfillment will devolve, not so much upon those who *do*, as upon those who *plan*. Planning means consideration of various possibilities or courses of action, then deciding on one of them.

More than ever before, this is the day of the decision-maker, in business as in all other aspects of life. Faithful followers may run the machines and know how to keep them operating. But these workers must be led and coordinated, and the leader's role is more important than ever as the world becomes more complex. The man or woman destined for leadership tomorrow, as always, is the one with the brains, courage, and character to win the authority to say, "Yes, that's it. Go ahead." Or, "No, it won't work. Try again." Or, "Plan A is good but Plan B is better suited to our purposes."

Until one of these statements—or a similar one—is made by someone who is willing to stand back of it and make it stick, people cannot work together because the all-important ingredient of leadership is lacking. Thus, the art of decision-making is increasingly important to progress as science, technology, and automation advance—and it shall remain so.

Ingredients of Decision-Making

Before we discuss specific steps in the decision-making process, let us discuss the general qualities and characteristics which lead to sound decision-making, and the kind of person who has them.

The characteristic or quality needed above all others in decision-makers is courage. I do not, of course, mean physical courage. That has little to do with decision-making in most instances. What I mean is moral courage—the kind that enables a man or woman to face up to responsibilities and take a stand when the situation requires it.

Lack of courage of this type excludes many otherwise highly qualified men and women from executive roles. According to a study of unsuccessful executives in more than 200 firms, conducted by the Laboratory of Psychological Studies of the Stevens Institute of Technology, *inability to make decisions* is one of the principal reasons executives fail. It is a much more common reason than lack of specific knowledge or technical know-how.

Human beings hate to make decisions. Indecision is generally more comfortable. All of us are conscious of this wish to put off deciding. Few of us are fully aware of the degree to which habitual inability to make decisions interferes with the realization of our full potentials and the attainment of our goals in life. Psychiatrists have discovered that every one of us indulges in all kinds of unconscious devices to cover up our indecisiveness.

"We procrastinate," Dr. Karen Horney says, "and just don't get around to doing things. We allow ourselves to be swayed by chance, or leave decisions to someone else. We also becloud the issues at times to such a degree that we leave no basis upon which to make a decision."

Decisions Are Painful

Why are decisions so painful that we sometimes go to ridiculous lengths just to avoid making them? One reason is that a decision of character, large or small, always involves the risk of being wrong; in business, one may lose his job and/or seriously affect the company's future. Another reason is that every decision involves judgment of goals and of values, with risks. Unless, however, a man has the courage to make choices and to take risks even when the stakes are high, he is not cut out for top-management responsibility.

Frequently, the chief executive awaits the views and reports of subordinates so as to have a crutch to lean upon; someone else to blame. Industrial management firms lend eloquent testimony to this attitude. Often the element of personal popularity enters into a decision. The "boss" may not wish to alienate his colleagues or stand aloof from them. There are countless examples where the desire to be a good fellow has influenced decisions rightly or wrongly.

But making difficult decisions is what executives are for. They are basically risk-takers. Because we have had people like this—men who have been willing to stake their futures on bold decisions—our nation's economy has grown and prospered. Take the risk-bearing function out of an executive's

127

job and his importance on the American scene would disappear overnight. There would no longer be any need for him.

Responsibility for the consequences of far-reaching decisions, of course, is a heavy burden for any man to bear. It is not surprising, therefore, to see top executives, even with many years' experience, displaying a reluctance to come to grips with a problem that calls for a decision—at least some kind of decision. Of all the famous last words in the annals of business, undoubtedly the most famous are these: *"He couldn't make up his mind."* The indecision these words describe is costing our country hundreds of millions of dollars every year.

It has thrown any number of companies into bankruptcy and cost thousands of executives and workers their jobs.

Procrastinating Techniques

The means we use to deceive others and ourselves into thinking that it is not yet time to face a major decision are myriad in number, but in many instances they can be recognized by telltale phrases which spring to the lips when the mind is not yet ready to function. Here are some of them:

"I'm going to need a lot more time to think this one over . . . You just can't rush into something like this overnight . . . I don't want to do anything that's going to upset the status quo around here . . . The time isn't ripe to go ahead yet . . . Frankly, it's my opinion that we ought to sit on this idea for a while . . . I'm going to have to study the situation much longer before I can come to any conclusion . . . Let's get a little more collective thinking on this . . . I'm going to have to wait until everybody can get all the facts in," and so on. The variations are legion. You hear them every day.

It is a curiously interesting paradox that sometimes these objections are justifiable reasons for not making a decision at the moment. They are sensible stop-look-listen signs to prevent catastrophes that might result from off-the-cuff, half-baked thinking.

But paralysis of decision-making can be fatal. Sleeping on a problem, for example, allows time for one's subconscious to

128

contribute to a solution, but when a manager turns a request to "let's sleep on it" into a Rip-van-Winkle hibernation, the corporation may die and be buried before the Great Executive wakes up.

Snap judgments are equally bad at the other extreme. Thus, there must be some kind of balance.

Herbert Bayard Swope, one of Bernard Baruch's closest advisers, always asked himself three questions in working to-

* * *

The most common source of mistakes in management decisions is the emphasis on finding the right answer rather than the right question.

In deciding which of two secretaries should go downstairs every morning to get coffee for the office—the one question would be: What is the prevailing social or cultural etiquette? In deciding the considerably more complex question: Shall there be a "coffee break" in the morning, there would be two questions: Does the "break" result in a gain or in a loss in work accomplished; that is, does the gain in working energy outweigh the lost time? And (if the loss outweighs the gain): Is it worth while to upset an established custom for the sake of the few minutes?

—Peter F. Drucker, The Practice of Management (Harper & Row)

* * *

ward a decision, as a protection against rushing ahead without adequate consideration. They were:

First: *Why should it be done at all?*

Second: *Why should it be done now?* and

Third: *Why should it be done this way?*

With Mr. Swope, these were honest questions demanding honest answers, rather than mere obstructionist devices. When his co-workers, however, "laid it on the line" and showed that something had to be done immediately, and that the recommended way of doing it offered maximum advantage and minimum disadvantage, no one could reach a decision more firmly and implement it more positively than this distinguished American publicist.

But, entirely too often, these warning devices are intemperate excuses rather than valid reasons for delay. They are seized upon by executives as a coverup for their more comfortable state of indecision. They are sometimes used as specious devices for avoiding that crucial hour, when the issue must be faced and the decision made, for better or worse.

Again, these cautionary phrases may reflect valid reasons for not acting. But more often, they constitute only excuses for delaying the inevitable, sometimes until too late.

Killing Ideas

Killing an idea may reflect any one of a number of things. It may be there is only one course of action, and killing it reflects a snap judgment whereby the decision is made quickly but without all the relevant information, often as a result of prejudice or bias. Or, an idea may represent only one of a number of alternative courses of action in the decision-making process; and by eliminating one or more of these alternatives quickly, the major decision becomes simpler and easier to make.

In his struggle to avoid complexity (and reality) the "simple-minded" executive oversimplifies. Here are a few of the phrases sometimes used by executives to kill ideas and make them feel more comfortable:

"We've tried that before and it didn't work."

"Too theoretical; not practical."

"It's not in the budget."

"We're not ready for it."

"Production won't accept it."

"Customers will never stand for it."

"Doesn't conform to our policy."

"Why something new now? Our sales are still rising."

"Won't work in our industry."

"Everybody else does it this way."

"It takes too much time (or work.)"

"It's never been done that way before; why stick our necks out?"

It's a sad day for the executive who hesitates to explore new ways and new ideas—thus coming to grips with his own failures in the decision-making process—when he wakes up one morning and reads that one of his competitors has already decided to go ahead with one of the "foolish" ideas he had so summarily rejected at first sight. Executive graveyards are littered with sad stories like "He kept the company on the launching pad until the end."

Let me emphasize again that the opposite of procrastination —rashness—can also lead to disaster. However, in business

*　　*　　*

There is no more miserable human being than one in whom nothing is habitual but indecision.

—William James

*　　*　　*

today it is far less common than perhaps it once was. Most of us are aware of the penalties of rushing headlong into an imprudent, overhasty decision without taking the time or getting the facts necessary for reaching a sound conclusion. The important point is not to let the virtue of valid caution be perverted into paralyzing timidity. The psychological climate prevailing in an industry or the country at large may often thwart a correct decision.

Gather the facts? Certainly, if you want to avoid snap judgments that may be costly. Wait until all the necessary and pertinent considerations are in? Yes, but be sure that what you are waiting for is really essential to your decision. And be sure you can afford to wait that long. Often, executives are obliged to make decisions on the basis of inadequate facts, incomplete evidence, and without proper clearance, because of the importance of the time element.

Need for Urgency

In connection with the timetable factor, there is no doubt that a sense of urgency must be the predominant characteristic of a good executive personality. Clarence B. Randall, president and chairman of Inland Steel for many years, stresses the need for this in his book, *Freedom's Faith* (Little, Brown & Co.):

"Some very able and conscientious men never make effective executives because their approach to difficult problems is judicial in its quality, rather than dynamic. They concentrate so exclusively on the necessity for doing the best thing that they do nothing.

"They lack the sense of urgency required in the fast-moving routine of modern administration. Wise as counselors, they perform an important function in cautioning their impetuous associates against pitfalls that otherwise might have been overlooked, but left to themselves they will never come up affirmatively with a positive program of action.

"Actually, in most business situations a half-dozen possible plans are proposed, any one of which would work reasonably well; and it is far more important to select one and get on with the job than it is to prolong the debate until the last shred of doubt as to which is the perfect best can be removed."

Presidents Roosevelt, Truman, Eisenhower, Kennedy, and Johnson are examples of the men who had the moral courage to make urgent decisions involving enormous consequences, decisions whose success or failure could be attributed to no one else.

Mistakes Are Not Final

Over and over again I have found that it is the human factor in decision-making that often afflicts an executive and prevents him from taking proper action. Fear of methodological blundering is not half so strong as fear of the consequences of doing the wrong thing.

But mistakes are rarely as final and devastating as they seem to be in the middle of the night after execution. After all, how else does one learn except through his mistakes? Mistakes are our most effective teacher. This is more than a cliche, it is a fundamental truth of human existence. Of course, if we make too many errors, or fail to benefit from those we have made, we have to suffer the consequences, and they may last for a while. But by and large, mistakes—when they are not extreme—are part and parcel of every executive's career upward. As in baseball, it's the percentage that counts.

What are the percentages? For my part, I believe that there is a great deal of truth in the statement that the difference between a successful executive and an unsuccessful one is the difference between being right 55 percent of the time and being right only 48 percent of the time. Some executives are satisfied with a batting average of .300, which they consider a good record in any league.

At any rate, if an executive can maintain a batting average of .600, he has little to worry about—unless, of course, his competitors have an average of .650. But frankly I do not believe even your competitors on the average score that high, however it may seem so at times.

On the other hand, if you are able to make four out of five decisions correctly, you are way up on top. Extremely few executives can point to a record as good as that.

Mistakes Will Happen

It is both enlightening and comforting to realize that, at best, the human decision-making process can never be the precise computing-machine procedure we would like it to be. Even the most brilliant and reflective of us are bound to make mistakes. This is a hard fact of reality. We have to live with it, and we must learn to accept it.

For one thing, human thinking is rarely if ever totally impersonal, objective, and unbiased. Man is not so much a rational being as he is a rationalizing being. His conscious thought processes are nearly always a means of justifying— finding logical and acceptable reasons for—his emotionally based needs, drives, and wishes. There is nothing wrong with this. Who is to say that human feelings are good or bad? It's just our nature—the way we are put together.

We can rarely judge facts or evidence without some degree of emotional involvement. As a result, we tend (to a certain uncontrollable extent) to accept data in the light of our personal drives and wishes, giving stronger weight or greater emphasis to factual information that is in accord with our individual feelings, and less weight or importance to equally objective evidence that is not in line with what we are seeking to accomplish.

That emotions have effects on choices is borne out by a study of practical decision-making in industry conducted by Dr. Herbert A. Simon and his colleagues at the Carnegie Institute of Technology. One of their findings is that we make our decisions conform with what we would like them to be, rather than with what they necessarily should be. We tend to stack the cards against ourselves (or in favor of ourselves) even though we do not realize it. This is largely done subconsciously, of course. We are never fully aware of the twist that our wishes build into our decisions.

We also stack the cards the way we want them to be stacked by other very subtle means, for better and for worse: by selecting the problems we want to decide upon first, by the way we proceed to delineate and define those problems, by the facts we choose to guide ourselves by or use to reinforce our position, by the way we postpone action, and finally by the people we pick to consult for advice or suggestions. Every step of the way there is room for error, or opportunity for impeccable judgment!

These are some of the reasons, therefore, why the most brilliant executive, even though trying to proceed objectively and deliberately toward chosen goals and keep his thinking as unbiased as possible, is apt to find the decision-making process imprecise and irrational much of the time—somewhat like shooting in the dark. And he must remember that there will always be somebody who will oppose every decision he will ever make.

His Loneliest Hours

Here's another important point to remember. Many of the executive's most important decisions are a choice between different sets of values. Which should take priority over others and why? As Professor David G. Moore of the Graduate School of Business Administration at Michigan State University has remarked:

"The executive's loneliest hours are spent in choosing, not between right and wrong, but between two rights or two wrongs. His most creative moments are those in which he successfully integrates values, bringing diverse ideas together into new arrangements."

Take the complexity of modern business with all its inter-reactions, the fragmentary and sometimes distorted way in which facts, figures, and other information finally reach the executive, the inadequacy of his channels of information and the obstacles to be found in every attempt at two-way communication, plus the fact that major decisions generally require predictions about the future—often concerning human behavior, with the knowledge that such predictions have been notoriously inaccurate throughout history—and it will be little wonder that decision-making is sometimes the ambiguous affair that Professor Moore has described it to be.

Here, again, are some more of the many ways in which errors can creep into the decision-making process.

No matter how hard we try to be as exact and as discerning as we can, we are bound to make mistakes. These are indeed some of the executive's "loneliest hours." A certain amount of good luck must be on the side of the successful decision-maker when he attempts to pinpoint the reasons why a particular decision was a good one, two, three, or sometimes 20 years later.

But good luck happens only to people who do things, not to those who sit wringing their hands in the hope that somebody or something else will take the need to decide away from them.

Give yourself, therefore, the best possible reasons to feel that you are as good a judge of what will be as anyone else. Then put everything you have into making your predictions come true.

Whether the decision is large or small, whether it takes an executive three minutes or three years to make the decision, he is apt to be confidently optimistic of the results. In fact, an amazing number of executives regard the outcome of their decisions as a certainty, according to the editors of *Fortune*. That magazine reported such comments as these in a survey of some of the nation's top decision-makers:

"I was born an optimist" . . . "Just keep on being bullish and you'll win" . . . "In the main I am an optimist about the

*   *   *

The belief that action has to be taken on a problem may in itself be pure superstition. For 20 years a large shipping company had difficulty filling one of its top jobs. But for 20 years the job was filled whenever it became vacant. In the 21st year a new president asked: What would happen if we did not fill it? The answer was: nothing. It then turned out that the position had been created to perform a job that had long since become unnecessary.

*   *   *

nation's economy and my own business" . . . "A lot of things happen in my business that prevent you from being consistently optimistic or pessimistic; however, I am an optimist."

Other executives were a little more guarded in their attitudes and talked in terms of probabilities or good probabilities. It is obvious, though, that there is little room for pessimism or skepticism in the executive makeup. Pessimists make poor executives, just as procrastinators never qualify.

It is equally clear that an executive must have an open mind if he is to keep his decisions as free as possible from undue bias. This is particularly important when he is sifting his information and weighing it. Otherwise the percentage of error will multiply the longer he deliberates. But once he has finally decided upon a course of action, he should close his mind tighter than a trapdoor, and keep it closed, unless or until he finds he has been wrong. Only then should he open the door again and initiate, as promptly as possible, corrective action.

Steps in Decision-Making

Granted that decision-making is an all-important executive function, and that choosing the right decision often spells the difference between success and failure, the next question that naturally arises is: Just how does one go about arriving at the best possible decision in a given situation at a given time?

Superficially, it seems that there are wide divergences of opinion in the answers that have been given to this question by successful executives. But I believe a further investigation will reveal that the differences derive mainly from differences in language used, and that the fundamental processes recommended are to a large extent similar.

Here is a formula, if you choose to call it that, which I have used in making decisions for myself in matters that have been important to me. My rule is that when you have to decide something, the way to do it is:

Define the problem.

Put it into the clearest language possible.

Examine it painstakingly. Get all the facts you can.

List the possible choices open to you, and what each choice will lead to.

Then make your decision on the basis of the values you believe in, and the course of action you honestly conclude the facts lead you to take.

Care and persistence in applying this formula to minor decisions will increase your capacity to apply it to larger decisions. Eventually, when one of your life's biggest decisions is thrust upon you, the time and effort you have taken in the past to develop the faculty of making logical, objective, and good decisions will insure wisdom in the more important matters.

Every decision you ever make will be the result of weighing two factors: advantages versus disadvantages, as the formula above emphasizes. Except for the borderline elements that may not be clear gains or losses, it is exactly like making up a balance sheet. Instead of balancing figures, you balance advantages against disadvantages. It is well to remember, however, that some benefits greatly outweigh corresponding disadvantages, and vice versa. The appropriate "weights" for each entry are not all equal. Be sure to weigh different factors according to their importance if you expect adequate decisions from the use of this method.

Ben Franklin's Methods

A man who was well aware of the differences in values was that wise old patriot, Benjamin Franklin, who said and wrote so many things that are forever true, today as well as in his day. In a letter to Joseph Priestley in 1772, Franklin had this to say about his own decision-making procedure:

"My way is to divide half a sheet of paper by a line into two columns, writing over one *Pro* and over the other *Con*. Then, during three or four days' consideration, I put down under the different heads short hints of the different motives, that at different times occur to me, for or against the measure. When I have thus got them all together in one view, I endeavor to estimate their respective weights; and where I find two, one on each side, that seem equal, I strike them both out. If I find a reason *pro* equal to some two reasons *con*, I strike out the three. If I judge some two reasons *con* equal to three reasons *pro*, I strike out the five; and thus proceeding I find at length where the balance lies; and if, after a day or two of further consideration, nothing new that is of importance occurs on either side, I come to a determination accordingly. And, though the weight of reasons cannot be taken with the precision of algebraic quantities, yet, when each is thus considered, separately and comparatively, and the whole lies before me, I think I can judge better and am less liable to make a rash step; and in fact I have found great advantage from this kind of equation, in what may be called *moral* or *prudential algebra*."

There are, of course, much longer and more detailed decision-making formulas. One example presented here for your consideration is that adopted by E. I. du Pont de Nemours & Company for analyzing its public relations projects. This shows the methodical manner in which a department of a large, complex organization moves toward decisions within the limits of its own departmental responsibilities and capabilities, in full coordination with other departments, and with the necessity always held clearly in mind of operating in the interests of the corporation as a whole.

Section A

1. What is the objective this project is designed to gain or approach? Is the objective sound and desirable?

2. If the project succeeds, will it reach or approach the objective? Are there collateral advantages?

3. Is the project feasible?

    a. Is it reasonable to expect it to succeed?

    b. Can it be done with existing personnel?

    c. Does it involve cooperation outside the department?

4. Are there disadvantages to the project?

    a. Is it counter to sound public-relations policy?

    b. Is it counter to company policy?

    c. Is the expense too high in relation to possible gain?

    d. Can it embarrass top management? sales? production? research?

5. How much will it cost? Where is the money coming from?

6. In what ways can the project fail? What are the foreseeable difficulties?

7. What are the penalties of failure?

    a. Will it embarrass the company if it fails?

    b. Will it embarrass the department if it fails?

Section B

1. Why do it at all? Is it worth attempting?

2. Why do it now? Is there any reason for moving fast?

3. Why do it this way? Are there other methods of approach that promise more?

4. Is this the best way that the amount of money involved could be utilized to promote the public relations of the Du Pont Company?

If it passes all these tests, there are two more questions in

Section C

1. Who, if anybody, outside the department must approve the project?

2. Who, if anybody, outside the department must be informed?

How the Unconscious Mind Works

It would be untrue to suggest that all business executives—or even a few business executives—consciously plod through a long, detailed, decision-making formula before arriving at decisions. Undoubtedly, if asked, most executives who have actually proved their outstanding capacity to make sound decisions, often at lightning speed, would say: "No, I never do anything like that! I simply get the important facts, estimate the situation and decide."

Yet I am sure that if we could peer into the unconscious workings of their minds when they were in the throes of decision-making, we would find that many of the steps outlined above are regularly taken in preparing for that critical event when the decision is to be made, one way or another. The benefit to you of the formulas quoted here and the others you should study will not be in their conscious, step-by-step application to minute-by-minute decisions you may make, but in the effect they will have in training your subconscious mind to run through a correct psychological process when the decision-making moment is forced upon you.

Here are additional suggestions that may help you.

1. When you think you have obtained a reasonable percentage of the facts, try making a tentative decision and then seeing whether the evidence at hand supports it.

2. A decision that would involve an outlay of $20 million would require far more probing than one involving just $20. Delve into the facts no further than seems reasonable and profitable. There is a point beyond which study and deliberation is time wasted in every type of decision you will be called upon to make.

3. In every important problem be sure to allow additional time by way of a safety margin before your deadline. Complications may arise which you could not have anticipated, which may require postponing that final hour. If you have this built-in safety factor in your time schedule, it will often relieve you of last-minute anxieties.

4. When you have gone as far as you reasonably can in your pursuit of knowledge, weigh the unknown facts or possibilities as best you can and take them into account in evaluating the known.

Facing the Problem Squarely

General Lucius D. Clay, chairman of the Continental Can Company, has said that "nine times out of ten the inefficient manager becomes so not because of lack of training or lack of information but because of evading hard decisions." Indecision and procrastination have never solved a single problem in the history of mankind, and they never will.

But they have succeeded in making matters worse by creating new problems out of the old unsolved problems, until it took men of exceptional talent or even genius to eventually unravel the difficulty.

If a company's problems remain unsolved for any appreciable length of time, that company goes out of business. This is not new. Thousands have done so. More often than not, these business tragedies could easily have been avoided if somewhere along the line one or two executives had faced up to their decision-making responsibilities. This is what an executive is for, this is what an executive must do—if he is to remain an executive.

My plea, then, to those who are willing to take on the responsibilities of leadership is: Practice the art of making decisions. Develop proper timing, wisdom, and courage; learning how to think is the discipline.

Our turbulent, precarious, and fast-changing world brings special attention to this art. It is needed; it is demanded.

For intercontinental statesmen, for national leaders, for community leaders, clergymen, and teachers, as well as for business executives, the art of decision-making is the *sine qua non* for human survival. The economic, social, political, and moral problems prevailing upon us are awful and magnificent. If we make the right decisions, the sky is the limit for the fulfillment of each individual potentiality, for corporate growth, for every nation's development; indeed, for the future of man.

CHAPTER 9

CREATIVE THINKING

By Alex F. Osborn

It was only about 500 years ago that Europe began to rate the power of thinking, and especially creative thinking, on a par with the power of brute force. It was this new attitude that gave vitality to the Renaissance.

North America was the lucky beneficiary of the world's creative upsurge. As the *New Yorker* has said, "Ideas are what the United States is made of." Without doubt, our new heights in standard of living have been reached through creative thinking.

One new idea inherited by America from Europe was a way to use fire by means of an internal combustion engine. This gave birth to our automotive industry, without which America's standard of living would be far lower. For it alone gives gainful occupation to over 12,000,000 of us.

Agricultural ideas have made far richer the rich soil of our country. The creative genius poured into farm machinery by the McCormicks and the Deeres has enabled each farm hand to turn out far more food than formerly. When America was young (1820), one farmer produced only enough food for four other people. Today, one farm worker produces enough food for 38 other people.

Who in 1900 could have foreseen the changes in America that have since come about? From horse and buggy to car and plane and jet . . . from railroads and railway mail to transatlantic telephone and radio and television . . . from slow boat to the *Queen Mary*. (And now, more passengers fly the Atlantic than cross by boat.)

From gas lamps to indirect lighting . . . from sulphur-and-molasses to sulfathiazole . . . from hand-wound victrolas to hi-fi . . . from palm-leaf fans to air conditioning . . . from coal stoves to electric ranges built into the wall . . . from cold cellars to home freezers . . . from ear trumpets to transistor-powered hearing aids.

And yet, it is only recently that the value of imagination has been fully recognized even in America. A few years ago, the Chrysler Corporation started to hail imagination as "the directing force" which "lights tomorrow's roads, explores to-day for clues to tomorrow, hunts better ways for you to live and travel."

And the Aluminum Company of America has a newly coined word, "imagineering," which means that "you let your imagination soar and then engineer it down to earth. You think about the things you used to make, and decide that if you don't find out some way to make them immeasurably better, you may never be asked by your customers to make them again."

Thus, competition has forced American business to recognize the importance of conscious creative effort. So much so, that, more and more, the heart and center of almost every successful manufacturing company is its creative research. Industrial research used to do but little more than take things apart in order to find out what caused what and why. The new research adds to such fact finding a definite and conscious creative function aimed to discover new facts, arrive at new combinations, find new applications.

Thanks to thinkers like Dr. James B. Conant, imagination's importance to science is now recognized as never before.

Creative Problem-Solving

It is only occasionally that an important new idea is accidentally stumbled upon, and it usually turns out that the stumbler had been hard on its trail. Seldom is it a case of aimless luck, as in the story of the plumber who carelessly dropped a piece of steel pipe into a batch of molten glass and, on pulling it out, found that he had hit upon a way to make glass tubing.

We cannot consciously increase the crop of fortunate accidents, but we can produce more ideas by conscious creative effort, and in this process, it pays to focus our aim. We should first make our target as clear as possible.

Sometimes we must originate the problem itself. At other times the problems are thrust upon us by force of circumstances. In scientific and in business organizations, problems are often assigned to staff members, with the targets well defined.

Sensitivity to problems is a valuable trait. The lack of it is illustrated in the story of a young man who had taken a course in creative problem-solving and had later told his instructor that he'd been fired from his job. When asked why, the ex-student said:

"I don't know. After taking your course, I was prepared all right. If they'd given me some problems to solve, I know I could have solved them. But they didn't give me problems. They just gave me one whale of a mess!"

One reason why Americans get better and better goods for their money is that our manufacturers reach out for targets—consciously search for problems, the solution of which can spell opportunity. For example, recognition of shrinking as a shortcoming in men's shirts led to the multimillion-dollar idea of Sanforizing. Here's the story of how the target was picked and how the aim was set:

The problem grew out of the manufacturer's inability to give consumers as good a fit in shirts as in collars. The trouble was that collars had always been washed after being made, while if shirts were washed that way, they would lose some of their fine finish—would look as though they were not new, but had been through the laundry. So, on his own initiative, Sanford Cluett decided to find a way to shrink cloth without putting it in water.

At the cotton mills Mr. Cluett saw that, in the finishing process, the cloth was always pulled through the various processes of bleaching and mercerization. In fact, the cloth was sewed together into strips as long as 14 miles, and then pulled through the mill. This naturally distorted the fabric. He discovered that if this distortion were taken out, most of the shrinkage would be eliminated. So he built a machine which automatically restored the cloth to equilibrium—in other words, pushed the stretch back.

The Sanforized process was designed for cotton goods only. Its success led to other aims. One result is a similar process called "Sanforset" which stabilizes rayon. A still-newer process eliminates felting in wool. This case typifies how we can reach out for targets by grasping problems, and how one target can create another.

Creative triumphs have come also from diving off the deep end in search of unseeable problems. Faraday went at it blind when, in 1831, he discovered how electricity could be produced. He had no target. He merely wondered what would happen if—between two poles of a horseshoe magnet—he were to mount a copper disc and make it spin. To his amazement, electric current was what the spinning disc produced.

Dr. Charles M. A. Stine did not know what he was after when he started the search which resulted in nylon. His associates have told me that his outstanding trait was curiosity. There would probably be no nylon had he not decided to start a blind hunt.

Doctor Stine inaugurated a program of fundamental research in the Du Pont Company without specific objective, but believing that out of new scientific knowledge important developments would spring. Among the men engaged in this research was Dr. Wallace H. Carothers, who wanted to make larger molecules than had ever been made before, whether or not they had any practical application. He broke the world's record for molecular size of synthetic substances by producing polyesters and polyamides.

Dr. Julian Hill noted that one of these polymers in plastic condition could be pulled out into a fiber. Over a hundred chemists, physicists, and engineers participated in the research which ensued on these new compounds, eventually giving the world the synthetic fiber nylon.

Now and then someone asks a question which leads to a precious answer, and yet his name is lost in oblivion. One example of this was reported by the Department of Agriculture. Baby pigs are often crushed by their mothers rolling over upon them. An unknown thinker-upper asked whether pig mortality in a farrowing house could not be remedied by simply tilting the floor. This led to a system which is now working well. Since mama pigs like to lie down with their backs uphill and the piglets like to travel downhill, the tilted floor tends to keep the baby from under the recumbent old lady.

The Department of Agriculture has reported that these tilted floors have cut down this cause of pig mortality by as much as 25 percent. The price of bacon would be higher had it not been for that unknown's going out of his way to create a target.

Clarification and Dissection

We need not only to pick our problem but also to point it up. We should make the target clear. "Specify your problem consciously," urged Brand Blanshard of Yale. "Coin it at the beginning into a perfectly definite question."

As John Dewey has said, "A problem well stated is half solved." Clarification not only throws light on the target but helps to put it in perspective.

By all means, let's write out the problem. To help force creative action, we might even write it to somebody else and commit ourselves to find an answer, if not the answer, by a certain date. And let's not stop with merely posing the problem. Also let's remember that before we can phrase a problem we must determine the real nature of the problem. Only then can we properly set our aim or aims.

Dr. Walter Reed is one of our immortals mainly because he took pains to set the *aim* in the war against yellow fever. The *problem* was thrust upon him. On arrival in Cuba as head of the yellow-fever commission, he went over the most recent death list and asked about each case. He found that the latest to die had not even been near any other victim.

"You mean to say this man had no contact whatsoever with the disease?" asked Major Reed.

"None," was the reply. "He was in the guardhouse for six days with six other men and he was the only one to catch it."

"Well, if you are right about this," said the Major, "then something must have crawled or jumped or flown through the guardhouse window, bitten that prisoner, and then gone back where it had come from. I am convinced the time has come to set aside our microscopes and learn how yellow fever spreads from man to man. The poison is probably carried by an insect, and that may be a mosquito."

After all the bleary-eyed efforts to track down the cause of yellow fever through the usual microscope techniques, Major

* * *

The importance of problem definition was stressed by Albert Einstein in these words: "The formulation of a problem is far more often essential than its solution, which may be merely a matter of mathematical or experimental skill."

* * *

Reed, in that one observation, had set the aim that led to solution. Through his finding the right focus—plus the heroism of the volunteers who served as human guinea pigs—a vaccine against yellow fever was eventually produced. And 40 years later, our soldiers were able to chase our enemy through infested jungles and yet be immune to that once dread disease.

As Charles F. Kettering has explained: "The process of research is to pull the problem apart into its different elements, a great many of which you already know about. When you get it pulled apart, you can work on things you don't know."

In problem definition we should begin with a wide focus and then use a narrow focus to define the subproblems. As Prof. John Arnold of Leland Stanford has said: "Knowing what you are looking for helps you to recognize it when you see it. But in the case of innovation, how do you know what you are looking for? You don't, unless you state your problem so broadly, so basically, so all-inclusively and generically, that you do not preclude even the remotest possibility—so that you do not precondition your mind to a narrow range of acceptable answers."

In line with Professor Arnold's teaching, Emerson's "better mousetrap" was really a subproblem. The initial problem could well have embraced a total need such as: "How to get rid of mice." Thus, the problem would at first include all possible means of mouse extermination—such as poisoning, asphyxiation, electrocution, and even cats. This all-inclusive problem could then be broken down into its basic components.

"How to make a better mousetrap" could become one of the subproblems. And then, within this subproblem, we could ask ourselves a series of specific questions. "How can I make it better looking?" . . . "Cheaper?" . . . "Easier to use?" . . . "Safer for the housewife?" . . . "Lighter in weight?" If we happened to have a research staff, we might well assign one of these aims to each man or group.

The Buffalo Pottery Company started with this problem: "How can we reduce manufacturing costs?" This problem was too broad. Manufacturing costs embrace nearly everything in a plant. So the next step was to break out the 31 items comprising "manufacturing costs." This list was then boiled down to the 17 factors most subject to cost reduction. The problem selected for initial creative attack was this: "What mechanical method can we think of to substitute for hand labor at points of manufacturing change?"

Although this was a specific problem, it concerned seven positions in the plant, and each position called for a specific solution. After this set of problems had been processed (for each of the seven positions), the 16 other opportunities for cost reduction were subjected to creative problem-solving, one at a time.

Here's an ultrascientific example from General Electric of the method of composing a problem so as to be limitless in approach and yet specific in purpose. The General Engineering Laboratory received a request from an operating department to suggest a device by which a lamp could be turned on when you walked into a room, "so you would not have to fumble trying to find the lamp switch and knock the lamp down and fall over a chair and break your leg." The brainstormers took two weeks to define the problem.

Finally, the brainstorm group came up with what has since been marketed under the trade name of "Touchtron." You simply touch the side of the lamp and the lamp turns on. You touch it again and the lamp turns off.

One psychological reason for taking time to contemplate a problem was brought out in the Rokeach experiments with 250

*   *   *

Scientific tests for aptitudes have revealed the relative universality of creative potential. The Human Engineering Laboratories analyzed the talents of large groups of rank-and-file mechanics and found that two-thirds of these rated above average in creative capacity. An analysis of almost all the psychological tests ever made points to the conclusion that creative talent is normally distributed—that all of us possess this talent to a lesser or greater degree—and that our creative efficacy varies more in ratio to our output of mental energy than in ratio to our inborn talent.

*   *   *

students at Michigan State College. These tests bore out the hypothesis that by taking more time for perception of a problem, a less-rigid and more-creative attack is more likely to ensue.

Walter Chrysler saved his small pay as a young railroad mechanic in order to buy a huge $5,000 Pierce-Arrow sedan—just to take it apart, put it together again, and see what he could see. He wanted to find a way to make a better motorcar and went at it, according to Ray Giles, by asking himself specific questions such as "Why wouldn't brakes on all four wheels stop the car even better?" . . . "Why not keep the lubricating oil in better condition by having it run through a filter all the while?" . . . "Wouldn't tires of bigger diameter give a smoother ride?"

"No wonder when that young fellow later brought out his first Chrysler automobile, it was the sensation of that year's auto show," concluded Ray Giles.

One Aim May Lead to Another

Just as one idea leads to another, one aim often leads to another. This has been true of even the greatest scientists. As Paul de Kruif has said, "Microbe hunters usually find other things than what they set out to look for."

I went through the General Motors research laboratory at Dayton. My guide was the director, Charles Kettering. We peeked into a little room where three men were at work around a little stationary engine, which was exhausting through the hole in a window. "What are they doing?" I asked Mr. Kettering.

"Oh, I told them they ought to be able to change gasoline so it would give the motorist five times as many miles per gallon." They never found what they were after, but they did hit on the idea of lead, and that resulted in Ethyl gasoline. Their search had changed its aim and as a result, instead of increasing the mileage of gasoline, they had decreased its knocking.

The Corning Glass people aimed to make globes for railroad lanters so strong that they would not crack even when bombarded by icy sleet. They hit that mark all right, and railroads became safer as a result. But in doing that, they perfected a new kind of glassware that could withstand the heat of ovens.

The women of America have since bought nearly 500 million pieces of Pyrex ware in which to bake, serve and store. That innovation then led to Flameware for top-of-stove use.

Research directors recognize that aims often change. Dr. Howard Fritz told me how one of his scientists had started on a pursuit which led to a byproduct of his work, which then became his life's work. The byproduct became the product known as Koroseal. This is not an unexpected turn of affairs in organized creativity, according to Doctor Fritz. As Dr. L. L. Thurstone has pointed out, problem-solving often calls for "reformulating the problem itself and then solving the new problem."

It pays to assay our aims. The U.S. Patent Office is crowded with "good" ideas that are no good for anything. Countless people have spent countless hours and pounds of creative energy on projects of no useful purpose.

Personally, I have too often set forth in search of will-o'-the-wisps. For example, I had in mind a certain new kind of dictionary. I talked with a few people who dealt in words, and they were enthusiastic about my target. I set myself to the task and spent hundreds of hours working out the first hundred words. Then I talked to a dictionary publisher. It soon became obvious that it would take 10 men almost a lifetime to complete my work; the cost would be too great and the market would be too limited.

Had I analyzed that aim in time, I could have invested those creative hours in something of greater promise.

Questions as Spurs to Ideation

The *question* technique has long been recognized as a way to induce imagination. Professors who have sought to make their teaching more creative have often employed this device. For example, when Walter Dill Scott was at Carnegie Institute of Technology, he was known for the hypothetical questions he asked students—even weird questions like "What if we had eyes both in the front and the back of our heads?" . . . "What if we could swim more easily than we could walk?"

In practical problem-solving we can give *conscious guidance* to our thinking by asking ourselves questions. This is the way that technique works: First you isolate the subject or problem you want to think about. Then you ask a series of questions about each step in that subject or problem. Here are the queries which the officers had to ask themselves: (1) *Why* is it necessary? (2) *Where* should it be done? (3) *When* should it be done? (4) *Who* should do it? (5) *What* should be done? (6) *How* should it be done?

152

A creative problem usually calls for far more questions, and necessarily looser questions, than the Army manualized. Imagination has to be guided by stabs such as "What about . . . ?" and "What if . . . ?" And always it must be prodded with "What else?" and again "What else?" By bombarding our imaginations with such queries, we can pile up a quantity of ore in the form of all kinds of ideas—good, bad and indifferent.

Out of that ore, our own judgment, or the judgment of others, can refine gold in the form of good ideas.

Even in preparation for, and analysis of, a creative problem, self-questioning can often bring us nearer to solution. In those earlier phases of procedure, we should think up the queries which could put our imagination on the right track. And even in evaluation, we can best assay our tentative solutions by thinking up the right questions to apply to our findings—questions such as "Can this be tested?" . . . "What kind of tests would be best?"

A research project based on the application of questions to problem-solving was conducted by Leland Stanford University by Dr. Donald W. Taylor and Dr. William L. Faust and reported in the *Journal of Experimental Psychology*. The technique used was essentially that of the "Twenty Questions" game.

As Dr. Frank Kingdon has said, "Questions are the creative acts of intelligence."

When it comes to piling up hypotheses, one basic question has to do with other uses. This is so important that in his book entitled *Psychology of Invention in the Mathematical Field*, Jacques Hadamard referred to "two kinds of invention" and commented as follows:

"One consists, a goal being given, in finding the means to reach it, so that the mind goes from the goal to the means, from the question to the solution. The other consists, on the contrary, in discovering a fact, then imagining what it could be useful for, so that, this time, mind goes from the means to the goal; the answer appears to us before the question. Now, paradoxical as it seems, that second kind of invention is the more general one and becomes more and more so as science advances."

Under the heading "other uses," there are many questions with which we can prime our imaginations—questions such as "In what *new* ways could we use this as is?" . . . "How could this be *modified* to fit a new use?" . . . "What *else* could be made from this?"

Every manufacturer is constantly on the hunt for other things to make out of his own basic material. This has been particularly true of rubber. Out of thousands of ideas considered, here are a few that have been turned down by one big company: rubber bed-blankets, rubber bathtubs, rubber bathtub covers, rubber curbstones, rubber clothespins, rubber birdhouses, rubber doorknobs, rubber coffins, and rubber gravestones.

The success of most synthetic materials is based on thinking up new ways in which other people can use the product. Du Pont's neoprene has been built up into great volume through thousands of new applications, some of which could come only from shooting wild. For example, a toy-maker makes a chocolate-flavored bone out of neoprene for dogs to chew upon. A doll-maker has covered some of his creations with a magic skin of neoprene, and in a color so natural that a child thinks of it as a real baby.

The list is endless—a lamb with a coat like wool, a dog named "Poochy," baby chicks, a whale that spouts water, a whale-like submarine, a ship with three smokestacks.

Likewise with cellophane and nylon. The latter, for example, has already displaced catgut on most tennis rackets. Fishing lines of nylon have become more and more popular. Every woman knows about nylon clothesline. Huge hawsers and mammoth grommets are made of nylon, too.

"To what use can waste be put?" Along this trail, the piling up of alternatives is particularly important. America's packing industry has been built on ingenuity in finding new uses for almost every byproduct except the "pig's squeal."

Likewise in the steel industry. Slag used to be a costly waste. Now it is salvaged for ballast in railroad beds, for making cement, and for processing into building blocks. The slag from the Tennessee plant near Birmingham is so rich in phosphorus content that it is now packaged and sold throughout the South as a soil conditioner.

"What use could be made of those gases?" was the question some steel man must have asked himself long ago as he stared at the ugly fumes arising from his stacks. What a development that started! Today, through the use of byproduct coke ovens, those gases are saved and are the source of literally thousands of products in the chemical and drug field. While most people think in terms of 50,000 end products from such salvaging, a friend of mine in the steel business believes that as many as 500,000 more uses may be developed in the future.

What to do with "rejects" is another creative challenge. Often it is easy to sell them as seconds. Ingenuity can sometimes provide a more profitable answer. And what to do with scrap likewise calls for imagination. L. A. Conley of B. F. Goodrich saw pieces of surgical tubing being thrown into the waste barrel. "Why not cut them into rubber bands of the size and width used by the millions to hold small items together?" he asked. Conley got $150 for his new-use suggestion.

The profit his company made from that idea was velvet— velvet scraped from stuff which otherwise was worthless.

And then, too, there are cases where a new use may turn a dud into a triumph. George Westinghouse thought up about 400 inventions, of which the only dud was a rotary engine. But he refused to throw it away. Instead, he added a new invention and started another business—simply by turning his useless engine into a new and better water meter.

Other Uses "As Is"?

"To what other uses could this be put?" is a good question to ask of our imagination in regard to a thing, a thought or a talent. For by adding uses, we can often add value. Then, too, by piling up alternatives by way of other uses, a still better use is likely to come to light.

Thinking up additional uses can often widen markets for old products. A well-known scouring pad got its start in the kitchen sink. A new tire-cleaning use then opened up another market—a big one, too, consisting of 30,000,000 white-walled tires.

New uses for telephones have likewise opened up gold mines. A transcribed record now announces the correct time and the latest weather report. For this additional use, the New York Telephone Company charged a nickel per call and added $2,000,000 per year to its revenue.

Sometimes the very life of a new product depends on thinking up many new uses. Helicopters might have turned out to be museum pieces, unless someone had thought up enough new jobs for them to do—jobs which they can do best, such as the new use of patrolling high-tension lines over the mountains.

Scotch Tape has grown from a little specialty into a great industry. Its manufacturer created a list of 325 unduplicated uses. Tom, Dick and Harry thought up a lot more. I happened to be the beneficiary of one of these ideas. The side of my face became partially paralyzed as the result of an icy draft. A nerve specialist in Canada told me that only time could cure my ailment, but that I could help myself meanwhile with Scotch Tape. He showed me how, before retiring, to push my face into proper shape and then strap it there.

Some great advances in science have come from finding a new use for an old thing.

In London, along about 1620, a woman was having a hard time delivering a baby. A doctor named Chamberlain appeared with something under his coat. He covered it with a sheet and quickly brought forth the baby. For nearly a century, the doctor's "iron hands" were kept a secret within the Chamberlain family—and yet similar tongs were on almost every hearthside. According to an obstetrician friend of mine, "Forceps have done more to shorten labor pains and to preserve life than any other surgical gadget ever thought up."

Lord Lister suspected Louis Pasteur as more or less guilty of boondoggling in trying to find a way to make wine stay sweet. But this work of Pasteur's led Lister to wonder whether a more important use could be found for Pasteur's findings. Specifically, he asked himself, "If germs ruin flavor, could germs be the cause of so many unexplained fatalities in surgery?" This *other* use of Pasteur's new theory led to proof that germs did invade wounds, and this truth became the key to the antiseptic surgery which immortalized Lister's name.

"What *new* use?" . . . "What *other* use?" All of us have enough creative power to pile up alternatives galore by sending our imagination along this highway and into its many byways.

CHAPTER 10

CHAIN OF COMMAND

By Burleigh B. Gardner and David G. Moore

The man-boss relationship is one of the basic elements in an organization. The concept of supervision in which one person directs others is fundamental to the system of division of duties and responsibilities. Basic, also, are the different roles and expectations for supervisor and supervised. Thus the supervisor has a primary responsibility for getting a job done. And he is expected to get it done according to the standards and requirements set by himself or set by the organization.

In addition, he has secondary responsibilities which control or restrict the way he must function in getting the job done. He may have to keep within certain costs, see that safety requirements are met, abide by union contracts or personnel policies, and so forth.

As a supervisor, he does these things by influencing those under him. He must direct them, judge them and motivate them. And unless he can do these effectively, the job does not get done. However, the supervisor expects certain things of his subordinates:

1. They will accept his right to give orders, to judge, to direct.
2. They will obey the orders, or at least try.

In turn, the supervised have certain responsibilities and expectations. They have the responsibility for trying to carry out the orders. They expect that the orders will be:

1. *Understandable*
2. *Possible*

3. *Reasonable*

4. *Related to their job and the work situation*

They also expect that they will not be held accountable for failure if the job is not understood, is impossible or unreasonable, or is beyond their ability.

Now these expectations are basically part of our culture—we all grow up in a society which teaches us what these roles are and what we can expect of either supervisors or subordinates. Thus the idea that the boss has the "right to give orders" is merely an expression of an established social code of behavior. Furthermore, the obedience of subordinates is also part of the social code.

In terms of the exchange system, when the employee accepts the job he accepts this relationship. In effect he says: "In return for the money and other benefits I receive, I will work certain hours and so many hours each day; I will do the work for which I've been hired, and I will take orders from the boss within the limits to which it is customary and morally right for him to give me orders."

If the boss exceeds these limits, the worker may openly defy him, in effect saying, "I'm not being paid to do that," or "You can't pay me enough to take that guff." Or in many cases the worker obeys grudgingly or evades the issue and later evens out the transaction by doing poor work, cutting his output, or by other nonsanctioned actions.

We have, then, the situation in which the boss gives orders because his role, or his job, requires that he give them; and the subordinate obeys because his role requires acceptance of the boss's right to give orders.

One thing is clear—the obedience to the boss is not solely a matter of giving in to a superior force. While the boss has at his control certain power of rewards and punishments, he has far from absolute power. He can hardly "make" anyone do anything, and the extent to which he can try to force obedience is controlled by custom, by rules of the organization, and by the climate of opinion within the work group itself. Thus, in reality, his authority over others rests not in the power which is placed in the position, but in the acceptance of that authority by subordinates.

In spite of the general acceptance of the authority relationship, it is clear that not any order nor any act of the boss is accepted. In fact, the problem of how to get subordinates to do what you want them to do is a constant problem with any supervisor.

How do you get them to come to work on time?

How do you get them to do more work?

How do you get them to obey the rules?

How do you get them to talk less and work more?

The supervisor's primary preoccupation is with how to get people to do things. Nevertheless, careful observation in almost any work situation will show that there is a vast body of acceptance of orders and of general obedience to the rules and directives set by management and imposed or enforced by the supervisors.

Turning now to the chain of command, we see that it is through the linkages of this man-boss relationship that the top man is linked with the bottom. Every person except one within the structure has a boss; and every boss, in turn, has his boss, until finally at the top of the heap we find that rare and practically sacred individual, the president, the owner, the big-shot-who-has-no-boss. (Of course, even presidents have their boards of directors; but a director is a different sort from your personal boss, who seems to be ever present, asking questions and "breathing down your neck.") In most companies or factories there is one Big Boss and below him rank after rank of smaller bosses down to the very bottom, where we find those unfortunates who have no one to boss, those who are so numerous and so unimportant that their names never appear on the organization's charts—the workers.

The Supervisory Hierarchy

The whole structure forms a neat pyramid, with the Big Boss at the top and each rank of lesser bosses increasing in numbers as they decrease in importance, until at the bottom of the supervisory structure there is the largest and perhaps the most misunderstood group, the foremen or first line supervisors. The whole forms a status system, with all foremen having a rank superior to the workers, all the next level outranking the foremen, and so on.

Although each department chief outranks every foreman, it does not follow that a foreman will take orders from any department chief or even from any superintendent. (At least in theory they do not, but it is pretty hard to say "no" to a superintendent.) Instead, each person has his own personal boss to whom he looks for orders and instructions, for praise and criticism, for rewards and punishments.

This extends on up to the top, so that each person is linked up to the Big Boss through a series of these man-boss relationships. This forms what is known as "the line of authority," or "chain of command" in the army. Since each level has more persons in it than the level above, each boss, as a rule, has more than one person reporting to him.

This gives the fan-shaped pattern so well known on the formal organization charts, with a number of lines of authority merging at each level, until finally they all merge into the supreme command of the Big Boss.

Just as the lines of authority converge toward the top of the structure, the lines of interest and attention converge also. In fact, everyone seems to be looking upward with his attention focused upon the people above him and especially upon his boss. His boss is the man who hands out the orders, assigns him to his work, gives him a pat on the back for a good job, and passes on a good word for him to the "higher-ups."

And his boss is the man who can give him a dirty job to do, criticize him for doing it poorly, and give him a bad name up the line. His boss is his link with those above him in the structure. Thus the likes and dislikes of the boss, his moods and opinions, his comings and goings, his least comment and gesture, or the way he is distracted by that cute little redhead from the next department—all these are subjects of interest to his subordinates.

Each subordinate is concerned over just how his boss feels about him. He wonders if his work is satisfactory, if he makes a good appearance, if his boss thinks he talks too much or not enough, or if he knows just what his boss does expect.

While each boss is thus the center of attention from his subordinates, he, in turn, is busy watching his own boss and wondering about him. As a result, he tends to look upon his subordinates in quite a different way. He rarely worries about their opinions of him; he does not lie awake at night wondering if he acted like a fool in front of them; he does not treasure their words of wisdom or of praise to be retold at the dinner table. He does not even remember that he is the center of their attention, and he is likely to be annoyed with them if they are upset by his indifference or demand a lot of his time.

Thus we have a series of man-boss relationships in which each person is intensely concerned with how his boss judges him and at the same time is busy judging his subordinates. Each is constantly looking at his subordinates, trying to determine how well they are doing their jobs and how they might do better work; and each is constantly being irritated and disturbed when they fall short of what he thinks they should be doing.

At the same time, his concept of the job is often being mixed up with what his boss will think and what he expects, until "doing a job" often becomes a matter of "doing what the boss thinks is good." This concern is not merely with what the boss expects in terms of the work itself but also with what he thinks is "proper" behavior. As a result, the boss at each level judges his subordinates not merely in terms of the work accomplished but in terms of "what would my boss think if he saw them?"

Now one fundamental concept of formal organization is that responsibility is drawn together into fewer and fewer hands as we progress from bottom to top of the organization. Thus, each supervisor has responsibility for the work of, and supervision of, several subordinates, but has only one boss. As a result, the man at the top has only a few whom he holds responsible and through whom his influence and authority reach down into the depth of the organization.

Fundamental to this supervisory-subordinate relationship is the belief that superior status attaches to the one who gives orders.

Thus the supervisor outranks his subordinates—in fact, he is referred to as the "superior." "Who is your superior?" is understood to mean "Who is your boss?"

The chain of command also forms the primary channel of communication for the organization. It provides the series of relationships through which the commands of the Big Boss are carried downward through the structure to its most distant points. And it is also up this line that information is carried back to the Big Boss, so that he is kept informed.

Thus, one of the major functions of the line is that of providing channels of communication extending from top to bottom throughout the structure.

The Limitations

It is not, however, the simple, direct channel of communication that it is often thought to be. By its very nature as a linkage of man boss relationships, it has a number of peculiarities which affect the quality, accuracy, and speed of its transmission. In fact, much of the transmission is so difficult that it is rare for a superior who is several steps removed from the work level to have a comprehensive knowledge of what goes on in the shop.

Such a statement may offend the many top executives who speak with glowing pride of how close they are to the work level, of how their subordinates trust them and tell them all. In any sizable plant, however, where there are hundreds or even thousands of workers at the bottom, it is obvious that the man at the top cannot possibly be kept informed of every detail. His knowledge of the work situation must be limited to only certain kinds of details or general information. The movement of information from the bottom to the top must be limited, and what goes up must be carefully selected.

Ideally, only those things are communicated to the Big Boss which are necessary for his decisions or which will help him to perform his special functions. Actually, this ideal is rarely achieved, and often important information never arrives at the top, or a lot of small details clutter up the channels.

Although this is a two-way channel with information moving both up and down, there is a striking difference between the kinds of information which go each way. From above comes, "The boss wants to know . . . ," and "The orders are . . ."; while from below comes, "This is what happened . . . ," "These are the difficulties . . ." and "Here are our successes or our alibis . . ."

Rare are the occasions when direct demands move up the line from the bottom or explanations for failures move down from the top.

The line as a channel of communication has an important function in two kinds of relationships: first, between each person in the structure and his job; and second, between each one and his boss. Probably everyone is aware of the first function, and each one does communicate to adjacent levels the obvious things they need to know to do their jobs. Because this function of communication through the line is more or less effective, the system works, people do their jobs, and goods are produced.

The second function of line communication is often ignored or misunderstood, however; and because it is overlooked, the man-boss relationship is often so unsatisfactory as to seriously impair efficiency and cooperation.

Communication Down

Because of the nature of the man-boss relationship, because each person is so dependent on his boss for recognition and communication up the line, because each person is so sensitive to his boss's moods, opinions, likes, and dislikes, there is often much confusion and misunderstanding in communication down the line. Since everyone below him is constantly trying to anticipate his wishes, trying to read his every word and gesture, the boss does not always have to put into words his ideas and what he expects of the job.

But as a result of this extreme sensitivity to the boss, there are, in any work situation, frequent misinterpretations, and the problem of impressing the boss sometimes becomes more important than getting the work done.

For example, we see the superintendent passing through the shop, convoyed by the foreman. Being in a jovial mood, he makes a conversational comment that "the girls seem happy this morning, the way they are talking and laughing."

The foreman thinks: "Is he hinting that I shouldn't allow them to talk? Does he think I don't keep proper discipline? Those girls ought to have sense enough to stop talking and act busy when he's around. Maybe I better move Mary off by herself because she always gets the others started talking."

The boss leaves, quite unaware that his comments have been interpreted as criticism. As soon as he is gone, the foreman bawls out the girls for talking and not paying attention to their work; he moves the Marys around, and it is weeks or even months before the final ripples of disturbance have died down.

Or, again, the foreman may come in some morning with a slight indisposition or with family matters on his mind, and he does not notice Joe, who is standing near the aisle. Joe, of course, was all set for the usual: "Good morning, Joe. How's everything?" Now he's all upset, and he thinks: "What's wrong? Wonder if he's sore about something. Did I do something wrong? Wonder if he saw me kidding with that new girl yesterday and got sore about that."

For the rest of the day Joe is so busy trying to figure out what might be wrong that his mind is only half on the job. Finally the boss speaks to Joe about something in a very matter-of-fact way. Joe heaves a sigh of relief and says, "Boss, when you didn't speak to me this morning, I thought you was sore about something."

And the foreman thinks, "These guys are just like a bunch of kids. Just because you don't go around waving and smiling all the time, they think you're sore at them. I wish they would grow up and pay as much attention to their jobs as they do to those little things."

Distortion Up the Line

At the same time, and also because of their sensitivity to the boss and their dependence on him, there is a good deal of distortion of the facts in communicating up the line. Along with a great concern for "giving the boss what he wants," there is a constant tendency to "cover up," to keep the boss from knowing about the things that go wrong or the things that do not get done.

No one wants to pass bad news up the line, because he feels that it reflects on him. He is supposed to handle his job so that there is no bad news; he has to give his superiors the impression that he is handling his job efficiently. As a result, he does not go running in to tell the boss what a poor job he did or how stupid he was. That is, he does not unless he thinks someone else will get to the boss first with the story. And when he does have to break some bad news to the boss, he will probably have gotten everything fixed up or developed a good alibi for his failure.

In this way, people at each level develop methods of defense, often complicated and ingenious, by means of which they protect themselves from criticism from those above.

Thus we see each individual in the line acting as a filter who sorts over the information coming to him and carefully selects what he will pass on to his boss. Since the boss responds most favorably to good news, there is a tendency for good news to go up the line quite easily and rapidly.

Information as to improvements in output, quality, costs, and so on are transmitted readily from level to level. On the other hand, bad news meets certain barriers; everyone is reluctant to communicate his mistakes or failures. The "what will the boss think of me" feeling acts as a brake upon full and rapid reporting of things which go wrong. It encourages delays; it fosters alibis; it develops skill in the tactful presentation of bad news.

166

Since the subordinates are interested in giving the boss what he wants to hear, any signs of interest in certain aspects of the work tend to stimulate the flow of information concerning them.

If the general foreman expresses interest, or merely curiosity, concerning a new machine or process, or concern over some problem, or interest in some worker, then in every contact with the foreman the boss is likely to hear something about the object of his interest. If he has looked on some new worker with favor, the foreman is likely to find some complimentary things to say about the worker; if the worker is learning the job rapidly, the foreman reports that he is a whizz; if he is slow but friendly with the others, he gets along well; if he is just average, he is coming along well; and so on.

If the general foreman did not think so much of a new machine the engineers wanted them to try out, the boss hears critical remarks. If the machine does the work, the operators find it hard to operate, or they cannot seem to get the hang of it, or the controls are wrong and it is tiring. If it does a poor job, then it is just a piece of junk and never will be worth anything.

Furthermore, the minute the boss shows a loss of interest in such details, he stops hearing about them. The moment he responds with obvious boredom or lack of interest, his subordinate is likely to sense it and to drop the topic and hunt around for something else to take its place.

As a result of this tendency, the boss may receive a considerable amount of minor and unimportant details about a few aspects of the job. Besides, since such information is usually conveyed merely for the purpose of interesting the boss, it is selected and faintly colored to fit that purpose.

Thus he gets snatches of slightly distorted information which makes him feel that he is keeping well informed about what is going on. (Many executives may feel that such a statement does them a gross injustice, and that they really do know all about their organizations. If they are at the intermediate levels in the structure, however, they will probably tell you confidentially that the Big Boss really is not in close touch with the job and its details.)

Since these selective processes are working in all communication from each subordinate to his superior, the taller the supervisory structure, the more filter stations the information must pass through before it reaches the top.

Thus, for a small concern with only two or three levels, there is much less selection than for a large concern with five or six levels. Then, too, the larger the concern, the larger the mass of details at the bottom, a mass which is beyond the powers of any one individual to comprehend in its entirety. Between the sheer volume of detail to be selected from and the successive stages of selection at each level, the man at the top ends up with only a vague and highly generalized picture of what is going on.

Keeping the Boss Informed

Everyone in the supervisory structure expects certain kinds of information from his subordinates; and while the precise details vary with the nature of the job and of the individual, there are certain general types of information which all desire.

For one thing, almost everyone in the structure wants to be informed concerning those things about which his boss will inquire. Nothing is more disturbing than to be forced to admit ignorance to your boss regarding events in your organization. When he calls you in and asks, "What about the trouble on X job yesterday?" and you have to reply that you did not know of any trouble there, you immediately feel that you have failed, that the boss is annoyed, and that he thinks you are not on top of your job.

On the other hand, when you can reply to his question with a detailed statement of the trouble, you feel that you have impressed him with your alertness and ability, have relieved him of any concern about the way you are handling the job, and have generally been a success. There is nothing quite so satisfying as having the right answers for the boss, and hav-

168

ing them on the spot without having to say, "I'll look into it and let you know."

Because of this, every subordinate is expected to be on the alert for those things which his boss should know in order to be able to give his boss an answer. If the foreman hears that the union is going up to the president on that case which has been kicked around in the department for the last two months, he warns the department chief. If there has been friction with some other department which is likely to be carried up the line, he warns his boss. If the monthly cost report will show some item out of line, the foreman warns his boss.

Whatever happens that may get up the line without passing through the successive levels must be anticipated and each level warned.

The line of authority is, then, a channel through which information moves by fits and starts, is sifted over at each level, and is, to a large extent, dependent upon face-to-face communication.

This means that the larger the organization and the more levels in the supervisory structure, the slower the flow of information either up or down the line. (I tell my boss something, and he sits on it a day or so before he tells his boss, and so on until it may be weeks before something gets through from bottom to top—that is, if it does not get completely lost on the way.)

To be sure, there are types of information or certain conditions when items may go bounding up to the top with very little delay. In any case, it is the type of channel which tends to limit the flow of information, slow it down, or censor it; and the longer the channel the greater these effects.

CHAPTER 11

EFFECTIVE TEAMWORK

By Douglas McGregor

The significance of unity of purpose within a managerial team is given some lip service by most executives, but it is not always recognized that this objective can only be achieved by a closely knit group. Most so-called managerial teams are not teams at all, but collections of individual relationships with the boss in which each individual is vying with every other for power, prestige, recognition, and personal autonomy. Under such conditions unity of purpose is a myth.

One research study of top-management groups found that 85 percent of the communications within the group took place between individual subordinates and the superior (up *and* down), and only 15 percent laterally between the subordinates. Many executives who talk about their "teams" of subordinates would be appalled to discover how low is the actual level of collaboration among them, and how high is the mutual suspicion and antagonism. Yet these same executives generally create the very conditions which would appall them if recognized. They do so by managing individuals rather than helping to create a genuine group.

The Individual or the Group?

The subject of groups within management tends to generate a good deal of feeling. There are those who have no use for group effort at all and who appear to believe that an organization can operate effectively on the basis of relationships between pairs of individuals. In many companies, for example, committees are held in low esteem. The definition of a camel as a horse put together by a committee reflects a common attitude.

William H. Whyte of *Fortune* magazine, in his book *Organization Man,* takes an even stronger position. He argues that group activity has a downward leveling effect on the individual, forces conformity and denies the expression of individualism, nullifies creative activity, and is in general a hampering and limiting form of human activity.

These views deny the realities of organizational life. Many activities simply cannot be carried on and many problems cannot be solved on an individual basis or in two-person relationships. The problem of the group versus the individual is not an either-or problem at all. There are kinds of activities which are appropriate to the individual, others that are appropriate to the pair, and others that are appropriate to larger groups.

Under the right conditions, there are positive advantages to be achieved from group effort. In addition, there are severe negative consequences when we ignore the necessity for group action and attempt to solve certain problems in terms of pair relationships.

In general we are remarkably inept in accomplishing objectives through group effort. This is not inevitable. It is a result of inadequate understanding and skill with respect to the unique aspects of group operation. We accept the fact that we have to learn how to operate successfully in our individual relationships with subordinates. If we gave no more time and attention to this phase of managerial activity than we do to group operations, we would experience the same low level of effectiveness in both.

Whyte's thesis that we have given undue emphasis to group phenomena, and in the process lost track of individuals, misses the point altogether. The real problem is that we have given so little attention to group behavior that management does not know how to create the conditions for individual growth and integrity in the group situation. The problem is one of ignorance based on under-, not overemphasis.

171

Inadequate Research

Research on group behavior was relatively slow in getting started. For many years, almost the only question that interested psychologists in this field was whether more work got done when people operated together or separately. The tasks selected for study—for example, the performance of mathematical computations—were often not group tasks at all. The researchers failed to differentiate between activities appropriate to the individual and activities appropriate to the group. As a result, the research findings led nowhere.

During the last couple of decades, there has been a concentrated effort to carry on productive research on group behavior, and it is beginning to pay off handsomely. Kurt Lewin and his students initiated this work in the 1930's by asking themselves some meaningful scientific questions: What behavior occurs in face-to-face task-oriented groups, and how does this behavior differ (if it does) from behavior in other situations? Are there variables of forces operating in the group situations which are unique to it? If there are, what are their consequences?

From these beginnings, there has emerged a major field of research endeavor that has produced an impressive body of knowledge. Lewin called this field "group dynamics" because he recognized what has subsequently been verified—that there are important aspects of group behavior which can be best understood by study of the group as a field of forces. He saw this subject as analogous to the physicist's "dynamics."

It often happens that a new field of study, as it turns up findings which challenge long-established and emotionally based convictions, encounters considerable hostility. The intensity of feeling generated by Darwin's study of evolution has died down today, and we regard this field as a legitimate and scientifically respectable one.

It is somewhat difficult for the younger generation to appreciate the intensity of feeling that was generated a half century ago over the issues which Darwin raised. Some of us, however, remember the Scopes trial in Tennessee, which literally filled the newspapers for some time. Freud's psychoanalysis generated hostilities which have not completely disappeared even today. The field of group dynamics has encountered similar difficulties.

It was natural, as the earlier researchers discovered, that there were characteristics of group effort which differentiated this form of human activity from others, to apply their growing insights to practical situations. They began to ask what people could do to be more effective in groups.

As this field of application grew, there were of course those who oversold it, and there were others who jumped on the bandwagon to exploit the findings for their own economic ends. Finally, there were the strong feelings of those who feared that emphasis on group behavior would undermine their power. Group dynamics acquired a bad name.

Effective and Ineffective Groups

If we take a balanced and reasonably objective view of the large body of research evidence on group behavior, certain things are clear. First, there are no mysterious and secret skills which will enable the "expert" to manipulate groups toward his own ends.

Knowledge in this field, like knowledge in any scientific field, can be misused, but the dangers of its misuse are substantially less than, for example, in the field of atomic physics. In fact, one of the major contributions of research on group behavior has been to show how such manipulative misuse tends to be self-defeating.

Second, despite the rantings of a few "converts," the field is not a cult. It has its own jargon, but consider in comparison the vocabulary that has grown up within the missile field in the past decade!

Third, groups can be effective decision-making and problem-solving entities. All the arguments to the effect that "only the individual" can be responsible, make decisions, innovate, are shibboleths. The fact that many, or even most, groups do not do these things well proves nothing but our lack of knowledge about group behavior and our lack of skill in operating within groups.

The basic questions which the serious researchers in this field are pursuing quite independently of the lunatic fringe are: What forces are uniquely operative in the face-to-face group situations? How do they operate and how can knowledge of them be applied to improve the functioning of groups? This is a worthwhile endeavor.

Let us attempt to lay aside for a moment our prejudice, pro or con, with respect to group activity and consider in everyday commonsense terms some of the things that are characteristic of a well-functioning, efficient group. Occasionally, one does encounter a really good top-management team, or series of staff meetings, or committee. What distinguishes such groups from other less-effective ones?

Characteristics of Effective Groups

1. The "atmosphere," which can be sensed in a few minutes of observation, tends to be informal, comfortable, relaxed. There are no obvious tensions. It is a working atmosphere in which people are involved and interested. There are no signs of boredom.

2. There is a lot of discussion in which virtually everyone participates, but it remains pertinent to the task of the group. If the discussion gets off the subject, someone will bring it back in short order.

3. The task or the objective of the group is well understood and accepted by the members. There will have been free discussion of the objective at some point until it was formulated in such a way that the members of the group could commit themselves to it.

4. The members listen to each other! The discussion does not have the quality of jumping from one idea to another unrelated one. Every idea is given a hearing. People do not appear to be afraid of being foolish by putting forth a creative thought even if it seems fairly extreme.

5. There is disagreement. The group is comfortable with this and shows no signs of having to avoid conflict or keep everything on a plane of sweetness and light. Disagreements

are not suppressed or overridden by premature group action. The reasons are carefully examined, and the group seeks to resolve them rather than to dominate the dissenter.

On the other hand, there is no "tyranny of the minority." Individuals who disagree do not appear to be trying to dominate the group or express hostility. Their disagreement is an expression of a genuine difference of opinion, and they expect a hearing in order that a solution may be found.

Sometimes there are basic disagreements which cannot be resolved. The group finds it possible to live with them, accepting them but not permitting them to block its efforts. Under

*   *   *

There is no room in management for the lone-wolf executive—the self-centered type of person who thinks of No. 1 first, last, and all the time. He may flash brilliantly for a brief while, but his star will not be in the ascendant for long.

All business is a group enterprise, and it demands the best efforts of every one of its members working in unison, like an orchestra, if it is to stay ahead and reach its goals.

—*J. C. Penney*

*   *   *

some conditions, action will be deferred to permit further study of an issue between the members.

On other occasions, where the disagreement cannot be resolved and action is necessary, it will be taken, but with open caution and recognition that the action may be subject to later reconsideration.

6. Most decisions are reached by a kind of consensus, in which it is clear that everybody is in general agreement and willing to go along. However, there is little tendency for individuals who oppose the action to keep their opposition private and thus let an apparent consensus mask real disagreement. Formal voting is at a minimum; the group does not accept a simple majority as a proper basis for action.

7. Criticism is frequent, frank, and relatively comfortable. There is little evidence of personal attack, either openly or in a hidden fashion. The criticism has a constructive flavor in that it is oriented toward removing an obstacle that faces the group and prevents it from getting the job done.

8. People are free in expressing their feelings as well as their ideas both on the problem and on the group's operation. There is little pussyfooting, there are few "hidden agendas." Everybody appears to know quite well how everybody else feels about any matter under discussion.

9. When action is taken, clear assignments are made and accepted.

10. The chairman of the group does not dominate it, nor, on the contrary, does the group defer unduly to him. In fact, as one observes the activity, it is clear that the leadership shifts from time to time, depending on the circumstances. Different members, because of their knowledge or experience, are in a position at various times to act as "resources" for the group. The members utilize them in this fashion, and they occupy leadership roles while they are thus being used.

There is little evidence of a struggle for power as the group operates. The issue is not who controls but how to get the job done.

11. The group is self-conscious about its own operations. Frequently, it will stop to examine how well it is doing or what may be interfering with its operation. The problem may be a matter of procedure, or it may be an individual whose behavior is interfering with the accomplishment of the group's objectives. Whatever it is, it gets open discussion until a solution is found.

Understanding and Skill Needed

These and other observable characteristics are generally found in the effective task group. Every one of them represents important ways of dealing with forces which are present in every group. A substantial amount of sensitivity, understanding, and skill is required of all the members—not of the leader alone—to create such a setting as this.

It has been my privilege to be a member of a staff of six or eight individuals comprising the faculty of a National-Training-ing-Laboratory-sponsored training program on a number of occasions. Each time I am impressed anew by the demonstration of effective group action given by these colleagues as they come together to design the program.

Normally a day is set aside for the purpose. The task is clear, but there is always the expectation that this program will contain innovations—perhaps major ones—which will make it not merely different, but better than anything that has been done before.

No one knows what these will be, or how they will evolve, but the group confidently expects to use the resources of its members to do a genuinely creative job. This confidence is rarely mistaken.

In addition to designing the program, there are dozens of decisions to be made, many necessary assignments of specific tasks and responsibilities, a variety of individual interests and desires to be integrated with the requirements of the program. Conflicts arise and are argued out, sometimes with a lot of heat.

These colleagues are individualists, and no one of them is prepared to have his individuality submerged. Nevertheless, there is the kind of commitment to the common purpose that yields genuine self-control.

The task is accomplished with amazing efficiency, yet there is plenty of kidding and good humor. Group "maintenance functions" are performed as the need arises. There is a chairman, but the leadership moves around the group as the situation dictates. Everyone participates actively, yet no one dominates the group. I have never known a vote to be taken except as a joke. Every decision is unanimous.

Most significant of all, each such group has a different composition. Some individuals may have worked together before, but there are always several new members. Within minutes of the start of the meeting, they are as much a part of the group as if they had been members for years.

It is truly an exhilarating experience to participate in such an activity. I usually come away wishing some of my good friends in management who have a jaundiced view of groups could have observed the meeting.

Characteristics of Ineffective Groups

Now let us look at the other end of the range. Consider a poor group—one that is relatively ineffective in accomplishing its purposes. What are some of the observable characteristics of its operation?

1. The "atmosphere" is likely to reflect either indifference and boredom (people whispering to each other or carrying on side conversations, individuals who are obviously not involved, etc.) or tension (undercurrents of hostility and antagonism, stiffness and undue formality, etc.). The group is clearly not challenged by its task or genuinely involved in it.

2. A few people tend to dominate the discussion. Often their contributions are way off the point. Little is done by anyone to keep the group clearly on the track.

3. From the things which are said, it is difficult to understand what the group task is or what its objectives are. These may have been stated by the chairman initially, but there is no evidence that the group either understands or accepts a common objective. On the contrary, it is usually evident that different people have different, private, and personal objectives which they are attempting to achieve in the group, and that these are often in conflict with each other and with the group's task.

4. People do not really listen to each other. Ideas are ignored and overridden. Discussion jumps around with little coherence and no sense of movement along a track. One gets the impression that there is much talking for effect—people make speeches which are obviously intended to impress someone else rather than remain relevant to the task at hand.

Conversation with members after the meeting will reveal that they have failed to express ideas or feelings which they may have had for fear they would be criticized or regarded as silly. Some members feel that the leader or the other members are constantly making judgments of them in terms of evaluations of the contributions they make, and so they are extremely careful about what they say.

5. Disagreements are generally not dealt with effectively by the group. They may be completely suppressed by a leader who fears conflict. On the other hand, they may result in open warfare, the consequence of which is domination by one subgroup over another. They may be "resolved" by a vote in which a very small majority wins the day, and a large minority remains completely unconvinced.

There may be a "tyranny of the minority," in which an individual or a small subgroup is so aggressive that the majority accedes to its wishes in order to preserve the peace or to get on with the task. In general, only the more-aggressive members get their ideas considered because the less-aggressive people tend either to keep quiet altogether or to give up after short, ineffectual attempts to be heard.

6. Actions are often taken prematurely before the real issues are either examined or resolved. There will be much grousing after the meeting by people who disliked the decision but failed to speak up about it in the meeting itself. A simple majority is considered sufficient for action, and the minority is expected to go along. Most of the time, however, the minority remains resentful and uncommitted to the decision.

7. Action decisions tend to be unclear—no one really knows who is going to do what. Even when assignments of responsibility are made, there is often considerable doubt as to whether they will be carried out.

8. The leadership remains clearly with the committee chairman. He may be weak or strong, but he sits always "at the head of the table."

9. Criticism may be present, but it is embarrassing and tension-producing. It often appears to involve personal hostility, and the members are uncomfortable with this and unable to cope with it. Criticism of ideas tends to be destructive.

Sometimes every idea proposed will be "clobbered" by someone else. Then no one is willing to stick his neck out.

10. Personal feelings are hidden rather than out in the open. The general attitude of the group is that these are inappropriate for discussion and would be too explosive if brought out on the table.

11. The group tends to avoid any discussion of its own "maintenance." There is often much discussion after the meeting of what was wrong and why, but these matters are seldom brought up and considered within the meeting itself, where they might be resolved.

Why Many Group Meetings Fail

Why is it that so many groups seem to resemble this example rather than the first one? There are a number of reasons. In the first place, most of us have rather low expectations of group accomplishments. Our experience with really effective groups has been so limited that we do not have clear standards of what could be.

In the second place, most of us have relatively little knowledge of what is important to good group functioning. We are not aware of current research findings concerning the significant requirements for effective group operations, and therefore the things we attempt to do to improve a given group are not always relevant.

One of the most important reasons for poor group functioning is the general fear of conflict and hostility, which leads us to behave in ways that hamper rather than help. Hostilities, hidden agendas, and other personal factors inimical to group functioning are very commonly present, particularly with a newly constituted group.

To ignore these or to suppress them is to let them determine the level of effectiveness of the group. Yet our fear of personal feuding and conflict is such that that is exactly what normally happens.

Another significant factor resulting in poor group activity is the mistaken idea that the effectiveness of the group

180

depends solely upon the leader. As a matter of fact, the research evidence indicates quite clearly that skillful and sensitive membership behavior is the real clue to effective group operation. In a really competent and skilled group, the members can, in fact, carry on a highly effective operation with no designated leader whatever.

Finally, along with our fears of conflict and hostility, is a lack of recognition of the necessity for paying attention to the maintenance of the group itself. Like any complex organization, a group requires attention to its functioning. If it is to operate at peak efficiency, it will require constant maintenance. Most groups deal with maintenance problems only in the post mortems outside the meetings, and these seldom result in action within the group.

Behind all these specifics, frequently, is a deeper attitude: Management by direction and control is jeopardized by effective group functioning. The principle of "divide and rule" is eminently sound if one wishes to exercise personal power over subordinates; it is the best way to control them.

If, however, the superior recognizes the existence of the intricate interdependence characteristic of modern industry, and if he is less interested in personal power than in creating conditions such that the human resources available to him will be utilized to achieve organizational purposes, he will seek to build a strong group.

He will recognize that the highest commitment to organizational objectives, and the most successful collaboration in achieving them, require unique kinds of interaction, which can occur only in a highly effective group setting. He will, in fact, discourage discussion or decision-making on many matters which affect his organization except in the group setting. He will give the idea of "the team" full expression, with all the connotations it carries on the football field.

The Potentialities of Teamwork

The face-to-face group is as significant a unit of organization as the individual. The two are not antithetical. In a genuinely effective group, the individual finds some of his deepest satisfactions. Through teamwork and group activity, many of the difficult organizational problems of coordination and control can be solved. However, these values can be realized only if certain requirements are met.

First, we will have to abandon the idea that individual and group values are necessarily opposed, that the latter can only be realized at the expense of the former. If we would look to the family, we might recognize the possibilities inherent in the opposite point of view.

Second, we will have to give serious attention to the matter of acquiring understanding of the factors which determine the effectiveness of group action and to the acquisition of skill

*   *   *

Knute Rockne said: "A football team is like a fine watch— all precisioned. If one small part is not working in harmony, the watch fails to function properly." The same holds true of a modern business team. Like the coach of a football team or the maker of a watch, the executive has the responsibility for making his group—as well as himself—function in harmony with the rest of the organization.

—J. C. Penney

*   *   *

in utilizing them. This means much more than offering courses in conference leadership. It means, above all, acquiring skills in group membership. The laboratory method of training developed by the National Training Laboratory is a particularly effective one for acquiring these skills.

Third, we will need to learn to distinguish between those activities which are appropriate for groups and those that are not.

Finally, we will need to distinguish between the team concept of management as a gimmick to be applied within the strategy of management by direction and control and the team concept as a natural correlate of management by integration and self-control. The one has nothing in common with the other.

Four Key Advantages

To the extent that these requirements are met, we will make some significant discoveries. For example:

1. Group target-setting offers advantages that cannot be achieved by individual target-setting alone. The two are supplementary, not mutually exclusive.

2. An effective managerial group provides the best possible environment for individual development. It is the natural place to broaden the manager's understanding of functions other than his own and to create a genuine appreciation of the need for collaboration. It is the best possible training ground for skill in problem solving and in social interaction.

3. Many significant objectives and measures of performance can be developed for the group which cannot be applied to the individual. The members of cohesive groups will work at least as hard to achieve group objectives as they will to achieve individual ones.

4. In an effective managerial team, the attitudes of "dog-eat-dog" competition, which are actually inimical to organizational accomplishment, can be minimized by the development of "unity of purpose" without reducing individual motivation.

It seems to me unlikely that the transition will be rapid from our conception of an organization as a pattern of individual relationships to one of a pattern of relationships among groups. We have too much to learn, and too many prejudices to overcome. I do believe, however, that such a transition is inevitable in the long run.

We cannot hope much longer to operate the complex, interdependent, collaborative enterprise which is the modern industrial company on the completely unrealistic premise that it consists of individual relationships. The costs of doing so—although they are mostly hidden and unrecognized—are completely unjustifiable.

When a few managements begin to discover the economic as well as the psychological advantages of really effective team operation, their competitive advantage will provide all the stimulus necessary to accelerate this transition.

Fads will come and go. The fundamental fact of man's capacity to collaborate with his fellows in the face-to-face group will survive the fads and one day be recognized. Then, and only then, will management discover how seriously it has underestimated the true potential of its human resources.

CHAPTER 12

THE ART OF DELEGATION

By Raymond Dreyfak

The Stevens Institute of Technology Laboratory of Psychological Studies some time ago decided to take a reverse approach to the question "What makes for executive success?" by first finding answers to the question "What makes a manager fail?"

Case histories of unsuccessful executives in more than 200 companies were carefully analyzed in an attempt to isolate specific "lacks" in executives that had resulted in failure. In the initial stages of the study, seven "lacks" cropped up immediately and seemed to head the list. First among these was the inability to delegate responsibility.

Hard to believe? Possibly. Yet the ability to delegate wisely, effectively and successfully is a much more difficult art than one might think—and one that, when properly used, can increase an executive's effectiveness two- or threefold, even more. Obviously, then, it is worth every executive's serious and continuing attention, for even though an executive may consider himself reasonably proficient in this field, there is always some room for improvement.

Let's start out, however, with a rather elementary illustration, because cases like this are actually much commoner than one might suppose.

Here is a case in point. The volume of orders pouring into a small plastics company was exceeding its capacity. The firm's main problem was to expand its plant and production facilities. The plant manager was charged with this responsibility.

He was an able man. But he suffered from the delusion that the only way to do a job right is to do it yourself.

Now, with the mammoth task of relocating before him, he was smart enough to know that only two alternatives were open. He could increase his workweek from 60 to 80 hours. Or he could delegate some of his authority to "free up" his own time commitments.

In the interests of sanity he chose delegation.

Unhappily this complicated, rather than solved, his problem. His first move was to create the title of production man-

*   *   *

Delegation *gives you an opportunity to take on additional work yourself; to expand your department or division.*

Delegation *relieves you of petty, routine details that are not part of your executive job and which can probably be done just as efficiently by someone else.*

Delegation *helps keep your department from becoming a bottleneck, which is very apt to happen when the executive insists on doing everything himself.*

Delegation *improves the morale of your employees by giving them a feeling of sharing responsibility.*

—*J. C. Penney*

*   *   *

ager. In the past, managing the production had been one of his key functions.

The man selected for the new job was an ideal choice, an experienced foreman with good qualifications. The "training program" began at once. But it never got off the ground.

Like most "indispensable" executives, the plant manager was constantly beset by telephone calls, small crises and problem-bearers. On and off for two months the increasingly befuddled foreman sat at his boss's side to observe the complicated charting and analysis techniques. The third month he was invited to try working up a schedule on his own.

Though he did a heroic job, his knowledge had been picked up on a haphazard, piecemeal basis. There were many gaps. Each gap presented a problem, so that in time the foreman became problem-bearer No. 1 on the plant manager's list. His boss's willingness (born out of habit) to solve the problems *for* him instead of *with* him eventually became a crutch.

The windup was that the work was delegated in theory but not in practice. Much extra time was devoted to it by the foreman. Very little time was saved by his superior. Other tasks—labor negotiations, specialized purchasing responsibilities, personnel selection—were delegated in the same manner.

"Delegated"? Not really.

The plant manager was more harassed and time-pressed than ever. And the "production manager" was completely frustrated. The only thing delegated to him was a title, and everybody knew it but his boss.

Eventually the plant manager was replaced. And indispensable as he was, the business didn't collapse. The new plant was built. Today the production manager is actually managing production.

The ironic part is that all along the plant manager had been deluding himself into believing he was really delegating. Unfortunately, he deluded himself out of a job.

What Is Delegation?

Delegation is easy to define, hard to practice.

"Delegation," says Earl Brooks, "is the process of establishing and maintaining effective working arrangements between a manager and people who report to him. Delegation results when the performance of specified work is entrusted to another, and the expected results are mutually understood."

Effective working arrangements is the key phrase. A great many executives pay lip service to delegation, but in practice they do not delegate at all—or, at best, delegate only on a limited basis.

Effective delegation implies a three-way satisfaction.

First, the delegator must be satisfied that the job is being done properly by his subordinate.

Next, the subordinate must be satisfied that the job is really "his baby." He must feel that it is so recognized by his superiors and that he is receiving full credit for its performance.

Finally, the job itself should play a clear role in furthering the company's profit objectives.

This last actually is the supreme test.

A branch manager delegated the running of weekly sales meetings to an assistant. He in turn sat in at each meeting as an observer, making small contributions as occasion arose. Eventually the assistant grew skilled at running the meetings. But the manager never relinquished his observer post. The delegation served no profitable purpose.

Henry O. Golightly, New York management consultant, says: "The outstanding executive knows which things in his company bring in the profits. He relates his own job to these things, and he can point to his personal contributions to the company's profit objective. Once this profit target is pinpointed, he devotes his main attention to its achievement. And he delegates secondary responsibilities to free his time for concentration on his primary goals."

When you fail to delegate, you fail to use your time as profitably as you otherwise might. This stalls your personal progress and at the same time undermines your subordinates' morale. Because of your static situation, their progress is also delayed.

Why Delegate?

Here are three things that effective delegation will do for you:

1. Delegation will bring your company's profit goals closer to achievement.

2. Delegation will bring your personal profit goals closer to achievement.

3. Delegation will bring your subordinates' profit goals closer to achievement.

The message is clear. It is profitable to delegate effectively.

A pharmaceutical company's research director had an idea which, if successful, would increase his firm's profits by 8 to 15 percent. But it would take his personal time and effort to direct the development and implementation of his brainchild.

He discussed his idea with his superior, the manufacturing vice-president, and received enthusiastic permission to go ahead with the project. He then proceeded to turn over 50 percent of his duties to two assistants. He did this patiently and systematically over a three-month period. When he was certain that the assistants could operate independently, the new project was launched. Here is the outcome:

. . . A new product line was successfully developed. During the first year it was responsible for an 11 percent profit growth. (Refer to Point 1 above)

. . . The company, in appreciation, promoted the research director to vice-president, awarded him a generous salary increase and a handsome bonus. (Refer to Point 2 above)

. . . One of the two assistants, responding brilliantly to his delegated assignments, has recently stepped into the vacated research-director slot. (Refer to Point 3 above)

Why delegate? Because it is profitable to do so. For *everyone* concerned.

A Few Roadblocks

John A. Patton, a working director for a number of leading corporations, has said:

"I have yet to meet the executive who will speak out against delegation, or one who will admit that he does not delegate. Yet to bump into a truly effective delegator is a rare experience. In my opinion, this is the executive who turns over the right task to the right man in a way that will ensure that the job is done right. He then devotes his freed-up time to furthering his own career by increasing his company's earnings."

Earl Brooks, writing for *Nation's Business,* puts it this way: "One of modern management's most important functions—effective delegating of work—is a subject for plenty of preaching but not enough practice."

Let's examine some of the obstacles in the way of good, sound delegation:

1. Self-delusion (the executive who just thinks he is delegating).
2. Resistance to change.
3. Lack of confidence in subordinates.
4. Fear of competition.
5. Fear of having weaknesses exposed.
6. Not enough time.
7. Old-school reluctance to impart knowledge.

Most executives will admit a recognition of these roadblocks, yet in the same breath swear that they do not apply to them. Yet one or more of the above shoes fit a great many executives. Let's examine them at close range.

1. Self-delusion. Many executives kid themselves into thinking they delegate. They pay lip service to delegation. They go through all the motions but in the end refuse to let go of the reins. Such executives hold back their companies, their subordinates and themselves.

2. Resistance to change. The change-resistor is complacent in the niche he has made for himself. In most cases he is set in his ways, and there is nobody from above prodding him for new ideas or increased productivity. Unconsciously he reasons, delegation implies work, new challenges, fresh problems. Who needs it?

If this rings an uncomfortably familiar bell, some soul-searching may be in order. An unruffled existence may seem more pleasant at the moment. But sooner or later that prod from above may come. If you are out of practice, you may be unable to cope with it. And just at that point, some full-of-vinegar young fellow may happen along to display all the drive and enthusiasm you lack.

3. Lack of confidence in subordinates. A textile company's executive vice-president discussed a special project with a division head. The manager begged out of the assignment.

"I'm overloaded with work," he protested.

"Delegate some of it," his chief advised.

"I wish I could," said the manager, "but it's top-priority stuff. I have no one I can trust with it."

The vice-president then said something that changed his mind. "Who was doing this vital work before you took over?" The division head mentioned the name of his former superior.

"The job was just as important then," his chief pointed out. "If he didn't have enough confidence in *his* subordinate to let

*   *   *

A good administrator not only learns to delegate authority, but he also seeks to share his thinking with as many others as possible. This is not an easy habit for some men to acquire, however. Strong characters, in particular, tend to regard thinking as their prerogative only.

—Clarence B. Randall

*   *   *

go of the responsibility, he would still be doing it himself, instead of being up there where he is now."

The division head made no further objection. "Let's talk about that new project," he said.

It is not unnatural for a successful executive to have an inflated opinion of himself and a deflated opinion of his subordinates.

John J. Corson of McKinsey & Co. has this to say on the subject in *Nation's Business.*

" 'If you want a thing done well, do it yourself' is a deeply rooted belief for many men. They rose to their present positions by excelling in one way or another. Their very success has given rise to habits of doing and a mistaken notion that the successful executive is the genius who has a thousand balls in the air at the same time—who calls the shots and keeps tabs on everything."

4. Fear of competition. An office manager in a cosmetics company was being considered for promotion. The executive who turned him down said: "He's the best office manager we ever had. But he has never groomed anyone to step into his shoes. It would take him months to start now, and the job we have to fill can't wait that long."

The manager lost out because he feared competition and did not understand progress. As Andrew Carnegie once said, "The great manager is the man who knows how to surround himself with men much abler than himself."

5. Fear of having weaknesses exposed. The one thing you can't delegate is a guilty conscience. If you are afraid of "stubbing your toe" on your own "Achilles heel," the place to attack the problem is at its root.

Yet many executives are reluctant to delegate because they are afraid it would bring their personal shortcomings to light.

If you have a weakness—and, being human, who doesn't?—delegation may even help you to shore up the vulnerable area. Your failure to delegate can only compound the ill. Attempting to cover up your weakness will simply hurt you twice instead of once.

6. Not enough time. This is the "manana" approach. "I know I should delegate more authority," one frowning executive admitted, "but I just can't seem to get to it." This executive's problem is really very simple. He doesn't delegate because he doesn't have the time. And the longer he goes without delegating, the less time he will have.

A government administrator has said: "The manager who fails to delegate is like a dog chasing his own tail. Eventually he is going to run himself down." This administrator uses his own system of forced delegation.

"When I see that my days are getting too long and my time cushion too short," he says, "I know that delegation is my only salvation. At this point I play a little game with myself. I pretend that I'm away on a trip. I inform my secretary to hold off all callers, and I devote the entire day to delegation. It's surprising how much you can accomplish in a day in this way."

7. Old-school reluctance to impart knowledge. Today's generation of executives, for the most part, appreciates that both company and individual growth are dependent on the growth of each member of the organization. However, there are still a minority of managers who persist in the archaic notion that their hard-won knowledge is too precious to share, and that the more closely they hoard it the more precious it becomes.

In practice the reverse is true. The most profitable way to put knowledge to work is by sharing it. And the best way you can share knowledge is by delegation.

How to Delegate

Now that the roadblocks to effective delegation have been established, let's mow them down. Here are eight tested and proven guidelines to help you delegate more simply and effectively:

1. Pick jobs to be delegated with deliberation.
2. Match the person to the job.
3. Motivate his job enthusiasm.
4. Build his confidence through training and guidance.
5. Define his duties clearly, but not rigidly.
6. Encourage his independence and initiative.
7. Be prepared for possible failure.
8. Maintain overall control.

The reward for adherence to these guidelines is upgraded productivity for you and your company. Now for a close-up view.

1. Pick jobs to be delegated with deliberation. A company planning a new product line was faced with a serious shortage of research talent. "Your No. 1 job," the president told

the personnel director, "is to recruit as many good research people as possible."

To free time for this task, the personnel man knew that he would have to turn over a portion of his work to a subordinate. In fact he knew exactly which jobs he wanted to unload.

Unfortunately, his decision was based more on impulse than need. His subordinate balked at the assignments. He recognized the jobs as those his superior disliked most. This executive had not delegated work; he had "palmed it off."

"Before turning over a job," an insurance company vice-president suggests, "ask yourself if you are doing it for your personal convenience or to build your company's profits and develop your subordinates. What you delegate can be just as important as how you delegate."

Here is another tip. Before assigning a job to a subordinate, make sure it is delegatable, and that your superior would register no objection to your relinquishing the task nor to the delegatee you chose.

2. Match the person to the job. "Yes" answers to these three questions will provide assurance that the person you selected is the right one for the job:

Is he well qualified and capable of understanding the assignment?

Does he really want the job?

Will the rest of your staff gracefully accept your choice?

If the job is going to overstrain the mental capacity of the person selected, or is going to require skills he does not have, you are inviting trouble from the start.

In assigning a job, convince yourself that the delegatee can really measure up to the standards you set. Don't take his word for it; find out for yourself. Test his knowledge and understanding of the work. Ask him specific questions. Press for specific answers. Don't simply show him what to do. Have him demonstrate his grasp of the assignment by doing it for you.

194

Next, assuming he is well qualified, ask yourself, "Does he *want* the job?" Many subordinates accept assignments because they fear the consequences of turning them down.

You may have no choice but to assign a job to a man whether he wants it or not. But the man who welcomes added responsibility as a steppingstone to his personal advancement will perform best. The individual who is in a happy rut and content to remain there may need constant prods and close surveillance.

What about Paul, Harry, and Tom when George's authority and responsibility are increased?

This is a factor often overlooked by delegators. In one company a vice-president gave the data-processing manager the task of performing a feasibility study on a piece of equipment. The man was well equipped for the job, but so were two others: the systems chief and an auditing manager. All men were of approximately equal status, and two felt slighted because they had not been consulted.

"Another commonly made mistake," says the head of a department store, "is that of delegating *indirectly*—that is, circumventing the man's supervisor. This can cause all kinds of problems and resentment." Most often this is done thoughtlessly and innocently. A busy executive is apt to think in terms of job requirements and overlook the sensitivities of human beings.

In one company a marketing vice-president who usually picked figures off a report for himself came into the department in search of someone to do the job for him. The department head was away from his desk, so the assignment went to an assistant. He could not have made a poorer choice. This man's co-workers were already smoldering over previous assignments given to him. They interpreted the move as a management acknowledgment that he was now the "fair-haired boy."

3. Motivate his job enthusiasm. There are a positive and a negative aspect to every delegated assignment:

Positive: The delegatee, given increased authority and responsibility, is in a position to add to his knowledge, make a contribution to the work of his superior and his company, and so prepare himself for an advancement opportunity.

Negative: He is going to have to work harder.

When you turn over new jobs, "accentuating the positive" will do much to generate job enthusiasm and a spirit of cooperation. A failure to play up the "what's-in-it-for-me" factor is tantamount to accentuating the negative. If the new assignment looks as if it were going to translate itself into all work and no gain, the reception is likely to be cool—or at best, lukewarm.

Which of these approaches, for instance, do you think will produce better results?

(a) "Bill, I want you to take on this job because I'm too busy to handle it myself."

or

(b) "Bill, I have to turn over Project X to somebody I can trust. The job is of special interest to the president; that's why I've always handled it myself. It requires seasoned judgment, and since you've already done some fine work in this area, I think you're the best man for the job. When I told the president that you'd be working up these figures from now on, he was pleased to hear it. Now here's what the job entails . . ."

4. Build his confidence through training and guidance. Confidence inspires enthusiasm. Says the training director of a large chemical company:

"We all have a yearning desire to know how we are doing on the job; or more important, how our superior thinks we are doing. A constant feedback of information will satisfy this important employee need. Good training and constructive guidance will insure that the feedback is favorable."

This counsel is specially applicable to people newly saddled with increased responsibility. Many people greet challenge and change with doubts, unvoiced apprehensions. And our company climate is a healthy one, we harbor a particular respect for our superior's ability, intelligence, and judgment. The employee who is handed an assignment that his boss handled before him is apt to wonder, "Am I qualified to take on this job? Will I be able to measure up to his standards? Do I have sufficient maturity and experience for this assignment?"

You can allay such misgivings from the start. One way is to give the delegatee all the knowledge and guidance he needs to do the job. Then, as the knowledge begins to take hold, you can shore up his confidence at regular intervals by letting him know that you are pleased with his progress and happy that you chose him for the assignment.

5. Define his duties clearly, but not rigidly. This requires a delicate balance. A job description that is too loose is likely

*   *   *

Proper delegation of work keeps you from becoming one of those harassed individuals whose desks are always overloaded with unfinished (or even unopened) business, whose briefcases are jammed at night with work that they didn't have time for during the day, and whom their families never see in the evening because they are busily poring over office "musts."

—*J. C. Penney*

*   *   *

to leave the delegatee confused about what is expected of him; a too-rigid definition may restrict his movement and the exercise of his initiative. A happy medium is the balance to aim for.

Avoiding rigidity, the subordinate's duties should be firmly enough established for you to be able to answer these questions:

Does he know the boundaries of his authority? For example, if he is now permitted to purchase certain supplies, has he been informed of the dollar-limitations imposed on him?

Does he have a good general idea of where his newly acquired province begins and ends? For example, if he is buying office supplies, would this include tabulating forms for the data-processing department and art supplies for the advertising department? Or just the supplies that are used in the general office?

Will he be faced with a problem of overlapping authority? For example, will he be the only one authorized to purchase office supplies? If not, does he know about the exceptions? Does he know the procedure to follow to avoid personality conflicts, inefficient buying, duplication or effort?

6. Encourage his independence and initiative. No bird ever learned to fly without first trying its wings. But some birds require a little prodding now and then.

An economist in a trading-stamp company delegated the preparation of a top-management report to an assistant. Although this man suffered from an overdose of reticence, his superior had implicit faith in his ability to do the job well. But transmitting this confidence to the assistant was another matter. The young man came to his boss continually, not so much for advice as for assurance that what he was doing was right.

It invariably was. The executive knew that his assistant was ready to operate on his own. The assistant, unfortunately, did not share this conviction.

Normally the report was scheduled for the 25th of the month. On this month the economist was called out of town on the 15th. Just prior to leaving for the airport, he summoned his assistant.

"George," he fibbed, "I just got a call from upstairs. They'd like the report on the 20th of this month. Now I'll be out of town, but I know you can handle it."

George started to protest, but his boss cut him short with a reassuring grin and a hasty excuse that he would have to rush if he wanted to make his plane.

When he returned from his trip, the report was flawlessly completed. George, having accomplished it completely on his own, was now able to throw away his "crutch." The necessary prod had been given.

Before a man can operate effectively, he needs a free rein to think for himself and work out his own problems. That doesn't imply that your subordinates will not need your guidance. But like any fledgling they are going to need that opportunity to fly for themselves.

When they do learn to fly, don't expect them to do it exactly the same way you do, even if you feel that your way is better.

Theodore Roosevelt once said, "The best executive is the one who has sense enough to pick good men to do what he wants done, and self-restraint enough to keep from meddling with them while they do it."

7. Be prepared for possible failure. When that bird of yours learns to fly, it is not unlikely that he will fall on his face a few times.

Your reaction to your delegatee's blunders can make all the difference in his future performance. An oil company executive says, "One of the best ways to win a subordinate's appreciation and support is to help him save face when he makes a fluff."

That doesn't mean you should turn your back on mistakes. Find out what went wrong and, most important, why. But the emphasis should be on building up, rather than tearing down, the delegatee's confidence.

Advance preparation for possible failure will help you to cope constructively with mistakes if any when they occur. It goes without saying that if they occur too often, more drastic action may be called for. This may mean that the work was not turned over properly or that you delegated to the wrong man. This, too, is always a possibility.

8. Maintain overall control. A common cause of misdelegation is the turning over of total responsibility and control along with the assignment. As long as you remain the delegatee's immediate superior, final authority should remain in your hands. Test your adherence to these five rules whenever you delegate:

Establish well-defined standards of operation and make sure they are understood.

See that your subordinate's output is edited and audited as required. Devote the same effort to guaranteeing that the work comes out right that you would if you had done it yourself. Make sure that performance standards are met, balances carried forward and checked. Whenever possible, build control checkpoints—proofs and balances, progress reports, work samples—right into the job procedure.

Set up a two-way flow of information. By keeping your subordinate well posted at all times, he will be encouraged to do the same for you.

Encourage a free discussion of problems. Establish a climate that will make your subordinate want to come to you when he needs help.

Review and evaluate your delegatee's performance periodically. Get him in on the act. Let it be known that freedom of movement does not imply freedom of accountability.

This, then, is the much-discussed and much-misused art of delegation. One executive likened his working day to a time bank. "When I delegate," he said, "I make a deposit of minutes so that I may make a subsequent withdrawal of hours."

Remember, without delegation personal advancement is impossible.

"The final test of a leader," says Walter Lippman, "is that he leave behind him in other men the conviction and will to carry on."

You can do this through effective delegation.

CHAPTER 13

PLANNING FOR COMPANY GROWTH

By Jesse Werner

Every year hundreds of businesses reach the point of no return. If you check the record you'll find that in retailing—

From 20 to 25 percent never last past the first year.

An additional 19 percent close before the end of the second year.

Ten percent more go out of business during their third year.

Less than 20 percent are still in business after the tenth year.

The life expectancy of small manufacturing firms or wholesalers is somewhat longer. Perhaps a fourth of them last for 10 years.

Why do so many fail? There are any number of reasons, including poor financial management, internal problems, selling difficulties, or inferior products. But there is at least one common thread running through all these reasons: lack of proper planning.

Effective planning is a key management function whether a business is just starting out or is in a growth stage. Success brings growth and growth means change. It is axiomatic that the business organization that does not adapt to change, and in adapting grow stronger and larger, will eventually perish. If it doesn't perish, it will be taken over by another, faster-growing company. The results are similar.

There are two reasons, then, why every company or business organization must plan.

One obvious reason is because it is not a success. It therefore is faced with failure unless it can revise its current tactics and strategy so that its profit and growth line will turn upward.

The other reason is, strangely enough, the converse of the first. It must plan because it *is* successful.

In the alert executive's book, success is a danger second only to failure. Why? Because success breeds contentment, and contentment breeds acceptance of the status quo. Since the one unfailing certainty about modern business is change,

*   *   *

GROWTH STOPPER NO. 1

As a company grows, it changes. To keep pace with the change, the organization must change, too. Otherwise growth stops.

The classic pattern is the owner-manager who starts a small business. He causes it to grow by his ability and drive. As it grows, he hires assistants. For a while the business continues to grow. Then it levels off. Try as he will, the owner cannot get it to grow further, no matter how hard he works personally. Why?

He has delayed revising his form of organization too long.

*   *   *

those firms that are happy with the present and prefer the comfort of the rut to restless anticipation of, and preparation for, the future are doomed to failure when their turn comes. And come it will eventually. The graveyard of business is littered with such epitaphs.

It is, of course, difficult to face up to the need for energetic planning when success is already a reality. Complacency is the natural, human result. No one welcomes change; many people dread it. Change means readjustment to new patterns

Comments appearing on this and subsequent pages are digested from an article by H. B. Maynard, management consultant, on how to avoid seven growth stoppers in *Business Management*, September 1962.

of conduct, new and different ways of doing things. It threatens feelings of security.

But anticipating and preparing for change now by planning for tomorrow's needs today is every bit as necessary when a company's chart shows rising sales and increasing profits as it is when the graph is heading inexorably downward.

Since every business, then, is vulnerable to change—which is nothing more than the opportunity to grow and expand, or else fail—growth, expansion, and planning for change must be the ever-present concern of every single executive.

Planning Is Not Projecting

The one thing planning most certainly is not is extrapolation of the present into the future.

An executive can ill afford to plan on this precarious basis.

He cannot expect to find the same economy, the same suppliers, the same customers, and the same competitors tomorrow that he has today. He cannot assume that the activities which meet today's needs will meet tomorrow's needs, too. Yet it is apparently a very human trait, shared by economists, salesmen, and most businessmen (who must think about the future), to assume that the future will resemble the present.

This is mere projection, of course. Anyone can continue a curve on a chart to infinity. The skill comes in predicting what sources are likely to change its shape. *This is planning.*

Responsibility for Planning

Almost everyone who works in a business and has a job of any importance does a certain amount of thinking about the future of his company and how he can help bring this future about. Foremen and supervisors prepare their job sheets; salesmen schedule their calls on prospects and customers; advertising managers set up timetables and deadlines for newspaper, magazine, radio and television ads; accountants collect and assemble data of all types that will end up in monthly, quarterly, and annual reports.

All of these tasks together provide, as it were, the day-to-day planning that is necessary if a company is to live and "breathe." This type of activity, however, is but the continuation of today into tomorrow. The kind of overall planning that we are concerned with is that which entails decisions to change the course of a business enterprise.

Planning for the Future

Kuan Fei, a Chinese poet who lived back in the third century, pointed out very succinctly the difficulties confronting the modern executive in his job of planning:

> *The plans*
> *Are man's;*
> *The odds*
> *Are God's.*

Any number of executives have had the unfortunate experience of seeing their most carefully laid plans "go up in smoke" because of certain changes that could not have been anticipated. But as one observer has noted, "The executive who has had that happen to him is outnumbered 12 to 1 by the executive who has himself gone down the drain, swept along by conditions for which he was totally unprepared simply because he *failed to plan at all.*"

If, then, we accept these two facts of business life (and we have no alternative but to accept them, since they are axiomatic) that—

1. Planning is the process by which profitable growth is sought and attained in a changing and uncertain world, and

2. It is one of management's prime responsibilities, since a company either grows or declines; there is no in-between position.

There are four major steps in planning for growth or expansion:

1. Gathering of all pertinent statistics and data.

2. Close analysis of these facts and figures.

3. Setting your objectives as to extent, size, type, cost, and estimated return.

4. Step-by-step planning of the overall operation; putting it into the works.

The first step in planning is to get acquainted with all the facts affecting your company. This is admittedly a big order, but one that must be painstakingly pursued if your planning is to be adequate. Nearly every management has a vast store of information about itself, its markets, the current state of the economy both at home and abroad, wherever it may have

*   *   *

GROWTH STOPPER NO. 2

Manufacturing managers long ago learned that to make the shop more efficient you have to: (1) observe what is being done now, (2) develop improved methods, and (3) teach the new methods to properly qualified operators. Many top managers, and sales managers, fail to see that this same approach can produce the same good results in a field sales force.

*   *   *

interests. Any information you do not have is generally obtainable from various sources.

Orderly planning obviously starts at the very beginning, with the collection and systematic assembly of this body of knowledge. It means, for instance—

1. Taking a financial inventory. This includes analyzing the company's assets and debits well beyond the ordinary financial level; change and growth trends over the last several years in terms of dollar sales, net profit, return on investment as well as sales, inventory turnovers and ratios, cash-flow changes, and increases in personnel.

These are, of course, general indices applicable to all types of businesses. Specialized aspects of your own business should also be analyzed, depending upon your particular operation.

You have to take into consideration, for example, your rate of depreciation of current assets, changes in your share of a special market, increase or decrease in the number of your customers by territory, or efficiency rates of similar plants.

2. Taking a personnel inventory. Your internal audit should include such necessary facts as the age and years of experience of your management personnel and key specialists. Take into account the availability of replacements for all executives, particularly aging executives.

3. Evaluating intangibles. These include such things as the comparative efficiency of the different operations of your company, the image it presents in the eyes of your employees, your customers, suppliers, the financial world, and the general public.

A systematic internal audit such as this, even if it were carried no further, is an invaluable aid in planning, because it pinpoints weak and strong spots and enables you to capitalize on the latter, strengthen the former.

Check Your Markets

The next part of your audit must be an objective evaluation of your markets and customers. It is a truism, but nonetheless a reality, that nobody can serve more than 100 percent of any market. The limit of growth is obviously, therefore, reached at that theoretical point. It is management's job to estimate as closely as possible what the total available market is, what proportion of that market is now held by the company, and how strong the existing and potential competitive forces are.

A third overall factor of great significance to any business in its planning is the economic condition of the country. As is quite evident to anyone who follows the financial and business press, there are any number of uncertainties confronting us when we attempt to forecast the prevailing economic climate in the near and distant future so far as it will affect the interests of our own business.

This is the reason that even the best-laid plans of "mice and men" occasionally go awry. Nevertheless, future trends and changes must be charted as intelligently as possible or your entire planning process will prove futile.

General data on business and economic trends are available from a number of sources, both governmental and private. Any competent economist has these sources readily available at his fingertips. Make full use of the most authoritative and reliable of these sources. Industries and areas have minor ups and downs of their own apart from general business trends, and figures and statistics for your own type of business or area will guide you as to what to expect in your own field.

Check these figures against those for American business as a whole during the period of years covered by your planning.

Setting Your Sights

Once the objective and factual audit of the company, its markets, and the economy has been completed, the second step of the planning process begins.

This is the establishment of your goals. These goals are of several kinds, depending on the length of time covered by your plans.

If your planning is on a typical short-term basis, your goals are normally those set forth in your annual budget. This is based on estimates of sales and profits for the next fiscal year and on how much it will cost to finance current operations and new capital investments. The budget, naturally, reflects specific steps or programs planned for the ensuing year, such as an increase or decrease in personnel, provisions for new equity financing, purchase and installation of new production equipment.

However, in addition to this short-range planning, a company should have before it a general, long-range plan. How long a period of time this should cover depends, in large measure, upon the type of enterprise it is. For some businesses, three years would be considered maximum. On the other hand, producers of basic raw materials from mines, quarries, and oil wells habitually think in terms of tens of years.

In industries where complex production units require several years to complete the final stages from drafting board to start-up, a multiyear planning period is by nature a necessity.

Size of the company also affects length of the planning period. The larger the firm, the longer its planning span is likely to be. Many of our largest manufacturing companies plan in terms of 25 years or more. For the average concern, however, five years is about as long a time as available facts will allow it to set its sights.

Hardest Part of the Job

Using the detailed budget prepared for the forthcoming year as a basis, a five-year plan then becomes merely a further projection of four years. This is where the hardest part of the planning takes place. It is extremely easy to put down some proposed sales figures that are larger than this year's, some proposed net profits that are well ahead of this year's, and some further expansions of existing facilities to take care of the vastly increased sales—and call this the company's long-range goal.

These are not goals. They're merely pious hopes. Goals can only be built up by a careful series of charted steps based on concrete judgments of what the market holds for you.

How to Grow

Growth of a business can take two forms: an increase in the sale of its present product lines and/or entry into new fields, whether related to present activities of the company or not.

In setting a company's course for growth over a several-year period, it is a rare enterprise indeed that can assume it will be serving exactly the same markets with the same type of products at the end of that period. Planning must therefore try to decide what the changes in the current market picture will mean to its present sales and how the company should react to the probable changes. As technology invades more and more of industry, the brutal fact must be faced that any sales product is likely to be superseded and become obsolete.

A business enterprise exists to serve customer needs. That enterprise which serves them best will always be the profitable one.

In some instances technological changes during the next few years may be so widespread that a product line will have to be completely withdrawn. If it is not possible for such a manufacturer to change his product so that it is competitive with the improved substitute gaining trade acceptance, no choice remains but to (1) either develop a still further-im-

*   *   *

GROWTH STOPPER NO. 3

The manager who wishes his company to grow must be careful when delegating authority to hire a key man. It is usually wise to let key people have some voice in choosing those with whom they must work. But if you are building for growth, recognize that a weaker man will not willingly choose a stronger man who may soon become a threat to his own position. A growth stopper? And how!

*   *   *

proved product or (2) direct the company's know-how into another field. This might be called "defensive diversification."

Besides resorting to defensive diversification at times, a healthy and self-confident management is always considering whether its total assets in manpower, money, and physical goods can be used as a basis for other profitable enterprises. Every long-range plan must include hard-headed thinking on such possibilities. Unusual opportunities can be far more readily seized upon when they are actively sought.

In fact, unless a company does analyze its "diversification potential," an opportunity may actually arise for making an acquisition or acquiring a new technology and pass unrecognized, until much too late to take advantage of it.

Growth in Present Sales Fields

If your goal is expansion in present sales fields, use as your springboard (a) the inventory of assets and liabilities we mentioned earlier, together with (b) the plans and programs that make up your budget for the next fiscal year. This will get you off to a knowledgeable start. However, you'll find it more practical to reverse your thinking from the customary way. Start with future trends of the economy, then mix in projections of your market demands and customer needs, and then finally proceed to evaluating your own firm's prospects for expansion and growth.

Let your thinking follow in that order for the most accurate results.

After you have figured as best you can what the country's economy will be like, how your own markets will stack up, and how your company's potential should fit into this general picture, you'll find obvious problems arising. For instance, if the field of industry your firm serves is expected to have an explosive growth in the southwest part of the country during the next few years, you're going to have to take into immediate consideration problems of sales distribution and freight costs, perhaps even the climatic conditions in their effect on your products.

You can begin to build up your final long-range goals in concrete fashion the moment you have solved these "circumstantial" or environment problems that are going to have a pretty important effect on your sales and profit curve. You will now have a reasonably clear-cut series of guide lines that will indicate probable target dates for the operations of every single one of your departments: marketing, manufacturing, research, personnel, financial, and even legal.

At the same time that you are doing all this, you must also project, or anticipate, the probable future actions of your competitors. You can only assume that they, as well as you, are eager to maintain and increase their share of the market, and that they intend to put their most strenuous efforts into obtaining a lion's share for themselves.

You'll also have to take into consideration future competitors who are likely to spring into being. This is not quite as hard to plan for as you might suppose, because most technological breakthroughs—or mere changes in popular tastes, styles and even fads (such as the universal hula hoop craze of recent vintage)—do not ordinarily burst into existence overnight. There are usually a number of warning bells in advance for the alert businessman to heed.

Long-range planning for growth in present sales fields should also take into account the possibility of buying other

*   *   *

GROWTH STOPPER NO. 4

A small manufacturer of a highly engineered line of metal fixtures found himself on the horns of a dilemma. His product had received a high degree of market acceptance. At the same time his shop was so inefficient that it had difficulty in producing the orders which were on the books. It was suggested to him that an industrial engineer could help straighten out the shop problem. He felt, however, that he could not afford an industrial engineer. So he borrowed money and put an addition on his plant. Shortly afterwards he went out of business.

Any industrial engineer worthy of the name will save his salary many times over by the savings he effects in company costs.

*   *   *

companies—or entering into joint ventures with them—in order to obtain new sources of raw materials, increase your share of the market, or otherwise improve your status in your product field. As markets change, companies sometimes find the only way they can preserve their profits is by merger, either horizontally (as when two hotel chains or two automobile manufacturers merge) or vertically (a move which can take either of two directions: backward toward raw materials or component parts, or forward toward market outlets as in the merger of one oil company with another to obtain its distribution centers).

Companies in technological fields must also plan for research expansion. There is probably no more valuable way to give proper guidance to a research program, as to its broad objectives, than in terms of long-range goals. Spelling out customer needs and demands that can be expected to arise, and the related needs of the company's own marketing and manufacturing departments, should provide plenty of opportunity for research.

Growth in New Fields

Expansion into new fields of activity is much more complex than planning for growth in present sales fields. Uncertainties always exist when entering new situations. But the fact remains that after a company has reached such a size that its share of the market can no longer be rapidly increased, top management must consider growth through new fields.

There are two possible approaches to new-field growth. One is through the company's own efforts, based on new technological developments. The other is by purchasing another company outright. Each of these methods has its attractive features.

One of the advantages of entering a new field on your own —"self-generated entry," as it were—is that it can be done on a modest scale, at least at first. Only a small investment in money and manpower may be required in the initial stages, since most of the work can be handled within the framework of the present company organization. The obvious disadvantages are that substantial returns will be slow in coming in and mistakes may be made, because every aspect of the new venture will have to be learned by your own personnel by painful trial and error.

Although outright acquisition of a company already in a new field has certain advantages, it is not without its disadvantages, too. For one thing it requires an immediate expenditure of cash, or it may result in a dilution of equity.

Moreover, an acquisition brings into the company a whole new group of people and procedures, and every organization that has gone through this sort of consolidation can testify that certain shocks are inevitable as each organization learns more about the other. It can be expected that personality clashes will result in loss of personnel and, at best, many months of decreased efficiency on the part of both organizations.

In fact, undiscerned and unanticipated problems may turn what originally appeared to be a profitable and safe venture into an unsuccessful one.

The benefits of an acquisition in a new field are that it brings with it the sort of know-how in manufacturing, marketing, and market acceptance that is otherwise hard to come by. Under normal circumstances acquisition of a going concern should return profits from the beginning, in contrast to the long and expensive build-up period required for entering a new field on your own.

Joint Ventures

Joint ventures are a modified form of acquisition that are often favored as a method of reducing the risks in entering a new field. If two companies can pool their complementary strengths, the result will tend to be a unit stronger than either company alone. But it is essential that each partner be able to make a contribution in fact, not just in theory. If the partnership fails to include the elements each one believes the other will provide, it will soon disintegrate.

Either joint project will then collapse, or else the stronger partner will absorb the whole enterprise.

A second important consideration with regard to joint ventures is that they demand the cooperative effort of two independent groups. Unless the rules under which the new venture will operate are closely and logically spelled out, difficulties will arise. Even with proper formal arrangements, however, if the two cooperating organizations have seriously varying business philosophies and types of management, it will probably be impossible for them to operate together for long.

In spite of all this, there is much to be gained by a joint venture, and the advantages are sometimes enormous. Pooling of resources, reduction of risks are factors that cannot be ignored. In certain situations, as when an American firm decides to enter a new foreign market, a joint venture may be the only way that the problem can be solved.

The key fact to be remembered is that long-range planning must be the prime responsibility of top management. It cannot be a staff function turned over to some individual or department outside the line organization. Why? Because the plan is essentially a series of guide lines for company action. The plan, therefore, does not really exist until it is put into action. It is evident that in any organization the people responsible for putting it into action must be the ones who decided on it originally. This can only be line management.

Evaluating the Plan

When the plan has been agreed to by all concerned and is ready to be put into action, last-minute changes may have to be made in it because of certain unexpected events. Here again, the individual or the department originally in charge of collecting and preparing the data for analysis can perform an inestimable service for management by flagging these events and noting their effect. The necessary modifications to the plan can then be considered and decided upon.

The original planning group can also help management with its timetable. The plan will involve estimates as to when certain targets or objectives are to be achieved. For example, if research has stated that laboratory work on a new product will be completed within 18 months, this will set the timetable for manufacturing, which will, in turn, require the marketing department to be ready to sell the product at a specified subsequent date. Obviously, if the product is not available from research at the time required, or if it does not have the planned features properly incorporated in it, major changes will have to be made in the marketing and manufacturing plans.

If the plan is to be an essential tool for management, continuous revision can prove, in fact, highly useful. It permits the highlighting of problems almost as rapidly as they occur and makes possible remedial action that is equally prompt.

Additional Benefits

While the long-range plan's greatest value is as an operating tool for management, it has many additional benefits for the company. The knowledge and thinking that have gone into it require the help of many people at all levels of management and of many types of specialists. If these people know that their efforts are to be incorporated into a plan of action for the entire enterprise, they are apt to bring their best and most enthusiastic thinking to bear on the project. They will

*   *   *

GROWTH STOPPER NO. 5

Prior to an installation, the necessity for the thorough training of all technicians who will establish time standards or piece rates is usually clearly recognized. Certainly, after the installation is completed and there is turnover among the technicians, the training of their replacements is no less important.

The need for training exists equally for new supervisors, new tool designers, new production-control men, and the like. This need is seldom recognized.

*   *   *

have the satisfaction of feeling more a part of their company's operations, and they will take a greater interest in its day-to-day operations as a direct result.

As we all know, a business is the collective result of many different operations working harmoniously and successfully toward profitable goals. This may be true in theory but it is apt not to be true in practice. It is often difficult for production people to accept the "whims" of the marketplace as reported by the sales force and make the necessary adjustments in product quickly and wholeheartedly.

In a good organization this sort of cooperative conduct is almost second-nature.

The existence of a long-range plan which production people and salesmen alike have helped create, therefore, can often be an important means of creating and maintaining greater departmental harmony and cooperation.

The company and its management, moreover, are usually under the scrutiny of many outside organizations. These include board members, banks, and investment houses.

The board of directors, for instance, will often be asked for approval of capital expenditures. From banks the company must obtain loans for its projects. Investment houses will wish to recommend its stock, or perhaps float an issue for the company.

In all of these cases one of the important points by which the company's management will be judged is the nature and caliber of its long-range plans. The more concrete and complete such plans are, the more likely it is to earn the respect of outsiders and their support in necessary financial matters.

A Word of Caution

Important as long-range planning is as a management aid, and valuable as the results may be that are obtained from using this technique, it must be admitted that it is no panacea that will restore certainty to an uncertain business world. Nor should it in any way be expected to. No planning method can forecast the future with even reasonable certainty, and no decisions for action can be expected to achieve every aimed-for result.

Furthermore, although the literature on long-range planning is a growing one, and many articles and books can be found recommending certain procedures and planning techniques, there are no known devices to fit every circumstance and every company.

Planning methods developed by each company must, of course, be arrived at by something of a trial-and-error process, and they will benefit correspondingly from a sound dose of common sense. There is no way for an outsider to know whether a long-range planning procedure and its applications will prove successful in a given company or not. The only people competent to make that decision are the management members themselves.

But there is one thing of which we can all be certain:

If the long-range plan becomes a central part of management thinking, and if, with increasing frequency, the predictions and proposed objectives of the plan become realities, then the program is an obvious success. The proof of that success will be the company's growth.

CHAPTER 14

SOLVING PROBLEMS

By E. F. Wells

Seemingly at the height of his genius, Louis Pasteur suffered a stroke. One-half of his brain was destroyed. Yet Pasteur went on to make some of his greatest discoveries *after* this shattering loss. There seems to be no limit to the miraculous powers of the human brain when it is disciplined and then allowed to soar.

In fact, the most amazing thing about you is your 50 ounces of gray matter that can remember, compute, analyze, judge, synthesize, imagine, and create. Although the mechanized brain can compute more rapidly and remember more accurately, according to Dr. Howard H. Aiken, head of Harvard's Computation Laboratory, no electronic brain will ever duplicate or even approach your finest achievement—*your power to think creatively!*

How It Works

For years Elias Howe struggled with the idea of a sewing machine. Everything he tried failed. He had sharpened the needle at both ends and drilled an eye in the middle. He had loosened the stitch, changed the bobbin, tightened the stitch, and again failed. Utterly defeated, he went home, ate, and disconsolately went to bed. That night he dreamed he was captured by savages who dragged him before their king. The king gave him just 24 hours to make a machine that would sew. If he failed, he would forfeit his life.

In his dream, Howe could see the savages approaching. He saw the long, pointed, awesome spears descend. The spears had eye-shaped holes in the tips. Wide awake now, Howe bounded from bed. He knew what was wrong with his machine! The eye of the needle should be near the point, not in the middle! Taking one of his wife's sewing needles, he raced to his workshop, filed the head of the needle to fit the machine, and confidently inserted it. It worked; the complicated problem was solved.

Dr. J. B. Rhine, the noted parapsychologist of Duke University, has said he believes that what we are inclined to call creativity or even genius is merely a process, a habitual way of using the mind. The difference between the man we recognize as a creative or inventive genius and the ordinary mortal is that the genius has made a determined effort over a long period of time. He has trained himself to think imaginatively,

*   *   *

FORMULA FOR CREATIVITY:

Need or problem—analysis experimentation and/or research—concentration or frustration—relaxation or sleep—insight or inspiration—proof or verification.

*   *   *

and he has persisted in his attempts, persisting even into a period of despair and frustration. There is a formula to creative problem solving, and frustration is often part of it.

To paraphrase Arthur Maroth, former chief engineer of Carnegie Hall, when you are angry enough at some object or situation to kick or swear, you are very close to invention. The difference between the creative and the rest of mankind is that the creative try to solve the problem, and the rest kick, swear, or shrug and pass on by.

In analyzing hundreds of creative and inventive individuals, preparatory to writing *How to Think Creatively*, Eliot D. Hutchinson found that usually these individuals, consciously or unconsciously, went through a series of activities before arriving at the moment of insight or inspiration. They recognized the need, analyzed the problem, gathered any necessary data, experimented or thought about it persistently, and then relaxed.

Naturally, the creative process does not always follow this formula; nothing is so whimsical as the subconscious portion of man's brain. Ideas can come from anywhere, at any time, but they come most frequently to the man who is searching for them, and they are most meaningful to the man who gives them serious consideration when they do come.

Recognizing the Need

After watching workmen continually dissecting Manhattan's streets, Fred Allen remarked, "What they ought to do is just put a zipper down the middle."

New York's mayor might not be too happy with that solution, but that's where creativeness begins—with the recognition of the problem, or the lack, or the need.

The irate cries of an infant inspired Walter Hunt to conceive the million-dollar safety pin. Blistered hands and limply liquid ice cream, the result of trying to row a picnic treat across the swashing Wisconsin lake to his girl friend, inspired Ole Evinrude to decide the world urgently needed an outboard motor.

Nothing is so irritating as the cynical Cassandras and the negative Nostradamuses who predict that soon all man's requirements will be met and production will decline. One need only look from his window or around his room to see half a dozen things that could be done more efficiently. When asked if technological progress could lead to overproduction, Edison replied: "There cannot be overproduction of anything which men and women want. And their wants are unlimited, except by the size of their stomachs!"

And the fuller their stomachs, the more sophisticated and imaginative their tastes.

Research and Experimentation

Robert Frost once said, "A poet might be made through all the years of trial and error, but any good poem is not made; it's born complete." It is important to note, however, that this complete poem is rarely born to anyone but a poet. Knowingly or unknowingly, through countless attempts, the poet has trained his mind to think rhythmically, rhymingly. He has disciplined it and prepared it for the moment of inspiration, and the harder he works, the more often is the great poem born complete.

For years, M. A. Rosanoff, long associated with Edison, endeavored to soften the wax of phonograph cylinders, and when the answer came, it was born complete like a perfect poem. "I had learned to think waxes," Rosanoff later stated, "and the solution had come without effort." True, it had come during a moment of relaxation; he was resting on the couch. So it may have come without effort, but it had not come until he had learned "to think waxes."

Certainly inspiration has been known to spark the mind without preparation, without research, without prolonged thought, but it appears most frequently, most brilliantly among those who have learned to think "in wax," "in paint," "in human relations," "in poetry," "in finance," or in whatever field they hope to be creative.

It is now believed that learning, or practice, or prolonged thought produces actual changes in the brain. Experiments at the University of California at Los Angeles indicate that certain so-called Golgi cells, like roots of growing plants, develop more and more fibers as learning proceeds. Artists appear to have an extra-high proportion of highly branched Golgi cells in their visual areas, while musicians show particularly dense growths in the auditory areas of their brains. It could be that these cortical changes are even necessary to the conception of a new and highly complicated idea.

Concentration and Frustration

On the day before he reached his revolutionary discovery linking time, space, matter, and energy, Einstein told a colleague he was so discouraged, he had decided to abandon the project.

Frustration may not be essential to inspiration, but the frequency with which it precedes insight would indicate that it serves some function. Possibly it is a part of the normal creative cycle; possibly the anger accompanying frustration improves the blood circulation, which increases brain action. In any case, some of the most impressive and profitable solutions have been in direct proportion to the degree of difficulty and frustration with which they were wrought.

Unfortunately, it is during this period of frustration that one is most likely to adopt a solution that is "almost right." It not only isn't good enough, it is often a greater handicap than no solution at all. As psychologist Kurt Lewin has phrased it, "When the problem can *almost* be solved by an easy method, the adoption of a more difficult method encounters unusual obstacles." It also prevents the subconscious mind from producing the correct solution, because once the almost is adopted, the subconscious dismisses the matter as solved.

Whenever it is necessary to adopt a temporary solution, recognize it as such and continue to search for the correct answer.

Relaxation

Apparently, in creative thinking a point is reached when it is essential for the conscious, critical portion of the brain to let go while the subconscious synthesizes or conceives. Einstein, after letting go, said that his space-time conclusions came to him while he was sick in bed—a time when the subconscious is particularly active.

Lenox Riley Lohr, former president of the National Broadcasting Company, stated that ideas come most readily "when you are doing something that keeps the mind alert without putting too much strain upon it. Shaving, driving a car, sawing a plank, or fishing . . ." Many problems have been solved while a man slept. Pressured by bills and desperate for a new plot, Robert Louis Stevenson had a horrifying dream which he put into words and sold as Dr. Jekyll and Mr. Hyde.

Once the well-known French mathematician Henri Fehr queried 69 of his colleagues, asking if they thought it possible to solve problems in dreams. Considering the exactness of mathematical problems, one would not expect a very high percentage to agree. Yet 51 replied "yes," and only 18 said "no."

Often a supervisor will obtain better ideas in one hour of creative relaxation than in eight hours at a desk. But acquiring a moment's idleness is the hardest part of creativity. To work is easy; all about you everyone appears feverishly employed. But to shake off the guilt of doing nothing to justify one's existence while merely staring into space—this requires courage or ingenuity, to say the least!

One chemist solved it by getting a pestle, a bowl, and some pale-blue powder, and conscientiously stirring these while he thought. For those without pestle or powder, the best technique is to think over a problem just prior to falling asleep and to anticipate having the answer in the morning.

Another way is to take a solitary lunch break, concentrating hard on the problem before leaving your desk and turning it over to your subconscious mind as a definite assignment; then dismissing it from consciousness while you enjoy a leisurely meal and a stroll back to the office. Another way is to give serious thought to problems requiring unique or imaginative solutions just prior to a weekend of golfing, boating, gardening, or anything that will relieve the inhibitions of the conscious mind and allow the inventive, unconscious systems of thought to reach the forefront.

Although, certainly, no one would disparage formal training, creativity is not dependent upon it. The originator of the steamboat, John Fitch, was a gunsmith. He had never even seen a steam engine, and the Wright Brothers were bicycle repairmen.

With this formula, everyone can be creative so long as he remembers that the need itself helps to create the inspiration that fulfills it. "We are told that talent creates its own opportunities," wrote Eric Hoffer in *The Passionate State of Mind*, "but it sometimes seems that intense desire creates not only its own opportunities, but its own talents."

How It's Hampered

Theater-magnate Max Reinhardt was the despair of his business adviser. The adviser vetoed most of Reinhardt's imaginative ideas. Once a friend remarked: "Say, I wish I had someone like that working for me, Max. He must save you thousands of dollars!"

"Most of the time he does," replied Reinhardt. "Ninety-nine percent of the time he's right and I'm wrong. But 1 percent of the time he's wrong and I'm right. And on that 1 percent we make our living."

The higher a man advances in business the more he needs conceptual skills for long-range, imaginative planning and creative problem-solving. Most businesses have more than the necessary requirement of critics, fellows who know what cannot be done, but there is a scarcity of the originators of bold ideas. The enemies of original thinking are mainly four, and any one of them is enough to stifle all thought, all creativity.

1. Avoid Excessive Caution

If during a period of managerial and financial upheaval the infant General Motors had listened to its cautious advisers, it would have discontinued a small new model called the Chevrolet.

Excessive fear of error contributes more to actual error than any other factor. Because when a man is excessively cautious, he is in a state of withdrawal. He may hope that things will remain as they are, but since change is his only certainty, his world must either shrink or expand. If he will not venture, then his world must contract.

The cautious usually pride themselves on their realistic evaluation of the experimental, reasoning that percentages deal harshly with new ideas. But if Du Pont had acquired caution when it lost heavily because of its early venture into paints, varnishes, and dyes, it would never have ventured into nylon.

If Lewis and Clark had not been prepared to strike out boldly into unexplored territory, well aware that their plans might go awry as some of them did—if they had waited until they had all the facts, insisting on something more tangible than an unchartered map—the Louisiana Territory might never have been secured. The United States might have remained forever a nation of 17 eastern states or even been conquered by the Republic of Texas.

2. Regimentation No Help

The regimented mind does no creative thinking. The regimented are ruled by tyranny, tyranny of the past, tyranny of rules, tyranny of statistical data, tyranny of opinion polls, tyranny of experts, and tyranny of the established. But this is not the era of rigidity. "During the past half-century," wrote Brig. Gen. David Sarnoff, "invention and technology have traveled farther than in all the previous history of man."

Few things there are which are not subject to improvement, except possibly the buggy, the stirrup, the buggy whip. The Wright Brothers may have thought they had solved the problem of flight, but they had only just begun.

It well may be that one of American business's greatest assets is its divine discontent; its unshakable conviction that "the best is yet to be done!" As chairman of the board of Radio Corporation of America, Sarnoff sagely said, "Today, in speaking of the future, it would be folly not to be audacious."

3. Excessive Criticism Cuts Creativity

"The thinking mind," wrote Alex Osborn in *Wake Up Your Mind,* "finds it easier to judge than to create. Nearly all of our education tends to develop our critical faculty. And our experience likewise builds up our judgment . . . And oddly enough, the more we exercise our judgment, the less likely we are to exercise our imagination." Criticism, and this includes self-criticism, can short-circuit creativity. The time for critical evaluation is after the moment of inspiration.

The creative process requires more than reason. It may begin with reason, and certainly it requires disciplined thought, but the moment comes when the imaginative, subconscious portion of the brain must be allowed to take over unhampered by the critical conscious. Man has been gifted with a brain that at the present time defies science. No one fully understands how it works any more than scientists completely understand how electricity works.

But this ought to keep no one from turning on the blaze when he can do so simply by releasing the switch.

4. Defeatism Another Enemy

Cyrus McCormick tried mining gold in what is now McCormick, South Carolina. He failed. He tried mining gold in the rich lode of his imagination and succeeded with the reaping machine. His friends could have told him, "It couldn't be done."

Those who deny their creative ideas for fear of making a mistake should remember that trial and error are a part of the creative process. Many errors are serviceable; some are even essential to ultimate success. In a series of interviews, heroes of Mt. Everest forcefully pointed out that the mountain couldn't have been scaled sooner because a certain number of mistakes had to be made before man could know enough to do it successfully.

Speaking of this, Lawrence A. Appley, in *Management in Action*, added, "If top management is intent upon making real progress, it has certainly learned that progress entails a certain amount of error." Creativity demands it.

How It's Helped

In a boarded-up room on the third floor of a bombed-out department store, eight men built the million-dollar Sony Manufacturing Company. They did it using materials salvaged from rubble and military surplus. What they lacked in materials they made up in creative brainpower.

George Bernard Shaw once slyly remarked that he had "made an international reputation by thinking once or twice a week." What Shaw failed to emphasize was that the thinking he did which produced such impressive results was creative thinking.

226

During the period of research, analysis, or experimentation, the creative imagination can often be triggered by any one of the following questions.

1. How else can this be used? The North Western Railway was near bankruptcy when Ben Heineman took charge. Cutting costs was the first order of business, and one of the most costly features was the task of turning a commuter train around for its return run. President Clyde Fitzpatrick solved the problem by deciding the diesel locomotive could serve two purposes. Outbound to the suburbs, it could pull the train, and inbound to Chicago, it would *push*.

2. How can two or more things be combined to create something new, something less expensive, something more efficient? After one man had invented the pencil, and a second had invented the eraser, a third thought of combining the two into a million-dollar idea. Frederick W. Taylor did not invent psychology, and he certainly didn't originate industry. But he was a pioneer in coupling the two.

3. How can this be modified, changed, or adapted so that it may be put to new uses? Much of Sony Manufacturing Company's success is built on the idea of "making it smaller." In 1957, it produced the world's first pocket radio—little larger than a pack of cigarettes. It then began working on midget TV's.

Du Pont could have been content with producing a filmy gauze of nylon; instead, it went on to produce a wealth of variety by modifying texture. A supervisor improved the reaction to his reports by changing the colors. He used red paper for emergency reports, pink for highly secret information, and blue for monthly statements.

In dealing with any problem, consider the following possible areas of change: color, size, shape, sound, strength, texture, speed, direction, material, weight, thickness, price, layout, personnel, and so forth. Henry Ford did not invent the automobile, but he adapted it to the multitudes, and altered forever both industry and modern life.

4. What can be substituted? What else or who else could do the job better or cheaper? At the Martin Company, an em-

ployee noticed that the $1.35 "heat sink clip," applied to bleed off damaging heat during soldering, looked pretty much like the clip his wife used in setting her hair. The hair clip cost 2 cents. Substituting it resulted in a saving of $1,330 a year. And McCormick & Company, Inc., makers of Schilling Spices, found during a promotional campaign that a mailing firm could handle the routine correspondence cheaper than they could.

5. What can be added, what taken away? Lockheed Aircraft reduced the cost of its correspondence by adding replies to general requests for information to the bottom of the letter requesting it. It has done away with the extra manifold copy by using backs of other letters being answered for the carbon copy.

6. Could this problem be reversed or turned upside down? After the disaster of Pearl Harbor, when the Japanese bombed U.S. planes before our pilots could get off the ground, the Air Force began asking, "How can we get the planes out of the hangars faster?" The problem wasn't solved until, finally, it was reversed. "How can we get the hangars away from the planes faster?" The answer to this last clever question was a diamond-shaped two-section hangar that pulls apart at the widest point. Mounted on rubber tires, the sections are powered to move at 35 miles an hour, leaving all planes ready to take off simultaneously.

Dr. Willis R. Whitney, founder of General Electric research laboratory, called this approach, "changing the problem." "If you cannot find a solvent for the ink," he advised, "change the ink!"

Creativity is not so much an aptitude as an attitude. At the outset, it requires a confident belief in one's own ability to solve the problem or fulfill the need. But it also requires an enlightened stubbornness to persist despite discouragement. Nothing worthwhile is ever achieved without effort. Sir William Herschel made 200 attempts before he produced a telescope that truly satisfied him. Edison tried 6,000 different species of vegetable fiber before he found a filament for the electric light bulb. Frank Munsey's remarkable publishing career might be tersely described as 40 failures, 40 successes, 40 millions.

No one knows better than the successful businessman that Disraeli spoke truly when he said, "All of my successes have been built on my failures." But the successful found the zest and enthusiasm to continue despite failure because they were totally absorbed in the original idea.

How Creativity Is Used

Mary Bickerdyke, the calicoed cyclone who nursed wounded Yankees through the Civil War, continually clashed with Dr. J. D. Irwin over the need for better food. The feud had flared into an undeclared war by the time she marched into his office to request a 20-day furlough in order to go North "and bring back fresh milk and eggs."

The dapper young doctor stared at her. How did that "old battle-ax" think she was going to keep milk fresh on a hot, slow freight? Well, he wouldn't bother pointing out to her that milk curdled, eggs rotted. He was, in fact, delighted, only too pleased to take her to General Hurlbut. Let the general listen to her. Here was proof the old gal was crazy!

But after listening to the plan, the general agreed to it, and before the 20-day furlough had expired, Nurse Bickerdyke was back, accompanied by a bizarre procession of more than 100 cows and 1,000 hens—all alive and more than able to furnish the army with fresh milk and eggs.

Simple? Yes, but just unconventional enough to elude the regimented mind. The timid could have thought of it, but they would never have dared incur the ridicule. As for the critical and the defeatists, they would have foreseen all the obstacles.

Problems are to be solved, and they can be solved if the imagination is not restricted by caution, fear, or cynicism. Don't be hidebound by the traditional way of doing things; don't be stopped because someone else has failed; don't listen to those who say it can't be done. Think about the problem enthusiastically, alert to the fantastic or even the obvious, and if you don't solve it the first time, return to it again when you are refreshed.

Far too many apply creative thinking only to inventive or artistic problems, but it is equally rewarding in the field of human relations. There can be no empathy and little persuasion without imagination. How else can a man view the world as seen by another and so know what will motivate, persuade, and inspire?

Once, in discrediting his own creativity, Lee Bristol of Bristol-Myers said, "Every man on our staff has better ideas than mine, but my job is to get them to agree." Mr. Bristol was underestimating himself, for to get high-powered executives or supervisors to agree requires a great deal of empathy, and empathy requires creative imagination.

One executive places his most difficult correspondence on the top of the stack, considers it thoughtfully, and if an answer does not come readily to mind, places it at the bottom of the stack. "I find," he explained, "that by the time I reach it again, my subconscious mind has formulated an answer." As is true of all devices using the subconscious, the more this technique is used, the better the results.

Auren Uris, in *Developing Your Executive Skills*, told of an executive faced with a low ceiling which prevented his installing a power conveyor. Undismayed, he had a pit dug which allowed for the high points of the machine. The imaginative, inventive supervisor is not deterred by clumsy floor plans, awkward storage areas. A door can be sealed, a new one created. There is no permanent restriction except the restriction placed upon you by the limit of your own imagination.

If there is one thing upon which the world agrees, it is that American businessmen are ingenious. One machine manufacturer, wondering how to induce more patrons to use the self-service laundromats, asked himself, "Where else could I put my machines?" So now when moviegoers patronize a large Arkansas drive-in theater, they can toss their clothes into a laundromat while they watch Elizabeth Taylor take Richard Burton to the cleaners.

When the Singer Sewing Machine was first introduced in India, the natives were indifferent until an enterprising Singer agent bought up thousands of yards of white cotton cloth.

He had the cloth impregnated with one word, translated into four different dialects. He sold this printed material at slightly below cost for loincloths and soon had hundreds of walking advertisements carrying the word Singer to the inhabitants.

But ingenious as American business is and has been in the past, no one has yet exhausted the possibilities of: Where else? What else? What if? How else? When else? Who else?

How Creativity Is Extended

General Robert E. Wood, later to become chairman of Sears Roebuck & Company, was in Panama during the building of the canal, and reading material was scarce. Desperate, the general began reading the U.S. census reports. To his imaginative mind, they represented something more than dry figures. He saw in them a population trend toward the South and West. He saw farmers moving to the cities. He saw the automobile changing the habits of the nation. Later he had the opportunity to put his knowledge to work, and, as a result, he persuaded Sears to build retail stores and to build them along the growing network of highways, along the path of the shifting population.

The alert executive should consider every chance thought, every idea that could result in a new product, a curtailment of effort, a time- or money-saver. Once conceived, of course, all ideas ought to be eyed skeptically, for many will be unusable, but as scientist-philosopher Alfred North Whitehead has said, "We had better entertain them all, however skeptically, for the thousandth idea may be the one that will change the world!"

An executive should also extend the uses of imagination by encouraging everyone who works under him to think creatively. It is easy to be skeptical when someone approaches you with a new plan, but Clarence Francis of General Foods found that skepticism can be far costlier than faith.

"Younger executives come to me with what they think are new ideas," he once said, "and out of my experience I could tell them why their ideas will not succeed. But instead of talking them out of their ideas, I have suggested that they be tried out in test areas in order to minimize losses. The joke of it is that half the time these youthful ideas, which I might have nipped in the bud, turn out either to be successful or to lead to other ideas that are successful."

Even if your people don't stumble onto a great money-saving idea, there are other important dividends to be gained from encouraging creativity, and the most important is the invigorating climate and increased mental alertness such an attitude produces.

Possibly one of the most profitable ways an executive can apply his own creativity is in devising methods to increase creativity among his people. One has hung a large blackboard in a prominent spot. One side states boldly, "What this outfit needs is . . . ," while the other side suggests, "Well, how about this?"

Other executives have found brainstorming sessions produce answers to cost reduction, increased sales, improved safety, better employee relationships, contemplated changes, and a host of seemingly insolvable problems. U.S. Steel Corporation and Reynolds Metals have used brainstorming to attack marketing problems, and a session at General Motors' AC Spark Plug Division produced more than 100 suggestions on how to smooth a casting.

As you know, the concept of brainstorming was originated by Alex Osborn, cofounder of Batten, Barton, Durstine & Osborn advertising agency. But if a brainstorming session is to be successful, critical expressions such as "Naw, that's been done before" or "Naw, that won't work" must be outlawed. Anything that remotely smacks of cynicism must be forbidden. Even far-fetched ideas should be welcomed, not only because they are sometimes the answer, but because the outlandish often suggests the right answer.

One winter, when Seattle telephone lines were dangerously ice-girded, an emergency brainstorming session was held. Ideas began to fly, and in the general excitement a normally shy young linesman said, "How about flying a helicopter over the wires?" He thought it might create enough vibration to shatter the ice, and he was right!

Other supervisors use suggestion boxes. In Los Angeles County alone, employee ideas saved the local government $152,445 in a single year.

Creativity is not necessarily correlated with intelligence. Dr. Catharine Cox Miles has offered evidence that some of the greatest geniuses had only slightly higher-than-average intelligence as it is presently measurable. The imaginative Cervantes, for example, is believed to have had an I.Q. of only 110, but fortunately for the world, Cervantes' alter ego, Don Quixote, accepted no barriers. Limits were merely windmills to be fought and conquered!

Democracy was never intended to be a spawning place for mediocrity; it was never intended to be the breeding hole of stagnant ideas. The free enterprise system encourages dynamic, creative thought; in fact, it depends upon it! Once when British philosopher Whitehead was asked what he considered America's contribution to the world, he thoughtfully replied, "Your diffusion of literacy and average comfort and well-being among the masses . . . is one of the major achievements in human history."

The diffusion of human comforts is the achievement of American businessmen, and it has been accomplished by men such as you, using their greatest of all instruments, the creative, imaginative portion of the human brain!

CHAPTER 15

CUSTOMER RELATIONS

By Peter F. Drucker

The purpose of a business is to create a customer. The purpose is to provide something for which an independent outsider, who can choose not to buy, is willing to exchange his purchasing power. And knowledge alone (excepting only the case of the complete monopoly) gives the products of any business that leadership position on which success and survival ultimately depend.

From the inside it is not easy to find out what a business gets paid for. Organized attempts to look at one's own business from the outside are needed.

As experienced a company as Radio Corporation of America (RCA) was convinced that the consumer would recognize and accept the RCA trademark on refrigerators and ranges when it entered the kitchen appliance business in the forties. RCA is of course one of the best-known consumer trademarks for radios and television sets. To a manufacturer these are as much "appliances" as are kitchen ranges. For the consumer they are an entirely different category of goods, carrying different value connotations.

Trademark acceptance in the market did not carry over from radios to ranges, and RCA had to withdraw from the kitchen appliance business. It is quite possible— indeed, likely —that the RCA trademark would have carried customer acceptance for tape recorders and photographic cameras. To a manufacturer, however, radios and cameras are entirely different goods.

There are scores of similar examples. What to the manufacturer is one market or one category of products is to the customer often a number of unrelated markets and a number of different satisfactions and values.

People inside a business can rarely be expected to recognize their own distinct knowledge; they take it for granted. What one knows how to do, by and large, comes easy. As a result the people in the business tend to assume, unthinkingly, that there is nothing to their knowledge or special ability; indeed, that everybody else must have it too. What looms large on their horizon are the things they find hard—that is, the things they are not particularly good at.

I am not saying that the people inside a business are bound to be wrong in their appraisal of what the business does and what it gets paid for. But they cannot take for granted that they are right. The least they can do is to test their judgment.

Market Realities

All this is hardly news for businessmen any more. For a decade now the "marketing view" has been widely publicized. It has even acquired a fancy name: the Total Marketing Approach.

Not everything that goes by that name deserves it. "Marketing" has become a fashionable term. But a gravedigger remains a gravedigger even when called a "mortician"—only the cost of the burial goes up. Many a sales manager has been renamed "marketing vice-president"—and all that happened was that costs and salaries went up.

A good deal of what is called "marketing" today is at best organized, systematic selling in which the major jobs—from sales forecasting to warehousing and advertising—are brought together and coordinated. This is all to the good. But its starting point is still our products, our customers, our technology. The starting point is still the inside.

Yet there have been enough serious efforts for us to know what we mean by the marketing analysis of a business, and how one goes about it.

Here, first, are the marketing realities that are most likely to be encountered:

1. What the people in the business think they know about customer and market is more likely to be wrong than right. There is only one person who really knows: the customer. Only by asking the customer, by watching him, by trying to understand his behavior can one find out who he is, what he does, how he buys, how he uses what he buys, what he expects, what he values, and so on.

2. The customer rarely buys what the business thinks it sells him. One reason for this is, of course, that nobody pays for a "product." What is paid for is satisfactions. But nobody can make or supply satisfactions as such—at best, only the means to attaining them can be sold and delivered.

Every few years this axiom is rediscovered by a newcomer to the advertising business who becomes an overnight sensation on Madison Avenue. For a few months he brushes aside what the company's executives tell him about the product and its virtues, and instead turns to the customer and, in effect, asks him: "And what do you look for? Maybe this product has it." The formula has never failed—not since it was used, many years ago, to promote an automobile with the slogan "Ask the Man Who Owns One"; that is, with the promise of customer satisfaction.

But it is so difficult for the people who make a product to accept that what they make and sell is the vehicle for customer satisfaction, rather than customer satisfaction itself, that the lesson is always immediately forgotten, until the next Madison Avenue sensation rediscovers it.

3. A corollary is that the goods or services which the manufacturer sees as direct competitors rarely adequately define what and whom he is really competing with. They cover both too much and too little.

Luxury cars—the Rolls Royce and the Cadillac, for instance —are obviously not in real competition with low-priced automobiles. However excellent the Rolls Royce and Cadillac may be as transportation, they are mainly being bought for the prestige satisfaction they give.

236

Because the customer buys satisfaction, all goods and services compete intensively with goods and services that look quite different, seem to serve entirely different functions, are made, distributed, sold differently—but are alternative means for the customer to obtain the same satisfaction.

That the Cadillac competes for the customer's money with mink coats, jewelry, the skiing vacation in the luxury resort, and other prestige satisfactions is an example—and one of the few both the general public and the businessman understand.

But the manufacturer of bowling equipment also does not, primarily, compete with the other manufacturers of bowling equipment. He makes physical equipment. But the customer buys an activity. He buys something to do rather than something to have. The competition is, therefore, all the other activities that compete for the rapidly growing "discretionary time" of an affluent, urban population—boating and lawn care, for instance, but also the continuing postgraduate education of already highly schooled adults (which has been the true growth industry in the United States these last 20 years).

That the bowling equipment makers were first in realizing the potential and growth of the discretionary-time market, first to promote a new family activity, explains their tremendous success in the fifties. That they, apparently, defined competition as other bowling equipment makers rather than as all suppliers of activity-satisfaction is in large part responsible for the abrupt decline of their fortunes in the sixties. They apparently had not even realized that other activities were invading the discretionary-time market, and they had not given thought to developing a successor-activity to a product that, in the activities market, was clearly becoming yesterday's product.

Even the direct competitors are, however, often overlooked. The big chemical companies, for instance, despite their careful industry intelligence, are capable of acting as if there were no competitors to worry about.

When in the early fifties the first of the volume plastics, polyethylene, established itself in the market, every major chemical company in America saw its tremendous growth potential. Everyone, it seems, arrived at about the same, almost unbelievable, growth forecast. But no one, it seems, realized that what was so obvious to him might not be totally invisible to the other chemical companies. Every major chemical company seems to have based its expansion plans in polyethylene on the assumption that no one else would expand capacity.

Demand for polyethylene actually grew faster than even the almost incredible forecasts of that time anticipated. But because everybody expanded on the assumption that his new plants would get the *entire* new business, there was such overcapacity that the price collapsed.

4. Another important corollary is that what the producer or supplier thinks the most important feature of a product to be—what they mean when they speak of its "quality"—may well be relatively unimportant to the customer. It is likely to be what is hard, difficult, and expensive to make. But the customer is not moved in the least by the manufacturer's troubles. His only question is—and should be: "What does this do for me?"

How difficult this is for businessmen to grasp, let alone to accept, the advertisements prove. One after the other stresses how complicated, how laborious it is to make this or that product. "Our engineers had to suspend the laws of nature to make this possible" is a constant theme. If this makes any impression on the customer, it is likely to be the opposite of the intended one. "If this is so hard to make right," he will say, "it probably doesn't work."

5. The customers have to be assumed to be rational. But their rationality is not necessarily that of the manufacturer; it is that of their own situation.

To assume—as has lately become fashionable—that customers are irrational is as dangerous a mistake as it is to assume that the customer's rationality is the same as that of the manufacturer or supplier—or that it should be.

A lot of pseudo-psychological nonsense has been spouted because the American housewife behaves as a different person when buying her groceries and when buying her lipstick. As

238

the weekly food buyer for the family, she tends to be highly price-conscious; she deserts the most familiar brand as soon as another offers a 5-cents-off special. Of course. She buys food as a "professional," as the general home manager. But who would want to be married to a woman who buys lipstick the same way? Not to use the same criterion in what are two entirely different roles—and yet both real, rather than make-believe—is the only possible behavior for a rational person.

It is the manufacturer's or supplier's job to find out why the customer behaves in what seems to be an irrational manner. It is his job either to adapt himself to the customer's rationality or to try to change it. But he must first understand and respect it.

6. No single product or company is very important to the market. Even the most-expensive and most-wanted product is just a small part of a whole array of available products, services, satisfactions. It is at most of minor interest to the customer. If he thinks of it at all. And the customer cares just as little for any one company or any one industry.

There is no social security in the market, no seniority, no old-age disability pensions. The market is a harsh employer, who will dismiss even the most faithful servant without a penny of severance pay. The sudden disintegration of a big company would greatly upset employees and suppliers, banks, labor unions, plant-cities, and governments. But it would hardly cause a ripple in the market.

For the businessman this is hard to swallow. What one does and produces is inevitably important to oneself. The businessman must see his company and its products as the center. The customer does not, as a rule, see them at all.

How many housewives have ever discussed the whiteness of their laundry over the back fence? Of all possible topics of housewifely conversation, this surely ranks close to the bottom. Yet not only do advertisements play that theme over and over again, but soap company executives all believe that how well their soap washes is a matter of major concern, continuing interest, and constant comparison to housewives—for the simple reason that it is, of course, a matter of real concern and interest to them (and should be).

7. All the statements so far imply that we know who the customer is. However, a marketing analysis has to be based on the assumption that a business normally does not know but needs to find out.

Not "who pays" but "who determines the buying decision" is the "customer."

The customer for the pharmaceutical industry used to be the druggist who compounded medicines either according to a doctor's prescription or according to his own formula. Today the determining buying decision for prescription drugs clearly lies with the physician. But is the patient purely passive— just the man who pays the bill for whatever the physician buys for him? Or is the patient—or at least the public—a major customer, what with all the interest in, and publicity for, the wonder drugs? Has the druggist lost completely his former customer status? The drug companies clearly do not agree in their answers to these questions; yet a different answer leads to very different measures.

The minimum number of customers with decisive impact on the buying decision is always two: The ultimate buyer and the distributive channel.

A manufacturer of processed foods, for instance, has two main customers: the housewife and the grocery store. Unless the grocer gives his products adequate shelf space, they cannot be bought by the housewife. It is self-deception on the part of the manufacturer to believe that the housewife will be so loyal to his brand that she would rather shop elsewhere than buy another well-known brand she finds prominently displayed on the shelves.

Which of these two, ultimate buyer or distributive channel, is the more important customer is often impossible to determine. There is, for instance, a good deal of evidence that national advertising, though ostensibly directed at the consumer, is most effective with the retailer; is indeed the best way to move him to promote a brand. But there is also plenty of evidence—contrary to all that is said about "hidden persuaders" —that distributors, no matter how powerfully supported by advertising, cannot sell a product that the consumer, for whatever reason, does not accept.

Who is the customer tends to be more complex and more difficult to determine for industrial than for consumer goods. Who is the ultimate consumer and who is the distributive channel for the manufacturer of power equipment for machinery: the purchasing agent of the machinery manufacturer who lets the contract, or the engineer who sets the specifications? Or the buyer of the completed machine?

While the latter is usually without power to decide from which maker the parts of the machine (e.g., the motor starter and the motor controls) should come, he almost always has power to veto any given supplier. All three—if not many more —are customers.

Each class of customers has different needs, wants, habits, expectations, value concepts, and so on. Yet each has to be sufficiently satisfied at least not to veto a purchase.

8. But what if no identifiable customer can be found for a business or an industry? A great many businesses have no one person or group of persons who could be called their customer.

Who, for example, is the customer of a major glass company which makes everything as long as it is glass? It may sell to everybody—from the buyer of automobile instrument-board lights to the collector of expensive hand-blown vases. It has no one customer, no one particular want to satisfy, no one particular value expectation to meet.

Similarly, in buying paper for a package, the printer, the packaging designer, the packaging converter, the customer's advertising agency, and the customer's sales and design people, all can—and do—decide what paper not to buy. And yet none of them makes the buying decision itself. None of these people buys paper as such. The decision is made indirectly, through deciding on shape, cost, carrying capacity of the package, graphic appearance, and so on. Who is actually the customer?

There are two large and important groups of industries in which it is difficult and sometimes impossible to identify the customer: materials industries and end-use supply (or equipment) makers.

Materials industries are organized around the exploitation of one raw material, such as petroleum or copper; or around one process such as the glassmaker, the steel mill, or the paper mill. Their products are of necessity material-determined rather than market-determined. The end-use industries, such as a manufacturer of adhesives—starches, bonding materials, glues, and so on—have no one process or material to exploit. Adhesives can be made from vegetable matter such as corn or potatoes, from animal fats, and from synthetic polymers, furnished by the petro-chemical industry. But there is still no easily identifiable, no distinct customer.

Adhesives are used in almost every industrial process. But to say—as one would have to say about the steel mill or the adhesives plant—that everyone is his customer is to say that no one is an *identifiable* customer.

The answer is not, however, that these businesses cannot be subjected to a marketing analysis. Rather, markets or end-uses, instead of customers, are the starting point for this analysis in materials and end-use industries.

Materials businesses—steel or copper, for instance—can usually be understood best in terms of markets. It is meaningful to say, for instance, that a certain percentage of all copper products go into the construction market—though they go to such a multitude of different customers and for such a variety of end-uses that these two dimensions may well defy analysis. It is meaningful to say that the adhesives all serve one end-use: to hold together the surfaces of different materials, though neither customer analysis nor market analysis may make much sense.

The view from outside has three dimensions rather than one. It asks not only "Who buys?" but "Where is it bought?" and "What is it being bought for?" *Every business can thus be defined as serving either customers, or markets, or end-uses.* Which of the three, however, is the appropriate dimension for a given business cannot be answered without study. Every marketing analysis of a business, therefore, should work through all three dimensions to find the one that fits best.

Again and again one finds (1) that a dimension which the people in the business may consider quite inappropriate—customers or end-uses in a paper company, for instance—is actually highly important; and (2) that superimposing the findings from the analysis of one of these dimensions on another one—e.g., analysis of a paper company in terms of paper end-uses, paper markets, and paper customers—yields powerful and productive insights.

Even where there is a clearly identifiable customer, one does well to examine the business also in relation to its markets or the end-uses of its products or services. This is the only way one can be sure of defining adequately what satisfaction it serves, for whom and how. It is often the only way to determine on what developments and factors its future will depend.

These market realities lead to one conclusion: *The most important questions about a business are those that try to penetrate the real world of the consumer, the world in which the manufacturer and his products barely exist.*

How to See the Unexpected

All the standard questions of a market study should, of course, be asked: Who is the customer? Where is the customer? How does he buy? What does he consider value? What purposes of the customer do our products satisfy? What role in the customer's life and work does our particular product play? How important is it to him?

Under what circumstances—age, for instance, or structure of the family—is this purpose most important to the customer? Under what circumstances is it least important to him? Who are the direct and the indirect competitors? What are they doing? What might they be doing tomorrow?

But the emphasis might be on different questions that are

rarely asked. They are the questions that force us to see the unexpected.

1. Who is the *noncustomer*, the man who does not buy our products even though he is (or might be) in the market? And can we find out why he is a noncustomer?

One illustration is the experience of a successful manufacturer and distributor of do-it-yourself home-repair and home-maintenance supplies and equipment. A market study brought out that his main customer was the newly married family with the first home of its own. It would be an eager customer for about five years and then gradually fade out. This seemed perfectly logical to the manufacturer. After all, these were the people who were most actively interested in the home. They had the energy to do manual work. And, having small children, they normally spent most of their evenings and weekends at home.

But when noncustomers—families married longer than five years—were actually looked at, they were found to be a potentially excellent market. They were noncustomers primarily because the company had chosen a distributive channel, especially the neighborhood hardware store, which was not easily accessible to them except Saturday morning. Saturday morning is not a good shopping time for men, once children, though still young, are past their infancy.

Putting the merchandise into shopping centers (which remain open in the evenings when, increasingly, the whole family goes shopping together) and adding mail-selling directly to the home more than doubled the manufacturer's sales. To be sure, a smaller percentage of the older homeowners buy, and the older family buys somewhat less per year. But at any one time there are many more people who have owned a home for five years or longer than there are new owners.

A smaller percentage of the older age group still yields a bigger business than a higher share of the younger market.

2. Equally important may be the question: What does the customer buy all together? What does he do with his money and with his time?

Normally companies want to know what share of the customer's total spending—his disposable income, his discretionary income, or his discretionary time*—goes for their products, and whether the share is going up or down. This is important, of course. But to have some idea how the customer disposes of all his money and time may tell a good deal more.

Asking this question brought out, for instance, that neither price nor quality was the determinant of purchasing decisions for the products of a major construction-materials company. What determined purchase was whether it could be accounted for as capital investment or as operating expense. What made the purchase possible for one group of potential customers, especially public bodies—namely, that the purchase appeared as an operating expense in their books—made it difficult for the other group, the private businesses, for whom a capital investment appears as an asset, while operating expenses interfere with profit figures in the books.

The same products had to be "packaged" differently for the two kinds of customers: Public bodies got a 10-year "rental" in which the initial investment was paid off as part of an annual rental charge; private businesses were offered a capital asset at a price which included 10 years' free maintenance.

This leads in turn to two questions that are not asked in the ordinary market survey or customer study:

3. What do customers—and noncustomers—buy from others? And what value do these purchases have for them? What satisfactions do they give? Do they, indeed, actually or potentially compete with the satisfactions our products or services are offering? Or do they give satisfactions our products or services—or products or services we could render—could provide too, perhaps even better?

What this question might unearth are the value preferences of the market. How important in his life is the satisfaction

---
*Which means respectively: cash remaining after taxes and other compulsory deductions from the pay check, cash available after "necessities" have been paid for; time available and not needed to make a living and to get the necessary rest (i.e., time available for leisure, recreation, education, and so on).

the customer obtains from us? Is the importance likely to grow or to diminish? And in what areas of satisfaction does he have new or inadequately satisfied wants?

4. This is, of course, very close to the crucial question: What product or service would fulfill the satisfaction areas of real importance—both those we now serve and those we might serve?

The most imaginative illustration I know is that of a South American soft drink bottler who, while doing well, noticed that he was rapidly approaching market saturation. He thereupon asked himself, "What new product would, in the present stage of our economy, most nearly resemble the satisfaction which soft drinks offered to the masses 50 years ago?" His answer was paperback books. The population, while still very poor, had become literate in the meantime. Yet books in South America are available only in a few stores in the large cities and then at prices which even the middle class can hardly afford.

Paperback books, this man concluded, are, for today's population, precisely the small luxury which soft drinks were for the barefoot Indians half a century back. And in respect to merchandising, mass distribution, mass display, and the need rapidly to return unsold merchandise, paperback books are almost exactly like bottled soft drinks. What the man learned about his business, in other words, is that it was not "soft drinks"; it was "mass merchandising."

Four additional areas demand investigation.

First: What would enable the customers to do without our product or services? What would force them to do without? On what in the customer's world—economy, business, market —do we, in other words, depend? Is it economics? Is it such trends as the constant shifts from goods into services, and from low price into high convenience in an affluent society? What is the outlook? And are we geared to take advantage of the factors favorable to us?

Second: What are the meaningful aggregates in the customer's mind and in his economy? What makes them aggregates?

Two examples will explain this question:

When the automatic dishwasher was first developed, the makers went to great trouble and expense to make this new kitchen appliance look just like the clothes washer—an appliance the housewife had enthusiastically accepted and was thoroughly familiar with. Since technically the two appliances are quite different, to make them look alike—especially in outside dimensions—was no mean achievement.

Yet the main reason why the dishwasher has—so far—been a disappointment to its manufacturers is the ingenuity that went into making it look exactly like its older cousin, the clothes washer. For while it looks alike, it costs twice as much. To the housewife who is no engineer—and sees no reason why she should be one—this makes no sense. If something has been made to look exactly like the automatic clothes washer, why then should it cost twice as much? In other words, the manufacturers put the automatic dishwasher into a set of aggregates in which it created price expectations it could not meet.

It is likely that the dishwasher would have done much better had it looked so different from the traditional kitchen appliances as to stand out clearly as something new, as something not belonging in this familiar aggregate: kitchen appliances.

Another example is the totally different experience Sears Roebuck has had with two kinds of insurance. When it introduced, in the thirties, automobile insurance as something sold through its retail stores—like any other merchandise—it was exceedingly successful. The Sears-owned insurance company rapidly became the second largest underwriter of automobile insurance in the United States.

When, 20 years later, it introduced life insurance, it met with considerable customer resistance and has not yet been able to repeat its earlier automobile-insurance success. To the customer, automobile insurance is essentially a product, an automobile accessory, and as much a part of the car as brakes or steering wheel. But life insurance is something different; it is finance rather than merchandise. It simply does not belong to the same aggregate as automobile insurance—that both have the word "insurance" in their name does not make them sufficiently alike.

Another case of mistaken aggregation by the manufacturer had a happier ending.

A manufacturer of garden products introduced a line for the rose grower—a special fertilizer, pesticide, and so on. A leading supplier, he expected the new line to be rapidly accepted. Almost every home gardener has roses and wants to take care of them. As "rose products" the new line was a failure. But as products for the care of flowers and shrubs in general, they began to sell well in a few places—even though the manufacturer in all his instructions stressed their exclusive application to roses.

When the manufacturer accepted the customer's verdict and offered the products for all flowers and shrubs, the line, which he was ready to give up as a failure, suddenly came to life. "Rose grower" clearly means "somebody else" to the suburban home owner.

"Aggregates," to use the terms of the psychologist, are "configurations." Their reality is in the eye of the beholder. They depend not on definition but on perception. The perceptions, and with them the aggregates of the manufacturer and of the customer, must be different; for they have different experiences and look for different things. Yet it is the customer's perception of aggregates that matters, that decides what he buys, when he buys, and whether he buys.

Another searchlight on the unexpected is the third question: Who are our noncompetitors—and why?

There is nothing that changes faster than industry structures. Yet few things appear to executives so much like a law of nature as the industry structure of the moment. The present membership of the electrical industry association or of the retail grocers institute is considered "the industry." Yet again and again total newcomers are suddenly the most effective competitors—especially when they offer the customer a basically different means of satisfying the same want.

In no time, industry structure—yesterday seemingly so solid—is fragmented. Yet the new one, as it stabilizes after a time, is again taken for the ultimate.

Here are two examples:

The manufacturers of printing presses paid apparently no attention to the new processes for office reproduction that began to come on the market after World War II. These were not "printing," and the equipment for the processes was not being sold to "printers." One of the large printing-press manufacturers was offered several reproduction processes by the inventors and turned them down without any study.

It was not until a large part of the printer's traditional work was being done by their former customers themselves on office reproduction equipment that the printing industry woke up to the fact that a competitor had appeared who was far more dangerous than another printing-press maker could have been.

Similarly, the fertilizer industry in the United States considered itself a "chemical business." The questions—Who are the noncompetitors? Are they likely to remain noncompetitors?—would at once have brought out that there is no reason why the petroleum companies are not in the fertilizer business. They furnish the most important raw material: ammonia (which is a by-product of natural gas). They are experts in mass distribution and have representation in the smallest hamlet in the country.

And it was increasingly clear, in the late fifties, that the petroleum companies needed additional products for their huge and expensive distribution system. Yet even when one of the big American companies went into the fertilizer field in Europe, the U.S. fertilizer companies were convinced that it couldn't happen at home—until they woke up one fine day to find that the mixed-fertilizer business in the United States was being taken over by the petroleum industry.

The question: Who is our noncompetitor? logically leads to the fourth question: Whose noncompetitor are we? Where are there opportunities we neither see nor exploit—because we do not consider them part of our industry at all?

Understanding the Customer

Finally one should always ask the question: What in the customer's behavior appears to me totally irrational? And what therefore is it in *his* reality that I fail to see?

I have yet to find a consumer-goods manufacturer, for instance, who understands why every important retailer will—indeed, must—insist on having a private brand of his own. The more successful the retailer is in selling national (i.e., manufacturers') brands, the more will he insist on carrying and promoting his own. Manufacturers ascribe this insistence to the retailer's shortsighted concern with profit margins instead of with total profit-dollars.

Yet retailers usually admit that the higher profit margin of the private brand is eaten up by higher inventory costs and by the cost of goods left over which, being the retailer's own, cannot be returned. This only confirms the manufacturer in his belief that the retailer is irrational.

Actually, the retailer is perfectly rational in fearing that complete dependence on national brands will endanger him, no matter how much profit he makes on them. Why should anyone want to come to his store if all he sees and gets there are the same nationally advertised and nationally sold brands he can buy every place else for the same price and of the same quality?

A store whose reputation rests exclusively on the brand names everybody else can carry has no reputation or identity at all. All it has is an address.

Attempting to understand seemingly irrational customer behavior forces the manufacturer to adopt the marketing view rather than merely talk about it. Moreover, it forces the manufacturer to take action according to the logic of the market rather than according to the logic of the supplier. He must adapt himself to the customer's behavior if he cannot turn it to his advantage. Or he has to embark on the more difficult job of changing the customer's habits and vision.

The retailer's desire for a private brand to establish his store's identity is in the retailer's own best interest. The manufacturer had therefore better adapt to it, and if possible, turn it to his own advantage. The dominant supplier in any given product range might himself become the supplier of the private brand too.

Whenever a manufacturer tries to impose what he considers rational on an apparent irrationality which turns out to be in the best interest of the customer, he is likely to lose the customer. At the least, the customer will resent his attempt as a gross abuse of economic power—which it is. For behavior, however, that is contrary to the customer's own best interests, the manufacturer, in the end, pays a heavy price.

As many examples show, forcing oneself to respect what looks like irrationality on the customer's part, forcing oneself to find the realities of the customer's situation that make it rational behavior may well be the most effective approach to seeing one's entire business from the point of view of market and customer. It is usually the quickest way to get outside one's own business and into market-focused action.

Marketing analysis is a good deal more than ordinary market research or customer research. It first tries to look at the entire business. And second, it tries to look not at our customer, our market, our products, but at the market, the customer, his purchases, his satisfactions, his values, his buying and spending patterns, his rationality.

CHAPTER 16

PUBLIC RELATIONS

By Howard Stephenson

There are all kinds of public relations—good, bad, and indifferent. What we are interested in, and what any company is interested in, is good public relations, of course. What is it? How do you go about getting it? Of what concern is it to the average executive?

I think we would all agree that "good public relations" means a state of good will—friendly relationship that entail respect and confidence—between a company and its various "publics," ranging from its own employees to its suppliers, dealers, stockholders and the community or country at large. Creating and maintaining this state of active good will, like liberty, has its price: *eternal vigilance*.

A company earns good public relations in only one way: through attitudes and actions that others understand, like, respect, and respond to. Its main public relations job is to get people to understand.

This takes more than words or stunts. No outside counselor can bring about good public relations by his own efforts. No head of a firm can accomplish it alone. A public relations executive can do no more than go through the motions until the spirit is there. Management must *want* good public relations and want to deserve it if it is to get it.

It has been said that an organization is the lengthened shadow of a man. That is the shadow. But the substance is the devotion to duty of many men and women, those who hold executive jobs in staff or line. These are the people who should be alert to public relations opportunities on their own jobs.

Any executive is likely to become involved, sooner or later, in one or more situations that demand "public relations sense." Here are a dozen typical real-life instances, from my own practice in public relations, and they each present their problems:

Executive family: A new vice-president is brought in from the outside. Will he win loyalty from others who aspired to the job?

Working force: It is rumored that the branch plant, employing 300 people, will be moved to another state.

Sales force: Quotas will be raised for the next quarter.

Dealers. The cooperative-dealer advertising-allowance plan has been scrapped.

Local community: Should a junior executive be given three days off to run the Jaycees' annual welfare project in town?

Professional: Our research head is asked to present a medal awarded by a technical society to a competing company's scientific consultant.

Customers: A defect has been found in a product. Retail stores in four states are heavily stocked.

Government: The city council will vote on an ordinance rezoning the industrial district. This might force the plant to move.

Press: A top executive's wife has been named correspondent in a divorce case, and the papers have wind of it.

Financial: A company director is gathering stock proxies, preparing to force the present management out at the next annual meeting.

Labor: A popular foreman is discharged for flagrant drunkenness. A wildcat strike is threatened.

Education: A nearby college asks for a substantial contribution toward making up its operational deficit.

No sleight of hand, engineering of consent, slickness, or rhetoric will solve any of these down-to-earth problems. Nor is there a science of public relations that can give workable answers. Public relations is an art, not a science. It is not a black art. It is not mysterious. Its success is gauged by the good will it creates.

An executive of normal talents, blessed with innate good will himself, would have an excellent chance of handling successfully any of the foregoing real-life situations, even though he had never heard the term public relations. But he will perform better if he acts from knowledge of standard procedures and not entirely by instinct or rule of thumb.

Is there, then, anything new about public relations? Why is it recognized in many companies as an essential function of top management?

Perhaps public relations is merely a rearrangement of some factors always known to business management. The catalyst

* * *

Everyone who works for a company is important to its public relations. Your employees can be builders of good will for the business, or they can destroy good will. Or they can be neither —just numbers on a time clock. Your employees are an important cog in any public relations undertaking, no matter which way you classify them.

* * *

for this new combination is the emphasis placed upon two-way communication. Or you may say that public relations essentially is an application in management problems of pieces of new knowledge gained in the social sciences. A manager need not be an anthropologist, yet some of the findings in anthropology may be of use to him in a real-life situation.

Before we go any further, however, let's take a look at public relations from the organizational point of view.

It is not easy to pin down public relations on an organizational chart, of course. For example, General Motors designates a vice-president in charge of public relations and advertising. Procter & Gamble links public and legal affairs together. At Texaco, a vice-president directs public relations and personnel. United States Steel Corporation puts its large public relations staff in charge of an assistant to the chairman. Air Reduction Company has a "director of relations."

Permeates a Company

One reason for this diversity is that public relations activity goes on constantly all through an organization. It is really a horizontal, not a vertical, responsibility. Some sizable corporations avoid the term public relations. They prefer to speak of communications. That does describe the means through which public relations is activated, but it does not tell the whole story. For every component of a business lives amid special public relations situations.

Frequently these have to be handled by communication of one sort or another. But in some cases the function narrows down to policy—to the company attitude—and basic decisions become more important than the mechanics by which they are implemented.

An advocate of putting public relations and advertising together, for instance, is on good historic ground. Both deal with words and pictures. Both are needed to advance the public's understanding. By and large, advertising tends to be dominated by the needs of marketing. The bulk of it is devoted to moving products or selling services. Public relations helps here, too, but can scarcely do this job alone. For public relations must meet other demands—those of suppliers, production, research, engineering, employees, finance. Thus public relations has a broader responsibility than that of merely sales or advertising.

Perhaps public relations and advertising come closest together in sales promotion. Here it is sometimes difficult to make a precise distinction.

For example, a new product line is to be shown at a press preview. Is this a public relations or a sales promotion activity? It is a point often argued, but from top management's point of view, not too significant. If public relations and sales promotion executives are working hand in hand, opportunities arise for each to help the other. Good managements usually make the going much easier by designating one or the other for final responsibility—and budget control—on a given project.

Professional public relations people tend to say that employees constitute the No. 1 public. Thus they consider all who work for the company their responsibility. This comes as news to many personnel managers, who got along just fine without any new "public relations" label.

For instance, who shall produce the employee magazine? Again, this holds more importance for the departments involved than for the top echelons. What is wanted is a good house organ, drawing on talents wherever they are available. Here a definite policy helps resolve any conflict of authority.

Public relations and legal staffs sometimes have a surprisingly common ground of activity. Both endeavor to keep the company out of trouble and, once in, to get it out. Professional public relations people often shy away from legal departments because the cautious legal mind seems to restrict and qualify communication. What one calls imaginative boldness the other may describe as unwarranted hyperbole. A working balance, provided there is good will on either side, however, can usually be reached to mutual satisfaction; it *must* be, if both functions are to contribute to company prosperity.

The financial community, to be sure, is important to any company whose shares are offered on the open market. The security analyst has developed impressive stature from his former role as statistician. Increasingly it is becoming desirable for companies to impart fullest understanding to the analysts whose advice is sought by large and small investors. This, too, is a public relations activity for a company.

The controller or treasurer finds opportunity to explain the company and to answer questions posed by security analysts. In many companies the public relations staff makes arrangements for a company spokesman to appear before a group of analysts. It likewise handles contacts with the working financial press. These functions can be handled by a company officer when no professional public relations man is available.

Even at the top, however, with the president or chairman, a public relations officer can do no more than the chief executive can do if he is qualified and can spare the time. As a rule, the head of a concern has more frequent need for a public relations specialist than do department or division heads. For he is the spokesman, the public personification of the company. His presentations must always be the finest that the best combination of brains available can muster. (There is in fact danger, at times, that a professional public relations man may become so preoccupied with the president's demands that he will miss opportunities to be otherwise useful.)

Functions Like a Coach

From this brief rundown of relationships within a company, it is clear that the role of the public relations executive, under whatever title, is that of helper, coach, and guide. But suppose a company does not have the budget or the inclination to hire one or more public relations specialists. Is it, then, necessary to sacrifice the good contributions that can come in prestige and profit through proper public relations?

By no means! Any executive worth his salt possesses some of the sensitivity toward others that makes a good public relations man. True, he may not be skilled in communication techniques, but he might be surprised to discover in himself more of this talent than he knew he possessed.

Suppose he were to try to "double in brass," though. Let's say he is a personnel director, or a controller, and receives that most terrifying request—to make a speech. He feels he cannot write, is no orator and he gets butterflies in his stomach whenever he has to stand up in a meeting.

Now a public speech is one of the most valuable public relations endeavors a company man can undertake. So here is a capsule secret:

Your audience is not as much interested in you as in what you have to say. Chances are it is made up of people who can't write well, can't speak well and also get butterflies. If you can get your mind off the impression you are going to make, and are filled with the subject you want to talk about, you can always make an acceptable speech.

An executive untrained in public relations can also write a publishable article for his trade or professional publication. He can serve on a public relations committee of an outside organization. He can do precisely what any public relations man can do: Persuade people to understand and accept an idea.

This is not to belittle public relations competence. But when the chips are down, an honest and earnest presentation, made with head and heart, will captivate. The big thing, for the executive, is to want to tell. If you want to tell, you can make yourself understood, with or without the assistance of professional public relations people.

As an executive, suppose you are on your own in a situation that demands public relations sense. You smell trouble. You expect complaints, criticism, opposition, perhaps a legal battle. There is nobody to go to. You have to act.

Before you act, get more information. That's a good rule. Find out what people really are saying and thinking, not what you imagine. Listen. Ask a few questions. Then listen some more. Try to uncover the attitudes of those who may oppose you. These may be different from what they first appeared to be.

In a Connecticut city, factory workers were on strike. Though the company had offered great concessions, the workers would not sign to go back. Why? The production superintendent decided he had to find out. His job was at stake. So he rang doorbells. He asked the neighbors of employees, who did not hesitate to talk. The trouble was—a personality.

A company official had been so "obnoxious" the workers had agreed never to deal with him.

The smart superintendent told this man the truth. Then he told the company president. Risky? Yes. But the "obnoxious" man bowed out. The workers signed. One man, by listening, broke a strike.

This is called two-way communication. By discovering what others are thinking, you can decide how to communicate with them. Let's look at this process of communication, the basic tool you use in public relations. It has five elements: the *sender* (you), the *message*, the *medium of communication* (word of mouth, letter, newspaper, radio, and so forth), the *recipient*, the *effect*.

When you send a message through the right medium and the other person understands it, this has an effect on him. It may change his mind. It may influence him to buy. It may help him decide to accept a job. But until he understands your message, it cannot have the intended effect.

Your Golden Key

You do not have to be a public relations expert to listen—to find out what the other fellow has on his mind. When you make communication work both ways, you are using the golden key. This is the only secret weapon you need. Too few executives use it.

So valuable, however, are the results of two-way communication in industry that large organizations of professional "askers" and "listeners" do a big business. They take "opinion polls." When the stakes are great enough to justify the expense, it is an excellent idea to employ a professional for this. In the course of an ordinary job, however, you can often do it yourself if you have a proper public relations sense.

The written questionnaire is a popular device for collecting opinions. It is useful in many situations. A few simple questions, asked of a large number of persons, may produce a dependable picture—enough to make or buttress a decision. The questionnaire has a weakness, however. People tend to give the answer they think you want. Beware of this. It is not sufficient reason for discarding questionnaires, but they should not be used blindly. The personal interview is harder, more expensive and takes longer—but pays off better in the long run.

Handling the Major Publics

Public relations people speak of not one public, but many. Among important groups or publics to be dealt with by a business are the owners, or stockholders, the managerial staff, hourly employees, the local community, government officials, and the news media (daily and weekly papers, radio and television). Each presents a set of continuing but ever-changing situations that call for public relations handling.

Few executives would feel comfortable about passing this responsibility entirely over to a public relations expert. If one is available, his breadth of experience may have great value. In the same way, a management consultant can be useful on plant layout, production, marketing, and other matters. But public relations problems won't go away, even if there is no specialist around.

During the past 20 years procedures have been worked out which are now fairly standard for dealing with each of the major publics. Alas, there is no formula that fits precisely any given case. But there are guidelines.

Take stockholders. In the old days a stockholder was a lamb. Management fed him dividends, and he was happy. But this is less true now. Present-day management must be alert to meet challenges by dissident stockholder groups. It must woo the stockholder before trouble begins. And it does.

When somebody invests in the shares of a corporation, he is likely to receive a warm and cordial letter of welcome. He may get a report every three months as to how management is doing. He is certain to receive one annually. This is much more attractive than its counterpart 20 years ago.

The investor may be invited to a meeting of shareholders in his own home town and shake hands with the president and other officers. He is urged to attend the annual meeting. If he does so, he may receive an electrically stimulated indoor garden, a bottle of whiskey or some other giveaway. He may get a free airplane ride, theater tickets or other tokens of regard. And he is sure of a fine meal.

Should he show up at a branch plant, or company headquarters, the red carpet awaits him. Depending upon the taste of management, the stockholder is made to feel wanted, respected, and honored.

Well, who owns the company? Isn't it he?

260

To the individual executive, the managerial staff to which he belongs is in itself a small public, whose needs for communication he must learn to serve. No matter where he ranks just now in the hierarchy, he must deal with those below, on the same level, and above him in status.

An executive is rather quickly typed by his associates. He becomes known as dependable or unpredictable; a yes-man, a no-man, or a maybe-man; diffident or aggressive; imaginative or sterile; cool, cold, warm, or a bit too warm; lazy or industrious—the image he projects within the executive family at the start may be extremely difficult to change later.

The executive who looks upon his role within the company as a matter of personal public relations gains an advantage. Every letter, memo, verbal or written report, conversation, order given or received is weighed in advance for its probable effect on his own relationships.

Don't Become a "Loner"

A key to maintaining good relationships is to demonstrate a genuine interest in other people's work. A person is tempted, with the complex duties he faces every day, to focus so narrowly on his own job that he may give a false impression of being a "loner," wrapped up in himself.

Wise Ben Franklin said that a good way to make a friend is to ask a favor. Surely just as effective is to do a favor. One more hint: The executive who makes a studious effort to learn all he can about every phase of the company's business demonstrates, by that very fact, a keen sense of public relations. When he reaches the point where others on his level come to him for information outside his own bailiwick, he has become that figure so essential in public relations—an opinion leader. This can be more important than a promotion in rank or a raise in salary.

Communication between management and employees is also a matter of public relations. Many activities, even when run outside a public relations department, have important public relations connotations. Such is the safety program. And the recreational program. And the open house, the group visit to a plant, the bulletin boards, the employee magazine or news-letter, the foremen's meeting, the union negotiations. Every activity that involves communications echoes in public relations.

Certainly this does not mean that public relations runs the show. It means, rather, that every participant on the executive level has a stake in the public relations effects of the activity.

A trend has developed to regard company publications—including indoctrination booklets, management reports to employees, and announcements of basic shifts in policy—as public relations responsibilities. A danger lies in this excellent tendency, however; namely, that executives with other duties may slough off their share of this one.

No matter who writes or pronounces the words, an executive has the primary responsibility toward those directly under him. A word of explanation, a small group discussion, a willingness to answer questions—these are the bits and pieces of the public relations effort, it is true; but they are essential.

No matter what his larger role, the individual executive does not lose the role of "father" to the staff that reports to him. This is one of the prizes of leadership. It would be folly to neglect this personal public relations opportunity.

The department or division head has a like obligation to management. It is part of his public relations service to let top management know what people in his bailiwick are doing, thinking—and especially, saying. This is a point at which the invaluable playback in two-way communication may fall down.

Too often for comfort, an executive short-circuits the communication line. Yet he knows and understands the feel, the climate in his own realm better than others. To impart this knowledge to those in higher echelons of management is to demonstrate a public relations sense.

What goes on in a company's plant holds very special interest for the local community. This interest is legitimate and will be satisfied one way or another. The high fence with a sign "Keep out. This means you" is largely a thing of the past.

Now it is standard practice to invite the neighbors in. This is better done in an organized manner, to permit proper safety and other controls.

The plant tour by high school students, developed by Frigidaire at its Dayton, Ohio, plant a generation ago, has been adapted in many communities. High school students to some extent comprise the future reservoir of man- and woman-power, not only in the hourly working force, but in administrative, research, and other phases of employment. Here is a public worth cultivating. Few plants are so small that they will not attract interested community groups.

A group on an escorted tour may be readily handled. But when a company extends its hospitality to the general public,

*   *   *

Public relations should be the concern of everyone connected with a business organization, not just the few who are directly responsible for it. Those who write letters, for example, are important factors in public relations. A thoughtless letter to a customer that some salesman may have spent years cultivating can undo all that work and turn a friend into an enemy—or, what is just as bad, a disgruntled customer.

*   *   *

at all hours, complications arise. What is needed here is a policy, a plan of operation, kept as simple as possible.

To be sure, this sort of friendly attitude was not born yesterday. Shredded Wheat was doing it at Niagara Falls in 1908. Since World War II the great advantages of the welcome mat have been capitalized on increasingly, however. From management's point of view, a plant that may expect unannounced visitors at any time tends to do a good housekeeping job.

An alert executive is not content to wait for visitors. He finds many ways to extend the company's influence into community life. Membership of company men in local organizations is commonplace. Frequently the company pays the dues and other expenses. Sooner or later many companies face a decision: Shall company executives be permitted or encouraged to enter local politics?

The trend is to do so. Such participation is on the increase. Here generalities will not do. The actual situation, the personality concerned, the local "climate" or attitude toward the company must be considered.

On the whole, opinion is gaining ground that executive time spent away from routine on civic affairs of various sorts is a good company investment. General Electric estimates that every employee—not only executives—has a circle of about 50 friends and acquaintances. These should also, the company reasons, become fast friends of General Electric.

The Problem of Local Contributions

To what extent should an executive encourage his company to make local contributions to worthy causes? Should a soliciting team from the United Fund or Community Chest be turned away? Should it be denied access to the working and administrative forces? Should an executive accept responsibility for collections in the plant? Should he serve as a fundraiser in the town or head up a total campaign?

Such questions are no longer answerable strictly in regard to the company's immediate interest. Social pressure is high to require any company employing a substantial number of persons to participate in this way.

A contributions policy helps enormously. When a request is made for money, it is fair and legitimate to ask penetrating questions: When was the charity founded? How many members? What's the budget for next year? Is the organization approved by the Better Business Bureau? Has it applied for membership in the United Fund or a similar body? How often are solicitations made? Does it have a paid staff, and if so what is the annual payroll? Is the treasurer bonded?

A charity organization that objects to such questioning probably does not have too many good answers.

In a sense, all community participation is a matter of "prevention," of protection against future hostility. A company

264

long accepted as a good neighbor lives in a better climate than any newcomer. The Ciba Company, planning to open a $17-million plant at Toms River, New Jersey, spent two years developing good relations in the community before construction even began. By the time production had started, the company was no stranger.

The time to get acquainted with a local government official is before he walks in and shows his badge. Obviously the head of maintenance has dealings with police and fire departments. But who in the company is on good terms with the sheriff? Who knows the councilman in every district? Who has taken the trouble to visit the tax office without being summoned? Who has shown interest in the city school system? And in the county school system? What about the highway department? And the water and sewage plants? Do executives of the company usually beg off jury duty?

Perhaps no public is more thoroughly ignored, as a public, than local officialdom. It is not that they are to be asked for favors or concessions. But they will do their jobs better if they know how a company operates, what a plant looks like inside, what the valid reasons are behind some company practices—don't forget that.

If they understand, they can sometimes assist. But if they have no contacts, the company may seem a mystery. And people are mistrustful of mysteries.

Meeting the Press!

From management's point of view, the press, including radio and television, represents the people, the general public. These are the media through which the company reaches the public with its messages. The company's purpose is to be understood. Hopefully, this understanding will create a favorable impression. Relations with the media, therefore, are crucial. No executive with a public relations sense underestimates their importance.

Many a reporter for a local newspaper would rather talk with a company executive other than the public relations head. This is understandable. First, he likes to get his news direct. Second, there is a chance he may bring out a newsy fact the company had not thought of or is not ready to reveal. The public relations man is cagey; another executive might be more relaxed.

How can this be dealt with, and bruises prevented?

An excellent policy is to let the reporter talk with whomever he chooses, but in the public relations man's presence. If there is no public relations man, one specific person should be designated as the principal contact with local newspapers, radio, and television. All inquiries should be directed to this official, usually the president or a vice-president. He will accompany the reporter on any other interviews.

This simple device works well. Editors find they like it, too. They like to know where to go for an answer, they are wary of an executive who seeks too much personal publicity.

Reporters and editors are busy people. They do not like to be hung up on a query when a deadline is approaching. It is worthwhile, therefore, to drop other matters and look after a reporter's needs promptly—even when he must be told nothing is available. If executives all down the line understand there is a company policy on news, and are required to comply, the sailing becomes fairly smooth.

Sailing never is smooth, however, when a disaster occurs. A bad accident, a decision to shut down a department, disappointment on a government contract—it is folly to attempt to suppress such news. The reporter has other sources. The advantage of telling the facts straightforwardly is that this minimizes the chance that they will be distorted. A reporter who is denied access to a plant where a disastrous event has occurred is not likely to forget this when he hears an unfavorable rumor the next time.

Usually it is a mistake to talk with a new reporter "off the record." With no bad intention, he well may misunderstand what is released for publication and what is not. Newspapers are rightfully sensitive to their duty to print the news. There is no such thing as forbidding an editor to publish something he believes to be true, so never attempt it. If the story is true, you're stuck with it. If it isn't, give the newspaper the facts. That's good public relations.

And whether you're dealing with the press or any other of your various publics, good public relations always pays off in the long run.

CHAPTER 17

LABOR RELATIONS

By James F. Lincoln

If we are to get the full cooperation of labor and management, there must be a radical change from the present relationship. Such a change will be difficult to get, however, because of past habits.

Both workers and managers must realize completely that their progress can only come from willing cooperation.

Cooperation, as we use the term, does not mean just the elimination of resistance to progress in efficiency. That is of small importance. Cooperation is the working together of all people in the organization in the same way that all the members of an athletic team work together to win a game. Cooperation does not mean elimination of featherbedding only. It means the enthusiastic finding of new methods, new tools, new ideas by all people, from top to bottom, in the organization. Cooperation means the enthusiastic use by all people in the company of their best ideas, skills and methods to reduce costs and improve quality in any way that is possible.

Such cooperation is present in athletics. It is present in the family. It is present in much top management. It is not present in the usual labor-management relations. When cooperation such as we describe is obtained, manufacturing efficiency will be enormously increased over present standards. Production costs will be a small fraction of what they are now. This will be the result of the worker's unrestricted productivity. By his expert knowledge and his desire for progress, he will also develop better methods and better machines for production. Because of his own natural human desire to develop his latent abilities, the worker also will develop himself greatly.

In one case well known to the author there has been a reduction in manhours per unit of production of well over 90 percent over a period of 25 years. This was not the result of greater physical skill only. It was the result of the development of better machines and tools of production, as well as new and better skills and designs. It was the result of the desire of all those involved in production to perfect their ideas and apply them to production.

Such a change in the attitude of workers from top to bottom is bound to be revolutionary in its results. It is, however, an obvious step. It has been delayed because the managers of

*   *   *

Management's benighted policy in dealing with the worker has been responsible for the present grave crisis in labor-management relations. The worker has had to go to the union to get the increase in standard of living and status that he should have gotten from management automatically. He has been forced to do so by management's continued resistance to progress through the union. That is how the present war between labor and management developed.

*   *   *

industry have largely failed in their leadership. Instead of there being management-workers leading wage-earning workers in cooperating to increase and distribute more of the goods of life to all, short-sighted managers and workers often have resisted such development. Because of its failure in leadership, management's position in the eyes of the worker also is far from what it should and must be.

Managers must regain their position as the accepted leaders of cooperating workers. The wage payer still can boss the wage earner, although this authority has been greatly lessened by the labor unions. Enthusiastic acceptance, however, of the leadership of management by the worker is in most companies lacking. To regain it will take some doing.

The first step that managers must take is to get their own thinking straight. If willing cooperation is wanted, the manager must begin it and lead it. He is dealing with experts who, in most cases, are far more skillful in doing their jobs than he would be. While it is possible to boss these experts in the usual lofty way, their eager cooperation will not be won by so doing. The manager must awaken their desire to cooperate with their fellow workers, including himself. Their full cooperation cannot be obtained in any other way.

If managers are to get such desire on the part of the worker, they must review the whole program of the company seriously.

A wage earner is no more interested than a manager is in making more money for other people. His job does not depend on pleasing the stockholders, so he has no interest in dividends. Neither is he interested in increasing the efficiency of operation when such increased efficiency will result in his losing his job because management has failed to get the necessary orders.

The worker is the same kind of person as the manager. He has the same needs, desires and fears. If the manager received the same treatment in all matters of income, security, advancement and dignity that he gives to the hourly worker, he would soon understand the real problem of management and have little difficulty in finding the solution.

Why Workers Are Rebellious

The first question, then, that management should answer is: What end has the company in view? What is it trying to do?

In the mind of the average wage earner today the answer is this:

"The company I work for is trying to make the largest possible profits by any method it can pursue. The profits go to absentee stockholders and top managers. They don't give a damn for the hourly workers who do the job, nor for the customer who pays all the costs."

270

With such a view, any desire to cooperate with management is unlikely. There is little reason for cooperation. The hourly worker will not go along. He sees no object in working but wages. He therefore will be uncooperative. He will be inefficient. He will be unimaginative. He will be rebellious.

The proper answer to the problem is self-evident. Industry must make sense to the worker if it is to engage his interest. It must serve purposes that he sees and approves if he is to cooperate eagerly in achieving them. It must have as its goal, first of all, progress, improvement in ways of living, better lives for everyone. This is, in fact, the achievement of American industry to some extent, and it should be seen clearly and

*   *   *

A generation ago the boss was in a dominant position. He often had greater knowledge, skill, and experience than the worker. But that time has largely passed. The worker today is an expert who has abilities that are far beyond the boss's. His contribution is completely necessary if industry is to succeed and progress.

*   *   *

adopted as the purpose of all industry. Cooperation must reward the worker in proportion to what he does.

This must not be forced on management by the union, as has been true so far. It must be the program of management. Management must also protect the needs of the worker by continuous employment, as it now protects the jobs of top management.

Perhaps these goals in the light of past custom seem impossible. They are not. They are being reached now by many companies. This is a natural development.

The changing of the goal of industry from profit to service by producing a better and better product at a lower and lower price is what most companies claim is their goal now. It is obvious, therefore, that at least in theory, service rather than profit has become the goal. The fact is, however, that this program of service at lower prices is like our acceptance of the

Sermon on the Mount; it is discussed on Sunday and forgotten on Monday. We industrialists are "practical men." We actually cannot get off the beam of profit. That is for the "eggheads." Here again we must change our ideas.

The goal of service to the customer, by giving him more and more for less and less, is not only right, it is completely practical. Where it is accepted, it is far more successful for all concerned than the policy of "all the traffic will bear." This program is necessary if we are to get the willing cooperation of labor. It is necessary also if we are to get the customer's cooperating approval and support.

Cooperation is essential to the "division of labor" that we call modern industry. No industry can progress without it. But there is all the difference imaginable between the grudging, distrustful, half-forced cooperation of men who must earn wages and men greedy for larger salaries, and the eager, wholehearted, vigorous and happy cooperation of men working together for a common purpose and rejoicing in their mutual success—their expanding company.

If we are to create the atmosphere in which this willing cooperation thrives, we must change completely the habits and conceptions that have guided management heretofore. Labor and management are properly not warring camps; they are parts of one organization in which they must and should cooperate fully and happily. They are like husband and wife in this necessity. To successfully meet the competition that our American economy now faces from abroad, we managers must have the wage earner's wholehearted cooperation.

In achieving this needed state of cooperation, management must take the lead. That is what management is for. Its job is to lead. In doing that in the case of labor-management relations, it will be necessary to change many policies that management has followed heretofore. Management must exploit neither the customer nor the worker. Industry must continuously increase its rewards to both. Such rewards must not be forced on managers by competitors nor by labor unions.

When outside force is necessary to lower costs and raise wages, management has failed in its job.

American industry has always been able to meet world competition, with its lower wages and lower material costs, whenever cooperation was achieved. Many American products now dominate the world market. All could meet world competition if cooperation such as some companies have achieved were universal.

A lower price on a better product is obtained by making such a result the desire of all the people in the whole organization. When the goal of a properly led company is better quality at a lower price, that goal will be reached. It is management's responsibility to organize or reorganize the company's program so as to accomplish just that.

If it does not or cannot do that, it should disappear—and eventually it will. Competition will destroy it in a free market. That is what competition is for.

Higher and higher reward should go to the employee in return for his contribution in producing the better and better product at a lower and lower cost. This progressively greater reward should go to all those in the organization, from bottom to top, depending on the contribution that each worker makes to the program of cost reduction and product improvement.

There can be no doubt that progress in industry can continue only while there is a new and growing source of buying that will absorb the products that can be made. This increased buying is done largely by the hourly worker as his income increases. If this greater income were reduced, his buying would decrease in proportion, and industry to that extent would disappear. The resulting economy would be far smaller than what we now have. All industry would be affected.

In spite of the need for ever-higher wages, leadership in industry has resisted every move toward giving a better income to the hourly worker. This needed buying power on which our economy is now based was forced on management by unions, not by the intelligent judgment of management.

If management had taken the lead in this matter, as it should have done, the present labor-management friction would never have developed. The workers' need for unions would not have occurred. The present war between worker and management would be impossible. The efficiency of production would be many times what we now see.

Let's Face Up to the Problem

Management must rectify this error. It will be harder to do so now than it would have been a generation ago. It can be done, however, and eventually must be. Many companies have done it already.

If management is to accomplish this end, it must recognize the problem and apply the proper answer. The answer is obvious if we will view it objectively, forgetting habit and previous custom. The worker is a man like the manager and will react to the same stimuli. He is not a man apart, in spite of the enmity that has been developed in him by the present labor-management friction. He is just as eager as any manager is to be part of a team that is properly organized and working for the advancement of our economy.

However, he is not particularly struck by the idea that he has a duty toward management that management does not have toward him. He has no desire to make profits for those who do not hold up their end in production, as is true of absentee stockholders and inactive people in the company.

Management, in regaining its position of leadership, must recognize that the position of the hourly worker has changed from what it was a generation ago. He is much more powerful and also much more skilled. Manufacturing has progressed greatly. The manufacturing organization is now a group of experts who have developed new machines and methods that have almost completely eliminated the previous methods that were used. Management is not dealing with servants. It is dealing with workers of unique ability, who because of their skill are completely necessary to efficient production.

It is only by cooperative use of this expert group that any company can meet world competition, or the competition in our own country.

Management cannot boss such people. It must lead them. Managers must be accepted leaders whose leadership is respected because of ability, and whose fairness and honesty cannot be questioned. Such management must see that the abuses to which the hourly worker has been subjected by custom are eliminated. Management must see that the reward to the worker is proper and is so understood and accepted by him.

The customary abuses of layoffs and improper use of profits are the most obvious conditions that must be changed. The reward of the worker by money and advancing position are additional ones. When the worker knows that he will be rewarded in direct proportion to this contribution and that his job is safe, his whole attitude toward his work and his managers changes. He wants to increase the rewards in which he

*　　*　　*

If management had cooperated in labor's advance, the wage rates would be the same as now. Fringe benefits would be the same as now. The leadership of management, however, would be unquestioned and, because of that, the efficiency of industry would be far beyond what is now usual. Foreign competition, which currently threatens our industrial future, would be largely eliminated, since we would by our efficiency outstrip it.

*　　*　　*

shares justly. The hourly worker does not want strikes. He does not want featherbedding. These abuses are his only means of reacting against the resistance that management has made to his progress. If managers were treated as unjustly as many managements have treated wage earners, they also would fight back, as the unions do, by any means at hand.

The abuses of labor union power are the natural reactions of human beings to the abuses to which management has subjected them. When the worker is convinced that the abuses that caused him to use such methods of reprisal no longer exist, he will join in a fair and honest program of cooperation, as he so much wants to do.

The fundamental task is to rectify the mistakes that management has made over the years. Labor once looked to management to lead. When management did not do so properly and fairly, the present reaction was inevitable. When management accepts its responsibility to lead in the proper way, there will be no lack of cooperation by the worker. He is a fellow player on the team and wants to be treated as such. He is not just a convenience to be used and discarded as management may decide from time to time.

Greater Efficiency Expands Markets

The question is frequently asked: If efficiency were increased to the degree that it is in some companies and could be in all, would not the number of jobs be so small that many workers could not find employment?

The answer is obvious. Efficiency cannot eliminate jobs because increased efficiency lowers costs, lower costs cause lower prices, lower prices expand the market; an expanding market raises employment.

Buying is controlled by price. There is no limit to human desires. Therefore, there is no limit to the market for any useful or desirable product if the price is low enough. There is no market for a product, no matter how useful, if the price is too high.

We see this fact illustrated in the number of second-hand cars that are sold, compared to new ones. If new cars were available at the price of second-hand cars, the market for new cars would expand many times. The same fact controls in the present market for ready-made clothes, which is many times that of custom-made clothes in spite of the greater attraction of clothes made for the individual by a tailor.

There are endless illustrations of this same fact to be seen on every hand. Cost is decisive. Cost controls the size of the market.

When the cost is reduced, as increased efficiency of cooperation reduces it, the market will be expanded indefinitely. World trade will increase tremendously. The demand for workers needed to satisfy this expanding market will constantly increase. There will be jobs without end. Prices will be falling, wages and profits rising, markets expanding, jobs increasing in number and variety, skills improving; lives will be ever richer in work, and leisure, and all human values.

Employment depends on the rate of buying. The rate of buying depends on price and quality. Both of these results depend on the skill and desire of the producer. The skill and desire of the producer depend on his desire for efficiency and his consequent development of his latent abilities.

There is no limit to the development of human beings and human cooperation, since man is so made by his Creator. Christ gave the world the program needed to accomplish these results. There is no mystery as to what we should do. We only need to adopt the Christian ethic.

When we accept the Christian ethic, we in management make the worker's progress a major aim of our policy. Our company must win in a competitive market. To develop a team that can win in such competition, we must care for the well-being and development of every man in the plant as an athletic coach looks out for every member of his team.

When we do that, an entirely different attitude develops in the worker. He responds as members of a team do—with his full cooperation. If he feels, as he must, that management is trying to help him in his striving for a better life, he will with great enthusiasm repay the management by greater efforts to help achieve the goals that management has. Such a reaction is automatic in man. It always occurs. Men automatically respond to sincerity with even greater sincerity. That is the reason that the Christian ethic is always successful in practice.

There are many forms and degrees of cooperation between the worker and management. The worker's attitude can vary all the way from passivity to highly imaginative contributions to efficiency and progress. When the first cautious thawing develops into genuine team spirit, however, the difference that it makes in an industry is the difference between the speed with which the union worker usually approaches his job after a coffee break and the agility with which he plays a game.

Enthusiastic cooperation of men in business and industry increases efficiency enormously. It multiplies production. It cuts costs. It raises wages, while it constantly lowers prices to the customer.

This difference in the spirit of the men is fundamental, but it is hard to measure or describe. However, it shows itself in the help that the hourly worker gives in developing new ways of production, in saving materials and time. It shows in the continuous operation of machines compared to the breakdowns on these same machines when the workers don't care. Like friendship between two persons, the spirit of cooperation is intangible, but its effects are great.

Today, because of habit, we industrial managers are all too apt to think of the wage earner as merely a member of a union that is trying to ruin the company by high wages and low productivity. Industrial leadership must meet this challenge. It must provide incentives that will inspire the individual wage earner to develop his latent abilities and give him the opportunity to rise as far as these developed abilities can carry him.

Installing an Incentive Program

Incentive is usually thought of in industry as a money payment for more production. Many other incentives, far more potent than money, are available to management. Money incentive, however, is the simplest to apply and therefore is far more popular than any other type.

Money incentive is often applied as piecework. The results obtained are various, and in many cases they are far from good. In other cases, piecework is at least partially successful in increasing production. It does not get to the bottom of the problem, however. Alone, it does little or nothing to create and encourage the willing cooperation of all the workers.

The problem that management has in applying incentive is to make sure that the program it uses is an incentive in the mind of the worker. Does he want to go along?

It does not follow that because managers think they are applying a good program to the workers, the workers necessarily think so too. If the plan does not inspire the individual worker to feel that he wants to do his best on the job, and keep on doing so, the incentive is far from successful. The attitude of the wage earner absolutely determines the success of any incentive program.

What, then, are the components of a successful incentive? First, the worker must feel that he actually wants to work more efficiently and produce more. He must feel that greater efficiency will reward him in a satisfactory way. He will feel this only when his greater efficiency does in fact bring him greater rewards, both in money and in other ways as well.

The worker also must feel that greater efficiency will not in any way endanger his employment. Any incentive plan is useless if fear of a layoff exists. That is still true even if the threat is only imagined in the worker's mind and does not actually exist.

The incentives that are most potent when properly offered and believed in by the worker are the following:

First: Money in proportion to production.

Second: Status as a reward for achievement.

Third: Publicity about the worker's contribution in skill and imagination and the reward that is given for it. This results in added status for the worker.

The success of any incentive, as we have noted, depends completely upon its acceptance by the worker. The incentive of itself will not assure results, no matter how good the managers may think it is. The worker is very suspicious of management. His experience with incentive plans has not been good. In general, managers have used incentive plans with the object of getting more production for less cost. The worker is no fool; he has seen that the object was to get him to work harder for less reward. He is apt, therefore, to be very skeptical of any incentive plan put forth by management.

It is well to keep in mind in applying any incentive system that money of itself is not as great an incentive to any of us as self-respect and status. We will all sacrifice money to keep our self-respect and to gain the respect and admiration of our contemporaries. This is shown by the enthusiasm of the amateur athlete in playing a game. The only reward he can have is self-respect and the respect of others whose good opinion he values. He will generally try harder than the professional, who gets paid for his performance.

The acceptance by Robert McNamara of the job of Secretary of Defense, which could cost him millions, is a good example of money being passed up to gain a hoped-for status.

We see many other cases in which a higher-paying job is passed up for employment that provides status but a lower salary. This can be illustrated by many people in education, the ministry and in government service. Money as a reward is far less attractive to most of us than the respect of those we know. This fact is important in the successful use of incentive plans in business and industry. Management has largely ignored it because many managers fail to think of a wage earner as they think of themselves.

Status is of great importance in all human relationships. The greatest incentive that money has, usually, is that it is a symbol of success, which gives the successful man status. The resulting status is the real incentive. The ability to gain status by accomplishments which, incidentally, bring more income is of far greater importance to a man than the income itself. Money alone can be an incentive to the miser only.

There are certain principles that must be followed if any incentive system is to succeed. The first is that literally no limit be set on the earnings that a worker can get, except the worker's own limitations. This has to do not only with the physical skill of the operator, but most of all with his development of new ideas that may increase production far more than physical skill can. The fear that the worker often has—that if his earnings go above a certain amount, the piecework price will be cut—now limits production tremendously in many plants.

Glorify such ability. Stimulate it. Encourage it. Do not penalize it.

It is, of course, proper to change a piecework price if management has changed the method of production so fundamentally as to justify the change. That is the only way that any change in a piecework price can be fairly made, and the change must be scrupulously fair to the worker. That is the only way the worker will regard it as fair and still work with energetic good will.

There is much to be considered in this area. The worker is the expert on the job he is doing. He knows much more about it than any manager when he really wants to. If he has been properly led, and the proper incentive is offered to him so that he actually wants to make the operation more efficient, his advice and help can be invaluable in finding better and more efficient ways to do the job. Under usual leadership he is not apt to give such help. His interest must be in the opposite direction. Here is a great opportunity for the progressive manager.

No Tips, Please

In using money as an incentive, it is necessary first to make sure that the plan fits the conditions involved. It is a mistake to give a man something to try to induce him to be more easily led by the giver. A wage earner is a man with the understanding and reactions of any other man. When management gives him money, with a notion of buying his loyalty, naturally he sees the motive and resents the insult. He has seen management continually resisting the union's demand for higher wages and other benefits. He will not easily believe that management has changed in character.

If money is to be an incentive to sincere cooperation, it is absolutely essential that the worker earn that money. His self-respect is not developed, nor is his efficiency induced, by tips.

The necessary development of competition between workers must be such that the more skillful worker's reward is in proportion to his contribution as compared to that of the less productive. Everyone in the group must feel it is a fair game and want to compete in it. If the men feel no pleasure, no fun, in the competition itself, the results of any incentive program that management may introduce will be far from what they could be. The possibilities of man, when he develops skills because of a desire to do so, are limitless, and so are the possibilities of enterprise in which men use their developing skills to increase the efficiency of the company.

The attitude of the usual worker in a union shop is to have a certain production as a limit. When he has produced so much, he stops. This may mean that the man—after producing the quota he sets—does nothing until the end of his shift, or it may be that the speed of production is held so low that he produces no greater amount during the shift. The result is the same. It is a very small fraction of what willingly cooperating men easily produce in the same length of time.

It is obvious that no incentive plan can succeed in such plants as long as a featherbedding attitude exists. Little or no progress can be made in efficiency as long as the worker's attitude remains as it often is. A man's desire to act is his incentive to action; a man who sees nothing to gain by working more efficiently cannot be given any incentive to increase his efficiency. If the desire is lacking in the men, management cannot put incentive into them by any incentive plan.

Only after management has eliminated the fears of layoffs and rewards to the wrong people that the worker now has, with a consequent desire to limit output, can an incentive program be used to stir his desire to produce more efficiently.

The plan should reward the man, not only for the number of pieces he makes, but also for all other assistance that he gives beyond his usual job. The accuracy of his work obviously adds to its value. His cooperation with management in improving methods of production is of far greater importance than any other skills. Both of these are obvious contributions he can make, and he should be properly rewarded for them.

There are other ways in which his cooperation earns a reward in any successful incentive system. His attendance and his health are largely in his own control and are of great importance to the efficiency of operation. His excellence in these regards should be properly acknowledged. Of the greatest importance to progress, however, is his development. This is not only the result of being trained to do his job better. Doing his job well is of relatively small importance. The great thing is the development of his latent abilities.

282

Given the opportunity for and proper recognition of his achievements, the progress he can make and, as a consequence, the progress his company can make because of his development are beyond the belief of those who have not seen it.

Incentive plans in general do not attempt to develop the potential powers of all the men in the plant. Management does not even recognize that possibility. That is where it overlooks its greatest opportunity.

A truly cooperative manager finds many ways to increase cooperation and reward achievement. Obviously, this cannot be done by a mechanical piecework plan only. There should be an overall bonus based on the contribution each person makes in any way that is helpful to overall efficiency.

If each person is properly rated on all these things and paid accordingly, there will not only be a fair reward to each worker but, much more important, there will be friendly and exciting competition between the workers, so that each tries to outdistance the others and contribute more. A spirit of teamwork will prevail, as it does between competing members of a football team. The results will seem miraculous when compared to the results of the usual cut-and-dried policy now followed.

Money incentive has been stressed, since it is used in almost all cases. If it is to be most effective, however, it must be combined with status and publicity. Promotion of the people in any company must be determined by their record made in production, both in skills and imagination. The worker must feel that higher status is a natural reward for achievement (as, of course, it should be), and management must make sure that outstanding achievement is fully recognized, is known throughout the plant and receives promotion.

When money, status and publicity are used accurately, and honestly by scrupulously just leadership, they are incentives that completely capture the worker's imagination. He will not only be a cooperating operator; he will also be a rapidly developing individual, with rapidly increasing ability.

In following out this program, we must act on the principles that Christ taught the world. The basis of this program is human fellowship, based on the brotherhood of man. This kind of quality is a practical fact; each one of us is a unique person, but we are all equally human. Here is a principle of human nature as real as any principle of physics. It becomes as obvious as the law of gravitation when we break away from the habit of thinking of labor and management as different things.

Eventually this spirit of brotherhood should prevail in all business and industry. Where they prevail now, there is a revolution in production and progress. Men find new ways of saving time and materials and increasing efficiency; production is many times greater, especially in shops where labor-management friction existed before. Costs are reduced, and prices cut, but profits, wages and bonuses are greatly expanded.

Men who are accomplishing such results are revealing obvious roads to a future progress that will make past and present accomplishments seem picayune.

CHAPTER 18

MORALE AND PRODUCTIVITY

By Thomas G. Spates

During the past 10 to 15 years while operating personnel officers have had their hands full keeping up with changes in social legislation, problems imposed by a "laboristic" economy, the complex techniques of personnel administration, and day-to-day service to their respective organizations, the behavioral scientists have been playing a major role in our progress.

They have been building a body of evidence in support of the lessons learned "the hard way" by many old-timers. They have been confirming the faith of those leaders who were motivated by spiritual conviction regarding the "right" and "wrong" ways to treat people at the places where they work. They have been increasing greatly our knowledge and our understanding of forces involved in morale, motivation, and productivity.

On at least one conclusion the behavioral scientists appear to be in practically unanimous agreement. The conclusion is that each of us does not *have* a personality; each of us *is* a personality. This means that it is grossly inaccurate to speak of people as having a "nice" or a "disagreeable" personality. We should be more specific—a bit more scientific. It means further that if you have any personnel forms—employment, appraisal, reference—that include "personality" along with cooperation, initiative, energy, judgment, as qualities of an individual, those forms are obsolete. Each of those qualities is an ingredient of total personality.

This conclusion imposes upon us an obligation to be more precise, to make up our minds what ingredients of personality we are interested in—not to use personality as a dumping place for the things that are left over in our analysis of desirable or critical qualities.

But the conclusion does not stop with that first observation. It goes on to say that most personalities are healthy. A healthy personality is that in which the almost infinite ingredients are in balance. You may think I'm a screwball, but I am in balance and, therefore, for the time being, anyway, a healthy personality. If a personality is to remain healthy, you cannot change one ingredient without altering some others. This is

*   *   *

Personnel work must not be allowed to become the property of a staff Santa Claus. It must be done by the people who are carrying the responsibilities of management. The men and women in the rank and file must be lifted up to a higher plane of understanding and responsibility, and the men and women who are their immediate bosses are the ones who must lift them.

—E. K. Hall, former vice-president, A.T.&T.

*   *   *

a conclusion of tremendous importance to the progress of personnel administration.

Let me illustrate by two different experiences. A California company gave me a most extraordinary assignment. They asked me to attend a three-day conference of their top management including members of the board of directors and at the final session give them an unreserved evaluation of what I had seen and heard. It was a tough assignment. They were wonderfully fine people, but some of the proceedings were painfully dull not only for me but also for most of the managers.

However, the part that seemed to call for special comment was a panel session devoted to a discussion of how to motivate creativity, during which an operating executive said, "In my division I demand enthusiasm." My reaction was role-played somewhat as follows:

"Okay, Mr. Authority, you are my boss. You demand enthusiasm from me and I want to keep my job. But God put only a little bit of enthusiasm into me. This ingredient can't be changed without altering some others. I'll try, but neither you nor I am smart enough to predict the consequences. What's more, for all you know, my little bit of enthusiasm in combination with other ingredients may serve your objectives far better than if I cooperate in meeting your demand."

This is not an argument against enthusiasm. It is a desirable ingredient particularly when applied to the attainment of good ends. The point is—it should be motivated if desirable by example and environment, not by compulsion. How much real respect, loyalty, cooperation, and enthusiasm does one get and hold for long by demanding them?

The personality ingredient conclusion of behavioral scientists is one about which I can get emotional. The reason is this, I was born left-handed. On my first day in school the teacher looked over the class, spotted me with the crayon in my left hand, thought: "Aha! Here is a nonconformist. This will never do." She tried persuasion. It didn't work. Being left-handed was a built-in part of me as a healthy, balanced personality.

So, one day the old buzzard snuck up behind me and scarred the knuckles of my left hand with the brass edge of a ruler. In repressing a natural impulse to retaliate against this cruel act, something had to give. It might have been my speech. In my case it was my eyes. Sick headaches, astigmatism, eyeglasses at age seven. In a different and startling way, this early educational experience caught up with me again in my early fifties. So, I have had more than just eyeglasses to remind me of my involuntary and primitive initiation into the behavioral sciences.

The lessons derived from the opening conclusion in the scientific approach to personnel administration should be clear. Leadership involves much more than the trite qualities so often prescribed. Because of the origin and uniqueness of each human personality, there rests upon leaders a responsibility with a quality of sacredness. Tampering with the ingredients of personality is a potentially grave and dangerous business. If, as one who directs the work of others, you are interested in both high morale and high productivity, over the long pull, you will avoid the compulsory method of changing personality ingredients.

Need for Participation

One of the two most important factors in the long-run morale and productivity of the individual is the experience of participating in matters affecting his interests. That conclusion has been confirmed in a host of scientific experiments. It is the essence of the Hawthorne Studies of 30 years ago as described in the voluminous report by Roethlisberger and Dickson entitled *Management and the Worker* (Harvard University Press). Other experiments and observations are described by Norman R. F. Maier, distinguished psychologist at the University of Michigan, in his fine but inaccurately titled work, *Principles of Human Relations;* in *Group Dynamics,* edited by Cartwright and Zander; and in the splendid work of the late Professor Nathaniel Cantor, *The Teaching-Learning Process.*

A classic example of the influence of participation on productivity is the experiment conducted in the Harwood Manufacturing Corporation at Marion, Virginia, and described in *Human Relations* 1948, 1, 512, by Lester Coch and J. R. P. French, Jr. This experiment was made because the economics of the business indicated the need for a product change.

For the experiment the production employees were divided into four groups which were equal on the basis of previous production records. One group knew nothing about the product change except the starting date. Another group elected representatives who were told of the changes and expected to report what they knew to the rest of the group. In two groups every member was informed, asked to discuss the problem and make suggestions. Some suggestions were used.

Within less than a week from the date of change, the participating groups were making over 70 units an hour compared with a previous rate of 60, and the increase was maintained between 70 and 75. Production of the "tell 'em nothing" group not only dropped to 50 units an hour, but 17 percent of its members quit in the first 40 days on the new product. Presumably they felt that they had been subjected to gross discrimination. After two weeks of low production the representation group leveled off at about 63 units.

We had a different but certainly no less impressive experience in a production unit of General Foods. A poultry processing plant for the Birds Eye Quick Frozen line was acquired in the Maryland Peninsula. Some local business leaders privately protested against the application of our personnel principles and policies to colored employees in the plant on the grounds that they would be "spoiled." By rejecting the protest, refusing to lower our standards of human values we, in time, influenced the raising of personnel standards in manufacturing and processing throughout the Peninsula.

Three years later the maximum, expected capacity of that plant had been more than doubled with no additional capital expenditure and only a 57 percent increase in the number of employees. The direct labor cost per unit of finished product showed a steady decline although wages had been increased each year.

Performance reviews were completed on every employee in the plant. On his review, one of the Negro boys who had spent several years in the Army wrote: "This is the first time in this part of the country that I have had the experience of being treated like an American citizen."

Better management leadership and response by employees to the experience of participation in a social-economic revolution on their home grounds are the only valid explanations for that phenomenal increase in production beyond maximum expectations based upon the physical equipment and facilities.

The skeptics regarding the economic advantages of participative administration point out that it slows down decision-making. Authoritarianism makes decisions easier and faster. We can have no serious argument with those conclusions. However, when you add to the time of making decisions the time it takes to get them efficiently executed, consultative supervision will win 100 to 1. The total elapsed time between recognition of the problem and its satisfactory operating solution is reduced by the higher morale and productivity arising from the individual self-respect which accompanies participation.

Importance of Attitude

Starting with analyses of the causes of accidents and continuing in other areas of human behavior, it has been concluded by scientific methods that at least 80 percent of everything that goes wrong in an organization is due to people who either *don't know, can't do,* or *don't care.* This means deficiencies in knowledge, skills, and attitude. In general terms those three deficiencies form a complete diagnosis of what makes things go wrong.

The 80 percent, however, is probably too conservative, as suggested by this experience while serving the United States Atomic Energy Commission as a member of its Advisory Committee on Personnel Management. At one of our monthly meetings in 1951, Dr. Lawrence R. Hafstad, one of our foremost atomic scientists, who later became General Motors' vice-president in charge of research, was explaining to us with charts and graphs the characteristics of a then secret project.

I was flabbergasted by the demonstrated capacity of the human mind to forecast, in detail, the performance of a new project in atomic energy for which there was no precedent. Dr. Hafstad was sensitive enough to detect my reaction. He interrupted his explanation with the remark that of all the intricate and complex problems with which they had to deal in this fantastic project, which has since become a successful reality, 75 percent were due to people. Later I wrote for permission to use that remark. Permission was granted and with this comment: "Based on our past several months' activity, Larry thinks the figure is closer to 90."

If there had ever been any question about it, the leaders of the Soviet Union have proven beyond a shadow of a doubt that of the three deficiencies in people that make things go wrong, knowledge and skills are relatively easy to teach and to learn. In the short span of 40 years they have transformed a country of predominantly illiterate peasants into the world's second ranking industrial power. In some areas of technology, they have even surpassed the United States. Colonel Nasser, too, gave us an impressive demonstration of the relative ease of acquiring knowledge and skills when he took over the Suez Canal and put it into smooth operation without the skilled British and Greek pilots upon whose services it was assumed he would be dependent.

These spectacular demonstrations and many more make it unmistakably clear that by all odds the paramount challenge to education and to leadership is in shaping and influencing *attitudes:* "We just don't give a damn"; "Who's going to knock himself out for that slave driver"; "It's no skin off my back"; "I'll show those good-for-nothin's who is the boss around here"; "I'm sure enough not going to open my mouth while he's in the room"; "It's okay if you can get away with it."

At all levels of organization, the most important attitude, the most important single factor in the morale and productivity of the individual is his mental attitude toward his boss. This leads to the question: What kind of boss is most likely to have high morale and high productivity and attain them from those whose work he directs?

What Kind of Boss?

Both the scientist and the empiricist have some common answers to that question. Contrary to early assumptions, high morale and high productivity do not necessarily coincide. You may have high morale with low productivity and low morale with high productivity. It is possible for employees to feel well disposed toward their boss and to restrict production because of powerful social pressures within their group. It is possible for employees to dislike not only their immediate boss but also the whole management and to have deeply personal reasons, of which pride is one, for turning out production equal to or better than the expected standards of quality and quantity.

In the long run, the goal of high morale and high productivity can be attained—and the best results in terms of both human and economic values will be achieved—by bosses in whose conduct the following actions and attitudes will predominate.

First, they will be interested in those whose work they direct as unique and different personalities. They will express their interest more in deeds than in words. They will even recognize and take account of the occasions upon which an individual may be different on Monday than he was on Friday for reasons external to the job.

There is an important distinction between being interested in people and liking them. It is folly to presume that a boss will like all employees. Furthermore, it is not essential to getting the job done.

Actually, a greater interest may be taken in employees who are not liked because they may present more of a challenge to the leadership qualities of wholesome curiosity and tolerance. Parenthetically, one of the causes of disappointment in college education not included in the recent excited demands for change is that too many instructors are interested only in their subject and not in the students. This is one of several valid analogies between personnel administration and the teaching-learning process.

Second, they will require high standards of performance. They will persist in asking and expecting of you the best you've got—the best of which you are capable. This requirement of bosses who attain high morale and productivity may come as a discomforting shock to the debunkers of "human relations" who view with alarm the debilitating consequences of their caricatured version of modern personnel administration with its backslapping, spoon-feeding hero.

The Timken Roller Bearing Company of Canton, Ohio, has demonstrated that extraordinary results can be achieved even in the field of collective bargaining by insisting upon high standards. Among the results achieved they report: freedom from wildcat strikes since 1946; avoidance of the industry strike of 1956 and the short one of 1955; operation of a unionized mill even during the general strike of 1952 with the local union president himself at work; improved productivity and uninterrupted deliveries to customers.

Among the deeds performed by our bosses with best results which would express their interest in those whose work is directed and would also help them to do their best are: keeping everyone informed on matters pertaining to the employment environment; listening attentively and with considerable but not unlimited patience to what the other fellow has to say about the job and the work; planning and scheduling for materials, supplies, equipment, and repairs in order to facilitate production rather than breathing down your neck emphasizing the need for it. The boss who presses hardest for production to the neglect of his planning responsibility is the least likely to get it, according to studies of behavioral scientists and to the teaching of practical experience.

Other studies and experiences have suggested that even the monotony of repetitive operations can be relieved if the boss is enough interested to delegate some of his duties to members of the work force. The benefits of delegation are not limited to heavy and complex operations. They carry all the way through the line organization to the lowest echelon of supervision.

In addition to its more obvious advantages of developing understudies, distributing job satisfactions, and facilitating execution of assignments, delegation is an expression of security and self-confidence on the part of the boss.

Many bosses even in top management refuse to delegate responsibility and authority because of an inner sense of insecurity, real or imagined. Example: The controller who was overconscious of his lack of a college education and compensated for a mild sense of guilt about it by making it necessary for everyone to come to him for the answers. He developed ulcers and the members of his department concluded they were in a dead-end street.

Results—low morale, low productivity, stagnation of ideas, need for new leadership.

Employees, being sensitive to their environment, respond with higher morale and productivity to the boss who radiates security and who, by delegation and other actions, helps to train them for higher jobs even though there is no immediate chance of promotion. We can be reasonably certain too that the secure boss will refrain from passing the buck either up or down in the fulfillment of his duties, and will thereby contribute to better results.

The foregoing comprise most, but not all, of the major actions and attitudes of bosses that scientists and empiricists agree are conducive to the best possible results in both spirit-

* * *

We all think we know how to get along with people. That is what we have been doing ever since we were born. The pity is that the man who is most sure he knows how to do it is often the man who is gumming the game worse than anyone else.

So long as a manager or a superintendent is in a defensive state of mind toward his people, he can't put over constructive ideas to his men and lead them into cooperation.

—E. K. Hall

* * *

ual and material values. In depth, perceptiveness, and practical applicability they differ from the old "key man" cliches.

These importantly practical findings are no longer just a matter of theory. They come from experiences and experiments in offices, shops, road gangs, and schoolrooms. These findings argue that the boss with the best results will analyze a situation before assigning accountability or blame. Let me illustrate that one with a simple role-playing incident.

You are my boss. You could be a vice-president or a laboratory instructor or anyone in between. You approach my place of work. It could be a desk, a bench, a packing line, a printing press, the warehouse, or even the woodpile. Whatever it is you see in front of me strikes you as being a "mess" and calls for your attention. When you are near enough for me to hear your voice, you say, with appropriate inflection, "Tom, what did you do?"

Right away my defenses are up. So, that's the kind of guy you are! If I am still a healthy personality, I'll use all of my ingenuity to keep you from finding out. It is possible that I wasn't even there when the "mess" occurred, but you have it all figured out in advance. Your action and attitude have cost you my respect, and I'll take it out on you in some form of sabotage if I am a healthy and skilled personality capable of high productivity, as the vast majority of employees potentially are.

Now let's assume that everything is exactly the same, except that your words, with appropriate facial expression are "What happened, Tom?" Oh brother, a single, simple exception, but what an exception that turns out to be, with a psychological difference. And what a lad this boss turns out to be. He will get the story straight. Intuitively, I know that I can trust him to be firm and fair. If discipline is in order, I will take it cheerfully. If it's higher production he wants, he'll get it.

Oh, yes, and finally this boss whose actions and attitudes are those of being interested, requiring high standards, informing, listening, delegating, planning, training, and analyzing will, also, of course, offer opportunities for participation in matters of mutual interest to those whose work he directs, and they will not have to pay initiation fees, dues, and assessments to anyone for this inherent right to consultative supervision. By making possible this finally included attitude-shaping experience of primary importance, this becomes the boss who, by all odds, is most likely to attain high morale and productivity and to contribute generously to the good success of the enterprise with which he is associated.

Are there real, live bosses who meet those difficult specifications? The answer is yes, but not nearly enough. I have had a few in my career. One was Richard Hellmann, a short, stocky German immigrant who, starting from a delicatessen shop in Harlem, built a multiplant business and earned a fortune by making honest mayonnaise and treating his associates considerately. He was the only boss I ever had who volunteered to spend some money to make my office feel "homier" and look more like his. That kind of "conformity" has appeal even to a rebellious nonconformist. Some years later in another company I was battling the treasurer for just a few more inches of elbow room in the office he was measuring off for me.

Although Richard Hellmann was a natural, it is inevitable that as time passes a steadily increasing proportion of high-incentive bosses will be made and will help to maintain and expand the way of excellence in human values. My studies and my experiences lead me to agree unreservedly with Adolf Berle, Jr., who says on page 187 of his brilliant analysis of

* * *

When the man in the ranks finds that the interest of the boss is not confined to the balance sheet, he soon ceases to center his own interest solely on the pay envelope.

—E. K. Hall

* * *

The 20th Century Capitalist Revolution, published by Harcourt, Brace and Company:

"There is solid ground for the expectation that 20 years from now the men of greatest renown in the United States will be the spiritual, philosophical, and intellectual leaders for the sufficient reason that they will be needed more than any other type of men. Society still tends both to produce and to honor the kinds of men it needs most."

A company in greater Philadelphia making a precision metal product not only was unionized but also suffered a violent strike. In fact, the strike was so bitter that the officers of the company had to be escorted through the gates of the property with a motorcycled police escort.

A year later I accepted the invitation of a superintendent to visit the factory, where a part used in the assembly of a finished product was made. It was only a short walking distance from the main plant and executive offices. The physical aspects of the factory seemed not to offer much incentive for high morale and productivity. But in making the rounds with this superintendent, you could literally feel the atmosphere of friendliness and mutual respect.

To satisfy my curiosity I inquired as to what went on in this factory a year ago during unionization and conflict at headquarters down the street. His reply was that they just stuck to their knitting and the union leaders didn't make a sale.

Imagine that! And under the same top management! The qualities of this leader, his standards of excellence in human values were powerful enough to more than counteract all the influences that led to loss of leadership and generation of severe antagonism in a nearby area of the same organization. Not only does this experience demonstrate the multiple value of high-incentive leadership, but it should also help to lay to rest that often-repeated platitude that "personnel administration can never be any better than the sum total of the character of the man at the head of a business."

Surely it is a big help when the head of the business has a high regard for human values. However, there will always be some bosses who refuse to be disheartened by shortcomings at the top. In spite of handicaps, on their own initiative and convictions, and confident of the results, they will practice sound personnel administration.

Another one of these high-incentive leaders I have known and admired is Howard P. Warren, former manager of the Minute Tapioca Plant of General Foods at Orange, Massachusetts. Years before the plant was acquired by General Foods, he was providing the state of Massachusetts with one of its best examples of sound personnel administration. In setting this example, he needed no advice from General Foods.

The story is told that from his office window one stormy winter day he noticed an AFL business agent at the entrance to the plant preparing to distribute union handbills. He went down, invited the agent in for a cup of coffee, and suggested that he distribute the handbills inside the plant where he would be more comfortable. The agent enjoyed the coffee and decided there wasn't much point in distributing the handbills in this plant. He was right. In Howard Warren's 36 years of leadership there, the employees never gave any indication of needing outside help. During all my years with General Foods, he was a dependable and generous source of encouragement and inspiration.

Two More Major Findings

Although this interpretation of the scientific approach to personnel administration is inadequate when account is taken of the vast literature available, it would be inexcusably so without mention of two more major findings.

The first concludes that outside activities—bowling, baseball, bands, picnics—promoted solely by management for employees, or in cooperation with them, have little or no effect on productivity. They may be good in themselves, but the expense should not be justified on the assumption that it will contribute to an increase in productive effort. These activities are no part of sound personnel administration. They may provide some temporary fun, entertainment, "uplift," contribute to "company spirit" or even sales promotion, but they should not be considered in the slightest degree a substitute for the true substance of personnel administration, including high-incentive leadership.

The second of these finally selected general findings probably comes as a real shocker to some of the debunkers of "human relations" and many people in management who have assumed that the goal of modern personnel administration has been to make employees happy. The concept of "the great big happy family" has had a strong appeal. "If contented cows give more milk, then happy employees should be more productive." Those always were thoroughly unscientific propositions. We have known too little about the ingredients of happiness for each of countless individuals, no two of whom are alike, to concoct a general formula for its attainment.

Excluding the cows and confining their studies to people, scientists now say that the happy employee is not necessarily the most productive. Once that is pointed out to you, it seems to make a lot of sense.

For example, you can visualize a "happy" employee at his desk, bench, or machine. He's just happy. In fact he is so happy with things as they are that he does not want to alter either the pace or the conditions of work. His resistance to change is likely to be almost insuperable because of the connection he has established, maybe erroneously, between his state of happiness and his work.

By contrast, the "unhappy" and "aggressive" employee who may attribute his unhappy state to his job will be pressing for change, improvements, innovations, better ways to get the job done. Apparently, supervisors should be thankful for having at least a few unhappy "agitators" under their direction rather than be irritated by their presence and trying to arrange a transfer. However, in sum, what this finding seems to be emphasizing is that high standards of human values are maintained, not with the irrational expectation of making everybody happy, but with an awareness of the highly complex and sometimes elusive nature of productivity incentives.

High Morale, High Productivity

For the enhancement of human values, the satisfaction of spiritual needs, the enrichment of material rewards, and the betterment of living standards, high morale and high productivity, both of which may be measured, are indispensable. Their attainment is a worthy and essential goal for all who direct the work of others, including educators.

Personality takes on a new meaning, breadth, and dignity when indentified with the whole individual rather than with one of many unequally vital ingredients. The concept of the normally healthy personality whose ingredients are in balance, even though the consequences may be repulsive to other healthy personalities, and which are not to be carelessly tampered with, adds a new dimension to the responsibilities and opportunities of leadership.

Knowledge and skills being relatively easy to acquire, we will follow the ways to our worthy and essential goal with the attitudes of personalities—their "leaping feelings and lagging thoughts"—as a focal point of our concern. *Success or failure will be determined largely by the mental attitude of employees toward their boss.* We are sure that participation is high on the list of experiences that shape that attitude. We know, within practical limits, the kind of boss that is most likely to attain high morale and high productivity.

Because there is much evidence to support the conclusion that leaders are made and not born, and the means for their development are at hand, we are confident that the numbers of democratic, cultural, and incentive leaders will increase at an accelerated rate.

There will be intensified concentration on day-to-day interpersonal relations within the employment environment and proportionately less concern with external activities. We won't mind if employees in large numbers should proclaim their individual happiness, but we will look upon it as an agreeable by-product rather than a major goal of our efforts.

While those who direct the work of others at all levels of organization are putting to productive use the findings of our behavioral scientists, they in turn will be receiving increasing support for their research and extending the frontiers of our knowledge and understanding of the forces related to morale, motivation, and productivity.

CHAPTER 19

HUMAN RELATIONS

By Herman W. Steinkraus

In recent years we have been living through one of the fastest periods of change that American business and industry have ever experienced. From the steam engine to electricity, to automobiles, to planes, to chemicals, to automation, to the atom, to the universe—all in rapid, massive jumps!

These developments we see all about us. But it is not so generally recognized that we have also been making parallel strides in the relations of employer and employee, comprising the whole field of what we have come to call human relations.

For many years managements were so busy with the technical side of their plants that they found little time to devote to the subject of their relations with their employees. The individual was just a production number. But today if any management takes this outmoded attitude, it soon finds itself submerged in all kinds of problems, even perhaps with a strike on its hands.

When companies were small, there was still a personal relationship possible between the boss and the worker—more frequently than not, one of good will. But as firms increased in size this changed, and employees no longer knew the top executives they worked for. This lack of understanding of the human side of business led to serious problems, and so we faced the necessity of learning more about this subject of human relations.

Now, books are written on it, courses are studied in business schools, and it has become an important part of business conferences. Just what do we mean by this term?

Human relations has been defined as the working together of management and employees in the spirit of mutual understanding and teamwork. Practically, it is the integration of people into groups that can work together harmoniously and productively for the economic benefit and social satisfaction of all.

If this relationship fails on the economic side, the company loses profits, and may have to go out of business. If it fails on the human-relations side, the employee will simply look for work elsewhere. It has long since been an exploded theory that employees go where companies pay the best wages. Money is not the major consideration, as we used to think it was. It is

*   *   *

When the worker has a real feeling of belonging, he is much more content with his work. Recognition and consultation minister to his psychological needs. As a result, his morale improves. The employer has a lower turnover of workers and better production. Efficiency increases while waste and spoilage decline. New ideas and better processes are suggested. Once again it is discovered that good human relations are really the best form of industrial relations.

*   *   *

a fact that people often choose to work where they get less wages, for a wide variety of reasons.

Today successful managements realize that their employees are more than production numbers; that they are human beings very sensitive to feelings of pride, recognition, and rewards, which strongly affect their attitude and their everyday performance.

It was the farsighted Andrew Carnegie who first emphasized the value of the individual worker to our economic system. He placed the worker above everything else in importance. He said, "You can take away our factories, take away our trade, our avenues of transportation, and our money—leave us nothing but our organization—and in four years we could reestablish ourselves."

That was indeed a radical thought in his day, when so little importance was placed on the individual employee. The boss could say, "We pay so much; take it or leave it." Who cared what the worker thought or felt? Labor was plentiful and cheap. As for pensions! Pay them anything after they are through? What a harebrained idea! What company has money to throw away like that?

And there was the long, long workday. I well remember as a boy when steelworkers worked in two shifts of 12 hours each. In a few industries, workers had already gone on a three-shift, eight-hour day, which the 12-hour workers eyed enviously. But what a long, bitter struggle it was before the steelworkers achieved this one improvement.

Indifferent to Employee Needs

Here and there some of the more progressive companies thought they were doing a lot if they gave a small life-insurance policy to each of their employees, just about enough to cover funeral expenses. As for vacations with pay, or sick benefits, there were practically none. If an employee did not please, he was fired; if he was fired, he was through. Severance pay was unheard of.

I remember well the indifference to the worker's family, the cold dinner pail, the layoffs, the insecurity. But a new day was to come, with emphasis on fair and humane relations, and in due time it arrived. Today, no company, large or small, can afford to neglect this important field.

We have come a long way since that time. Yet some of the first major moves intended for the benefit of employees were bitter failures. The reason was managements did not know enough about human nature. They wanted to give benefits as a great gesture of generosity; the workers did not want things given to them that way.

In a number of outstanding cases, which are now history, whole communities were built for workers, with new plants, model homes, recreation halls, parks, and playgrounds—everything was offered free, and model housing provided at the lowest rent. But one by one these paternalistic ventures failed, and the well-intentioned men who planned them were left brokenhearted. They could not understand why even their most loyal, older employees preferred to live less well, but independently, in their own homes in their own way.

So, gradually, the age of paternalism faded away. But one great thing remained—for the first time employees had won respectful recognition. As a group they had status. They no longer had to bargain as individuals but could stand together as a body. So we witnessed the rapid growth of unions.

Most of the employer class met this new organization with determined resistance, but it was impossible to fight the trend. The weakling was soon a young giant. In general, the only companies which successfully withstood unionization were small ones, or those with a strong personal leadership.

I remember the day when Fred Crawford, of Cleveland, rebelling at what he felt was a threat to personal liberty, put on a striped prison uniform, and in this garb addressed a mass meeting of his employees. He held them by the force of his own brilliant personality. And who can forget that picture of Sewell Avery being carried forcibly out of his own office?

Rise of the Unions

But in the period between the two World Wars, more and more companies did accept unions, and we saw an unending procession of benefits won by union demands. During the second World War, unions were strengthened still further by the government action of placing contracts only with plants willing to unionize. When the war was over, many companies thought they could throw out their unions, but it did not work out that way. The union had come to stay.

It could and did demand, bargain, and threaten, while management argued and fought back. Too often the result was a crippling strike, ending in losses all around, for there never was a truer statement than the one that "nobody wins a strike." Everyone loses, just as in history nations who thought they had won a war often lived to see they had really lost it.

By now we should be beyond this unintelligent use of force to settle disputes, and should be able to settle our industrial problems by use of our God-given brains and intelligence. We should be far beyond resorting to this crude and, at best, temporary expedient, which has far outlived its usefulness.

Actually, we cannot much longer afford the kind of strikes we have had in this last decade. With high taxes, rising costs, and our grave international problems, this is a poor time to indulge in practices that weaken our national economy. We would do well to pull together instead of apart in these times. It is difficult to believe that there is something fine and American in these long and devastating strikes, which give little or no consideration to the general public. Without a doubt this is our *most serious single human-relations problem*, and one which must be solved soon or drastic steps will have to be taken. Usually the long strike is not planned as such, but called only as a show of strength. How often the statement is made, "It will be all over in a few days." Then it isn't; it drags into costly weeks and months.

Strikes Are Contagious

When a company has one strike, it is much more likely to have a second, and a third; then it spreads to nearby companies, and whole areas get to be known as strike areas, a good place to keep away from.

We have many aids to avoid strikes, techniques of negotiation, and well-worked-out voluntary arbitration and conciliation media. While it is much better to have such a healthy atmosphere in the company that crises do not arise, if they do, a resort to conciliation or voluntary arbitration is obviously better than a strike.

In this connection, I have felt for a long time that it would be highly beneficial if the Department of Labor in Washington were changed to the Department of Labor and Management. Labor *per se* no longer has to be bolstered, as it once was, by the government. It is labor and management working together that gets the production out. It seems to me that such a step would be a progressive one. We have modernized our plants;

perhaps we need now to modernize our thinking about other matters, too.

Let's be realistic. Unions are here to stay. They represent a very large segment of all workers, and we shall have to deal with them. The question is, *how* to deal with them? Are there any techniques that can help us?

Fortunately there are, and the heartening thing is that it is possible to establish good human relations in any plant, so that there is such a healthy atmosphere that there is no occasion for serious friction or strikes to develop. I could cite many, many instances, but closest at hand is my experience in our own company, and its over-90 years of steady production and no strikes—even, at times, when the whole valley was out on strike.

A strike in any firm is certainly the low-water mark of human relations; therefore it is highly desirable to avoid the loss of time, money, and prestige it results in. It is too late to start to establish good relations when you are sitting down at a bargaining table to negotiate a contract. The groundwork has to be laid long before that.

Take It Step by Step

First, you have to be willing to want better human relations badly enough to work for them. Think about them in your company, and make out a clear company policy on all matters pertaining to the welfare of the employee. State it clearly. Put it in print. Let it be known. And, most important of all, stand by it at all times. Let the president or major executive of the company sit in on labor sessions frequently.

I also believe that labor relations are not legal relations; they are human relations. The legal department is not the one to negotiate labor contracts. Advise, yes, but not direct.

In my opinion, based on over 30 years of dealing with large international unions—including those in steel, auto, and mining—contract negotiations should be conducted by line men who are close to top management. Of course, however, they can call for the assistance of various staff men, including legal counsel, for that part of the contract in which special skills are required.

During the war I considered labor relations the most important single task of our top management, and as president of my company I kept very close to the bargaining for around 10,000 employees. That we never had a strike when they were being called all around us, I believe, is due to the fact that our employees had learned to trust us. They believed we would do what was fair for both sides and negotiations were for the purpose of finding out just what that was—and agreeing to it.

All Executives Must Be Trained

Secondly, if you want to establish sound human relations, you must train all your executives in a special human-relations study program. There are many ways at hand—taking existing courses, reading books, sharing conferences. It is most important to keep up-to-date. Anyone who has dealt with labor leaders knows how thoroughly prepared and well informed *they* are.

We always tried to keep our bargaining sessions completely free from name-calling or explosions of anger. If these threatened to occur, we would immediately call a recess until things had calmed down.

Furthermore, our principal objective was not to squeeze things down to the lowest common denominator, but rather to arrive at a contract that both sides could feel happy about. We never tried to bury the other side. We wanted to develop good will and avoid the feeling on the part of either labor or management that the other side had been licked.

I remember one instance after a particularly hard-fought negotiation tussle that lasted for weeks until we finally arrived at an agreement. We shook hands all around. Then the union representative came up to me and said: "One matter I meant to bring up, and we never got to it. I suppose it is too late now."

I asked him what it was, and on learning it was something not too major, I said: "We concede that. You can have it."

Naturally he was delighted.

When I got home, my right-hand man called me up in consternation. "Why did you do that?" he asked. "The company didn't have to give in on that."

"I know," I said, "that is exactly why I did it. We had won enough. I wanted them to feel we were very fair and to give them something extra to take back to tell the employees about."

I realize such a tactic sounds soft. But the fact is, it works. The good will gained by that simple gesture lasted a long time.

So far we have considered this subject from the point of view of management. Now let us turn to the employee for a

* * *

The recognition of the worker's rights should begin with the employment office. The reception given to the applicant and even the physical surroundings of the office are important. The thoughtful employer makes it his rule that the employment office is well situated and decently furnished. Applicants are welcomed, not merely tolerated. Prospective employees should understand that company policy tolerates no discrimination for reasons of religion, race, national origin, or any other consideration alien to ability to do the work. Every effort is made to find their aptitudes and experience and to put the right man on the right job.

* * *

moment. What is it that motivates him? What is he really after? What makes him a happy worker? If we are to establish good human relations, he has to be happy in his work.

As far back as the surveys of 1949, it was proved that money was not the first consideration. We all know people who work in a certain place for less money than they might get elsewhere.

If it is not money, then, what is it the worker chiefly wants? It is a group of intangibles, which are to him very important. They are the same things that you and I and every human being wants, and the worker wants them more than we realize.

308

First, he wants respect. He wants to be regarded as a person—an important person with basic rights that mean as much to him as the same rights do to the president of the company. He wants to feel that his services, even though small, are needed and important to the company. He wants to be noticed.

That reminds me of an incident that once happened to me in our own plant. I had just made a speech the night before to a group of our people, in which I emphasized the point that everyone on our payroll was important to us, or we would not have him on our payroll. The next morning a sweeper stopped me as I was going down an aisle of the plant and said, "You didn't mean what you said last night about the importance of every job, did you? Now look at my job; I just sweep. How can that be called important?"

I said to him: "Of course it is. I meant just what I said. Now your job is partly keeping those long aisles clean of pieces of round rod, which fall away from those machines sometimes and roll into the aisles. Suppose you failed to do your job well, and one of our people stepped on a piece of rod and fell down and broke a leg or a back. You sweep, and help keep the plant clean and safe. Don't you think that is important?"

"Gee!" he said, "I never thought of it that way."

Giving Them Job Pride

On the importance of status to a person, here is a small suggestion. Give him as good a title for his job as you can. Think of the most honorable yet properly descriptive title you can give a man, so that his wife and children can speak with pride of "father's job."

For instance, machine operator is better sounding than machine hand; supervisor is better than foreman. That does not mean to use high-sounding titles which are not justified— merely better designations for jobs whenever possible.

If I could live my business career over again, one thing I am sure I would do. I would recognize and praise much more. Does anyone get too much praise? I hardly think so. And how far the friendly word goes!

I was always touched by the genuine appreciation felt on occasions when I would drop into a company meeting, or some social occasion of the employees, or take a moment to stop and chat with some worker at his job as I passed by. Years later I have had the employee tell me about it, recalling details of the conversation.

To him it was important.

This sort of personal touch was, of course, the secret of good relations in the early days of American enterprise, when com-

*　　*　　*

Experience has shown that in most cases intelligent handling of union-management relations can minimize conflicts and promote cooperation. The union can become an integral part of a program of teamwork, communication, and participation. Then it will be a spokesman for the workers, but not one that is hostile to the employer.

*　　*　　*

panies were small, and each employee was known by his boss. Large multiunit plants have indeed increased our problem.

However, if one cannot do this sort of thing naturally and sincerely, it is better not to attempt it at all. Any patronizing of employees is fatal, for they are very keen in detecting the "put-on" or the "phony."

The other day I was told a story by a banker who had occasion to call on the president of a certain company in connection with a bank loan. There was some commotion outside, and the president went over to the window and looked out. There he saw a group of workers below milling about, picketing. He looked down on them and muttered, "Scum!"

"You know," the banker told me, "I never went near that company again. I just didn't want to do business with a man like that."

How impossible it would be for an executive with such feelings to sit down at a bargaining table and convince his employees of his sincerity and good will.

A step beyond having good will is to translate it into practical means of expression. It is absolutely essential to have stated policies of recognition for jobs well done, rewards for ideas, a policy of promotion from within, and news publicity for accomplishments—not only that a job may be appreciated, but that others may know about it. Our local newspapers have always been most cooperative in giving over much space for employee news, though we had our own monthly plant newspaper as well.

Also, for many years, I wrote a periodic letter to each employee that went to his home, with all kinds of company news and plans in it, stating company opinions about various subjects, the sort of conversation I would carry on if we had the opportunity—which, of course, we did not have—of talking personally with each other. Often members of a family would mention items in these letters, so I know they reached home, were read, and did make a friendly contact.

We never wanted our people to hear from the outside what we were going to do. We wanted to tell them first. This may sound unimportant, but actually it is not. I have seen too many companies where the motto seemed to be "Tell them nothing." This opens up the whole subject of communications, which is now viewed with a new importance, but is too big a subject to go into here. A whole book could be written on this subject. In a few words, it is important that workers know at all times what is going on if they are to work happily and confidently.

Those are some of the intangibles the worker wants, and *he wants them as much as good pay.*

New Craving for Security

Finally, the employee wants security. This desire for a feeling of security, and particularly job security, is something more noticeable with young people than with old. The employee wants all the protection the company can give him—for himself, for his job, for his family—as against layoffs, less pay, automation, or any other factors that might threaten his well-being.

This is a fundamental desire. This too, I feel sure, is here to stay. I frankly admit I have done my share of grousing and bemoaning about this demand for "security." Certainly it is far removed from the pioneer spirit, and the risks our forefathers took. But I have long since learned that you can't fight human nature, and this desire seems to have roots that are pretty deep.

I noticed it first when young college graduates would come in from an interview about some job. The first question they would ask would be about retirement pay and the company benefits. I was appalled. What the job offered in opportunity seemed far less important to them.

Well, I am not so appalled any more. This craving for security seems to be linked with self-preservation and preservation of one's family in a changing world. Perhaps it is further brought about by our many population changes. Never before have there been so many shifts of plants, involving the uprooting of many homes each year and changing them from one place to another. Finding new jobs, losing others, and the fear of automation are among the problems of today.

As for automation, it is a safe guess that it is also here to stay, and if I could give free advice to my union friends, it would be that they might be wise to accept it, and learn how to live with it, instead of opposing it; finding the solution in the spirit of cooperation, not of conflict and strikes.

If I may add one more thought, everyone has social instincts. We all want to belong. In fact we are the biggest nation of belongers in the world. Workers like to feel part of a group, to be included. That is why we belong to churches, lodges, clubs, unions, athletic teams, and so forth.

The "Brass Family"

So let us give our employees plenty of things to belong to. In our company we offered all kinds of activities, and new ones we encouraged rather than discouraged. Somehow (this was

312

a brass plant) we came to be called the "Brass Family," and I believe the company was referred to more often that way than by its proper business title. I do think that this feeling of belonging on the part of our employees made them both happier and more efficient in their jobs.

All these characteristics are deeply rooted in the nature of man. The better they are understood and accepted by management, the smoother will be the operation of the company, and the happier the human relations in that company.

You cannot measure such things with a yardstick. There is no mechanical scale to apply to human endeavor. You can measure the output of a machine, but you cannot measure the capacity of a man.

It is a fact that properly inspired people can accomplish vastly more than they ever thought they could. It has been estimated that this latent capacity is 40 to 50 percent greater, on the average, than is being utilized today.

When understanding, pride of accomplishment, and job satisfaction are added to the individual skills of the worker, the results can be really astounding.

CHAPTER 20

EMPLOYEE COUNSELING

By Dr. Howard Wilson

Not too long ago the *Journal of the American Medical Association* carried an article that should have been of great interest to every executive who read it. For it dealt with one of his company's biggest problems and, at the same time, major headaches: employee complaints.

One day, it seems, five employees of a large East Coast company went to their "bosses" to complain about their jobs. When these complaints were carefully listened to and analyzed, it was found that only one of them was actually caused by working conditions. Here is what was at the basis of the other four:

A stenographer was upset to the point of being panicky because her boy friend had been postponing marriage for so long that she was fearful of losing him.

A foreman had become sick with guilt because he feared he was to blame for his wife's state of depression, as a result of which she had threatened to kill their two children.

A young salesman was torn by feelings of shame because he was unable to decide which of two girls to marry, both of whom were in love with him.

A middle-aged executive had become preoccupied with the fear that he might have inherited the same tendency to heart disease that had killed his father and, at the same time, some of the paranoiac traits of his mother.

Such cases are by no means unusual. They are found every day in the "best-regulated" companies and among the "best-regulated" personnel. The world is full of troubled people and, like their happier fellowmen, they are to be found on every company payroll. Your company and the one next door are probably no exception.

Oh, you won't hear these people airing their personal problems and anxieties very often in undisguised form. They're apt to keep their worries to themselves until they happen to explode someday over "working conditions." Likely as not what they are really exploding about is not the particular "spark" that sent them running to their "boss" with a long list of job complaints, but rather something far deeper in their subconscious that had been building up to a state of increased tension for weeks, months, or even years.

Try to Help Them

Apart from our natural sympathy for troubled people and our desire to help them, the stern realities of company interests and employee morale require management people to assume a certain amount of responsibility for doing what they can for them. The key question is: How does one go about it?

Employee counseling is one of a leader's major responsibilities, whether he realizes it or not. It is obvious that if a young woman worker is upset over her relations with her boy friend, who has suddenly given her the cold shoulder, she isn't going to be very efficient in her job duties. Blunders are likely to appear in her work.

It is equally obvious that waste, spoilage, and general inefficiency are the results whenever any employee—whether his work is routine or specialized—is unable to concentrate on his job because of worry, anxiety, tension, resentment, or any of the hundred-and-one other sicknesses of the mind.

Counseling with these employees whenever the occasion warrants, listening to their problems, and helping them reach a solution that will reduce their conflicts is not merely humanitarianism, therefore. It is good, hard business sense as well.

Employee counseling, however, is by no means confined to the emotionally disturbed employee. It is a catchall method for handling every type of worker problem confronting the executive, whether personal or job-rated. Counseling is also a useful method for appraising the performance of employees and helping them reach specific goals or develop to their greatest potential.

In fact, counseling and employee appraisal go hand in hand. Without counseling of some kind, rating can rarely prove as effective a criterion of employee performance as it has been set up to be. Just what is counseling?

The term itself is not always properly understood because it is relatively new in the language of business and industry. The first formal counseling program in industry is supposed to have appeared during the first World War. During the second World War, counseling rapidly expanded until it was considered a valuable personnel tool. Today a number of companies have trained, professional counselors, usually assigned to the personnel department, whose full-time job it is to help employees who come to them with their problems, whether arising on or off the job.

Requires Special Skills

In those companies—and there are any number of them— where professional counseling services are not provided, it is the happy (or unhappy) lot of the department head or supervisor to have to double in the role frequently. "Happy," because it can be considered a privilege to be able to assist someone in distress; "unhappy," because to do an effective job of counseling one has to acquire special skills apart from those a manager is usually expected to have.

In any event, counseling is something every executive or manager must know as much about as possible for two very simple reasons:

1. He is often counseling in some manner or form almost every day of the week if he is sensitive to the needs and concerns of his people.

2. He can do it better and more effectively when he understands the right way to go about it; how to listen and

"interview" properly, so that the employee or subordinate will leave the session a happier individual and a more effective "company man."

As you may know, there are two types of counseling. One is called directive counseling, the other nondirective counseling. Many of us are familiar with the first kind, which might be called the advice-giving method. After listening to an employee's problem, the counselor or interviewer decides what he thinks the interviewee should do about it, and then recommends a course of action that he believes will solve the particular problem, relieve the interviewee's tensions, or eliminate the cause of the difficulty. Note the dominant role played by the counselor, who directs the session, shares the interviewee's experience, and offers advice.

But no matter how well meant our advice to others may be, it is a known fact that rarely is it followed unless it happens to coincide with the other's own pattern of conduct or frame of reference. Hence directive counseling, except when a problem is posed that only the counselor himself can solve or answer, does not often achieve the success it might if the interviewee were allowed, instead, to reach a solution of his own making.

This is the goal of the second type of counseling: *nondirective.*

A Listening Role

Sometimes called the employee-centered method of counseling, the nondirective approach is one in which the counselor encourages an employee to think through, talk through, and explain his difficulty for one basic purpose: to enable him to gain a better understanding of the problem himself and see its underlying implications more fully. The role of the counselor here becomes a passive one, in which he "listens the employee out" in an understanding and sympathetic manner. He does not offer the employee suggestions or advice, but rather encourages him to determine his own course of action, and work out his own individual "plan of salvation."

Since nine out of ten of us are going to do this anyway in such a situation, the nondirective method of counseling is usually found to be more realistic, more practical, and more meaningful to the counselee as well. Except, of course, in those instances in which action on the part of the counselor or interviewer himself is called for, as might be the case in certain kinds of job-related problems.

If nondirective counseling is more realistic and effective, then, as many of us believe, why isn't it used more widely in business and industry today?

Well, there are several reasons. In the first place, business itself is organized primarily on a directional basis—authoritarian levels of "command," so to speak. Most people believe

*   *   *

The counseling session should be relaxed and devoid of emotions. If the employee becomes too emotional during the session, the interviewer should change the topic and get on more neutral ground. Many counselors find that if the employee becomes emotional, they should remain cool and intellectual; if the employee talks loud and fast, they should talk softly and slowly. The interviewer can often change the tempo of the session by doing the opposite of what the employee does.

*   *   *

it has to be to get things done. The boss is, therefore, regarded as a sort of superior who "tells" rather than asks his people to do things. In nondirective counseling he would be called upon to play an entirely different role from that which he is accustomed—or expected—to assume. He naturally might balk at this.

Second, it means that the superior must ordinarily acquire a special set of skills for this "passive" type of counseling. The art of listening properly is but one of these skills that can only be attained after many hours of study, practice, and training. Of course mastery of nondirective methods is much easier for some people than others, because they have always been essentially nondirective in their approach with other people. On the other hand, I have known "bosses" who have found it almost impossible to use this approach to counseling because it is not in tune with their personalities and outlook.

Third, the use of nondirective counseling requires a great deal of face-to-face time with an employee, because it is a much slower method than direct counseling by its very nature. Most supervisors do not have the time required to spend in this way with individual employees, or else they feel they should not take this much time away from their other duties.

Cooperative Counseling

As a result, a third method of counseling has been developed. It is called cooperative counseling and is a combination of both the direct and the nondirect approaches.

Suppose I explain the cooperative method this way. The supervisor or manager adopts the directive technique in instances like these:

When the employee describes his problem, the counselor admits that the problem is of the type stated (if it really is) by giving his own supporting evidence to prove it.

When the employee deserves credit for the way he has handled some particular situation, the counselor gives him the credit he feels is due.

Then, however, the counselor will shift to the nondirective method and use a modified version of this approach by throwing the discussion to the employee until he thinks he has accomplished his objective. During the entire session or interview he is thus continually shifting from being directive to being nondirective. He's directive whenever he is telling, and nondirective whenever he is *asking*.

For a great many "bosses" and supervisors this combination of *tell* and *ask* has obvious advantages. It allows them to be dominating as well as passive, keeps the interview on the beam, and saves valuable working time. Moreover, it leaves the final solution to the counselor himself on the theory that a person "convinced against his will is of the same opinion still."

Direct vs. Nondirect in Operation

Now let me give you some actual examples of both the directive and the nondirective approaches. It will help clear the picture I have painted and clothe it with more realism. Both of these examples have to do with exit interviews and are reprinted from Erwin Schoenfeld's article on "The Nondirective Exit Interview," as it appeared in the American Management Association's magazine *Personnel*.

The purpose of an exit interview, of course, is to find the causes of employee turnover and thereby spot administrative or supervisory problems, clear up petty misunderstandings, and correct any morale problem that may exist.

As you might expect, however, conducting the exit interview so that it will achieve the desired results is extremely difficult. Both the interviewer and the interviewee are under emotional stress because of the somewhat unpleasant circumstances of the occasion. Getting the interviewee to speak his mind openly and frankly is almost impossible sometimes, because he hesitates to point an accusing finger when he is dependent upon his employer for references.

Notice, therefore, in the following examples how much more effective the nondirective approach can be than the directive. (*I* stands for the interviewer, *E* for the employee.)

TRADITIONAL DIRECTIVE APPROACH

I: Well, Mary, you're leaving today, I hear.

E: Yes, I am. My mother is sick, and I have to take care of her.

I: I'm sorry to learn that. I hope she'll be better soon.

E: Thank you. I do too.

I: But don't you think you could have given us a little more notice? I understand your mother has been ailing for some time. It's not as though she had been taken ill all of a sudden.

E: I would have liked to, but it just did not work out that way.

I: Well, you know the company expects you to give adequate notice when you leave. I don't think you're acting properly at all.

E: I'm sorry, but I couldn't work it out any other way.

I: All right, then. Good-bye and good luck.

E: Good-bye, and thank you.

NONDIRECTIVE APPROACH

I: Come right in, Mary. This is your last day with the company, I see.

E: That's right. This is my last day here.

I: I understand from your supervisor that your mother is ill. I'm certainly sorry to hear that.

E: Yes, she's not feeling too well, and I sure have my hands full these days.

I: Of course, with your mother ill there must be many more burdens on your shoulders.

E: You don't know the half of it. With mother out sick now, I've got to take care of the whole household—shopping, washing, ironing, cleaning—just about everything. I'm worn out, what with working here in the office until five and all the things I have to do at home.

I: That certainly doesn't leave you much time for anything else.

E: I would have given you a couple of days' notice if I weren't needed so badly at home.

I: Yes, I can see that, as things are, you weren't able to give much advance notice.

E: No. And besides, you don't need me.

I: Oh, really?

E: Yes. If you ask me, I don't think anybody cares whether I stay here or not.

I: You feel you are not going to be missed at all?

E: That's just it. In my department the supervisor leaves everything up to the assistant supervisor, and she's a part of the gang. They eat lunch together, and since they all live in the same part of town all they ever talk about is their boy friends.

I: That sort of leaves you out of things.

E: Yes. Just because I live in a different neighborhood they don't seem to care about me at all. They never ask me to go along for lunch, so I have to eat alone.

I: Eating all by yourself isn't much fun . . .

E: I'll say. After mother gets better I'm going to find a job where the girls aren't so standoffish. I want to work with a bunch of friendly girls, not like it is here . . .

TRADITIONAL DIRECTIVE APPROACH

I: So, Bill, you've resigned, I hear.

E: Yes, I got a better job closer to home.

I: Better than your job here? What kind of a job is it?

E: Well, for one thing, there's more money.

I: More money than you're getting with us?

E: I'll say. You don't pay the going rate here.

I: I don't know how you can say that. Didn't you know that in the last wage survey, of all the firms in this area our pay scale compared favorably with all the others?

E: Is that so? Well, I've got a friend with the Dalton Company doing the same kind of work as I'm doing, and he gets 23 cents an hour more.

NONDIRECTIVE APPROACH

I: Hello, Bill, I hear you've resigned your job.

E: Yes, I've found a better job closer to home.

I: That's interesting. Can you tell me a little more about it?

E: There's not much to say about it except that you pay such low wages here and I think I can get more pay elsewhere.

I: You feel that the pay scale here is not as high as it should be?

E: You're darn right. I've been doing work that's usually done by the boys in Grade 6, but I was just paid my old Grade 7 rate.

I: If a person does Grade 6 work he should get Grade 6 pay.

E: That's what I told the foreman, but he said he couldn't do anything about it at that time. I spoke to him again a few weeks later and he said he would take care of it, but I guess he never got around to it.

I: You think the foreman should have taken the time to adjust your job grade?

E: Oh, he takes care of those boys that belong to his car pool, but he doesn't care about the others.

Friendly and Helpful

Now these examples are necessarily brief, but they are detailed enough to give you a pretty good idea of how a non-directive interview should be conducted.

From this it can easily be seen that the most important element in any counseling session is the interviewer's attitude. He must constantly watch and guard against any sudden emotional shifts that might be provoked by what the interviewee says. If the interviewer can project the feeling to the employee that he accepts him as an individual, that he feels there is more good in him than bad, that he does more things right than wrong, that there are more things about him deserving of praise than criticism, and that he wants to help the employee improve or overcome his problem—then he, the interviewer, should have little trouble reaching the goal of his interview.

Remember that in the great majority of instances—

Employees' jobs are highly important to them.

Employees want to please and improve.

Employees want to do a good job.

Employees want to get along with their supervisor or "boss" and fellow employees.

Here are a few other important points to keep in mind while counseling.

Employees are people, and people are different. They are different in their experiences, education, attitudes, interests, understanding, needs, and training—plus many other ways.

Employees also differ in what they can do, what they want to do, and what they feel they should do. The mere fact that one of them can do something is no reason another can also. Because one of them wants to do something is no reason another of them necessarily wants to do it too.

Keep in mind, moreover, that "bosses" can't change employees; employees can only change themselves. However, the manager or executive can often help them become better, more effective employees by causing them to be discontented with themselves as they are, and then motivating them to want to change by showing them the way through careful guidance and instruction.

Counsel in Private

No counseling session can be more effective than the environment in which it is conducted and the attitude with which it is conducted.

The environment should not only be private; it must appear private. Complete privacy is essential if an employee is to feel at ease in discussing personal problems or confidential matters. The atmosphere must also be relaxed and informal, and the employee should be put at ease both physically and mentally before any serious discussion can begin. Counseling across a desk, for instance, presents a psychological barrier that stifles free discussion.

Above all, there should be no interruptions or distractions during the interview. This includes telephone calls as well as personal visits by other people.

The effectiveness of the session depends largely, of course, upon the attitude of the interviewer. We have stressed this point before, but it is worth repeating. The counselor must (repeat must) strive to be:

1. *Natural*—he should conduct the interview in a way that comes natural to him and in a way that puts him—as well as the employee—at ease.
2. *Friendly*—the session must be conducted on a friendly note that gives the employee the feeling of being accepted as a person.
3. *Positive*—there is no room for negativism or any semblance of hostility in the counseling session. The objective should be that of cooperatively working out good, workable solutions to whatever problem is being discussed.
4. *Helpful*—any counselor who tries to be genuinely helpful to a counselee rarely meets any resistance.
5. *Permissive*—the employee must be made to feel free to express his views, feelings, and attitudes in the awareness that the counselor will understand and accept the employee's frame of reference. The counselor must carefully refrain from attempting to pass judgment on the employee, regardless of how strong the temptation may be at times.

Planning the Session

Many counselors find it helpful to plan their sessions well in advance. A tentative outline or checklist of points to be covered is often useful to guide the discussion in the most effective direction. Obviously it pays to have whatever facts are necessary ready at hand before the session starts, because there will be no time during the discussion when you can stop to send for them if they should be required.

The interview hour should be set at least two or three days in advance for the mutual convenience of both parties. A definite time limit should be set for the counseling period. It should usually last no less than half an hour if anything of value is to be accomplished, and should not exceed an hour if the employee's attention is not to wane. Sometimes several sessions covering fewer points can prove more effective than one long session in which you try to cover them all.

Every good counseling session is based on mutual understanding and acceptance on the part of the interviewer and interviewee alike. It should be a two-way process that results in a true give-and-take learning situation. It has been said that for a counseling interview to be really effective the employee should do about 90 percent of the talking. One of the greatest criticisms of most industrial counseling is that the counselor does too much of the talking and plays too dominant a role.

Getting the Employee to Talk

How do you keep the employee talking, once he has begun?

There is a special technique that must be mastered to accomplish this effectively. Here are some of the points of this technique to keep in mind.

1. *Avoid unnecessary questions.* Whenever you ask a question, it interrupts the flow of thought and changes the direction of the employee's thinking. Rarely will you get the entire story from the employee if he is interrupted. In fact, questions sometimes increase the barriers between the counselor and the employee. If you do use questions, avoid those that can be answered by a "yes" or "no," and try instead to use those that encourage a more complete expression of fact and feeling.

2. *Use brief, neutral responses.* By this we mean such responses as "I see" . . . "I understand" . . . "That must have been interesting" . . . Colorless and unemotional replies like these will help keep the discussion moving on the same track.

3. *Respond by manner.* Another way to encourage an employee to continue talking is to reply by a nod of the head, a smile, a pause, and so forth.

4. *Repeat the employee's last remark.* If the employee stops talking before you think he has completely expressed himself or his feelings, this device of mirroring back his last thought or expression in his own words—and then

pausing—will usually cause the employee to begin talking again.

5. *Rephrase the expression, feeling, or attitude.* By mirroring back in your own words a summary of the employee's expression, feeling, or attitude in the form of a question—such as "You feel you are not making sufficient progress?" . . . "You feel, then, you were not treated fairly?"—you will often be able to get the employee to continue and elaborate on what he has said.

6. *Use silence and pauses effectively.* Silence is a powerful communicator. If you remain silent when the employee stops talking, you will often find that he will start to talk again.

After you have heard the employee talk himself out, it will help to restate his ideas and feelings, ask any questions you wish, correct any inaccuracies, and clear up any doubtful points so as to be sure you will have had a successful counseling session.

Be Patient

Always remember in trying to effect any change in people that the change process is extremely difficult and takes a great deal of effort, time, planning, examining, and replanning. Counseling is only successful if there is an acceptance and essential readjustment on the part of the people who are to be changed.

Even when we personally want to change ourselves, and are strongly motivated and are with ourselves 24 hours a day, we find it difficult to bring about the desired changes, so we should recognize that it is even more difficult to effect significant changes in our fellowman. We should have faith that if the new is better, eventually people will recognize and accept it and be the better for it.

CHAPTER 21

HUMAN BEHAVIOR

By Harold J. Leavitt

Suppose we asked this question of many kinds of people: "What are the fundamental, unexceptionable truths of human behavior?" Suppose one asked it of college students, union members, top- and middle-level managers, foremen, salesmen, nurses, and housewives. The answers would include generalizations like these:

People are products of their environment.

People want security.

All people want is bread and butter.

People are fundamentally lazy.

People are fundamentally selfish.

People only do what they have to do.

People are creatures of habit.

People are products of their heredity.

Some of these answers seem to contradict others, but at another level the contradictions disappear. If one organizes them, one comes out with essentially the same generalizations that many modern psychologists would offer. For three major ideas are implicit in that list:

The first is the idea of *causality*, the idea that human behavior is caused, just as the behavior of physical objects is caused by forces that act on those physical objects. Causality is implicit in the beliefs that environment and heredity affect behavior and that what is outside influences what is inside.

Second, there is the idea of *directedness,* the idea that human behavior is not only caused but is also pointed toward something, that behavior is goal directed, that people want things.

Third, the list includes the concept of *motivation,* that underlying behavior one finds a "push" or a "motive" or a "want" or a "need" or a "drive."

Part of a Double Play

These three ideas can provide the beginning of a system for conceptualizing human behavior. With the help of these ideas, human behavior can be viewed as part of a double play from cause to motive to behavior-toward-a-goal. And it is also helpful to think of the three as generally forming a closed circuit. Arrival at a goal eliminates the cause, which eliminates the motive, which eliminates the behavior. Thus, for instance, a man's stomach is empty; the emptiness stimulates impulses interpreted as "feeling hungry"; the feeling of hunger stimulates action in the direction of food; he gets food. The food fills his stomach, causing cessation of the "feeling hungry" impulses, which in turn eliminates the behavior in search of food.

This closed circuit conception includes one major danger. Many "psychological" as distinct from "physical" goals are not finite and specific. One can consume a specific quantity of food and thereby temporarily stop feeling hungry for more. It is doubtful, however, that one can consume a specific quantity of prestige, for instance, and feel sated. Prestige and other "psychological" goals seem to be ephemeral and boundless; enough may never be obtained to inactivate the causes and hence the motive.

These assumptions of causality, motivation, and direction are nevertheless useful assumptions if they are accepted as universal. Causality, motivation, and direction can be thought of as applying equally to all people, of all ages, in all cultures, at all times. When one makes such assumptions they should lead one, upon observing human behavior, always to seek motive and, behind motive, cause.

329

There are many different perspectives on these assumptions, but the basic assumptions remain intact. For example, one can say that behavior is an attempt to get rid of tension. Tension then equals motivation; and the objective of behavior is to eliminate the necessity for behaving. Words like "motives" or "needs" or "drives" are rough synonyms for each other as well as for words like "tensions" or "discomforts" or "disequilibriums." Behavior is thus seen as an effort to eliminate tensions by seeking goals that neutralize the causes of tensions.

Thinking about motivation in terms of tension and discomfort inside the person is useful in another way. It puts the emphasis on the push from inside the person rather than on the pull from outside. Managers, for instance, often encounter problems with subordinates who "don't know what they want." They feel restless and disturbed but can't seem to say what it is they are after. Most of us behave this way a good deal of the time, feeling the push of tension from inside but not being able to identify the precise goal that would eliminate the tension. We search vaguely, trying one job or another, one boss or another, one idea or another, until—if we are lucky— we hit on something that does the trick.

Only then may we be able to tie up that particular feeling of tension with some specific goal, so that next time we can head directly for where we want to go. The baby, after all, doesn't start out saying, "I want a bottle." He starts out saying, "I feel discomfort somewhere inside." He then goes on to try all the different behaviors he can muster until he discovers that the bottle eliminates that particular discomfort. Only then can he identify this goal and narrow down his behavior so that he can get to his goal without exhausting himself.

But no matter how one views these concepts, they suggest that the ultimate condition of man can be thought of as an equilibrium condition in which he need not behave. This ultimate will be unattainable so long as one fly after another goes on landing on man's rump to stir up some new need and to force him to go on swishing his tail.

Of course the same landscape can be drawn from a brighter perspective. The tendency not to behave unless one has to can also account for man's capacity to learn. It can account for the baby's ability to become an increasingly efficient food finder. The diffuse kicking, squalling, and rolling give way over a few years to the simpler and more efficient behavior of learning to find and open the cookie jar. If people were not thus naturally stingy in their expenditures of energy, if they did not abhor unnecessary effort, if they were not lazy, then their factories would probably be no more efficient today than they were 50 years ago, if the factories existed at all.

This picture leaves no room for purely "self-starting" behavior. Something must always show up to eliminate needs. Nor does it allow for the idea of "habit," if habit means uncaused or undirected repetitive behavior. If the word "habit" is to fit here, it will have to mean something like "characteristic ways of trying to satisfy certain needs." The disorderly file clerk is not, then, just disorderly because he has disorderly habits. He is disorderly because he has learned to try to satisfy his needs by what we consider disorderly means. Nor is the inmate of the booby hatch just a different kind of human being from those on the outside. He is in there because his best methods for satisfying his needs have landed him there.

So these three assumptions (cause, motivation, direction) become theoretical starting points. Perhaps they are worth careful thought. For the reader should consider the implications of these ideas for such concepts as "free will," "habit," and "insane behavior." Accepting these assumptions will probably require some revision of the usual meaning of these ideas.

Three Assumptions

This chapter makes three interrelated assumptions about human behavior:

1. *Behavior is caused.*
2. *Behavior is motivated.*
3. *Behavior is goal directed.*

In the process some alternative assumptions have been implicitly discarded. We have discarded the ideas that behavior is "self-starting" and that it is "random," i.e., that it is going nowhere, for no reason.

Moreover, the three assumptions are assumed to be inter-related in a circular sequence: from cause to motivation to goal direction. Arrival at the goal inactivates the cause, and hence eliminates the motive, and hence eliminates the goal-directed behavior, although some goals may not be finite.

Many different words can be used to deal with these three ideas. Words like "drive," "tension," "need," and "disequilibrium," for example, are all approximate synonyms for the word "motive."

While people are alike, they are also different. They are alike in that their behavior is caused, motivated, and goal directed and their physical equipment is roughly similar. They are different to the extent that they are subject to different kinds of stimulation, that they vary in kinds and degrees of motivation, that they behave in many different ways to achieve many different goals, and that they have different sizes and powers in their physical equipment. The purpose of this section is to try to account (only at the broadest level) for the range and kinds of differences that every manager has observed among those around him.

The Range of Motives

Consider the variety of motives which seem to occur in human behavior. Consider, for example, the class of behavior called "work." What are the motives for work; what are the tensions or discomforts that people try to eliminate through work? Why should people sacrifice so much of the good life to walk into the plant morning after morning, year after year? Clearly, different individuals will give different answers to such questions, and each answer may be perfectly true for each person. Clearly, too, any single individual may come up with a variety of motives to fit his particular case. Direct questioning of a random portion of the American population would certainly include such answers as these:

I work for money and the food, shelter, and goods money buys.

I work for status and recognition.

I work to belong; to be part of a group.

I work to get to the top.

I work because it's only right that people should work.

I work for knowledge and understanding.

I work for security.

I work for the feeling of accomplishment I get from a job well done.

This list is not exhaustive. Some of the statements are concrete and specific; others are vague and shadowy. Some seem to overlap one another in meaning. Perhaps the reader will, nevertheless, go along with the generalization that most people work for some variety of reasons like these and that most people would also be willing to do some work for almost any one of the reasons listed, even if the others did not exist. But perhaps before he will go along, the reader may want to add at least one qualification: these motives may be real only for *most people in America this year*. Although some of them may be universal, others may be specific to our culture or to certain subgroups within our culture. This would be a valid qualification.

The Classes of Needs

Looking back over the list of motives, one can classify them into at least two major groups. Some arise from needs that are essentially physical and "basic": needs for food, for water, for warmth. One could add others: needs to urinate, to defecate, to sleep, and so on. These are clear-cut, unambiguous needs; they are physiological; they are universal; they are present in infants as well as adults; they are even present in most other classes of animals. They seem unquestionably to be part of the person's original inborn equipment.

The second large class of needs, however, is less easily definable. Needs for achievement, status, and "belongingness" are much more "psychological," more clearly limited to human beings, and for the most part not immediately observable in the newborn. They also seem highly individualistic—much more so than the basic physical needs. They seem to be present to an extreme degree in some people and almost nonexistent in others. We do not ordinarily characterize one another as "food seekers," but we do often characterize a person as a "power seeker" or a "prestige seeker."

In fact, our judgment of the intensities of psychological needs in other people makes up a large part of our judgment of their personalities. Application blanks for industrial jobs seldom include questions about how much water a man drinks or how many sandwiches he eats for lunch. But they do include questions about his ambitions and his social interests.

It is in these so-called psychological needs that the bulk of industrially significant personality differences lies; we must try to account for the differential development of these needs in different individuals. This problem could lead us quickly to the question of the importance of heredity and environment, but that would be an unprofitable venture. If the reader prefers to believe that the psychological needs are acquired out of our environment, such a belief will not affect the position taken here. If he prefers to believe that the seeds of psychological needs lie in the genes and that environment only fertilizes and nurtures them, that position is also tenable.

The Development of Personality

The most important issue seems to be this one: Can we, with as few assumptions as possible, account for the development of individually different adult personalities? For the back-slapping sales manager and the quick, methodical comptroller?

A theory, it has been said, is as good as its ratio of predictions to assumptions. To economize on assumptions, we may assume here that only the basic physical needs are inherited and then go on from there. It is then possible to account broadly for the elaborate complex of needs that exists in a 20-year-old while assuming that all he had to begin with were (1) his basic physical needs and (2) his body. In his "body" we must include his sense organs, plus his memory—a mechanism for retaining information picked up by the sense organs—plus a decision-making mechanism, plus a tendency to be stingy in the expenditure of energy, plus a muscular system that allows the person to move and act upon his environment. If that is the person's original basic equipment, it is almost enough to account for the accessories he will have added by the time he is 10 or 20 or 40. But he still needs one more characteristic, a characteristic that is not so much a part of the person as of the relationship between the person and the world.

This characteristic is *dependency*—the dependency of a newborn infant on parents for satisfaction of his needs; the dependency of the growing child on parents, teachers, and friends; of husband on wife; and of people in industry on their bosses; and vice versa.

If the human infant came into the world with almost complete physical development, like some other animal young, then we might have to devise quite a different theory to ac-

* * *

An understanding of people—of why they are what they are, of why they behave the way they do—is one of the most vital attributes to executive success I know of. People are the principal asset of any company, whether it makes things to sell, sells things made by other people, or supplies intangible services. Nothing moves until your people can make it move.

—J. C. Penney, founder and director, J. C. Penney Co.

* * *

count for the adult personality. In fact, if the infant could fend for himself from the start, the adult personality would be noticeably different from what it is.

But any infant who survives to adulthood has necessarily passed through a period in which he was almost entirely dependent upon other people for the satisfaction of his basic physical needs. And this dependency, coupled with the presence of physical needs and a good but incomplete physical plant, may give us the leverage to account for the development of a great many secondary and tertiary mental needs. To see how this dependency lever might work, consider this entirely hypothetical illustration:

Suppose that you suffer from a magical ailment. The major symptom of the ailment is paralysis—complete paralysis. But though you are paralyzed, your head is perfectly clear and your senses are perfectly keen. You can hear, you can see, you can feel, you can think—but you can't move.

You have a brother who possesses a magical gift. Whenever his hand is on your shoulder you are cured; you can move as well as anyone else. But when he takes his hand away the paralysis immediately returns.

Assume that your brother is a nice guy; he spends a good deal of his time with his hand on your shoulder, and he goes through considerable inconvenience to do this. Through his help you can lead something approximating a normal life. You have not had this disease very long, but by now you have gotten over the shock that it entailed, and you are trying to settle down to the best life you can work out.

This morning you awake, but of course you cannot move. You lie in bed until your brother comes in to put his hand on your shoulder. Whereupon you rise, dress, and wash. You have breakfast, chat, and read the morning paper. You do everything that you may have done before you had the disease.

Over breakfast your brother announces that he forgot to tell you he has a dentist's appointment this morning. He will have to leave the house about 10. He probably will not be back until noon. This is a matter of no great concern to you, since it's just a two-hour absence.

With his hand on your shoulder you arrange a comfortable place in which you can sit while your brother is gone. You set an easy chair by the window, put your feet on an ottoman, and tune in a radio to a program you particularly like. You open the window to let the warm air and sun in and to see what's going on outside. You settle down for the two-hour absence.

Your brother leaves.

For half an hour or so, as you expected, things are fine. You are perfectly comfortable; there's enough activity outdoors to keep you interested; and the radio program is good.

At 10:30 the program changes to the thing you hate most—hillbilly music—but that's of no major concern. A fly manages to get through a hole in the screen and begins to buzz around your nose.

By 11 o'clock there's a little itch from a rough place in the chair, but that's bearable, too. The fly is still around. The hillbilly music goes on. At 11:30 the sky clouds over. The air gets cold and windy. At 11:45 it's raining hard. You're getting wet and cold. If you could shiver, you would. The itches increase. Your bladder begins to get a little too full for comfort.

But you reassure yourself: 15 minutes more.

At noon you're waiting hopefully for your brother's step, but you don't hear it. He doesn't show at 12:15. The cold and the wet and the itches and the bladder and the fly and the radio become almost unbearable. By 12:45 you're on the verge of explosion. One o'clock and no brother, but more rain, more discomfort.

At just about 1:30 you hear footfalls. Brother walks in, puts his hand on your shoulder, and says: "I was caught in a traffic jam. I'm sorry I'm late."

Now let the reader seriously ask himself these questions:

1. Just how would you feel about your brother at this moment?

2. What do you think you would do to your brother at this moment?

Your answers probably fall into one of these major categories: (1) I would feel angry and resentful. (2) I would feel extremely relieved; extremely grateful that he had finally arrived. (3) I would feel mixed up: angry and resentful, on the one hand, and relieved and grateful, on the other.

To the action question, answers range from: (1) I would sock him on the nose to (2) I would throw my arms around him and kiss him.

Each of these answers is appropriate and understandable. Together they represent the necessary conflict of feelings that derive from the complete dependency of one individual on another. The person who says he would feel angry and hostile will probably be ready to admit that those would be predominant but not exclusive feelings. While he feels angry, he may at the same time feel affectionate and grateful. The man who says he will feel grateful and relieved will probably admit that he is also angry and irritated. Some admixture of these almost polar feelings will probably be present in everyone. This is the peculiar phenomenon of ambivalence, of the simultaneous existence of opposite feelings in the same place at the same time.

Similarly, at the action level, the man who says, "I would sock my brother on the nose," might be willing to add, "But I might feel awfully sorry afterward." And the man who says, "I would throw my arms around him," might add that his embrace would include a touch of a bear hug.

Suppose further that this sort of incident happened often, for month after month. Might you then develop an increasing wish for independence from your brother? Might you also seek ways of controlling your brother, of "getting something on him," so that you would not have to count impotently on his good will? And suppose he was a particularly bad brother who didn't care much for you? Wouldn't that intensify your wishes for independence from him or power over him?

Extreme dependency thus serves as a lever for initiating other kinds of needs. To the extent that dependency yields ready satisfaction of existing needs that one cannot satisfy independently—to that extent one's feelings are likely to be positive, friendly, affectionate, protective, grateful, and one is likely to develop strong social needs. To the extent that dependency does not satisfy but rather frustrates—to that extent one is likely to develop feelings of anger and hostility and to wish more strongly for independence and autonomy, to develop strong egoistic needs.

The infant suffers from this kind of magical paralysis. He is entirely dependent on adults for the satisfaction of his inborn physical needs. But because no parent can be entirely satisfying (or entirely frustrating), each child must necessarily develop some mixture of plus and minus feelings, first toward the parents and then, since the parents very often are the world, toward the world.

No parents can entirely satisfy or entirely frustrate an infant for these reasons: Infants who encounter only frustration in their very early attempts to satisfy their needs simply do not survive. Children who don't get fed die. At the other end of the scale, however, no infant can hope for perfect satisfaction. No parent has the prescience to foresee all the infant's wants before they arise or the patience to satisfy every want he does foresee. So no adult in the world grew up through complete frustration in infancy or through complete satisfaction.

The working range is the range between the extremes on the satisfaction-frustration scale. Parents can consciously or inadvertently work predominantly near one end of the scale or the other. And the extent to which the predominance actually is at one end or the other, together with the physiological givens, probably accounts for the general pattern of early personality development in any particular child. Teachers, bosses, and other people perform in the same range later to finish off personality development.

To be more accurate, one can put it this way: Some infants face a world that is mostly nonsatisfying, nonpredictable, and noncontrollable from the beginning. Some infants face a world that is more satisfying, more predictable, and more controllable. Children faced with an unpredictable and uncontrollable world are more likely to grow fearful and hostile early. They are more likely to wish strongly for independence. And they are more likely to be concerned with egoistic needs, with mechanisms by which independence may be gained, i.e., with power, ingratiation, acquisition of goods, and so on.

On the other hand, children whose early years are mostly satisfying are more likely to be secure and dependent. They are more likely to develop predominantly social needs, with only secondary concern (unless they learn it later) about autonomy and independence.

These acquired sets of feelings can now be thought of as two new classes of learned needs. One set is of essentially social needs, for dependency, for affiliation with people (because people satisfy needs), for affection, and the like. The other set is egoistic, i.e., concerned with the self in relation to other people rather than with other people per se. In this class belong the emerging needs for independence, for power (over other people), for prestige (as one kind of power over other people), for knowledge (another kind of power), and the like.

The Extent of Parental Control

Theoretically, the relative development of one of these sets of needs or the other in a child is partially controllable by an outsider, the parent. He can encourage social needs by satisfying physical needs, and he can encourage egoistic needs by frustrating physical needs. In practice, the problem is not quite so simple. For one thing, frustration of physical needs in infancy is likely to be accompanied by two by-products— hostility and fearfulness—as well as by a wish for independence.

Moreover, if one were really to frustrate continuously, he would soon have to frustrate not only physical needs but the egoistic needs that begin to emerge from the early frustrations. So now the frustrating parent, having developed in his child a wish for independence, must withhold the right to independence. The next step then is the child who wants independence but cannot successfully get it. Nothing he does for himself is right or successful. Where then? Perhaps a retreat from the world, a kind of internal or fantasy independence. When he grows up a little this behavior may earn him a complicated psychiatric label.

There is another key factor in this picture. When a child, or an adult for that matter, is prevented from getting what he wants, he is apt to become angry and to attack the thing that blocks him. The child strikes out blindly at Mama, the adolescent uses his fists, the adult often attacks with words. Suppose our hypothetical parent frustrates the child so that he wants to attack the parent. He kicks and he bites and he howls. Does the parent now decide to satisfy or to frustrate this new behavior? Does he let himself be attacked successfully, or does he frustrate the attack by using his superior force to retaliate? If he does the first, what becomes of his dignity? If he does the second, what does he teach the child? Probably he teaches the child that he must suppress or repress his hostility. But the *suppression* of hostility is not the same as the *absence* of hostility.

340

The child who is not allowed to kick still feels like kicking. Extend this behavior over time, day after day, incident after incident, and the pattern becomes one of internalized, non-expressed, "sat-upon" hatred and anger, sometimes with a cover of equanimity and calm.

This is not to say that the child is forever what he becomes in, say, his first year of life. On the contrary, the child is always something more than his history. And present needs plus dependency can account for the development of new needs in adults as well as in children. But the outgrowth of very early experiences (experiences in trying to satisfy one's physical needs through a wholly dependent relationship) is a foundation for the broad outlines of later personality. The first years have a good deal to do with determining whether or not the child feels essentially secure or insecure about his place in the world and essentially optimistic or pessimistic about other people.

Dependency in Industry

The things people learn in this first and most important dependency relationship probably also have a good deal to do with the way they face and deal with the less extreme dependency relationships of later life—like the relationship one has with his superiors in industrial organizations.

In fact, if we want to put this story in managerial terms, we need only to go over the last few pages and change a few labels. We can read "manager" for "parent," and "employee" for "child." And then we go on to tone down all the consequences a few notches. The employee, a "used" model of a child, enters a less extreme dependency relationship when he goes to work, and he enters with already existent social and egoistic as well as physical needs. If people in the company are "good brothers," the probability that the employee will learn to feel trustful and affiliative is pretty good—if he is already reasonably trustful of people with power. If people in the company are "bad brothers," his predominant local feelings (superimposed in a complicated way on the general feelings he brought in) are more likely to be hostile and competitive.

It is important to point out here that this view about early dependency may conflict with some widespread beliefs about training both children and employees. For example, this position suggests that strong discipline for the infant will probably lead to hostility and fear and to active power and independence seeking.

It suggests further that a history of frustration probably makes later frustrations more difficult to take rather than easier. And, in a situation in which great psychological pressure is to be put on a man, holders of this position would place their money on the man who had not gone through an infantile school of hard psychological knocks. They would pick the man whose parental relationships and preferably his later ones had been comfortable and relatively free from psychological want. (Incidentally, the evidence from studies of successful executives is consonant with this view. Successful executives tend to come from harmonious, higher-income homes and to have liked their families and teachers.) For the first year or two, the best way to "spoil" a child would therefore seem to be to deny him what he wants. The best way not to "spoil" him is to help him get everything he wants. And, if one considers the new employee instead of the new baby, the same conclusions might hold.

The Hierarchy of Needs

One outstanding psychologist has pointed out that certain needs take operational precedence over others if both are unsatisfied at the same time. The ambitious man who is lost in the desert pays attention to his thirst, not his ambition. In general, the ordering of needs seems to be from the physical needs, which take first place when unsatisfied, to the social needs, to the egoistic needs, and, within what we have called the egoistic group, to those needs involving "self-fulfillment" —that is, to needs for knowledge or understanding or the successful completion of tasks.

Suppose that such a hierarchy does operate; suppose we begin to get interested in social relationships after our bellies are filled, and in achievement after our social relationships are secure. What implications does the hierarchy have for management? One implication is that when management tries to reward or punish, it had better reward or punish the needs that are operational and not those above or below that operational level. If I feel psychologically safe about my physical needs, threats or rewards will have effects different from those produced by the same threats or rewards in someone who is operating primarily at the level of physical safety. Conversely, if my next meal is the problem that is real to me, don't expect me to be diverted with offers of promotion or threats to my status.

It has been suggested, in fact, that the general level of operational needs in a society changes as the society develops and that managers often lag behind that development in their methods of management. They may thus use incentives or threats that would have worked in the less developed America of a hundred years ago, but are as meaningless in our present affluent society as a penny is to today's teenagers. Our society, in other words, is probably at a stage in which social or egoistic needs are more operational for most of us than physical or safety needs.

In Summary

People are born with physical needs. They later either acquire or blossom out with a host of other social and egoistic needs. These new psychological needs can be thought of as outgrowths of (1) physical needs, (2) the nervous system of the physical body, plus (3) dependency on other people.

The child is dependent on adults. Adults can make that dependency predominantly satisfying or predominantly frustrating. Satisfaction builds security and social needs; frustration builds insecurity, hostility, and egoistic needs.

The dependency conditions of infancy recur in later life in industry and elsewhere. The same infantile learning formula may prevail at the adult level.

But the operational needs of adults may be different. For the needs we respond to tend to form a hierarchy, with physical needs taking precedence *if they are severely threatened.* But if we are physically secure, social, followed by egoistic, needs become the ones we work to satisfy.

CHAPTER 22

THE ART OF CRITICISM

By Walter E. Elliott

It's doubtful if a single facet of an executive's responsibility is not, in some way, linked up with the subject of criticism. The degree of good results hinges on one's degree of awareness surrounding this subject. Successful selection, indoctrination, training, performance review, discipline, motivation, cooperation from peers and superiors, selling of new ideas for improvement (both vertically and horizontally), all depend on how well one practices the art of constructive criticism.

And the "practice" includes being on the receiving end as well as the "dishing out" end!

The practice of constructive criticism appears easy for the one on the outside looking in. It is logical to reason that every normal person wants to improve, is interested in promoting his own best interests, senses that his own security is enhanced to the degree that his company prospers.

The real truth is that all of us fit the definition of "middle-age" . . . the age when one would rather die than give up the things that hurt him most!

In his book *Successful Human Relations*, Dr. William Reilly says you can classify all situations dealing with criticism under three main headings:

When you're right and the other fellow's wrong.

When you're partly right and the other fellow's partly right.

When you're wrong and the other fellow's right.

He emphasizes that the more wrong we are, the easier it should be for us to admit it and take criticism constructively.

The truth is that the more wrong we feel, the more difficult it is for us to take criticism.

This important foible of human nature is at the heart of the knotty problem of constructive criticism. Unless we see and recognize this principle, we are like the navigator approaching an iceberg, completely unaware that about four-fifths of it is under water, ready to sink our ship without warning.

A better comparison might be that of the expert rifleman, standing in a boat and aiming directly at a fish beneath the surface. No matter how good his technical skill, no matter how accurate his gun, he will miss the fish and become increasingly frustrated unless he knows the law of light refraction. Knowing that light bends, he aims several feet in front of where the fish appears to be and obtains more accurate results.

So, the more one knows about the "law" of criticism, the less frustrated he is when he has to motivate others to his viewpoint.

The "law" of criticism is akin to the "law" of electricity. Apply the law of electricity correctly and you get light at the end of a copper wire. Misuse the law and you get a terrific shock.

Positive vs. Negative Criticism

This booklet explores the art of criticism. It's an "art" since Webster defines art as "Ingenuity in adapting natural things to man's use." Of all the arts, criticism is one of the least developed on a wide scale. Down through the centuries, it has been used more like a meat cleaver in the hands of a butcher than a scalpel in the hands of a surgeon.

As far back in history as written records appear, man has traveled the dead-end road of misdirected criticism. The ancient Pharisees actually believed it their moral duty to try to correct people and make them good by criticism. When they held themselves aloof from others, they did it for the sake of the wrongdoers. "The sinner must be shown that sin estranges" was their reasoning.

Even though the founder of Christianity was the first to

warn His disciples to "beware of the leaven of the Pharisees," the majority of His followers, down through the ages, have been among the first to pronounce critical judgments and attempt to convert others by criticism. More military, class, family, and industrial wars have probably originated from this "need to convert" than from all other causes put together. Chopping off the heads of Moors during the Crusades was one of the more extreme forms in which the need to criticize found expression.

The dead-end road of negative criticism is always attractive to the one who enjoys dishing it out. First, he is "doing something for the other person's good." Second, it gives him a sense of satisfaction to feel superior to the one criticized.

The reason it is a dead-end road is that it creates more problems than it solves. Either it crushes the self-image of the one criticized, causing completely negative results, or it spotlights the excessive criticizer for what he really is; namely, a person filled with inferiority feelings who needs an outlet for his pent-up emotions.

If you get a sense of satisfaction from dishing out criticism by aloofness, sarcasm, etc., you are on a dead-end road to leadership. But if you hate to criticize, yet know it is your responsibility to do so in order to develop subordinates, to help your superior or peers avoid serious mistakes, then you are on the right road.

How to know if we are on the right road is the real difficulty. We all tend to shy away from the faintest possibility that ulterior motives and childlike emotions could dwell within us. All of us are to some degree like the woman looking out her window and criticizing the gray-streaked clothing hanging on her neighbor's clothesline. While the other's clothes may have been far from perfect, they would have appeared whiter had she first *washed her own windows*.

Clean Your Own Windows First

One basic truth of human behavior is that every one of us has many uncleaned windows. One dirty window has already been touched upon; namely, feelings of inferiority or insecurity that make us seek excuses to criticize others. Another dirty window is that of looking too narrowly through the framework of our own environment.

Most people would rather die than admit their brand of politics or religion is based on something else than their own logical reasoning. Even in their brand of cigarettes some would "rather fight than switch"!

Little wonder that the world's greatest psychologist once said, "Judge not, lest ye be judged." To be a truly impartial judge would take the wisdom of Solomon. It is simple to judge that a thickness of metal is below the accepted norm. It is not so easy to get the person causing the variation to learn from his mistake, yet not feel belittled as a person when criticized for making it.

What's Your "PCQ"?

Before we explore the keys to handling criticism constructively, let's check out your positive criticism quotient. You may find it much lower than your "I.Q." Read the following statements and decide if they are true or false:

	True	False
1. We can all agree on the nature of common sense.		
2. Sound logic is the one sure way to convince others.		
3. It is right to humiliate publicly those who show disrespect for others.		
4. The beliefs of some people are so absurd that one is justified in denouncing those beliefs.		
5. One should not be courteous to people who are extremely disagreeable.		
6. The best way to convince a person he is wrong is to tell him so and then prove it.		
7. Conscience gives the same command to everyone.		

	True	False
8. What will make one person happy can safely be assumed to make others happy.	....	....
9. Most persons must be told what to do.	....	....
10. It is best to call a "spade a spade."	....	....
11. Appeals to negative emotions are more effective than appeals to positive emotions.	....	....
12. The opinions of the majority have little influence on an intelligent person.	....	....
13. Good results often ensue from "making an example" out of one person in order to impress the others.	....	....

The more of these statements you agree to, the greater is the likelihood that you create a "backlash" when you approach the task of criticizing.

Criticizing Subordinates

Let's start off with an imaginary situation. Suppose you have only $50 plus a train ticket to Chicago. As soon as you arrive, you try to get a job before your money runs out. You take a quick look at the want ads and secure a minimum-paying job. You start the next day at 7:30 a.m. You are placed on a job you have never done before. During the course of the first few hours, what's the one phrase that most likely describes the "feeling" you are apt to have?

It is the "fear of not making good."

While you continue to have that fear, it lessens as time goes on. You don't get fired. Apparently, you are going to "get by." At the end of six weeks, what phrase now most likely describes your "overall feeling"?

It is "hope for advancement."

So far, so good. In fact, most managers strongly agree that the only fear on an employee's mind is his loss of income—that his only hope is for a larger income. This belief is so strong

348

in the minds of some that their entire approach toward discipline and promotion hinges on it.

But there is a third word that goes with "fear" and "hope." That is the word "pride." If you look, you can see it in the lowest group of society. Some psychologists maintain this is even stronger than fear or hope. At least it is equally strong. And the lower down the social scale one is, the stronger this protective device is apt to become. Succeed in completely killing a man's pride, and you have opened up a Pandora's box containing all possible negative reactions, from mental, emotional, or physical breakdowns to suicide.

Down through the lowest ranks of our society, people use their job as a yardstick to help make themselves feel important. They are saying, "My job is the thing that makes me feel worthwhile. It proves that I'm important and the world needs me." The art of criticism is getting a man to improve his job without undermining his feelings that his job is important, that he is important and that the world needs him. This goes for presidents of firms as well as for the rest of us.

It's a little sad sometimes to see how much importance is placed on the insignificant things by those who feel they are not very important. But it's even sadder to see executives belittle these things which are desperately important to such "insignificant" individuals. More strikes, slowdowns, apathy, resentment, absenteeism, and lowered production can be attributed to this oversight than to any other cause.

Simply overlooking the things which are so vital to the pride of such "insignificant" individuals is negative criticism of the first order.

Another oversight caused by indifference toward the things which "insignificant" people feel significant is that of making people feel wrong when they already know they are wrong.

I know a plant manager whose company was plagued by the attitudes of workers who felt their union was their only real boss. An opinion survey uncovered a number of minor areas where management had overlooked certain wise practices, as well as where practices of employees were way off base.

The plant manager ironed out the whole difficulty in a one-hour meeting with all the employees, largely because he started off by saying:

"Thanks to your participating in the survey, you have pointed out certain mistakes we've been making in our dealings with your union. We in management were wrong. We made some mistakes. Here is what we intend to do to rectify those mistakes . . ."

Tough words for anyone to say! Most people feel this would open up a series of additional demands. Instead, it opened up the minds of the employees. As the hour progressed, some of the very ringleaders who had made it so rough for management came forth and volunteered that they also had made some mistakes and would like to rectify their own. A suggestion-improvement committee was formed, over and beyond the formal bargaining committee. Within six months production was breaking all previous records.

The average manager would have taken the opposite approach. He would have played down management's mistakes and "straightened out" those he "knew" were wrong. But by helping the other men feel "right," even when he knew they were "wrong," he made it easier for them to admit their own mistakes.

Criticizing Peers and Superiors

Pride is often just as strong in those who "have arrived." It merely takes different forms of expression.

I once walked into the office of a company president who was worth over a million dollars. He had invented a product, built a company of 300 employees, sold out for a half million dollars and been retained at a $50,000 yearly salary. He had a pleasing personality and had risen quite high in his city's social circles; and intelligence tests proved him to be near the genius level. Yet he could not take criticism when the pressure was on. He also made it extremely uncomfortable for key subordinates by falling back on his authority and refusing to delegate responsibility.

While all his key people rated him as one who "acted superior," deep personality tests showed unconscious feelings of inferiority. During a lengthy interview in which he denied any such feelings, he suddenly said, "Well, if I do have such feelings, I'm sure it's not because I'm only five feet six tall."

Further probing disclosed he had been fighting such feelings all his life. In high school he had tried out for football. The coach wouldn't even give him a uniform. He finally bought his own and ended up as the city's all-star quarterback.

The same thing happened in basketball, where he became the best dribbler on the team. His need to "prove himself" drove him to acquire five college degrees and ultimate business success. Yet not a single person on his staff had the faintest suspicion that his pride, which had been so badly injured in his growing-up days, was still acting as a trigger whenever he was made to feel he was the least bit wrong.

You can safely count on the fact that every one of us, no matter how successful, has some ghosts in the closet which we unconsciously keep hidden from view. The entire process of growing up has been one of being made to feel more wrong than right. The more unconscious we are of the incidents that made us feel "wrong," the more they are covered up by excessive pride.

The saving of our physical skin today has become of less importance to us than the saving of our "social face." Pride causes a hankering for the right to enjoy our self-respect, which comes from outside ourselves in the form of recognition, praise, or esteem. Whether we are bums, presidents, or somewhere in between, we are equally less sure of ourselves than we would like to be, and equally as hungry for approval.

This brings us to the point of how to handle the hundreds of different situations where the need to criticize is our responsibility, despite the pride that is involved. Instead of trying to do the impossible—trying to learn each person's particular weakness and making allowance for it—we at least can pay attention to several underlying principles that are true for everyone. These are basic rules we can use, whether the person is a child, an adult, a subordinate, or a boss.

Rule 1: Anticipate Closed-Mindedness

The first rule to know is that most people's minds will snap shut the moment they are made to feel "wrong." Those who agreed to the statements in the quiz earlier in this chapter are the first to be surprised when those they criticize go on the defensive.

Some who agreed to these statements are so self-centered they simply cannot put themselves in the place of the other person. Because they are so self-centered, they would be the very first to close their minds if others took the identical approach toward them. This is why many brilliant engineers and accountants fail to rise to supervisory positions. Their entire learning was based on approaching technical problems by getting logical facts. Their trouble is they try to apply this same approach to people.

The people they try to convince are backed into an emotional corner by such engineers, where they only have a choice of fighting, giving in, or running away. Let this happen too often and the superior will finally find some way to eliminate the engineering supervisor, no matter how "logical" is his reasoning.

In the course of the past 20 years, I have seen dozens of frustrated engineers and accountants blaming everyone but themselves for their lack of promotion to broader administrative posts. They believe those of higher authority are either stupid or are consciously attempting to hold them back in advancement. While they actually may have more technical know-how to run the company than the president, they cannot "sell" their ideas without closing everyone's mind to their objectives.

Their entire trouble stems from their assuming that their peers and superiors are too "grown up" to retain the vestiges of their childhood environment.

Rule 2: Know the Predominating Feeling

The second rule to know is that the predominating feeling of everyone who is about to be criticized will be "saying" one of three things, no matter how self-assured his pride causes him to seem:

"I'm feeling hurt."
"I'm feeling angry."
"I'm feeling scared."

Suppose you as a supervisor clump down the aisle with an angry look in your eye and yell at Susie to come into the private spot reserved for "talking things over." (It's one of the rules not to reprimand in public, you know.) Susie follows you to the spot. She already is feeling hurt, fearful or angry even before she learns why she has been called in.

Regardless of the penalty that might be imposed, Susie feels the blow of losing face in the eyes of her group. Inside, Susie feels "he doesn't like me." (That's the hurt which is worse than whatever the mistake may prove to be.) She says to herself, "If it wasn't for his position, I would tell him off." (That's the anger.)

And then she feels, "But I don't dare because he might find some excuse to fire me." (That's the fear.)

So she suppresses these feelings, while apparently listening to what her boss has to say. She already is backed into such an emotional corner that she can't listen objectively to what he does say. Thus, when she bursts into tears and runs to the lady's room, the boss thinks he has done a good job by either correcting her or scaring her into doing better.

The chances are he has made a worse employee out of her. While she may never repeat that same mistake again, her bad feelings are most likely to show up later in a dozen ways that are even worse.

Unless the supervisor anticipates and lays the groundwork for reducing these negative feelings before he starts, he is not fulfilling his responsibility to either her, his employer, or himself.

About Empathy

A little-understood word in psychology is *empathy*. It means understanding to the point where you are so closely identified with the real feelings of the other person that you can almost feel his exact feelings.

Few people have this naturally. As an infant, we know a pin hurts us, but we cannot possibly realize that the same pin hurts someone else. In the ideal course of growing up, people gradually become aware that others also are hurt by the pin. In the case of many, their emotions are so arrested that they remain infants emotionally while becoming adults chronologically. The world is full of such self-centered people.

Most of us are not too far behind. Very few people are more concerned with a famine in India than they are over their own sore thumb. The more we are wrapped up in our own "bad feelings" toward ourselves, the more impossible it is to feel empathy toward others.

Roy Pearson, dean of the Andover Newton Theological School, was quoted in *Think* magazine on the subject of why executives fail. Among three basic causes, he lists the inability to communicate. He says, "The primary facet in communicating is 'empathy.'" The executive who fails is the one who can never persuade anybody of anything because he never seeks out the "truth" in the other person's position, as this other person sees it. Not taking the trouble to sense the differing viewpoints of others, he is constantly touching their sore spots, completely unaware that they are taking his remarks as negative criticism.

It is difficult to see that, while it is always right to be truthful, it is not always right to speak the truth. Every person has his own "safety zones" he protects in some special way against critical attack. Dr. Hilton Shepherd, psychologist, divides these into five "zones":

Zone 1—Oneself

Zone 2—Family

Zone 3—Friends

Zone 4—Acquaintances

Zone 5—Special groups

"Sensitivity," says Dr. Shepherd, "varies with distance, identification, and emotional attachment. So defenses are correspondingly affected. As attacks are aimed at Zone 1, they become almost explosive (except for forced self-control).

Other zones are defended less aggressively, but the inner feelings (resistances) are still there . . . and strong enough to affect behavior radically!"

The one-way communicator simply can't understand this and so is behind the 8-ball without ever knowing it. He is the first to blame everyone else as being noncooperative.

Rule 3: Expect "Stored Up Bad Feelings"

The third rule to know is that all of us tend to "store up" our "bad feelings." When we do, they are bound to pop out sooner or later and cause us to give someone else a hard time. Everyone knows how we can store up our own bad feelings during the day rather than let them out on our overcritical boss. Then we take them out on the wife or kids.

At other times, we store them up over family situations and take them out on the job. We've been taught that we shouldn't express these bad feelings. Actually, the only real danger lies in storing up or repressing them rather than facing the fact that we do have them.

One of the most important things for parents or supervisors to know is that they must help their children, or subordinates, feel free to express their bad feelings at the time they happen, rather than bottle them up because of fear of criticism. Do this and they will be better able to take constructive criticism the way it is intended. Meanwhile, expect others to have such bad feelings no matter how helpful you mean to be when having to criticize them.

A sense of understanding, achievement, and empathy are the most important ingredients in anyone's emotional diet. Give these three in large enough doses from the first day an employee is hired and he will be more able to take criticism objectively.

Rule 4: Seek Out the Real Motivation

The main reason why criticism has so often failed in the past is that we have failed to take the real motivation into account. We've dealt with "bad actions" only. Dealing with a man's bad feelings does not mean we ignore his bad actions; but the bad feelings must always come first.

I know a plant manager who had a foreman who was such a show-off that all his subordinates hated him. Because the manager didn't want the workers to feel management countenanced such behavior, he made it a point once a week to go into his department and criticize him. He felt this would reduce "his inflated ego."

While the foreman quit acting like a show-off, his efficiency began dropping in other ways. When the manager was shown that the foreman's real motivation for showing off was caused by feelings of inadequacy, the plant manager changed tactics. He began to look for things the man was doing well and complimented him at least once every week. Within a year, this man became one of his best foremen.

This was all because the manager began to take his real motivation into consideration as a result of understanding the true cause behind the man's outward actions.

Rule 5: Feel for the One Criticizing

The fifth rule to know is that the average person who is about to criticize you is likely to be tensed up with his own feelings of insecurity.

Suppose your boss calls you into his office and criticizes you for making an apparent (to him) wrong decision. You know he is wrong. Your first impulse is to go on the defensive and show him where he is wrong. It's only natural to do this. The most difficult thing would be to immediately tell him he may be 100 percent right! (If you're smart, you'll know that no matter how wrong he is, he wouldn't have called you in unless he had felt justified in dishing out the criticism.)

Accuse him of being wrong and you only make him feel worse within himself. Admit that he may be right and you take the edge off his own feelings of insecurity. Then you proceed to ask factual questions in a tactful way. Gradually, as all the facts come out, he sees where he went off half-cocked without your even "telling him" he was wrong. In the future you will find he thinks twice before he "jumps in" so hastily.

Meanwhile, he has more respect for you, rather than labeling you as one who "alibis," "can't take criticism," or "passes the buck." What's more important, as all the facts emerge, if you find you really were wrong, you don't "lose face" by having to "eat crow."

From the very beginning, you admitted you might have been wrong. Thus it becomes less difficult to admit you really were wrong! So, right or wrong, you can afford to admit immediately you may have been wrong. No one in an emotionally tense situation can be absolutely sure of all the facts, anyway.

This is why it takes a very big person to accept criticism. The small potatoes just can't keep their own negative emotions out of the situation and admit they may have been wrong. Admitting the possibility of a mistake is not an indication of subservience but an indication of sound emotional maturity.

Summary for Taking Criticism

There are only two reasons why people criticize us. Either they are sincerely interested in helping us, or they are using us as a scapegoat for their own disturbed feelings.

In the beginning, therefore, assume the other person does want to help us. From this vantage point, we can determine in what ways the criticism is true and in what respects it is not. We can learn all we can from it and try to benefit from our new knowledge.

If, however, we see growing evidence that the criticism is due to the other's own inner hostilities, do not resent it, but understand him. Go on from there and make the best of the situation. Remember that every one of us is "akin" to the man standing on the street corner with his dog. A gold-plated Cadillac rounds the corner and splashes him with mud. In a rage over his hurt pride and at the man in the Cadillac, he strikes out with his foot and kicks his dog.

Every day most of us in some way get the same treatment as does the dog. If we expect it, and understand the real reasons behind it, we will automatically discount 90 percent of the unjust criticism we receive.

Good Relations for the "Tough-minded"

One of the greatest misconceptions in some teachings about human relations is that people should not be criticized. Many executives take courses and become overconcerned with trying to make everyone happy, sugar-coating reality, avoiding their responsibility of constructive criticism.

The truth is that morale is worse in such companies, in which the resulting inefficiency is bound to "run rampant," than in firms with harsh authority as the rule rather than the exception. The greatest disservice an executive can do for his company is to overuse the "kid glove" treatment.

For generations, ideal management practices have gradually evolved through a series of bumbling experiments. What is coming out of these years of experiment is something called "broad" versus "close" supervision. The philosophy of "close" supervision still predominates in our industrial society. It is the ancient authoritarian system, in which each boss feels he must closely direct and criticize each subordinate. The result is that subordinates need more and more rigid criticism, more rules with "teeth," more threats of some sort to get them to match the standards expected.

This, of course, is the very reason for more and more people falling back on unions for security. It is management by "personality" rather than by impersonal standards.

The concept behind "broad" supervision is that most people can be trusted to do the right thing once the climate is created in which they are encouraged to think for themselves, where they feel identified with the goals common to management, where the known standards expected are agreed upon by everyone from the very beginning. Those who consistently fail to match the clearly known standards know they are falling short, without ever being told they are.

Thus the standards become the "boss" and not the degrees of perfection bound to exist among a group of executives with widely varying degrees of perfectionism. This eliminates the feeling that one is being criticized "because the boss dislikes me personally." The small minority who fail to match up under such a climate know they are "out" because the rules give everyone four balls and three strikes. As in baseball everyone works under the framework of known standards. It's results that count.

What this all means is that leaders should give more personal attention to adequately training their subordinates to think for themselves, hold more group and individual meetings to talk over the end results desired, encourage employees to suggest better ways for reaching common goals. When they do this, they have far less reason to give "negative criticism."

The value of this approach can easily be seen by asking managers one simple question: "If you were to leave the department for half a day, would efficiency be reduced?" Those who say "no" would be correct. Those who say "yes" would also be correct. However, a study of those who say "no" will reveal that they are the ones who consistently achieve higher production than those who say "yes."

The reason is that those who say "no" have been devoting their time to the broader responsibility of training, establishing better interdepartmental cooperation and personal understanding with their subordinates. Those who say "yes" will be found to have spent the bulk of their time "checking up" on subordinates, giving more detailed and frequent orders, becoming a "stock chaser."

A morale survey would reveal that more of such a supervisor's men would feel they were "a mere cog in the wheel" than those under the supervision of one who gets better results by not hovering over his people like an old mother hen.

A Final Word of Caution

One of mankind's greatest needs is to advance the idea that disagreement is not necessarily criticism. The one who disagrees with our thinking causes us to feel threatened. We take it as criticism.

The subordinate who disagrees is not necessarily disloyal. The boss who won't agree is not against us just because we are who we are. Most of society's accomplishments are not due to cooperation alone, but to the disagreement among men on different ways to reach the same total objective. Disagreement should be judged, not by the act, but by the motivation behind it.

If you are sure you are right, then search out the reasons for resistance. Is it because of inertia, misunderstanding, poor judgment, insecurity, or because there is a fallacy in your own attitudes or thinking?

Only if you do this, can you give or take criticism objectively and gain from it.

CHAPTER 23

SELECTING PERSONNEL

By Robert N. McMurry

Frank O'Brien was the top salesman in his division. He was the winner in every contest and was a regular commuter to Bermuda as a reward for his prowess in the field. Hence when a vacancy in field management opened up, everyone agreed that he was the outstanding candidate.

At the start of his new assignment, he was a whirlwind; everyone liked him; his enthusiasm was infectious; his unit was off to a flying start. But six months later reaction began to set in. Morale began to sag. His men began to complain that he did not answer their questions or take action on their complaints. New men received little or no field training. Because he wanted each of his men to be fond of him personally, he was reluctant to administer discipline, even for offenses obvious to everyone.

Soon it was rumored he had formed a group of pets and favorites, who were given the best assignments.

In the meantime he was working night and day to increase sales. As a superlative personal salesman, he did this the only way he knew: He used his men as bird dogs and tried to close every major sale himself. But to no avail. As his men's morale slumped, so did sales. His reaction was to work even harder. Ultimately the breaking point was reached.

Accustomed as he was to fortify himself with an occasional drink, his need for the bottle increased, parallel with his anxieties and tensions. The end was abrupt. He came to a meeting with his superior in an advanced stage of intoxication, and the game was up for Frank.

The fault was not Frank's; it was his management's. They had failed to perceive that selling and managing are two very different activities qualitatively. Success in one does not necessarily guarantee success in the other. In fact, the reverse was true in Frank's case.

As a personal salesman, he had never learned to work *through* his subordinates. As a natural wooer of others, he could not bear to take action which might forfeit for him the affection (and support) of his men. All he knew was how to do the job himself. This was sufficient in selling, but woefully inadequate in a management role. Consequently he failed. In doing so, the company lost both a manager and a salesman (he obviously could never go back to his sales job). Hence there was no place for him to go but out.

Such episodes, costly as they may be to the employer, are doubly costly to the man himself. Failure is disastrous to everyone, and for men like Frank who are not too sure of themselves to begin with, the experience can be catastrophic. He will never be quite the same; his self-confidence has suffered a shattering blow.

He will probably never try to be a manager again; nor is it likely that he will have the opportunity. To be fired is hardly a recommendation, and this experience will remain a black mark on his record till the end of his career. A man is permitted only a limited number of firings in his life. A second one like this, and he will be truly finished.

Most tragic, however, is the effect of the experience upon him personally; it has transformed a sober, industrious, good producer and family man into a potential lush. Why?

Because his supervisors did not understand the most elementary principles of employee selection and placement.

Errors in selection and placement constitute one of the greatest, albeit often overlooked, sources of cost to American industry. This type of error is made in choosing people for positions at every level of the organization: from common laborers and clerical help to technicians and specialists, and to supervisors and executives. These errors are made not only with new employees brought in from the outside but with present employees who are being transferred or promoted.

Cost Is Hidden

Mistakes of this character are costly both to the employer and to the individual. From a purely fiscal point of view, these mistakes represent a substantial hidden cost to the employer. It is hidden because rarely are such costs attributed to their true cause: inadequate selection and placement procedures. Instead, most of them are charged to operating expenses.

If, for example, due to improper selection and placement, an employee leaves or is dismissed, every cent spent on his recruitment, selection, placement, training, and replacement is just as definitely lost as though the currency represented were burned.

But these are not the only costs. Nearly all new employees are overpaid during their early weeks and months on the job because they are rarely fully efficient. This investment is also lost when the employee leaves or is separated.

For most employers, the greatest costs arise from the selection of "marginal men"—often "the best of the worst"—who subsequently turn out to be marginal employees. These are the persons who in later years are not quite bad enough to dismiss but *not quite good enough to keep*. They are not particularly proficient in whatever their assignment may be, and they are certainly not promotable. Often they are the chronic complainers and troublemakers.

A greater cost, however, arises from the intangible consequences of improper hiring and placement procedures. These include the mistakes the employee makes and the adverse effect on his and his associates' morale when he is not suited to the job. Often when the employee has contact with customers and the public, he can create a great deal of ill will for the enterprise.

Another of the major intangible costs is the amount of time lost. Normally it takes months, sometimes years, before it becomes evident that a mistake has been made and a replacement

363

is necessary. All of this time is lost, since with the new incumbent an equal amount of time will be required to break him in.

The greatest of all costs, as in Frank's case, fall on the individual. He is frequently the worst sufferer. Either he fails in the position to which he has been assigned—thus creating a black mark on his record, with very adverse effects on his morale and self-confidence—or, because his deficiencies are not so serious that he is an outright failure, he struggles on and tries to handle a position for which he is not qualified.

May Result in Illness

This can be very costly to him psychologically. It may subject him to intolerable tensions and pressures, which can result in physical or psychological illness. A high proportion of men who suffer from the various psychogenic disorders such as ulcers, colitis and allergy are men who have been, to some degree, misplaced, and who have reacted to their consequent tensions by developing these psychogenic disorders.

They are, so to speak, victims of the "battle fatigue of business."

In addition, what is even more tragic, many react to the demands of their positions for which they are not qualified by taking flight into excessive eating, smoking, or drinking, by engaging in unnecessary travel, or else by driving themselves unmercifully to handle petty details, which could and should have been delegated to subordinates.

The primary objective of every enterprise is to build and maintain a work force that will be *stable* (have a minimum amount of turnover), be *productive* (be composed of personnel who are willing to do a day's work for a day's pay), and *satisfied* (will like their jobs and maintain a reasonably high level of morale).

To accomplish this, at least five conditions must prevail. First, and obviously, the employees must have been properly recruited, selected, and placed. Second, they must know their jobs—the precise nature of their duties, responsibilities, and scope of authority—and know what constitutes a satisfactory standard of performance.

Third, they must be adequately trained. Fourth, their compensation must be at least consistent with the going rate in the industry and the community, and when possible contain some incentive. Fifth, the supervision provided them must be technically competent and inherently capable of proper leadership to ensure that each employee's activities are properly disciplined and directed.

Of these five essentials, the first—proper recruitment, selection, and placement—is of primary importance.

The chief reason initial selection is of such major importance is that if the person hired is not basically qualified, no amount of care in placement, training, incentives, or direction and supervision will make him successful. It is impossible to build a successful organization if the basic human material obtained is of limited potential or is defective in any way. Many employers engage in wishful thinking and believe that they can rehabilitate employees who suffer from obvious limitations. This is unwise on two grounds.

First, few businesses are so constituted that they can effectively operate as rehabilitation centers. Second, with the exception of relatively minor limitations, most human beings are rather resistive to change. They do not respond very well to efforts to better them. In some cases, unfortunately, people even tend to spontaneously deteriorate after they are hired as a result of illness, aging, or various adverse environmental influences.

Even when the employer's initial selection methods have been sound, he may be guilty of improperly placing the individual. The man or woman may have been assigned to an activity that is temperamentally unsatisfying. For example, a man who is well qualified for protected, well-structured, inside activities such as accounting or recordkeeping may be asked to go out into the field and do door-to-door selling involving cold canvassing. This situation is often disastrous. Not only does the man fail on the job, but, as already indicated, the act of failing may have a serious effect on his morale and self-confidence, as it did in the case of Frank.

In other instances, well-qualified people are placed in positions that do not provide an adequate challenge. (It is just as undesirable to place a person in a position for which he is overqualified as in one for which he is underqualified.) The greatest tragedy, as we have said, occurs, however, when a man or woman who is well qualified to handle a position at one level is promoted "over his head." That is what happened to Frank.

No Easy Task

If selection and placement are to be effective, then, it must be realized that these procedures are far from simple ones. For one thing, jobs vary widely in their demands upon a person. Likewise, as everyone knows, human beings are infinitely complex. Even the most sophisticated computer, for example, does not have as many internal interconnections as does the human brain.

Furthermore, employees never work within a vacuum. They are constantly called upon to relate themselves to other employees, customers, and the public; they live in a highly complex social and home environment. Therefore, if people are to be properly placed vocationally, allowance must be made for their physical qualifications; their levels of intelligence; the extent of their technical knowledge, training, education, skills, and experience; their levels of energy, drive, and initiative; their personality makeup (character and emotional maturity); their courage, strength, and decisiveness (ability to lead and command); their motivations (goals in life); their values (what they regard as good, beautiful, moral, personally acceptable, and so forth); and their off-the-job environment (domestic, social, and economic).

Close Match Needed

If selection is to be wholly effective, it must aim to effect as closely as possible a match between the job and the prospective incumbent. The purpose of this is twofold.

It is to ensure that the incumbent can perform the job; that he has the requisite physical qualifications for the job; has appropriate (not too much nor too little) intelligence; has adequate experience, skills, training, and education; is willing to accept the hours, the travel, the need to relocate which may be features of the job; and has no crippling physical handicaps or ailments.

It is also to ensure that the incumbent will perform the job satisfactorily, as well as find the work temperamentally satisfying; will have adequate energy, initiative, and drive; will have sufficient courage, strength of character, and decisiveness; will have the proper character traits (habits); will be suitably motivated; will be free from emotional immaturity and tendencies toward unrealistic behavior; will have a value system that does not conflict with the values of his superiors or employers; will have an off-the-job environment that will be supportive and compatible; and can relate himself satisfactorily to his supervision.

The essence of good selection is the *accurate prediction of the probable success of a given individual in a particular job or hierarchy of jobs.* In short, whenever an applicant is offered a position, it should be only after the person doing the hiring has convinced himself that, if hired, the candidate will remain with the company for a reasonable period of time, do a day's work for a day's pay, and be satisfied, happy, and cooperative in his work.

Because of the complexity of this matching procedure—because of the number of variables involved—no single simple technique such as a battery of psychological tests will be of sufficient breadth and scope to provide all of the information needed for the prediction analysis. One must have the facts to go by.

These include a detailed knowledge of the demands of the job: (1) its special working conditions (travel, relocation, etc.); (2) technical aspects; (3) physical aspects; (4) intellectual requirements; (5) the extent to which energy, initiative, and drive are needed; (6) the extent to which strength of character, decisiveness, and leadership are needed; (7) the competence, expectations, and value systems of supervision and management (the degree to which the candidate must conform if he and his supervision are to be compatible).

Also a detailed knowledge of the candidate himself (who is usually a total stranger) is required.

This must include a knowledge of (1) his physical condition; (2) his level of intelligence; (3) his schooling, skills, and experience; (4) his willingness to accept any special features of the job (night and weekend work, travel, need to relocate); (5) his character makeup (habit pattern); (6) his principal motivations; (7) the extent to which he is emotionally mature and capable of realistic thinking and behavior; (8) the extent to which his off-the-job environment will be supportive, encouraging, and compatible; (9) the degree to which his values will be consistent with those of his superiors in the company.

If these facts about the job and the individual are to be valid and sufficiently comprehensive, they must be systematically assembled. Facts about the job and its environment must be based upon a knowledge of its duties, responsibilities, and scope of authority; the degree to which it is, or is not, structured, routinized, and regimented (the amount of leadership and decision-making required); the closeness and competence of supervision (the timespan of discretion allowed the incumbent); the expectations, values, and tolerance for competition of supervision (to ensure compatibility).

Checking the Applicant

Correspondingly, facts about the candidate must be gathered from several sources. They are:

1. *The candidate himself* by means of preliminary screening or "knock-out" questions, his answers on the application form, what he reveals on psychological tests and inventories, and also what he reveals in the course of a patterned interview.

2. *People who know him well* occupationally or have records of his performance, including previous supervisors and employers (through telephone checks), professors, school counselors and principals (through personal or telephone interviews, or from transcripts).

3. *Members of his family* (as the result of a home interview). This is an important but often neglected step.

To sum it up, then, there must be accurate specifications covering the kind of incumbent needed—both quantitatively (overqualification is as dangerous as underqualification) and qualitatively (the proper *constellation* of skills, experience, physical qualifications, character makeup, motivations, maturity, values, and home environment must be established).

These specifications determine where, what kind of, and how many applicants are to be recruited for a position.

Next, it is necessary to undertake a comprehensive recruitment program to ensure a sufficient number of applicants for the employer to be reasonably discriminating in his choice of candidates.

If the company has not set up a comprehensive recruitment program, it may be faced with the alternative of accepting a second-rate, or marginal, candidate, or else taking no one at all. This is why it is extremely ill-advised to depend on walk-ins or referrals by employees and friends for most positions. While their quality may be somewhat superior to that of the "run of the mill," it is still unlikely that there will be enough applicants who will meet discriminating job standards.

Secondly, in addition to those applicants who are generally of poor quality, it may be necessary to exclude a number of others who are highly qualified, but not for the type of activity under consideration. Finally, some of those who are qualified and have the requisite pattern of attributes will not be interested in the opening.

Therefore, one of the first prerequisites of a good selection program is an adequate number of applicants.

The number of candidates it is necessary to consider will vary widely according to the type of position to be filled. A rough indication of the ratio of number of candidates that need to be seen in order to obtain one qualified employee is illustrated by these estimates:

Lower-level jobs may require 15 to 20 applicants to obtain the right man.

Middle-range jobs may require 25 to 50 applicants to get the right man.

Technical jobs may require 50 to 100 applicants to fill the job opening.

Most sales jobs require 100 to 150 applicants to fill the position.

Many executive jobs require 150 to 200 applicants to fill the position.

In order to obtain the requisite number of candidates, it is often necessary to use a variety of recruitment methods, either singly or in combination. For low-level (laboring) applicants, simple media such as signs outside the plant, newspaper advertisements, appeals to present employees, car cards on busses, contacts with private and public-placement bureaus and, in some cases, radio should be adequately productive.

At the clerical level, essentially the same approaches can be used, except that greater emphasis will probably be placed upon the more sophisticated techniques—newspaper advertisements, school-placement bureaus, contacts with agencies and, in some instances, radio.

The Telephone-in Ad

For sales, supervisory, and technical personnel, it is generally better to employ newspaper advertising, supplemented by contacts with trade associations, schools, and agencies. Particularly in the case of salesmen, but also of considerable value in the case of engineers and other technical personnel, is the use of the "Sunday Telephone-in Newspaper Advertisement."

Such an advertisement is placed for publication on Sunday, and the applicant is told not to write but to telephone in on that day between the hours of 10 and 4. This has proved effective because it catches salesmen who are home over the weekend and, since it requires a minimum of effort on the part of the candidate, results in an increase of 200 to 500 percent over the number of responses obtained by write-in methods. Its primary advantage, however, is that it permits the telephone screening of candidates by a series of "knock-out" questions, so that much of the preliminary work can be accomplished on the telephone.

The recruitment of scarce technical personnel, such as electronic engineers and top-level executives, is best handled through professional executive recruiting services that specialize in this.

Assuming, now, that the employer has done a thorough job of recruiting, he should have an adequate number of candidates for the position he seeks to fill. Even at the hourly rated level—to say nothing of higher-rated jobs—it is not economical to spend a great deal of time with each of the candidates brought in by the recruiting program. Consequently, it is necessary to establish a simple but fast method of screening out the obviously unqualified. This screening procedure usually has three basic steps. They are:

1. The use of "knock-out" screening questions on the telephone or with walk-ins. These questions cover what the applicant wants to do; his experience, training, and education; his wage demands; and his availability (willingness to work unusual hours, travel, relocate, and so forth).

2. The use of "sight screening" techniques when the applicant is first seen in order to exclude those whose appearance and manner are unsatisfactory.

3. The use of a written description of the job, which is shown the applicant at the outset (principally for sales and executive positions) to exclude those who are not interested in the position once they learn its nature and are in a position to ask further questions about it.

Narrowing It Down

Knock-out questions will normally eliminate 60 to 80 percent of the applicants. However, not all of those hold forth promise for employment. Therefore six additional screening devices are required.

The first of these is the application blank.

Each candidate is asked to complete a comprehensive personal data sheet, listing his age, marital status, number of dependents, his schooling, military experience, work record, and such miscellaneous items as his home ownership and the amount of insurance he carries. This permits a further finer screening of the candidates, and is used principally to determine the extent to which the candidate can do the job. This second screening will eliminate an additional 5 to 15 percent of the candidates.

For further screening purposes, each candidate is asked to complete a rather comprehensive health questionnaire. Its purpose is to exclude at the outset those candidates who suffer from such physical ailments as epilepsy and tuberculosis, and hence could not pass the company's medical examination. (There is little to be gained by examining in detail the qualifications of candidates who will subsequently be rejected by the company physician.)

Further Screening Techniques

The information on this form provides a basis for an intensive medical examination later by the company physician (after the candidate has proved otherwise desirable). The actual physical examination is normally postponed until the last because it is a time-consuming and costly step in the selection procedure. Furthermore, in the majority of cases, if the candidate suffers from any serious illness or physical limitation, it will be picked up in the interview or on some preceding step, so that it will not be necessary to subject him to the physical examination.

As a fourth screening device, use is made of psychological tests. While, as indicated, tests of this character are not sufficiently broad and comprehensive to serve as the *sole* measure of a candidate's qualifications, they can, however, help measure specific attributes, skills, and aptitudes in the candidate.

As a fifth screening device and as a source of information relative to the candidate's truthfulness, job competence, and performance, as well as his reasons for leaving previous positions, it is recommended that reference checks be made with schools and previous employers. (If the candidate has attended college, he should also be requested to provide a transcript of his school record.) These reference checks are conducted prior to the formal job interview. Whenever possible, to minimize bias, two or more independent reference checks should be made. These are conducted by telephone. Normally such reference checks cover:

—A restatement of what the applicant has stated on his application form to confirm its truthfulness.

—An inquiry into other features of his performance (his industry, ability to get along with others, leadership, job competence).

—An inquiry into his reasons for leaving his jobs and whether or not the previous employer would rehire him (if not, why not).

—An inquiry into such off-the-job factors as the extent to which he may have had financial, domestic, health, drinking, or gambling problems.

These telephone inquiries are far superior to conventional letters of reference (usually personal references are of little value because everyone has at least three friends who will speak well of him) because:

—They are conducted (in the case of employment checks) with the person who knows the applicant best, his immediate superior.

—They are conducted in advance of the interview so that if discrepancies appear between statements on the application and the reports of former employers, they can be clarified in the interview.

—People will often say things they would not put in writing.

—Followup questions can be asked of the school or employer.

—An estimate can be made of the extent to which the candidate and his superior were compatible.

—Since (when possible) more than one independent check is made, bias on the part of the superior is minimized.

The foregoing screening steps, including the knock-out questions, will exclude, with the expenditure of relatively little time on the part of the interviewer, the majority of the more obviously unqualified candidates. At the factory level, at least 75 percent will be excluded; at the clerical level, perhaps 85 percent; and at the sales, supervisory, and executive level, 90 to 95 percent of the candidates.

At the conclusion of these introductory screening steps, not only have the obviously unqualified been eliminated, but a general, factual overview has been obtained of the candidate. Assuming that the candidate meets the initial requirements, he is now ready for the key element of the selection program: the Patterned Interview. Its objective is to:

—Round out and supplement the information already obtained.

—Integrate the data into a coherent whole.

—Provide facts to serve as a basis for an interpretation of the candidate's record and the ascertainment of his character makeup (the totality of his habits), his motivation, and the extent of his emotional maturity (especially his self-reliance and capacity to be realistic in his thinking and acting).

Kingpin of the Procedure

The Patterned Interview is the most critical instrument in the entire selection program. It is also the most time-consuming. It requires from 25 minutes at the factory level to 2½ hours at the executive level. It covers in detail the applicant's:

1. *Work record* from the present back to his first job, with special reference to dates of employment, how he got each job, exactly what he did and what changes took place in his work, his earnings at the start and finish of his employment, who his superiors were and what they were like, what he liked about each job, what he disliked about each job, how much time he lost on each job and why, and why he left each job.

2. *Record in service*, with special reference to: how he happened to enter the service, his rank at entering and leaving, whether he has remained in the reserve, what he liked about the service, what he disliked about it, what injuries or illnesses he suffered, and to what disciplinary action he was subjected while in the service.

374

3. *Schooling,* with special reference to his courses and school activities while in high school, his courses and school activities while in college, the sources of his expenses while in college, the reasons for his failure to complete any courses, and any special or supplementary training he has received.

4. *Early home environment,* with special reference to his parents' marital status (separated, divorced, or widowed), his father's occupation and economic status (was it necessary for him to contribute to the support of the family?), his place in the birth order of the children (was he an only, oldest, middle, or youngest child?), his activities as a boy (church membership, vacation activities, membership in the Boy Scouts, etc.), and his age at leaving home and becoming fully self-supporting.

5. *Domestic status,* with special reference to the dates of his marriage, separation, divorce, remarriage; the manner in which he met his wife and her age, the number and ages of his dependents; the nature of any domestic conflicts which may exist; his membership in church, civic, fraternal, and trade organizations; his hobbies, recreational and social activities; and his drinking habits.

6. *Financial status,* with special reference to his place of residence (does he own, rent, board, live with relatives?), what his home cost, what mortgage or rent he pays, what other property he has, what other sources of income, what debts, what it costs him to live per month, his net worth, whether he contributes to the support of others, whether his wife is gainfully employed, and if so what her earnings are, and how much insurance he has.

7. *Health condition,* with special reference to his health as a child; his health as an adult; specific health conditions such as hay fever, asthma, allergies, and ulcers; his proneness to accidents; and the health of his wife and other family members.

On the basis of this information, supplemented and checked against data from other sources (the knock-out questions, the application, the reference checks, and the psychological tests), the interviewer is now in a position to form relevant judgments concerning the candidate's *will-do* qualifications (the most important elements in making valid predictions relative to what the candidate will do if employed). These findings permit surprisingly valid judgments concerning the applicant's character traits, motivations, level of energy, and degree of emotional maturity. Specifically, these attributes may be defined as follows:

Character traits: The sum total of the applicant's habits. The best basis for predicting what a man will do in the future is to ascertain what he has done in the past. The habits most significant for predicting job success are vocational stability, industry, perseverance, ability to get along with others, loyalty, self-reliance, and leadership.

Motivations: These, while subject to change as his environment alters, can be ascertained as they currently exist by a study of his field of interests, his vocational likes and dislikes, and his life goals. The principal needs of most people are for security, status, recognition and prestige, money, power, competition (an opportunity to win), opportunities to investigate, perfectionism, and opportunities to serve.

Level of energy: This indicates the amount of drive and initiative he may be expected to show. Energy level, like habits, is estimated by observing the push and drive the person has shown in the past and is currently showing.

Emotional maturity: The applicant's capacity to deal with reality on a mature, adult basis and to learn and profit from his mistakes. This is ascertained by observing the extent to which he has given evidence of being emotionally mature in the past. The manner in which emotional immaturity is most likely to manifest itself is in excessive selfishness, disregard for consequences, extreme pleasure-mindedness, excessive passivity and dependence, unwillingness to accept responsibility, excessive tendencies toward wishful thinking, abnormally strong and uncontrolled destructive tendencies, and excessive show-off (exhibitionistic) tendencies.

Editor's Note: Samples of the Patterned Interview discussed here may be obtained from The Dartnell Corporation, 4660 North Ravenswood, Chicago 60640.

The At-Home Interview

Assuming that the data assembled thus far indicate that the candidate is genuinely promising as a candidate for the position, a final step is taken to ascertain the influence of the candidate's off-the-job environment on his probable success (this step is taken only with supervisory, sales, and executive personnel). This constitutes the "home interview." It is designed to permit an estimate of the extent to which the candidate's off-the-job circumstances can be expected to be advantageous to him on the job. (Unfortunately, some home environments have quite the opposite effect, with the result that an otherwise well-qualified man may fail because of adverse home circumstances.)

If a true picture is to be obtained of the applicant's home environment, it is necessary for the interviewer to visit the home in person (obviously always by invitation). It is essential not only that the wife be met and appraised but the entire family be seen. This is because:

—If the wife is seen alone at a dinner or in an office, she is likely to be on her good behavior and not her usual self.

—She may not be the potential source of trouble; some other family member may be.

—When the family is seen on its home grounds, its members express themselves more freely and the "climate" of the home can be more readily assessed.

The home is visited ostensibly to inform the family about the position being offered the candidate (its nature, the opportunities it offers, some of its disadvantages, such as travel or relocation). Of greater importance, however, it is visited to ascertain who is dominant in the home; who handles the family finances, has the final voice in major purchases, has the major use of the family car, decides where vacations are to be spent, decides who is to be entertained and whose relatives visit or live in the home.

It is also important to find out the attitudes of the various family members toward the candidate:

1. Is he admired, respected, and obeyed, or is he a "Casper Milquetoast"?

2. Are his wife and other family members supportive, encouraging, and helpful, or are they negative and disparaging?

3. Is the home appropriate for the candidate's station in life?

4. Are there evidences of friction and tension among the family members?

5. Are there "problem conditions" in the home (illness, retarded children, or other distractions)?

The attitudes of the various family members toward the job are also important. Do they question its suitability for the candidate on the ground that it may lower the family's status, the hours are undesirable, the level of pay is inadequate or the basis of compensation (commission) is unsatisfactory, too much travel is required, relocation may be necessary?

The crucial step in the selection of anyone, regardless of the level or type of position to be filled, is the ascertainment of the degree to which the candidate's qualifications match the demands of the position to be filled as set out in the initial specifications. This step is critical because it is assumed that if the candidate's qualifications match the demands of the position to be filled with reasonable exactitude, the likelihood of his success is good. As is evident from the foregoing treatment, all of the major aspects of an employee's adjustment to his job, as well as the influence of his home environment, must be taken into account if the prediction as to his success is to be valid. Therefore, it is a reasonable assumption that if the candidate fits the position for which he is being considered in terms of all, or even a majority of, the factors, his likelihood of success is good.

On the other hand, because of the number, intangibility, variety, scope, and complexity of the factors which must be taken into account in making predictions of this sort, no simple numerical formula or weighting procedure can be established which can be followed blindly in deciding whether or not—or how well—a particular candidate is suited to the position for which he is being considered. In the final analysis, the ultimate determinant is the soundness of the judgment of the interviewer—how much common sense he can apply in balancing and weighing the various factors.

No selection procedure, no matter how sophisticated, can ever predict infallibly; there are too many uncontrollable variables in the situation. Furthermore, the period covered by the prediction often extends from one to 20 years.

The greatest contribution of this hiring procedure lies, paradoxically, in its value in the prediction of failure. In this respect the efficiency of the technique is very high. The reason for this is that if a candidate is manifestly deficient in any of the attributes required for success in a particular position, he is almost certain to fail. The prediction of success is much more difficult. Most candidates succeed in concealing at least some of their weaknesses. Therefore, in the majority of instances the candidate, if employed, will prove less rather than more satisfactory than originally anticipated. Hence, if the interviewer has any reasonable doubts concerning his probable success, he will do well to exclude him rather than to anticipate (wishfully) that his performance will prove superior to that hoped for.

CHAPTER 24

SOLVING PERSONALITY PROBLEMS

By Robert C. Sampson

There is much more to the mind than intelligence. Whatever a man does, he does it first with his mind. The mind is an organ of survival, the perceiving, feeling, and thinking part of consciousness. Unless it stops thinking—and some minds do—the mind thinks continuously and constantly about what the senses (sight, hearing, smell, taste, touch) feed it.

We use our minds mainly to find ways of getting what we want and to avoid what we do not want, producing thoughts and explanations to justify or cover up our feelings even from ourselves. It is, therefore, also an organ of self-destruction through thoughts kept secret from ourselves because we do not want to know what we are doing. Nathaniel Cantor says:

"To recognize responsibility which has not been met, decisions which have been avoided, and errors which have been committed, is to accept feelings of guilt, shame, and lack of esteem. This is not comfortable and we quickly seek and find ways of disguising, concealing or distorting the actual situation to save face. Whether one is aware of what takes place or not, the fact is that the discomfort is only temporarily resolved. In one way or another it will affect subsequent behavior."

According to Erich Fromm, the mind is the seat of the potentialities characteristic of man, his *power of:* "With his power of reason he can penetrate the surface phenomena and understand their essence. With his power of love he can break through the wall which separates one person from another. With his power of imagination he can visualize things not yet existing; he can plan and thus begin to create." Edward Glover, an English physician, says that the normal personality is not only (1) able to love someone other than himself, but also (2) has satisfactory working capacity, (3) is unhampered by mental conflict, and (4) is free of physical symptoms of anxiety.

Combining the observations of Fromm and Glover we find that a normal personality, in addition to being free of mental and physical symptoms of anxiety, is conscientious (satisfactory working capacity), cooperative (power of love), curious (power of reason), and creative (power of imagination) —qualities that are so necessary for effective executive and management work.

Values of the Mind

Our mind is a marvelous instrument for learning and thinking. It feeds on a tenuous network of values which give both direction and manner of thought and action as well as meaning to our efforts. These values, learned for the most part in infancy, are so much a part of us that the mind is usually a prisoner of our basic assumptions, blind to our biases and prejudices.

As management people, we tend to hold to middle-class values. These vestiges of the aristocracy-serf culture from Western Europe provide us with a set of stereotypes of class, race, religion, and sex which lead us to believe fallaciously that we "understand" others. Nor can we comprehend other values, as, for example, that blue-collar workers have less interest in success (but not in interesting work), in people per se, and in words and emotions as determinants of behavior. (So we try to deal with them and train them in terms of our values and then blame them for not learning.)

Our mind reasons properly; however, it shapes and changes what comes into it so that in the end we believe what we have to believe. Only with great difficulty can we get enough insight into ourselves, unless our values are shaken by some unusual situation, to analyze our own values objectively.

A child finds himself in conflict with himself in accepting

the moral values of his parents. His training is filled with rewards and punishments and lectures. Often with scoldings and threats he is scared into "loving" his parents, the very ones who frighten him.

It is in this atmosphere he gets his ethical preachments: Play the game fairly and may the better person win; never take unfair advantage of your competitor; never tell a lie; always admit your error; win or lose graciously and with a smile—or whatever his parents may do as far as ethical values are concerned.

Important to the development of the child, however, is not what he is told but rather the feelings of the parents both toward the child and toward each other, and their feelings about ethical values and their perceptions of the world and work, people, and power.

Few of us are able to comprehend how feelings, more than words, convey values to the child. A child imitates what he sees, not what he hears. Take manners, for example. A child can be taught to say "please" and "thank you" and convey superior or subservient feelings while using the words. A person who has not had manners drilled into him can often be more gracious even though brusque, because he conveys a genuine feeling in his concern about others.

Integrity is another good case in point. Moral values and codes of conduct are learned from the attitudes, feelings, and behavior of parents, then internalized into a conscience not from their preachments or punishments. And no school, with its stress on competition in tests and grades, the symbols of success rather than excellence itself, can teach manners or moral values in any meaningful way for a value system that is already well crystallized by the time the child enters kindergarten.

Yet the values themselves are in conflict, and a person is always wavering uncertainly, consciously or unconsciously, between such basic values as honesty-dishonesty, generosity-selfishness, cooperation-rivalry, helpfulness-destructiveness, conformity-nonconformity.

382

Emotional Structure

Of the three—mind, values, and emotions—the emotional structure is probably the most pervasive and elusive. We are even more blind to our emotional pattern than to our value system. Emotions are experienced by the mind, including feelings such as fear, anxiety, anger, joy, surprise.

Again, the pattern forms in early childhood, just as the network of values does. Man's self-image triad—the way he sees himself, what he would like to be, and his conscience—is quite different from his real self. The self-image determines how he perceives reality (selective perception makes things he does seem reasonable to him), perceives others, and generates self-fulfilling prophecies about others (based on his values and emotions). Preservation of the self-image is the fundamental motive in human behavior. The self-image, as opposed to the real self, demonstrates how personality traits, values, attitudes, drives, mental habits, and emotions are all inextricably interrelated. The mind is used to take care of emotional needs above everything else.

Of all the emotions, anxiety, with its painful uneasiness of the mind, uncertainty about self, appears to be the most difficult in man's conflict with himself. There are distinct differences between fear, normal anxiety, and undue anxiety or "anxious minds," a term which covers chronic undue anxiety.

Normal anxiety, similar to such states as fatigue and excitement, is part of a reasonably mature personality. Anxiety arises over an intangible threat with no objective basis, fear over something tangible. Fear, a conscious act, causes release of adrenalin, slows down the digestive processes, and dries the mouth, whereas anxiety, often resulting in being restless, upset, uneasy, or tense, increases salivation and gastric secretions.

The stress of both, however, overshadows and hinders thoughts and actions, although there is usually a greater tendency to grapple with fear and resolve it. Normal anxiety also fluctuates within a person between, for instance, indecisiveness and resoluteness, self-doubt and self-confidence.

High-level anxiety is typical of childhood, rising to higher levels during adolescence and declining considerably in adults, when it rises again around sixty.

Anxiety About the Future

Anxiety is normal about such future matters as death, permanent illness, economic security, or new experiences. It is normal for man not to be too concerned about world developments, the state of affairs in the nation, or even in his home town, unless there is a major crisis which threatens him personally.

In spite of our stereotype of ourselves which leads us to proclaim that we are for progress and improvement, it is normal to be apprehensive about change. What will it do to my job? My status? Anxiety is inherent though often not openly expressed or recognized.

It is normal for a member of management to be concerned about his own future. Anxiety regarding loss of job is generally present. As men rise on the management ladder, anxiety increases, not because they occupy more precarious positions but because they have so much more to lose if they fail. No one (except perhaps an incentive expert) maintains any longer that money and other material benefits motivate the manager once he gets beyond his needs for economic comfort, unless he is avaricious.

Struggling to get ahead in his own lonely little world, the manager sees fewer and fewer jobs as he approaches the apex of the management pyramid. He can see the years running out and has heard all too often that death of a career begins at forty. He can no longer believe in the Horatio Alger myth that there is always room at the top for the hard worker and clean liver. The more the ambitious man has of success, the more he wants of it. For every rung that he has climbed up the ladder of success, a drop of a rung or two may appear to him like a drop to the bottom. The place where he is now must be preserved with all its accretions of power, prestige, prominence, and position to fortify his self-image.

Anxiety About the Present

Our Founding Fathers granted that life and liberty were attainable, but viewed happiness as a never-attainable goal. They called it the *pursuit* of happiness. We are still pursuing it, in spite of greater abundance in our affluent society. Jules Coleman, a Yale University psychiatrist, puts it this way:

"Almost everybody—far from being happy—is actually *unhappy* most of the time."

Anxiety about the present includes such matters as sex, ridicule, blame, conflict at home or on the job. Performing new, difficult, or strange tasks may produce serious anxiety. Failure to carry out a task successfully will cause anxiety, no matter how well it may be masked. Harold J. Leavitt makes this observation:

"Less deep but equally important conflicts occur in everyday decision-making situations. There emotional and logical mechanisms get mixed into one another. It often then becomes hard to tell how much of our commitment to a course of action is objective and logical and how much of it is an effort to maintain our psychological balance. For human beings seem to want to maintain balance, to avoid dissonance between mutually contradictory beliefs and ideas. Hence, when we make a difficult decision, we tend to build up our support for our solution and to find more and more reasons for feeling we were right in rejecting the alternative."

The power struggle generates anxiety for a manager. Rivalry and competition make it impossible for anyone to feel secure in his relationships with others in the organization. Superiors and subordinates cannot understand each other. The panic which usually ensues when a mistake is made is testimony to the anxiety. Nor are a manager's relationships with his peers such that he has any self-confidence in his or their cooperation. The power orientation of managing only compounds man's anxiety about cooperation.

Too many people have been forced into the anxiety of insecurity or mediocrity by being given work which has no interest for them. This is not to say that there is not a considerable amount of boredom in every job. Boredom becomes a threat to emotional equilibrium when a man does not have enough important work to do or when he cannot see it as a necessary part of his larger job. The man who avoids doing the routine and the boring is already at the brink of undue anxiety.

Finally, tasks that have been slighted or not completed, deadlines that have not been met, promises that have not been kept, things that need to be done but cannot be worked in, misstatements left uncorrected, misrepresentations about others, white lies, all add up to a heavy load of executive guilt even for the manager with a high degree of self-confidence.

Little imagination is needed to visualize the anxieties, fears, and worries of an insecure executive. Nothing assails the self-image more viciously than the constant accumulation of the emotional trilogy of anxiety, inadequacy, and guilt.

Serious Conflicts

When man's emotions play tricks on him, he is in serious conflict with himself. He cannot communicate accurately and effectively with himself and others. Rather than see himself as part of the world, he tends to regard himself as the center of the world, with everyone else a part.

When he loses his emotional equilibrium, he develops an anxious mind which overreacts to his senses and overshadows his thoughts and actions. With his sense of security gone, he fears fear itself. An anxious mind is a great threat to health and well-being, yet man is unable to acknowledge it to the point of seeking assistance for emotional difficulties. He finds it hard to admit that he does not have full control of all his faculties.

Therefore, when he is told he has an emotional problem, instead of accepting it as an ailment that can be treated, he looks to his "nerves," or to some organ of his body, or fate, or job pressure, or someone else, as the cause of his unsettled state. He generally believes that he can pull himself out of it any time he chooses. The fact that a person cannot get control of himself "if he wants to" is beyond the understanding of most people.

On the other hand, the popular notion that the primary concern of mental health is mental illness, with hallucinations about the past, present, or future, creates the stereotype of the hopeless problem that should be institutionalized. Superstition based on ignorance and fear makes every phrase used to designate emotional problems, such as mental illness, emotionally disturbed, neurotic, psychoneurotic, and psychosomatic generally taboo.

Most of us are too blocked and naive to have any real understanding of emotional difficulties in ourselves or others. In an experiment at the University of Chicago, it is reported that the majority of people offered "natural" explanations for almost every mental disorder presented in short case descriptions.

The tendency to deny the existence of severe mental illness is, according to John A. Clausen, "clearly illustrated in a study of interpretations made by wives confronted by the mental illness of the husband. Grossly psychotic symptoms are often interpreted as reflections of physical illness, as 'understandable' reactions to situational stress or as indications of meanness or weakness in the spouse."

Power Pathology

The thing that makes man the human animal is his capacity for love of another human being. A man has the capacity for love, Fromm's power of love, because he loves himself just enough to accept others and understand them, to trust others and to relate himself openly with them. When a person has lost his power of love, he needs power over others. *Power over* is a weakness, not a strength, for then one must use others to satisfy the needs of his anxious mind. Fromm says:

"Where potency is lacking, man's relatedness to the world is perverted into a desire to dominate, to exert power over others as though they were things. Domination is coupled with death, potency with life. Domination springs from impotence and in turn reinforces it, for if an individual can force somebody else to serve him, his own need to be productive is increasingly paralyzed."

Power over can be an all-consuming, totally unsatisfying pastime in the business world. A man obsessed with business and making money, driven by elements he cannot comprehend, all too often finds that insecurity, illness, loneliness, and unhappiness are at the pinnacle of success. The compulsive power-seeker often comes out on top in the power struggle. According to C. Knight Aldrich:

"The man whose past unsolved conflicts add a 'neurotic' component to his basic 'normal' competitive drive has an advantage over his associate . . . If considerations of integrity, influence and so on balance out, the man with the single-minded devotion to competition wins . . . Home for the neurotic competitor represents either no competition and bores him; a handicap to his competitive efforts, which makes him nervous; or an alternative competitive field."

But even though a man may not be a compulsive success-seeker, he causes discomfort in others for, at a minimum, he is likely not to be understanding of others. He may also be a victim of some sort of compulsive behavior, repeating over and over irrational actions because he is too ridden with anxieties to perceive any other course of action.

Anxious Minds

Manifestations of undue anxiety come in a surprisingly strange assortment and degree of mental and physical ailments. We have our "affections of the spirit," with inexplicable variations in mood, energy, worries, inability to make decisions, and feeling left out of things, to being persistently hotheaded, suspicious, or pessimistic.

Mental manifestations of anxious minds range from the power-seeker to the dependent conformist; the work addict to the lazy man; the single-minded success-seeker to the unambitious; rebel to the reactionary; compulsive liar to the guilt-ridden confessor; or the man who is too insecure to take his vacation to the persistent pleasure-seeker. "Affections of the body" resulting from the anxious mind are more evident. For those of us who claim no greater difficulties than an occasional headache or upset stomach, it is but a short, quick step to physical manifestations of anxious minds such as excess weight, chronic indigestion, heart trouble, or ulcers.

The popular notion that executive pressures take a terrific toll, that the stress and strain of carrying so much responsibility makes executives the prime target for heart attacks, has been upset by two Du Pont doctors.

After a three-year study of 90,000 Du Pont Company employees, they find that the attack rate in the low-salaried management group was 4 per 1,000 per year, and in the top-salaried group 2 per 1,000 per year. The reasons? Top men may get more satisfaction from their jobs, while managers at lower levels with a minimum of responsibility may suffer from feelings of resentment and frustration due to lack of personal fulfillment; and top-executive jobs may go to the better adjusted, whose personality and emotional structure enable them to cope better with life's stresses.

Emotional Threshold

It is not easy to understand just how fragile a man's ego is. Each person has his emotional threshold—his *power over* "boiling point"—established early in the formation of his personality. Although there are instances where some great crisis has pushed a man beyond his threshold, more often than not it results from a myriad of little anxieties, emotional challenges, pitfalls, and road blocks strewn across the path of experience. Multiplying frustrations and disappointments take their toll—the straw that breaks the camel's back.

Depending on the level of the emotional threshold and life's experiences, there are five stages in life that involve sufficient frustration and tension for a person to go through his emotional threshold. The first stage is in the teens, when a person is trying to get free, to rebel from parental restrictions, and faces at the same time the uncertainties of the outside world. If he survives this period without going through his threshold, his next hurdle comes in the middle or late twenties.

389

This is a period of increasing responsibilities, when one is trying to gain a place in the business and social world and at the same time establish a satisfactory adjustment in one's love life. The third critical stage comes when a man starts supervising others.

The fourth stage is about age 45, when a man must face up to the realities of life and can no longer dream about the big success he would like to achieve. This is the period when one must come to terms with oneself and accept the fact that one is not going to go much further up the ladder but must endure the rather drab things one is doing now until retirement.

The last stage comes at retirement, when a man finally comes to face a life where he can no longer make a contribution, or at least for pay, and must with whatever capacities he has left face boredom and loss of place in the world.

Karl Menninger lists five levels of progressively more serious emotional conditions:

1. The first level of departure from normal is "nervousness" with a slight but definite disturbance in "adaptive control" and in "coping."

2. "Neuroses," the second level, "rarely result in resignation or hospitalization" but do require "expensive compensatory living devices, tension-reducing devices. These are painful symptoms and sometimes pain the environment almost as much as the patient."

3. At the third level there are "the outbursts, the attacks, the assaults, and the social offenses which result from a considerable degree of ego failure."

4. At the fourth level "there is disruption of orderly thought as well as behavior; there are demoralization and confusion."

5. The fifth level is "beyond 'psychosis,' in the obsolescent sense, the abandonment of the will to live."

Freud put quotation marks around *normal* by eliminating the black-and-white division between "neurotics" and "normal" people. The insane person is rational and responsible in many areas, and the "normal" person is irrational, inhibited, and anxious in some areas. The Anxious Mind, however, is controlled and impelled by incomprehensible fears.

Because it is unable to put in clear terms what is the matter, time and energy are spent attempting to find answers to vague and fuzzy questions. Chronic emotional distress lays a heavy hand on man's potential, warping his working, cooperating, thinking, and learning capacities. Most common is chronic exhaustion which is not helped by rest or sleep; second is chronic restlessness and inability to concentrate on tasks that require attention.

About two-thirds of the people a physician sees, according to Dr. Menninger, are those whose anxiety is expressed through clinical changes in the organs of their bodies, physical manifestations of an anxious mind. Those with primarily mental manifestations make up a large part of the other third of those who take their complaints to doctors.

CHAPTER 25

THE ART OF LISTENING

By Ralph G. Nichols and Leonard A. Stevens

Management Development Associates of New York, which has as clients some of the nation's largest industries, recently asked the top executives of a large manufacturing plant in the Chicago area to survey the role that listening plays in their work. Later, Edward Walther, a partner of the management firm, went to the plant and at an executive seminar asked, "What do you think about this business of listening?" A series of discussions followed.

"Frankly, I had never thought of listening as an important subject by itself," said one man. "But now that I am aware of it, I think that perhaps 80 percent of my work depends upon my listening to someone, or upon someone else's listening to me."

"I've been thinking back about things that have gone wrong over the past couple of years," said another executive, "and I suddenly realize that many of the troubles have resulted from someone's not hearing something, or getting it in a distorted way."

"It's interesting to me," said one man, "that we have considered so many facets of communication in the company, but have inadvertently overlooked listening. I've about decided that it's the most important link in the company's communications, and it's obviously the weakest one."

The Awakening to Listening

These comments are part of an awakening that is taking place in a number of management circles across America.

Business is hung together by its communication system. This communication, businessmen are frequently discovering, depends more upon the spoken word than upon the written word. The effectiveness of the spoken word depends upon how people listen.

In the business world men are saying that, above all, an executive must know how to listen.

Frank E. Fischer, an official of the American Management Association, points out that management has "talked too much and listened too little."

In a recent issue of the magazine, *Nation's Business,* an article written about the basic skills that future industrial managers will need places listening at the top of the list.

The editors of *Fortune* magazine have been pointing out for a number of years that lack of listening is a major weakness in the business world.

When one such statement was made by *Fortune,* the Bureau of National Affairs polled 160 executives around the country in order to find how they felt about the magazine's contention. Ninety-six percent of the executives agreed that management in general has failed to listen to people.

"All right," says the executive who has decided listening is important, "I am a bad listener. But what do I do about it?"

The answers to this question all too often are dreary echoes of what we heard at school: "Pay attention!" "Open up your ears!" "Try to understand the other fellow!" "Keep an open mind!"

But these recommendations mean little to a busy executive. They indicate nothing about the skill of listening and give no concrete suggestions for its improvement. For the sister communication skills, reading, writing and speaking, ample literature and specific training programs are readily available to the executive, but for listening he has had practically nothing with which to work.

However, this situation is changing. Industrial-training people are developing programs for listening improvement.

Universities and special management-training schools are offering communication courses that include attention to the subject of listening.

A number of industrial firms have developed or are developing listening-improvement programs for their executives. General Electric Company and Western Electric Company, Inc., are two examples.

And there are signs that a considerable body of literature is developing to help management people with listening improvement. This book itself is one step toward building up that literature.

Awareness First

A basic step for improving most skills is taken by building awareness of the skill's importance. The same holds true for training people to listen in business. This skill's importance, of course, varies from business to business, but there are a number of general areas where the need for good listening is universal.

On an elementary level, listening is important in the everyday communication of information. When people in business fail to hear and understand each other, the results are costly.

Not long ago in a major midwestern industrial concern that manufactures parts for heavy machinery, an order from a customer was received by telephone. The order, once it was put into writing, stated that 60 machine parts of a particular kind were to be shipped to a firm almost 1,500 miles away. Each of the parts weighed nearly 100 pounds. They were crated and forwarded to the buyer by railroad freight.

Several days later a representative of the buying firm phoned the manufacturer. "What on earth is the idea?" he asked. "I sent a truck down to the freight depot to pick up your shipment. Before I knew it, our trucker was making several trips. I assumed he could do the job in one trip, but then I learned there were 60 crates waiting for him instead of the six I had ordered. Will you arrange immediately to get the extra ones out of here? They're using up valuable floor space."

The order had been received on the telephone by a man in the manufacturer's sales department. He had relayed the order orally to a person who wrote it down as 60 rather than six. The company paid for forwarding and returning 54 heavy crates and a valuable customer was irritated.

Here is another example of the cost of bad listening:

When a Long Island, New York, plant hired a number of new employees a few years ago to work over a forge used for heating tool steel, a meeting was held to instruct the men verbally in the use of grappling irons. The men used the irons, with removable wooden handles, to hold the steel in the forge. When a man finished with a hot grappling iron, the instructor carefully emphasized that he was to hang it on the wall to the right of the forge. As the irons cooled, they were to be moved to the left wall. And when an employee needed a grappling iron, he, of course, would take it from the left wall.

Shortly after the meeting an employee hung a hot grappling iron on the wrong wall. Another man walked into the room, reached up and grabbed the hot iron. The metal burned and stuck to the skin of his hand. Unable to let go, he fainted and fell, with the grappling iron still stuck in his hand. By the time the man was found, the burns were so serious that they impaired his ability to work for the remainder of his life.

At a hearing after the accident, the man who had placed the iron on the wrong wall swore he hadn't heard anybody say hot irons were to be hung to the right of the forge. However, other employees testified to his presence when the instructions were given. Also, the instructor testified that the guilty man from all appearances had been listening intently while the instructions were given.

This kind of inefficient listening, if it could be tallied in terms of dollars and cents, undoubtedly costs the nation's industry millions of dollars a year. Not only does it cause expensive mistakes such as the two above, but it also creates a fear of the spoken word, which in turn causes businessmen to write out even the simplest of communications.

Bigness Demands More Listening

If we move from the basic information-passing function of oral communication to its broader aspects in industry, we find that listening plays an increasingly important role.

As any industrial firm grows, horizontal communication from one division of the company to another becomes more of a problem to maintain. Each division becomes larger and at the same time, in many cases, more autonomous. Very often the growth of different divisions results in their actual physical separation. Purchasing is on one floor. Sales is on another floor. Engineering is in another building. Eventually the people in the different divisions get out of touch with one another. The situation often reaches the point where the people of one division do not even know those in another.

This kind of separation is a barrier to communication, and it results, all too often, in the right hand not knowing what the left is doing, even within a single company with a single purpose.

Of course, between widely separated divisions there is communication, but it often must flow from one division toward the top of a company and back down into another division. Or it may flow through a coordinating department that keeps in touch with all divisions. These communication routes serve purposes, but still the important people of different divisions do not really get acquainted with one another, and there is a stiffness of communication that dampens the flow of many useful ideas.

On the other hand, when an effort is being made to bring the important people of different divisions together, they get acquainted, and a freedom of communication develops that can be a valuable asset to the entire company.

Here's an example of what can happen when personal oral communication has no way of flowing between separated divisions:

In a northern New York State firm manufacturing replacement parts for farm machinery, a man in the engineering department had an idea for making what he thought would be a valuable improvement in some of the company products. He suggested replacing cotter pins with lock rings on a number of parts. To the people of his department the idea seemed worthwhile, and the changes it required seemed minor. The idea was put into writing and was circulated through other departments of the company. There were no objections, so the change was made.

When the first lock rings appeared on new parts, an executive in the sales department saw the change and ran to the firm's sales manager. "Good lord," he said, "who ever let this get through? Farmers are not going to like these lock rings. If they lose a cotter pin they can replace it with a nail or a piece of wire. If they lose one of these rings, they'll be licked if another one isn't available."

As it turned out, the executive was right. Farmers objected to the change, and the manufacturer eventually had to revert to cotter pins. The whole incident was costly, both in terms of making the changes and in terms of lost customers.

The executive who predicted the trouble said to me recently: "This place has become so large that I seldom meet up with an engineer. Information like that about the cotter pins often seems so insignificant that it gets lost in formal communication channels. But if we could sit down and just chew things over—and, of course, listen to each other—such problems would often be ironed out before they ever got started."

Of course many companies furnish opportunities for the personnel of different divisions to meet and "chew things over." One large company in the Midwest brings its superintendents from various divisions together one afternoon a week. Most of the superintendents are involved in manufacturing different things. Each weekly meeting begins on a formal basis, but later the men are encouraged to talk informally with each other while they have coffee.

"I'll be talking with a fellow I never knew before these meetings were held," said one of the superintendents recently, "and he'll start telling me about how he solved a problem over in his plant. Suddenly I'll wake up to the fact that he's talking about something that has been bothering me for a long time.

By the time I've heard him out, he's told me how to take care of my own problem."

Here's where listening becomes a valuable tool for the smoother functioning of industrial management. Emphasis can be placed on listening at formal meetings designed to strengthen horizontal communication; or at informal gatherings, such as in a company lunchroom where people from different divisions eat; or in routine, day-by-day contacts as they naturally occur between people in separate divisions. Awareness to the value of listening in such situations is the key.

Upward Communication

As an industrial firm grows, and horizontal communication becomes difficult, problems also occur in a vertical direction. When men talk about industrial communication today, the terms "upward" and "downward" communication are often heard. When the top man says something to his subordinates, this is "downward" communication. When the process is reversed, it is "upward" communication.

In a small company these two avenues of communication are fairly simple to control. The head man may even walk among all of his employees, talk with them and listen to what they have to say. But when a company grows large, the two avenues become long and complicated. The distance, measured in numbers of people, between the top man and employees down below plays havoc with communication.

Downward communication has many mediums through which it can travel. There are sound systems for making announcements. Company magazines and newspapers are now flourishing, and the head men can use them for writing messages to employees. Management may write a message to employees, reproduce it and enclose a copy in each pay envelope. There are bulletin boards to convey messages downward. The top men can call meetings of employees and talk to them. Managers can give a message to subordinates with the order to "pass it on down." There are many ways of talking to employees. It has been estimated that industry in America spends well over $100,000,000 a year on downward communication.

But with all the money spent, downward communication is a frustrating affair in most instances. The top man says something, and through one avenue or another the communication goes downward—but then no answer comes back. It's similar to your talking to a person who doesn't react to you. The more you talk the more uncertain you become of what you are saying.

Upward communication in industry has few effective avenues on which to travel. There are suggestion boxes, which pick up messages directed to the top. Meetings of employees are held, but it is difficult to encourage the employees to say what is really on their minds. The top management may conduct attitude surveys to find out what the employees are thinking about, but such surveys usually can't work on a continuing basis to record rapid changes in attitudes, and also the surveys must be exceptionally well conducted to be of real value.

There's one more avenue for upward communication to take, and at first glance it seems like the obvious avenue to use. It has direct communication lines from bottom to top that are operative all the time that business is carried on. The lines work like this: The man working at the bench talks to his foreman, the foreman talks to his superintendent, the superintendent to his boss, and, relayed from person to person, the information eventually reaches the top.

Sounds like a good system, but it seldom works well because the people who form the human communication chain upward often do not know how to listen.

When there is poor listening, this avenue of upward communication fails for at least three reasons:

1. *Without good listeners, people do not talk freely; therefore the flow of communication upward is seldom set into motion.*

2. *However, if the flow should start, only one bad listener is needed to stop the movement toward the top.*

3. *Even if the flow should continue to the top, the messages are likely to be badly distorted along the way.*

The Boss Finds It Hard to Listen

Poor listening habits may be brought into industry by employees who received no training at school in the skills of listening, but once the habits have arrived they may be intensified by the social structure of industry itself.

For example, a boss, because of his position in the chain of command, may find it difficult to be a good listener when a subordinate is talking. Indeed, the boss may give lip service to his being a good listener by announcing: "My door is always open. Walk in anytime." But in spite of the announcement, his ears often remain closed to what is said by subordinates who accept the invitation.

In part, at least, this bad listening situation may result from a boss's assumptions about his position as a leader of men. In our society we talk about how leaders should understand the people under them; therefore leaders should listen. On the other hand, the leader is a man who "should be all-knowing," we say. In order to become a leader he should have "all the answers at his fingertips." If a man in a position of leadership feels strongly about this concept, he is likely to find it difficult to listen to those below him.

Inside himself he may fear that the act of listening will indicate weakness on his part—that as a person who should have all the answers he shouldn't have to listen.

Another barrier to good listening in upward communication is that the upward chain of talkers and listeners contains what we have termed "emotional filters," and inevitably they cause distortion of messages.

"Nearly every man in an organization's chain of command has his ideas of how things should be run," said an official of Western Electric recently. "What the man hears is likely to be interpreted in the light of these ideas."

Often without conscious recognition of the fact, listeners may accept, reject, and change some of what they hear. In industry the social structure of an organization may even accentuate such listening distortion.

400

A foreman hears his men continually discussing a policy that has been put into effect by top management. The men consider the policy unfair. The foreman tries to pass the information upward, thinking that perhaps the policy can be reviewed and changed before a grievance action occurs. But somewhere along the line there's a man who is afraid that his boss won't want to be bothered with gripes coming from the men below. So he changes the message around a little to keep his boss from getting upset.

Eventually the message, through such editing, gets turned completely around and top management hears that the policy is being accepted with open arms by all the men in the plant.

It would be absurd to assume that the lines of upward communication could be made to operate without hitches, but there is no reason to think that they cannot be improved.

If the people involved can be better listeners, if they can understand the importance of listening, the lines of communication will be improved. More and better listening on the part of top management is especially vital to encourage improvement all down the line.

Listening Irons Out Problems

And here we touch upon an important by-product of improved listening on the part of management.

"I try to get our foremen to simply sit down, shut up and listen to their men when problems arise," said the top superintendent of a large Indiana manufacturing plant recently. "I learned from hard experience that listening can be an asset.

"A man will come into your office wanting to talk about something. He has a problem on his mind that's been bothering him for several days.

"Now, if you can let him talk—no interruptions, just let him go—you can almost bet that he'll walk out of your office without a problem. You won't have to say much either. As the fellow talks, he'll slowly show himself what the answer to the problem is, or he might find that he doesn't even have a problem.

"Other times a man will strut up to you. He's mad. He objects to this and he can't stand that. If you start arguing with him, trying to defend yourself or someone else, the man may go away, but he'll still be mad, and probably he'll be back with the same objections turned into monsters.

"In the same situation if you can get hold of yourself and hear the man out, try to understand him, his objections will very often vanish into thin air. Either they didn't exist to begin with, or the man discovers as he talks that the objections are so minor that he shouldn't even be bothering with them."

Dr. Arthur Kellner, a New York industrial psychologist, explains: "When a person with a problem talks to someone who does not listen, his 'self-concept' is challenged and his problem becomes more acute. However, when such a person can talk to an interested listener, his 'self-concept' is preserved, or even enhanced, and he goes away feeling better."

People all up and down the line of industrial organizations need to be heard; they need to feel free to talk to their superiors and be met with sympathetic understanding. This requires, on the part of superiors, a measure of what we call "nondirective" listening. The listener hears, tries to understand (and later shows the understanding by taking action if it's required); but during an oral discourse, the listener refrains from firing his own thoughts back at the person talking.

CHAPTER 26

MANAGING PEOPLE

By Theodore V. Houser

There's one quality I have found over the years to be the trademark of practically every successful executive I have known. It is the ability to manage people effectively.

Sound easy? Perhaps; but it isn't.

No one is born with this ability; it has to be acquired. Yet not one person in 10 thousand has ever taken the trouble to acquire it. That's one of the principal reasons the search for executive talent is such a costly and never-ending one. Skilled managers of people, the backbone of every business organization, are scarce—so scarce, in fact, that some companies will think nothing of outright piracy to get them.

The importance of knowing how to manage people properly and efficiently—how to manipulate them, if you will—has long been recognized by business and industrial leaders. Even in the days of the elder Rockefeller, good management was being defined as "showing average people how to do the work of superior people."

Andrew Carnegie certainly subscribed to this principle. Otherwise, he would hardly have paid the legendary Charles Schwab close to $20,000 a week to produce steel.

"Charlie" was no expert on steel. Others in the company knew more about making it than he. Nor was he a financial genius, nor an administrative wizard.

But he did know how to motivate people, how to stimulate employees so that they would increase production of their own accord.

In the opinion of his boss, at least, Schwab had a "positive genius" for handling people, and for that ability Carnegie, who knew the value of a penny if anyone did, was willing to pay $1 million a year.

What does it take to manage people effectively?

Lots of things. One, of course, is patience. There are any number of times when people will tax your disposition to the utmost. To paraphrase the wry comments of an old friend of mine, John McCaffrey, who headed International Harvester for many years:

The trouble with business is it's full of people. A machine will never go off in a corner and sulk—but people will.

A machine will never make a mistake—but people will.

A machine will never show up late for work, take time off, leave early or argue with the boss—but people do.

It's not the hundred-and-one problems of production and distribution that keep executives awake at night trying to

* * *

The man who can put himself in place of the other man, who can understand the workings of other minds, need never worry about what the future has in store for him.
—Owen D. Young

* * *

solve them; it's the problems of working with people, the human problems of their jobs.

Obviously this job of managing people, which may often cause you sleepless nights, is a big one—perhaps the biggest of all the management arts. Here is what some leading executives have said on the subject, as reported in a countrywide survey by Daniel Starch, prominent consultant and lecturer in business research and author of *How to Develop Your Executive Ability*.

Alfred P. Sloan (General Motors): "The most important thing I have learned about management is that an executive must arouse the individual initiative of the men working under him."

Walter Gifford (American Telephone and Telegraph): "A good executive must be a first-rate judge of men. Perhaps his most important task is the selection of his department heads. If he does this wisely and successfully, a good part of his task is done. Having selected them, he must trust, inspire, and lead them. A successful general is one under whose leadership a staff and the rank-and-file will work and die with enthusiasm."

William L. Batt (former president of SKF Industries): "The ability to influence people is a foremost requirement for every executive."

Granted, then, that business or company management is largely "people management," how do you go about this human engineering job of getting things done most effectively through others, so that willing teamwork will replace grudging cooperation, the "what's-in-it-for-me" attitude?

How to Motivate People

The first principle—in fact, the basic principle—to remember in dealing with people is what Starch rather aptly calls the "law of egocentrism." This is a ten-dollar word for self-interest in our book, but apparently not in Starch's, for he considers egocentrism to be "more inclusive than either self-interest or self-preservation. It indicates the way a person from birth accumulates experience and becomes a personality of his own. All of his experiences are woven into and around that core—the *I* or *ego*. And, furthermore, all a person does and wants must serve that ego in the broadest sense or it will not survive."

Egocentrism is a useful word to remember. The secret of getting others to do as you want them to do lies in your ability to penetrate and understand this hidden world that each of us carries around within himself.

Of course, we are all different from each other in many respects; that's what makes each of us an individual. But at the same time all of us resemble each other in many respects. That's what makes us card-carrying members of the human race.

If it were not for our basic resemblances to one another, which are far more consequential than our outward or superficial differences, it would be impossible to have any understanding whatsoever of others, or even to be able to communicate with them.

It is because we are all basically similar that we can penetrate each other's egocentric or hidden world and understand what makes others tick, so that we can help make them tick "louder" at times—or at least more effectively. To accomplish this it takes two things:

A willingness and ability to put ourselves in other people's shoes and try to see things through *their* eyes—understand their needs, wants, strivings from their own point of view.

The skill in harnessing these needs and desires to departmental and company goals so that they will act as levers to raise performance to a higher plateau. In other words, motivation by an appeal to people's self-interest to become better and more efficient workers.

Why all this bother to treat employees with kid gloves? They're paid to do their jobs, aren't they?

Certainly they are. And they'll do them. But they'll do them better, more quickly, more accurately, and more willingly when they feel they have a personal interest or stake in what they are doing. That's human nature.

Therefore, given the proper motivation, they'll be more likely to put in a little more effort, "walk that extra mile," than they would otherwise. It's that type of teamwork that can make one department of a company shine above all the others.

The responsibility for performance like this is the best indication there is that the head of the department is cut out for higher things.

Motivating employees by appealing to their own "selfish" self-interests is nothing more than common sense. It is the most practical way to raise their production and efficiency. It is more potent even than monetary rewards as a means of getting the work out—right.

406

The Craving for Recognition

There's not a single one of us who doesn't "die a little" if he fails to receive proper recognition when he deserves it. As the noted psychologist, William James, put it, "The deepest principle of human nature is the craving to be appreciated."

Even when we ask for criticism, what we are really looking for—or hoping for—is praise and recognition.

Praise (as distinguished from flattery), when judiciously and properly administered, is probably the most effective way to motivate anyone, whether he is a vice-president or a young apprentice. Even the most crabbed or sour-faced person thrives on it, whether he shows it or not (don't let appearances deceive you).

No one is going to do a better job merely because he is expected to—or is being paid to.

There is only one way to get a person to do a better job, and that is by motivating him to, by appealing to his self-interest, his ego. One of the most effective ways is through encouragement, recognition of his accomplishments, praise. They're as necessary to morale as sunshine is to flowers. A character in one of Shakespeare's plays may not have been far wrong when he said, "Our praises are our wages."

Most of us firmly believe that people, like children, will sometimes become conceited or bigheaded if praised. As one prominent industrial psychologist points out:

"This is absolutely incorrect. It is discouragement, belittling, and faultfinding that produce conceit."

The reason we have such mistaken notions about the "dangers" of praise and encouragement, we are told, is that we are all so eager to have it entirely for ourselves so as to feed our self-esteem that we "selfishly conclude it is bad for others. Some even like to pretend they are so modest that they do not want the honest praise that is due them."

Praise, then—provided it is not indiscriminate and therefore meaningless—is one of the most potent ways to appeal to people's self-interest in making a *job* of their jobs. To be most effective, however, it should be directed at the performance, not the person himself.

CHAPTER 27

HANDLING TENSIONS

By Murray Morison

Tensions can be your greatest force for good or one of your most efficient means of self-destruction.

How well you learn to control and direct this force will spell the difference.

In this chapter you will learn:

1. *Just what tension is.*

2. *How this force can affect your life for good or evil.*

3. *How you can control and direct your tensions to best serve yourself.*

First, let's go back a few hundred thousand years. Despite some of the more obvious unpleasantries, life for man then was quite simple. You could easily tell the good from the bad. And you knew what to do about it.

You would get up from your couch of sticks each morning, crawl to the mouth of the cave and peer out. There was your world, all clear and simple. The good—the game for you to capture and eat for breakfast; or the bad—the saber-toothed tiger looking for *you* for his breakfast.

Not only was your world simple but so were decisions. You had to decide only two things, whether to run or to fight.

Freud would have been happy. If you saw a cave woman you liked and if you were fast enough, or she clever enough to let you, you had only to whack her on the head and drag her into your cave.

In those days tension was all good. It quickly equipped the body for maximum fight or flight. Tension stopped the activity of the stomach and pumped the large quantities of blood normally used for digestion from the stomach into the structural muscles. Adrenalin was poured in large quantities into the blood stream, glucose was more rapidly metabolized, our hearing, eyesight, and even thinking became more acute. In short, we were quickly readied for flight or fight, and as we took either action, these chemicals were quickly burned up.

Tension then was a wonderful mechanism—essential to our survival.

What went wrong? Something nature never figured on happened. We became civilized, social inhibitions set in. If you didn't like a man, it was no longer socially acceptable to walk up and club him. Now, instead of tension being used up in a good healthy fight, it turned inward and started to gnaw at our bodies.

The advent of the industrial revolution was also the advent of tension diseases: hypertension, nervous headaches, ulcers, gastritis, coronary artery disease, as well as all the other "civilized" diseases.

Dr. Paul Dudley White, world-famous heart specialist, was asked what modern diseases he considered the most damaging. Without hesitation he replied, "Tension."

"Tension?" replied the interviewer. "I didn't know tension was a disease."

"Tension," replied Dr. White, "I consider a 'civilized' disease, and it is the primary, secondary, or contributing factor behind such killers as coronary artery disease, heart disease, stroke, hypertension, ulcers, and almost all emotional disorders. It has even been indicated to be a primary factor in such time-destroyers as the common cold and headache."

In a report in the *Journal of the American Medical Association,* it was found that 70 percent of all patients treated in the larger medical centers in the United States were suffering from conditions either caused by uncontrolled tension, or aggravated by it.

What can tension cost you? Quite possibly your life.

What does it cost business in absenteeism, wrong decisions, general inefficiency? Untold millions of dollars.

At the Illinois Bell Telephone Company, a study was made of the common cold. Thirty-three hundred girls were interviewed about food, sleep, and recent emotional experiences that could have caused tension. The one common denominator for 90 percent of the 3,300 girls was that from 12 to 36 hours before the first symptoms of their colds, they had had traumatic emotional experiences that had caused tension.

What sort of experiences? Some of the girls had had disturbing fights with their husbands or boy friends. Simple tension? Sure, but the cost to the telephone company over a year was thousands and thousands of dollars in lost time.

Just What Is Tension?

Tension is the mental-physical product of unresolved emotional conflict. Without proper release tension builds up—becomes cumulative. Cumulative tension is always harmful.

Cumulative tension affects the small microscopic nerves called fibrils that control the capillaries, causing them to constrict and so decrease the blood supply to our entire body. Tension affects the hormonal output of the endocrine glands, increasing the output of some hormones and decreasing the output of others, and generally raising havoc with the chemical balance of the entire body.

This chemical imbalance, which is the direct result of unresolved tension, is unquestionably the primary or contributing cause of almost all our modern diseases, both mental and physical, even to the extent of lowering the body's resistance to contagious diseases. Unresolved cumulative tension sets in motion a cycle that is both psychosomatic and somapsychic ("mind-body" and "body-mind"). For example, the ulcer-prone executive: Tension causes spasms of the stomach wall (psychosomatic); this causes pain, the executive feels the pain and starts to worry (somapsychic); this worry causes more spasms, which cause more pain, which causes more worry.

410

And so, on and on in an ever-increasing spiral of ill health which will lead eventually to complete incapacity or death.

I recently asked four leading gastroenterologists, "If your ulcer patient could and would follow your instructions, and were free of all social restrictions, what treatment would you prescribe?"

Three of the four said, in effect, "Get a new wife and a new job," and the fourth said, "Leave everything and become a beachcomber on some Pacific island."

The facts are, however, that few of us can or are willing to take these drastic measures. What then? The answer, I think, is obvious. *Learn to control and constructively direct your tensions.*

How? Dr. George S. Stevenson, consultant to the National Association for Mental Health, has said: "Everyone experiences tensions in appropriate circumstances. It is the proper use and direction of these everyday tensions that drive so many of us to strive for perfection and accomplishment. They are the emotional motivating forces behind persistence and determination. Tensions mobilize the individual's mental and physical forces for defense against real or imagined threats, and are basic, indispensable, self-protective measures."

Establishing Healthy Habits

There are many roads to the control of tension. Remember, though, none of them will get you there without the deliberate formation of new and healthy habit patterns on your part.

It is an accepted fact among gastroenterologists that most ulcer patients can be cured by the simple procedure of hospitalization. Take a patient away from his environment and his ulcer heals itself. The trouble is, once he returns to his home and office, the ulcer also returns.

What then is the answer?

The answer, I think, is obvious. We must learn how to control and direct our tensions. As psychiatrists have pointed out, "Everyone has tensions, and whether or not they become bene-

411

ficial or damaging depends on the individual's ability to control and direct this primitive force."

A few nights ago I was having dinner with some close friends and, as often happens, the conversation turned to business and a mutual acquaintance—Vince. We all agreed that Vince was an exceptional businessman. In a matter of only a few years he had moved from a tiny boat-brokerage business operating out of his home to one of the largest boat-building companies in the country.

"The amazing thing about Vince," one of my friends commented, "is that he operates best when he's backed against the wall. He makes his greatest gains when things are the darkest. When other men might take to drink, Vince comes alive, his decisions are brilliant, he doesn't seem to need or want sleep, and what is most amazing, his enthusiasm becomes contagious and his whole organization surges ahead. Then, as soon as things become financially secure, he seems to go into a mental slump and everything grinds to a halt."

Vince is a man I consider a "tension addict." He is a man who has not only learned to get the maximum constructive stimulation out of tension—but craves this stimulation. As in primitive days, Vince finds tension essential to his survival.

Like Vince, you can learn to make beneficial use of tension. You, too, can eliminate your slumps by developing good mental habit patterns. One of the first steps in controlling tension is to try to develop a more tranquil state of mind.

Dr. Alfred Adler describes the tranquil personality as having a psychological balance wheel, the spokes of which he calls love, work, play, and worship. Too much or too little of any of these will throw the wheel out of balance and bring on emotion tensions.

Dr. David Fink, in his book, *Release from Nervous Tension*, says:

"Tranquillity comes from personality growth through the assimilation of new experiences. When a person experiences something he cannot understand or accept, or something he cannot incorporate into his established system of thinking or

412

feeling, he cannot digest this new experience and cannot assimilate it. This, then, becomes a traumatic, damaging experience—damaging not in itself but in the way one reacts to it. There are any number of 'normal' tension-causing reactions to a new situation. You may behave as if it had never happened, you can react by retreating from all new similar experiences, or you may react with habits of hostility. One thing, however, remains constant and that is, until the traumatic experience is reincorporated and assimilated, the result is internal conflict and nervous tension."

Tranquillity, we might point out, is the positive result of learning to control tension. In our review of Ed's experiences that cooperated in building tension, we covered these six principles for preventing the formation of cumulative tension:

1. Allow extra time.
2. Recognize your limitations, and either change them or learn to live with them.
3. Avoid tension-causing situations.
4. Learn to say "no."
5. Departmentalize your life—take one job at a time.
6. Whenever possible pick associates—both business and personal—you find stimulating.

As we have also noted, subconscious conflicts bring about chemical changes in the body that create tension. Tension that is not released through the natural outlets of "fight or flight" can build into a paralyzing disease, with the all-too-common symptoms of muddled thinking, illogical decisions, increased irritability toward your associates, plus the cumulative and dangerous physical symptoms that cause or contribute to all of our "civilized diseases." As we have further seen, we cannot consider the mind and body separate entities because of their tremendous influence on each other.

CHAPTER 28

GETTING ALONG WITH SUPERIORS

By Stanley Arnold and Ray Josephs

No matter how high a man goes in the business world, he is never truly his own boss. There is always someone to whom he is accountable—whether that person is a general foreman, department head, division officer, vice-president, president or chairman of the board. And even the latter must answer to the board of directors, the stockholders, and, in turn, to the community for his business decisions.

Even though you are now well on your way up the "ladder," you must continue to sell yourself to your boss, so that he can sell you to his boss. And in order to do this effectively, you must continually sell yourself to your subordinates, your fellow executives, your customers, your suppliers, your community and even your family.

Such a challenge can be a tremendous stimulant, the "plus" ingredient that adds spice and variety to your career—or it can be a burden and a drag on your performance if you do not know how to meet it.

You may have reached your present position by seniority, by having done an outstanding job in your previous assignment, by being in the right place at the right time, or by long-range planning, in which your current job is still several rungs away from the top.

Of the hundreds of successful executives we have encountered as consultants to top management, probably less than 1 percent reached their goals through sheer luck or family connections. They had mastered the techniques of thorough preparation, determined perseverance and good human relations.

They knew early in their careers that the higher you go, the tougher the competition is, and the better prepared you must be to sell yourself to all of your many publics, by no means the last of whom is your boss. So let's put them under the microscope for a few minutes.

How to Size Up Your Boss

To sell yourself to your boss, you must know what type of person he really is and how best to deal with him. You may assume you know him "inside out," without realizing that underneath he is very different. The average boss's on-the-job personality may be hidden by a variety of outward characteristics.

Do you recognize your boss, by any chance, in any of these descriptions? If you do, are you approaching him successfully —or in a way guaranteed to antagonize him?

The *dominant boss* is self-confident in manner; makes quick, unexplained decisions; rejects backtalk and suggestions. He can't tolerate half-way acceptance, or "Yes, but . . ." answers; wants convincing enthusiasm and full support.

Be subtle in your dealings with this type of boss. Don't fight back and don't force him to admit mistakes. Roundabout is quicker than full-speed-ahead with him. Watch personal confidences, or he'll rule your personal life, too.

The *administrator* is great on leadership, planning, coordination and direction; wants his staff to follow through explicitly. Beating last year's quotas has top priority with him, and if you can suggest improvements, especially based on other departments' successes, he's amenable.

Harmony and cooperation rate high in his book, even at the expense of ability. Show him you can get along with the team, and you'll win his admiration.

The *schoolteacher* type usually puts you on your own; takes mistakes, especially by beginners, calmly; would rather praise than criticize. He can be either easygoing or a stern disciplinarian if occasion warrants.

415

A good pupil delights him. Don't give him fast answers. Let him see that your ideas are the result of his guidance. A wonderful trainer, he can be a tremendous help in your advancement as one of his "pupils."

The *specialist* is given to long technical discussions, is precise, literal and sets high standards. He's more interested in results than credit, but seems to fear big projects, preferring familiar techniques, tools, and details. Distrusting sudden inspiration, he sometimes lacks human understanding and common sense. Often more impressed with how a thing is done than whether it works.

To get along with this kind of boss, often found in technical firms, take a cue from him. Concentrate on details, learn to express yourself clearly in frequent memos, preferably outlined in 1-2-3 fashion.

The *social type* sometimes flatters others into doing his work, is bored by routine details, loves meeting people under all circumstances. To him, who you know may be more important than what you know. Often up to his ears in office politics, he may surround himself with fair-haired boys. He's frequently out on three-hour lunches or client dinners, takes business hangovers as an essential part of his job.

You'll spot him more often in sales and contact departments. Take the opportunity to learn all you can; assume additional responsibility. Build him into a friend; assure him that his ability to make friends is indispensable, and his regard for you will, no doubt, increase.

The *worrier* refuses to trust anyone with his work, is always keyed up and overburdened, can be unreasonable about neatness and promptness. Subconsciously, he feels that his limitations may become apparent. Hence he refuses to delegate, clings to familiar red-tape methods, looks for new ways to make himself feel important. A loaded briefcase is his constant companion. He regards anyone who shuns evening and weekend work as a clockwatcher.

Never let him suspect you are trying to take over any of his work. Do things his way, and let him infer that you know how burdened he is. Do more than you're paid for to prove your dedication—and be sure he knows it.

The *seniority* type unquestioningly obeys all rules, knows the job by heart, frequently mentions how things "used to be done." Since his position is largely due to lengthy service, he prefers conformity to change. Security, pensions, and retirement are major concerns. His admiration for steady pluggers is genuine, but he distrusts brilliance or flashiness.

Let him teach you all he can about the company—it will do you no harm to listen, and may do you much good. Seek his advice, encourage him to feel paternal toward you, and he'll push your career.

The *"two-way"* boss can help your career, despite his occasional use of sarcasm and criticism that is hard to take. Lacking self-confidence, he assumes a domineering attitude toward subordinates, and defers to higher-ups. Big talk and pretense build his ego. He wants credit without too much responsibility and is obsessed with a fear of failure.

Use praise whenever possible to build his confidence and give him support. Tell him how his suggestions produced your ideas, giving him credit even when he may not deserve it. Show him you understand him, and he will respond.

In analyzing your boss, you may reach the not uncommon conclusion that he is a combination of several types. But remember, no matter what his idiosyncrasies, a sympathetic understanding of his problems can lead you to fresh thinking and a better adjustment. Developing this empathy is essential in selling yourself to the boss.

Five Ways of Talking Back to the Boss

Getting along with the boss doesn't mean being a yes-man, and you can perform one of your most valuable services as a manager or executive by learning how to disagree with him when you are convinced it is essential.

Every boss is looking for ways to improve company profits, increase individual and group efficiency, keep subordinates on the ball without unfair pressure, and prove to his own superiors that real progress is being made under his leadership. Thus he cannot afford to reject ideas that might help achieve these goals. He must listen to your ideas, no matter how much they may disturb him. Here are five ways you can approach him with suggestions or requests:

1. *Adopt his viewpoint.* Present your ideas from his point of view, even if your suggestions are diametrically opposed. Be sure to stress the fact that you are not criticizing him or his judgment.

2. *Keep it impersonal.* No one likes to be criticized in a way that reflects on his personality, habits, or character. Don't risk hitting the boss's sensitive spots and losing the argument. Analyze your suggestion from all angles first and present it so that he can't possibly think you're suggesting a "head examination."

3. *Time it properly.* Mother had it down pat when she fed Dad his favorite dinner before breaking the news of a domestic crisis. Timing is a matter of good office tactics, speaking up when your statements will appear in the best light.

4. *Use the right channels.* Sometimes it's a matter of making yourself heard when you're stuck in a quiet backwater, rather than some disagreement with the boss. Since every company has its hierarchy, it's a waste of time to take your case to the wrong person. Try asking for advice, if the one who can help you the most seems inaccessible. This is a difficult approach to resist, but be sure your prospective adviser understands that you have valid reasons for choosing him for the role.

5. *Be honest.* Everyone wants job satisfaction, but do you really know what you are "griping" about? Don't mistake a symptom for the cause. A pro and con listing of the good and bad things about your setup will reveal exactly where the true cause of dissatisfaction lies—and may even suggest a totally different solution.

Once you've nailed down the facts, don't clutter up your request with a lot of irrelevancies (about what other management people are getting or personal reasons for needing a raise, for instance). Your boss wants a level-headed, self-confident approach from his executive personnel as well as other employees—and it's amazing how rarely he gets it.

CHAPTER 29

COMMUNICATING EFFECTIVELY

By E. J. Thomas

It was only a few decades ago that many companies felt it "wasn't good business" to tell the public what they were doing.

Gradually, over the years, a new trend set in. Corporations discovered they were being judged not only by their products but by their "public image." And the people making this judgment were all-important—they were the customers.

This brought about a new mood in American business, and it was all to the good. The job of explaining how business and industry were contributing to the country's economy began to receive greater attention than ever before.

This new "inform-the-public" attitude of many corporations opened the door to wider and deeper public understanding of the problems of running a business. It also imposed an added responsibility on business leaders: the need to give stockholders, employees, customers and the communities in which they did business a clearer picture of their operations, goals, and prospects for the future.

Today, effective communication is a vital part of the life-blood of a corporation, standing shoulder to shoulder with such important functions as production, sales, finance, research, and development. In fact, communication plays an essential role in determining how successful these functions will be; it is the "cement which binds a company together." Without it, departments and divisions begin pulling in different directions.

Stop the free flow of ideas and information within a company; stop the transmission belt which conveys the company's policies and goals to its workers, shareholders, and customers, and the company will eventually stagnate and die.

If I were asked to define effective communication, I would begin by saying what it is not. It is not propaganda. It is not distorting facts to fit a company's policy. It is not an off-and-on device which is used to brainwash employees or mislead the public.

The best definition I know is, *the art of informing and persuading others*. And we must make sure that what we say mirrors our day-to-day practices and policies, whether we are trying to influence large or small groups, the public, or our own personnel. For the hard fact is that the public image of a corporation—both locally and nationally—is built on the foundation of its actions, and this includes producing a product which delivers value and service.

It is no secret that communications can be effective only in an atmosphere of trust. If a company is autocratic, if it reports facts dishonestly or fails to keep faith with its workers, it will soon find itself the victim of "corporate arthritis." Production delays, dwindling sales, and a general breakdown in company performance will follow.

If, over a long period of time, a company has been indifferent to the interests of the public or its workers, it will have an uphill struggle to win their support and confidence. On the other hand, a company that has established a reputation for honesty and trustworthiness, for fair dealing with its employees and customers, will have no trouble getting people to believe its statements.

I'm a strong believer in personal contact, especially in employee relations. Through the years at Goodyear I got to know thousands of our people on a first-name basis. And the better I got to know them, the more I thought of them not as Goodyear employees but as heads of families, with a real stake in the future of our company.

A cheery "good morning" to them is not enough. An infrequent pat on the back isn't, either. Nor can a company forget about its employees all year and then expect to win their confidence at the annual picnic.

To get the best out of our associates, we must know their problems and aspirations and take a genuine interest in them. We must let them know continually that their contributions are vital to the overall effort.

To keep the channels of communication open at 68 Goodyear plants in this country and abroad, almost every method and medium are used—frequently. They take in the entire range of communications—a broad spectrum of internal and external publications including newspapers, magazines, and newsletters; personal contacts ranging from informal talks to

*   *   *

How many communicators really understand the basic underlying principle of communication? How many well-conceived, well-planned programs of communication really consist of a one-way stream of information that inundates, and frustrates, and frequently irritates the poor individual on the receiving end? Remember, unless you are receiving as well as transmitting—unless you are getting a playback—you really aren't communicating at all.

—D. G. Mitchell, president, General Telephone & Electronics

*   *   *

staff and policy meetings at various levels; training and orientation sessions; a constant flow of releases to outside news media; and numerous other methods.

This, of course, is the machinery we use in telling our company's story. But communication is more than this. It always gets back to people. It is someone listening to what is being said, or someone reading what has been written. So we must be careful that what we say is clear and covers the subject fully, or people will grasp only a part of what we mean to say.

There are many myths about communicating with employees which still linger in the thinking of a few. And since it is employee communications that I wish to stress particularly in this article, let's look at one of these outmoded myths right now.

421

It is part of the folklore of American business that most workers aren't interested in their company. This myth has been shattered by surveys which show that most employees want more information relating to their role in the company. Their primary interests, of course, center around the wages they earn, the hours they work, vacations, hospitalization plans, and retirement programs.

But their curiosity doesn't end there. They want to know more about things which could affect their advancement in the company and the security of their employment—such as new plants, new products, and promotional opportunities. Moreover, they want more information about the history of the company and its organizational makeup.

Fortunately, most companies today are not only willing but eager to supply this information. For we have discovered there is a direct tie-in between job satisfaction and productivity.

Makes Him a Better Worker

I found that the more an employee knows about our company—the better he understands its goals, its corporate ideals, its background, and its place in the community—the better worker he is.

Why is this? It is safe to assume that if a man feels he is part of a common effort—that he is participating not passively but dynamically—he will be a loyal employee. This kind of employee is the best salesman a company can have, both inside and outside the plant.

I am reminded of an incident that occurred when I was taking some prospective customers through one of our Akron plants.

We were walking down an aisle when a fork truck approached, and its driver, a fellow who stands six feet four, yelled, "Get out of the way you so-and-so, or I'll run you down."

A look of surprise crossed the visitors' faces.

"You may be big enough," I said, "but I don't think you will do it."

422

We had gone only a little way when the driver returned.

"Eddie," he said, "I got to thinking that maybe these people are customers and might misunderstand. They probably don't realize I've known you for a long time and that I've always talked to you this way."

Then he turned to my guests and said, "If you are customers, I'll tell you we make the best tires there are—and if you buy any other kind you are just damn fools."

Well, we got the order, and while we'll never know for sure, that truck driver may have provided that intangible something that made the sale.

We are all aware that this kind of loyalty can be translated into greater productivity. This is reflected in better craftsmanship in the plant, in greater enthusiasm in the laboratory, in a spirit of competitiveness in the sales field, and in stronger leadership at the executive level.

The important thing here is that an employee identifies himself with his company, that he is made to feel a part of it, and that he is not just a number, an automaton operating a computer or some other piece of machinery.

Those of us in management have the responsibility for bringing out the best in others, regardless of the job. We also have the obligation to see that the people associated with us have an environment in which they can be happy—because this is where they spend most of their waking hours.

When people are achieving some measure of their potential, and are happy people, they are good employees, and they are making their company and their associates look good, too. It's quite evident, therefore, that if you improve a worker's morale, strengthen his sense of belonging, you create a cooperative spirit that results in better work.

The reverse is also true. When the communication machinery of a company becomes rusty, when workers feel "left out" and unimportant, productivity is bound to suffer. If production slumps for no visible reason, it may be time, therefore, to consider overhauling your company's policies and your entire employee-communications program.

Time and time again I have found that too many people forget communication is a two-way process—that it involves listening as well as talking. Unfortunately, however, the art of listening is often pushed into the back seat when the subject of communications is brought up.

It goes without saying that those in management must do a certain amount of talking so that orders and policies can be set into motion. But we should never stop listening, asking, and picking up fresh ideas that can be used in current or future programs. This means that we must encourage people to communicate *upwards* as well as downwards.

It has been my experience that ideas and opinions are best exchanged in an atmosphere unhampered by suspicion or embarrassment. One of the main things all of us must remember is to put people at ease. If they "tighten up," if they're not themselves, we'll never really communicate with them.

As soon as we do get people to "open up," therefore, by making them feel at ease, it's up to us to do our own share of listening.

The importance of developing listening skill was summed up by Dr. Earl Planty, executive counselor for the pharmaceutical firm of Johnson & Johnson, who said: "By far the most effective method by which executives can tap ideas of subordinates is sympathetic listening in day-to-day informal contacts within and outside the work-place. There is no system which will do the job in an easier manner . . . Nothing can equal an executive's willingness to hear."

No one should delude himself, however, into thinking that listening is easy. It isn't. The overrelaxed listener merely appears to tune in. He listens with half his mind. He is thinking about something else, and much of what is said is lost.

The skillful listener trains himself to "tune in completely," to find out if the speaker has any worthwhile ideas, ideas that can be harnessed to a workable program.

The half-listeners are the ones whose departments are continually plagued with unnecessary or false crises, where nothing ever seems to run smoothly. Eventually, they will be let out or shunted to a job far from the mainstream of important activity. This is the price they pay for being unreceptive to others' ideas.

Listening to people is a vital part of any business. I have found that if there is a promotion to be made or an opening to be filled, you can be pretty sure of making the right choice if you have kept your ear to the ground.

One thing we should not forget is that supervisors are a major link in the communications chain between management and employees. They are usually the ones who will explain the policies made by management.

"First-line supervisors and foremen," said L. W. Tate, vice-president of the Dallas Railway and Terminal Company, "are in the best position to feel the pulse of the workers in their daily contacts on the job."

Companies operate under a handicap when their executives listen only for what they want to hear. Because they have never learned to become good listeners, they will never become good communicators. How many men do you know who make a decision first, then try to justify their reasoning? They are opinion-dodgers, men who have never learned to benefit from the stimulus of fresh ideas.

If we want to communicate effectively with others, the one guidepost we must keep in mind is clarity. The best criterion for good communicating is: Is it easy to understand?

In this day of increasing complexity in the business community, there is a tendency to overwork long, technical words. Usually they serve only as roadblocks to understanding.

If a communicator is to do his job well, he must stay clear of high-sounding words. He shouldn't be afraid to use "shirt-sleeves" English.

He must be willing to call a road a road, not a "vehicular artery."

If we are to avoid muddied communications, the use of everyday English should not be limited to workers in the plant, but used when we are talking to associates. In today's fast-moving world it is important that we "de-fog" our language, that we speak in clear and simple terms to get to the heart of the problems that face us.

One myth that has come down through the years is that a direct, simple explanation of serious or even profound matters is "talking down." The King James version of the Bible, one of the most readable books ever written, shows how foolish this is.

Simplicity Enhances Understanding

Actually, we are not "patronizing" anyone when we put an idea in simple and vigorous words. To the contrary, it shows we are anxious to make our points quickly and clearly.

How do we achieve this clarity—the ability to speak and write straightforwardly? If we stop to remember that effective communication consists of relaying sharply defined ideas, the battle is half won. This means organizing our thoughts before we speak or write. In order to do this, we must first get the facts straight. Then we must arrange them in logical order. Finally, and perhaps the most difficult part, we must convey them clearly and concisely.

Don't Be Afraid to "Be Yourself"

Here I would advise everyone—from the district manager in Boston to the newly hired trainee—to use his own language; the language he uses at home and in the car pool. Those who are timid about "being themselves" when they write letters or memorandums should remember that everyone has some language talent, their own way of using words effectively. And they should put this talent to work.

By and large, those of us who want to communicate more effectively would do well to heed the advice of Dr. Rudolf Flesch, who admonishes us to use:

The familiar word in place of the unfamiliar.

The concrete word in place of the abstract.

The short word in place of the long.

The single word in place of a circumlocution.

We must remember that fancy language does not cover up or excuse fuzzy ideas, decisions or actions. It results only in additional vagueness.

There is no mystery about good communication. Neither is there a quick "Open Sesame," approach. Leo Rosten, the author who was named "Communicator of the Year" by the University of Chicago alumni recently, said in his acceptance speech:

"The communicator is the person who can make himself clear to himself first. Most people are not clear because they really don't know what they are trying to say . . . Good style

*   *   *

Despite the great amount of unanimity as to the importance of effective communications within a company, much of it has been left to chance and taken for granted. The problem seems always to be in someone else's backyard. "Our men always know what's going on . . . We're a small outfit; communication with us is no problem." And so forth.

It was while working in one of these "no problem" companies that a salesman discovered, after being on the road for five weeks, that for the last three weeks his plant had been closed down two days out of each week. And who told him? Right—a customer!

— *Walter E. Brunauer, sales executive*

*   *   *

is not much more than clean, clear thinking. And the person who retains that stubbornness which says, 'I don't understand that,' learns how to make it clear to himself and then make it clear to others."

Mr. Rosten made several other observations executives would do well to take note of. In his opinion, the best communicators are those who have managed to retain what he calls their infantile directness, "who have resisted the crippling effects of education." He said the effective communicator manages to retain a stubborn resistance against the "confusion and baloney" of his time.

I'm convinced a company will slip into low gear if it confines the exchange of ideas to the strict pyramid of an organizational chart. You can't put communications in a straitjacket and hope to keep a corporation on the move.

Informal lines of communication are just as important as formal lines, for it is in the relaxed conference, free of ceremony, that some of the most worthwhile ideas are spawned.

We must keep our door open to associates and others if we want to take advantage of new blood and the challenge of different opinions. The executive who remains aloof, who makes his own rules and brooks no dissent, will create nothing more than a corporate group that seeks only to agree rather than to offer productive ideas.

In short, there is no substitute for personal contact to strengthen a company's cooperative effort and sharpen its competitive spirit.

But as the size and scope of an enterprise increase, so does the task of maintaining direct and effective communications.

A counterpart of this dilemma may be seen in the governments of large nations. As the machinery of governments becomes increasingly complex and departmentalized, the greater the chances are that directives will become distorted or watered down as they filter through the various levels of command.

So it is with business. The more departments and administrators there are, the more difficult it is to keep the channels of communication open.

What can business leaders do to unclog the lines?

First, as a company grows in size, it must work overtime to keep information flowing freely, not only up and down the line of management, but out to those in the field and shop. We must keep in mind that decisions, ideas, and directives lose much of their usefulness and vigor because of delay.

Second, we must strive to communicate in the most direct way, even if this means that on some occasions formal organizational channels must be ignored.

And third, we must remember that effective employee communication must not rely exclusively on letters, memos, the plant newspaper, or the bulletin board. The best and most direct communication is face to face.

CHAPTER 30

LETTERS, MEMOS, AND REPORTS

By J. C. Aspley

One of my early jobs was with a Cleveland manufacturer of office duplicating machines, criticizing and rewriting promotional letters submitted by users of our equipment. This was a free service, intended to help users get the most from their investment.

These users had bought the equipment with the intention of using the mails to expand their business. But when it came to writing letters that brought back inquiries and orders, they were all thumbs. Their letters usually lacked that "something" needed to make them effective. It was our job to tell them what was wrong and show them how to write letters that would get results.

In order to "process" the hundreds of letters that were submitted and give the prompt service expected, we relied on form paragraphs. This was practical since most of the letters fell into these broad classifications:

1. *"Gimme" Letters*—the kind that were obviously selfish. They asked the recipient to do something for no better reason than that the writer wanted him to do it. They talked "we" instead of "you."

2. *Stuffy Letters*—those that bogged down with stereotyped phrases such as "we beg to state" and "beg to remain." They talked about things that did not matter to the person to whom the letter was addressed. They just did not win or hold interest.

3. *Rambling Letters*—you know the kind; you have to read them twice to find out what they are all about. The mes-

sage is buried in a mass of words—too often words that mean different things to different people.

Then, too, many of the letters lacked direction. They gave the impression that the writer started to write before he knew what he intended to say. And when he did get down to communicating his ideas, he used words to conceal his thoughts rather than to transmit them. Lack of planning stood out in every line.

The problem of an executive, therefore, is simple. To measure up to his responsibility, he must tactfully point out faults that defeat the object of a letter and show the writer how he can make his letters more purposeful, more effective. For in this modern, streamlined age, every letter should be a sales letter—it should sell either goods or good will.

In my work as a correspondence executive, and in building a publishing business by mail, my task has been to train others to write letters that get results. At the same time, and more important, to prepare letters that have won for the business a reputation for integrity and fair dealing.

Almost anyone with a grammar school education can write a passable business letter. But today, an average letter is not good enough. Our letters and reports have to be above average. They have to be effective.

What do we mean by an effective letter—or an effective report? Well, we are talking about a letter that does more than merely conform with the rules of good diction and composition. We are talking about a letter that is more than just a friendly letter (important as that may be). We are talking about a letter that gets and holds attention, that arouses interest, establishes confidence, and has a clear purpose. In short, an effective letter is one that gets action, that *makes things happen.*

If it is a sales letter, we expect it to bring back an order or at least an expression of interest. We don't want it to be like the salesman who calls on a prospective buyer and reports, "I got a pleasant reception and am sure we will get an order eventually." Pleasant receptions, unfortunately, are not negotiable at the bank, and "eventually" is a long time off.

If it is a collection letter, we expect it to do one of two things: Get a check, or get a firm promise to pay on a certain date. At the same time, we want to hold the customer's good will. He might be in a temporary bind for cash, but there is always the chance he will develop into a halo account.

If it is about a complaint, an effective letter does more than smooth ruffled feathers. It tries to turn the complainer into a booster by making him feel kindly toward the house. It avoids irritating expressions such as "I can't understand why you complain," "You must be mistaken," or, worst of all, "I was surprised to receive your complaint." The person who takes the trouble to write about his complaint is really interested in helping your company maintain its record for quality products and good service. Complaints are important; they should be treated that way.

If it is a report we are writing, we can make it more effective by being more objective. Keep it factual. Keep it brief. Assume that the person to whom you are reporting has sufficient intelligence to make his own decisions. Our job is to give him facts, not judgments.

No matter what the purpose of a letter may be, it stands as an advertisement for your company, and especially for the person whose name is signed to it. It is a well-proven fact that in business, today more than ever, we are judged by the letters we write. Our reputation for integrity, business acumen, ability to communicate, and, most important, our understanding of good human relations are all there for everyone to read in the letters we write.

To the recipient of your letters you are the company. It is important that all those in a business organization who correspond with people be instructed in writing letters and reports that project a favorable image of their company to the public.

The Man Across the Desk

The ability to write effective letters depends in large measure on understanding the person to whom we are writing. Imagine he is sitting across the desk. Judging from his letters, what sort of person is he? Is he a friendly fellow or a sourpuss? Is he profit-minded or more concerned with his standing in the community? Is he a know-it-all or a chap who will accept a suggestion gracefully? Is he a penny-pincher who doesn't believe a quality product has everything in its favor, including the price, or is he a free spender?

With a picture of the man across the desk in mind (even though it's skimpy), what is the best way to get him to do what you want done? What is the best way to approach him, the best way to present your case? What is important to him? What benefits (in a sales letter) will influence him? Should you try to lead him, or is he one of those "take-over" fellows who resent anyone else's trying to make up their minds for them?

Those who have studied human nature know that people often fall into categories. They react the same way to a certain approach; they are motivated by the same facts. They think the same, but what they read does not mean the same. That is what makes a correspondent's job interesting and challenging. He is dealing with human nature. And that is why any person who handles correspondence is so important to the growth and welfare of a business. He is a public-relations man, a teacher, and a leader all rolled into one.

Now to Plan the Letter

A good letter needs a good plan. That means giving it some thought *before* you start to dictate. What is the customer's problem? What is the best solution to his problem? What is the key—the heart of the problem?

The heart of the customer's problem is the key to your letter. It is what matters most to your customer and, therefore, matters most to you.

In the army, soldiers are taught to stop and make an estimate of the situation before making a decision. For the same reason, a good correspondent analyzes the situation confronting him, gathers his facts and plans his strategy before he begins to dictate. He knows exactly what he will say. He has all the facts at hand. He does not have to stop in the middle of dictation to do research work.

This is especially important if you dictate to a secretary. It is just plain bad management to have her sit gazing into space while you take off on a fact-hunting safari.

If it is an important letter—and every letter should be important—you may find it useful to jot down the points you intend to cover and the order in which you will cover them. This will ensure your covering every one of them.

If I were training young men on the way up to write letters that would mark them for promotion, I would stress the need to think and write incisively. Get to the main point. Build your letters around it. Stay off side tracks; they don't go anywhere.

To write a really outstanding letter takes study and thought. I know a vice-president of an insurance company who has a reputation for writing exceptionally good letters to his agents. I asked him how he did it.

"Very simple," he said. "I leave the house at 6:30 every morning, get down to the office before the turmoil begins, and go through the morning mail. Routine correspondence I pass to my secretary, who is very good at that sort of thing. Then I study the remaining letters to determine how best to handle each of them.

"First, I underscore those points in the letter that call for an answer. I number these according to the order of their importance. I doublescore the key point—the point I will peg my letter on. When I am ready to begin dictating, I have worked out an effective answer for every letter. If I need supporting material, I get it or have an assistant get it before I start my dictation."

This means a little more work. The few extra minutes we spend thinking about a letter can make our letters a credit to us. We want every letter we write to build and help brighten our reputation for writing effective letters.

Attitude vs. Aptitude

So you are ready to dictate. But before you begin, there is one other thing to be considered. Do you have the right attitude toward the writer of the letter you are about to answer? Your attitude is bound to determine the tone of your letter, and we all know it is not only what we say, but also *how* we say it, that matters.

Some of us anger too easily. We tackle a stack of correspondence with a chip on our shoulder. We pick up a letter written by a customer who has an exaggerated sense of importance. We think: "Now here's where I will put that so-and-so in his place. Who does he think he is, anyway?"

Or we run into a letter that criticizes the company unfairly. We develop a slow burn. "I'll just lay that Little Lord Fauntleroy on his back, but quick." And we proceed to do exactly that.

You may have aptitude, but with a negative attitude you can only lose. While I do not string along with those who hold "the customer is always right," I am mindful that one of the world's largest retail establishments here in Chicago was built upon the policy "Give the lady what she wants." There is no percentage in proving that a customer is wrong and you are right. Give him a chance to save face.

Then there is this matter of humility. However highly we may rate ourselves, let's be careful not to let it show. For the same reason that you dislike a conceited person or a person who goes out of his way to impress you with his importance, customers dislike us and our company when we write as though we were in love with ourselves.

Another bobbytrap to be avoided if you want your letters to make good, is the craving to be amusing and witty. Few people have the same sense of humor. Jokes that go over big on Broadway go over like a lead balloon on Park Avenue. We want those with whom we do business to respect us, to think of us as trustworthy and capable business friends. We don't want them to write us off as the village jester.

One more thing about attitudes: It's wise not to overwork the perpendicular pronoun. It is not only bad taste but also bad human relations.

I got a letter the other day that began with I and had 14 other I's before the end. You knew without being told that there was a man who really loved himself. Because of this evident love for himself, I took a violent dislike to him.

A Word About Style

Some writers worry too much about the way they write and not enough about what they write. They think it is important to have a "style." They study letters by topnotch advertising men and the world's great authors and thinkers to acquire style.

From a literary standpoint, style is important. But a stylist has a tendency to write over the heads of the people he wishes to reach. He dotes on long words and flowery phrases sometimes that make a person say: "Isn't that beautifully put? But will the meaning be understood?"

The best style is based on being yourself. When you write a letter, "put yourself into the envelope." Favor short words, preferably of Anglo-Saxon origin, rather than the less understandable words of Latin and French extraction. In short, write to be understood by even the slowest-witted customer or recipient.

There is a rule of long standing, to write as you talk. This is said to be the best way to give the letter a friendly tone and to avoid stuffy, stiff letters. But don't be a backslapper. There is such a thing as being too friendly.

Training Others to Write Effective Letters

Let's now consider how we can help others—those we supervise—make their letters and reports more effective.

Any of us who have the responsibility for upgrading the letters that go out from our office make two mistakes.

1. We like to believe that when we tell a correspondent a thing once, he understands its importance and can be depended upon to follow through.

2. We approach the problem negatively. We overdo criticism. Criticism tends to frustrate people. Our job is to build confidence in people and stimulate their interest in writing better letters and reports.

One of the principles of apprentice training that came out of World War II was the importance of repetition. Some people are slow to understand. They forget. They are easily confused.

So it was found that to train people effectively you had to: Tell them what to do and why they should do it; show them how to do it; let them do it.

You don't try to stuff them the way you would a sausage. Rather, you lead them step by step toward an objective. You first clear their minds of any preconceived notions they may hold and then proceed to condition them to accept and understand the principles you advocate. Trainees, it was found, then welcomed criticism which they otherwise might have resented.

This procedure calls for a program. Such a program might include group discussions, lectures, training films, and other devices, but the heart of the program should be the periodical review (with constructive criticism) of all outgoing letters.

Have each employee in the training group make an extra copy of all the letters he or she writes during a stated period— say a week. If you are coaching a number of persons, each can be given a different period. That will spread the work for the executive or supervisor. If only a few are being coached, staggering the work should not be necessary, however.

These extra copies come to your desk for "review" (some folks resent criticism). You have previously explained and sold the plan to the group, so they now appreciate the benefits to them personally of being able to write a more effective letter. They want to get ahead. What better starting point is there than being able to write action-getting letters and concise reports?

In some cases, the executive might suggest that a letter be rewritten (even though the original has been mailed). This is good practice.

If group discussions are a part of the program, the executive will find it useful to tally the weaknesses in a batch of letters and make the tally the basis for a brief talk. But again, be constructive. Make it appear easy to write better letters.

Handle the program so that each member of the group gets a feeling of participation. It is his program and to his good.

Another device to get groups of employees interested in better letters is to select one or two especially good letters for group discussion. Underscore those portions of the letter you wish discussed and keep the discussion on target. This flatters the person who wrote the letter. It also offsets the critical aspects of your reviews. You might even give an inexpensive prize—such as a copy of *How to Keep the Fog Out of Writing* (Dartnell Press)—for the best letter of the month. It all adds to the fun and keeps up group interest.

Such a program means time and effort, but it is worth it. The letters that go out from your company are an important phase of its public relations. Thousands of dollars are spent to build the best possible image of a company in the minds of customers and the public. A letter-improvement program, such as we are considering, does the same sort of job for your business at very little cost. A company, no less than a man, is judged by its letters. Better letters mean better business.

CHAPTER 31

IMPROVING READING ABILITY

By Hilda Whitener Yoder

It is said of Theodore Roosevelt that his intake of print was swift and photographic—that he could span a double-page spread of a new book in a minute and a half and then quote the text almost verbatim. The story is told by Edward Weeks, editor of *The Atlantic Monthly,* that in Budapest in 1910 Roosevelt had to speak at a dinner attended by Hungarian statesmen and noblemen. He launched into Hungary's past, citing names of medieval heroes and their exploits. The performance brought the audience to its feet.

After the banquet T. R.'s secretary asked him when he had found time to read up on that subject. "I didn't bone up on it," said T. R. "When I was in college I read a book on Hungarian history, and as I stood up before that group, the book seemed to open before my eyes."

Perhaps we can't all be Teddy Roosevelts; few are blessed with his photographic memory. But the chances are that executives who are stuffing their briefcases with more and more material to take home could drastically cut down on much of this homework simply by developing more efficient reading habits.

Hundreds of articles have been written about reading during the past few years. Writers have belabored every phase of the subject, from the way in which a child is conditioned by his parents' attitude to the reading efficiency of the mature executive.

This concentrated attention has been of benefit, for out of it has come a body of data useful in self-evaluation. However, nearly every article on the subject in popular magazines and books stresses reading speed alone. This is an oversimplification. The ability to read is the end result of other techniques, and those who are professionally engaged in improving reading are somewhat appalled at the emphasis on correcting the average person's reading habits by learning to read *fast*. There is considerable justification, however, in the average executive's complaint that reading still takes too much time.

Let us look at some facts about reading speeds: During attendance at school, one's reading speed begins with 50 words per minute reached during first grade. The average rate for college freshmen is 350 words per minute. But some of us never attain this speed, and many of us who do, fail to retain it. If your speed is now 180 words a minute, then consider the number of years that you have been reading material of increasing difficulty with a steadily growing handicap.

Test Yourself Here

To evaluate your speed, try a little test at this point: The 500-word selection immediately following, between the headings "Starting Time" and "Finishing Time," is of standard difficulty as found in newspapers and general magazines. It largely follows an interview with the present writer for *Business Week* and highlights some of the problems of reading speed and comprehension confronting businessmen. Before reading it, note the time you start and then enter your finishing time at the end of the example. Consult the accompanying table to find your reading speed.

Starting Time ....

Chances are good that you are stuffing your briefcase with more and more material to read at home. In virtually all middle- and top-level jobs, the flood of "required reading" has steadily increased.

Yet most businessmen could cut drastically—or even eliminate—the amount of such work they do take home. The secret: developing more efficient reading habits.

Statistics show that most businessmen read below the college level—attaining only 300 words a minute or less, and that their comprehension of the material is far too low. And 90 percent of them could at least double their reading speed and —much more important—boost their comprehension considerably.

To a slow reader, increasing speed and comprehension may seem impossible. He is likely to feel that the ability to read fast is a God-given talent possessed by only a favored few.

Actually, the rapid reader has received no such mystic blessing. The way a person reads is nothing more than a habit. And the slow, poor reader, by study and application, can usually become a good reader.

One way to change your reading habits is to go to a good clinic or teacher for a special course. This may well double— or even triple—the average executive's reading speed. One reason for this is the fact that methods for analyzing reading faults have been developed on a highly scientific plane. Here is just one example: The actual movements of your eye can be photographed, giving a graphic picture of such things as the number of fixations per line of type, backtracking, length of time to read a specific number of words.

But can you improve your reading skill on your own, without going to a professional source? Yes—if you are willing to study and practice. Just reading a book about how to improve your reading won't work, any more than just reading about exercise will strengthen your muscles.

Here are the broad principles involved: Authorities have found that most businessmen are likely to be perfectionists in reading—they read every word because they are afraid of missing something. Reading whole thoughts and phrases increases both speed and comprehension.

The best way to do this is by reading material of about standard difficulty, such as most popular magazines or light novels. Time yourself, see how much you have read in, say, 10 minutes. Next day, read the same length of time, but try to read more text.

440

While doing this, concentrate on moving forward. Don't regress, or look back, trying to pick up something you missed. You will have trouble getting the full meaning at first, but the important thing is to jostle yourself out of old habits.

One way to test your comprehension is to have someone ask you questions on what you have just read. A better way is to do this reading from books specifically designed to improve your skill. They include tests on comprehension.

Finishing Time ....:

Minutes	Words per minute
5	100
4½	110
4	125
3½	143
3	166
2½	200
2	250
1½	333
1	500

Does your ability to comprehend what you read need some improvement? More will be said on this point later. However, to evaluate your comprehension of the test material you have just read, circle the answers to the following true-false questions about it. (Answers are given on page 442.)

1. To cut his homework, a businessman needs to develop better reading habits.   T   F

2. Ninety-nine percent of businessmen can improve their reading.   T   F

3. Good reading is a matter of good habits.   T   F

4. Reading habits can be analyzed.   T   F

5. Reading techniques can be improved just by knowing your difficulties.   T   F

6. Perfectionists who must note every detail tend to be poor readers.   T   F

7. Reading can be improved by looking for whole thoughts and phrases. T F

8. The best way to improve reading is to choose for daily practice a book you find difficult to read. T F

9. Looking back for a missed idea is a "must." T F

10. Comprehension can be developed by reading books written for this purpose. T F

Answers to comprehension test: 1-T, 2-F, 3-T, 4-T, 5-F, 6-T, 7-T, 8-F, 9-F, 10-T.

Allow yourself 10 points for each question you answered correctly, and consult the accompanying table for your rating:

Score (Percent)	Rating
60 or lower	Poor
70	Passing
80	Good
90	Very good
100	Excellent

Reading Habits

There are perfectionists who compulsively insist on seeing and analyzing every word. This trait is admirable in, say, a proofreader, since his exacting profession consists in precisely this duty. But it is wasted effort in a magazine editor constantly dealing with piles of manuscripts.

In the course of a corrective session, one such executive was strongly advised to give his hair-shirt conscience a rest— counsel which, after the first guilt feelings were over, he was happy to take.

On the other hand, sloppy attitudes toward a job are likely to produce sloppy reading habits. The unconscientious reader hits only the high spots and shows poor comprehension of what he is reading. This defect is found particularly in students who only scan assigned reading and attempt to cram at the last minute. Pressure can produce results, but they are likely to be short-term. Everyone knows of lawyers who are able to duel with expert witnesses on apparently equal terms but 10 days later cannot answer the simplest question on the specialty they briefly had to master.

Perhaps the greatest complaint a reading-improvement specialist receives from all types of students is, "I can't seem to concentrate." One can only reply that the reading-concentration relationship is a two-way street, and that one of the great services of improved reading performance is a concomitant increase in powers of concentration.

Admittedly it is an uphill battle today, when so many of the tangibles and intangibles of urban living tend to break down concentration; but it is a fight that is well worth waging.

Comprehension

In training for improvement in reading, speed should initially be definitely de-emphasized. This sounds strange to those who have been dazzled by advertisements for some mechanical device which purports to be able to double or triple their reading speed, or to guarantee a fantastic rate, such as a thousand words a minute.

In promotional literature of this sort, the importance of the material to be read, and the understanding of it, invariably go unmentioned. The basis of most such aids is a shield which goes down the page, forcing the reader to keep ahead of it. This ignores the fact that the eyes must make a certain number of fixations or stops in each line. Thus harassed, the student has no time to assimilate material. He becomes utterly confused and either gives up the effort at self-improvement in short order or ruins his reading habits completely.

The sound teacher puts emphasis where it belongs—on comprehension. Speed can come later. The student driver is hardly ever taught the use of controls when the car is going full speed.

Your reading comprehension will, of course, be most complete if you have a background of knowledge and experience in the subject matter to which you are addressing yourself. Such background will naturally determine the degree of complexity which any material has for you and the choice of, say, the advanced or elementary reference material to which you turn. But, assuming that enough familiarity exists to make the subject meaningful, there are certain rules you can follow in training and practicing for comprehension.

In the case of a book, for example, your first objective should be to find the central thought of each chapter, section and paragraph. To do this, you should, as William D. Baker puts it, make use of all of the author's "signposts." Many of these signposts are obvious—for example, the chapter heads. Divisions within chapters are usually clearly defined by subheadings, set off in special type. Further subheads are usually indicated typographically. Another kind of signpost is the

* * *

No man can pretend to be educated who has not read, and who does not continue to read, consistently.
—*Frank C. Baxter*

* * *

paragraph topic sentence, often the first sentence in the paragraph.

Mortimer J. Adler puts it this way: "Every book has a skeleton hidden between its boards. Your job is to find it." Make use, Adler says, of all the help the author gives you—preface, table of contents, chapter introductions.

As you read, keep the author's major and minor themes in mind, and try to determine what is essential to his argument and what is merely added as supplementary and reinforcing information. And, above all, keep an eye out for generalizations, lest by quick surface reading you be misled by an opening broad statement whose meaning is greatly narrowed by the specifics in the body of the text.

This is, of course, a hazard of newspaper reading, where the attention-getting headline and opening teaser paragraph may give an exaggerated and misleading impression. Many readers skim over great quantities of the newspaper and magazine material in a frantic attempt to read everything they feel they should know in order to achieve the shifting and illusive goal of being "well informed." What happens is that they may get a sensational version or erroneous interpretation of what is really being said.

Retention

Retention of material read is obviously linked to comprehension and to the degree with which you can associate it with something in your experience.

Experts in reading improvement have found that a most effective procedure to guard against forgetting is that of "recall"—stopping reading periodically to check memory. Experiments with college students have shown that even though this procedure seems to slow a student's progress, it will lead him to recall more with greater accuracy. And if he thinks through the ideas in his own words, rather than in those of the author, the additional thinking will strengthen his recollection and, at the same time, will check his understanding of what he has learned.

Barely learning a formula or a vocabulary means that it will soon be forgotten. But, as Glock points out, "overlearning"—that is, further practice checks on memory and understanding even though you believe learning is adequate for the present—increases remembering many-fold. Students who cram, who learn something only for an examination and think no more about it, lose what they have learned very quickly.

These remarks on recall may seem a contradiction of the statement made in our timing example about concentrating on moving forward without trying to pick up something you missed. But the point there was to jostle you out of poor reading habits and test your comprehension at the end of any piece you chose for timing. And all of this, of course, leads up to the important step of choosing a method of reading to suit the purpose at hand.

Before reading an article, you must decide what your purpose is in reading it, then select the method of reading. If you are reading to kill time, you can read rapidly without noting details. If you are reading technical material, slow reading may be the only sensible manner.

Methods of Reading

A skilled reader should be able to read short stories, novels, and other light material at 400 to 500 words per minute. But, when you attempt to memorize facts or understand formulas, you should probably read at the rate of 100 to 200 words per minute. For a textbook which is not especially difficult, or for an editorial, you should probably gear your reading to 250 to 350 words per minute.

A very rapid rate can be attained—several thousand words per minute—when skimming an article to find a single phrase or to decide whether it is material which you would like to read carefully.

The most important technique in rapid reading is to read thoughts instead of words. This takes a great deal of practice, especially for a meticulous person and for the perfectionist who, as already mentioned, feels he must hang on to every word. For practice, use easy material such as short general-interest magazine articles. Read them rapidly and then recall what you have read. Force yourself by timing.

The idea is to teach the reader to make fewer stops, taking in more words at one time. Poor reading may be compared to trying to run fast with very short steps, a process which is tiring and ineffectual. A person gains more speed if he takes longer and more rhythmical steps, consequently covering more territory. A good reader does this naturally, but a slow reader must be taught.

He must learn to select the important words on each line, ignoring those words which have been repeated and those which do not contribute to the meaning of the article. This should be done aloud in the beginning until the technique is firmly established.

Do not confuse this method of reading with skimming or prereading, which is reading only certain phrases or sentences. It is to be used for thorough, accurate reading which should also be done speedily.

CHAPTER 32

PUBLIC SPEAKING

By Ralph C. Smedley

You never know when lightning may strike you—and you never know when you may be called upon to make a speech or "say a few words." It is an ever-present danger.

Every time you attend a meeting at which speeches are in order, you risk being called upon to make a few remarks about something or somebody. And in these days of multiplied meetings of numberless organizations, committees, and groups—business, professional, civic, community, church, charity, and all the rest—the only sure defense against having to "say a few words" is to keep away from such assemblies.

In view of the executive's constantly expanding horizon of responsibilities toward his community as well as his job, however, such a course of escapism is hardly feasible or desirable. It would require a rare ingenuity to be able to shun all the dangers of making a speech that become part and parcel of the executive life.

Besides, what fun would there be in becoming a recluse—an avoider of meetings, an "assemblyphobiac"?

There is only one solution, then, that will bring an executive "safety" and peace of mind so far as this matter of making a speech is concerned, and that is: *Always be prepared.*

It is said that Napoleon, during his campaigns, had the habit of conferring unexpected honors upon any of his soldiers who performed a deed of heroism and thus won his favor on the battlefield. Any of them might suddenly find himself called before his commander and dubbed a Knight of the Legion or a field marshal without a word of warning. As a result, the story goes, many a man carried a field marshal's baton in his knapsack so as to be ready if and when the time came, for every man counted himself a potential field marshal.

In similar manner today, every business or professional man should prepare himself—at least in some measure—to be able to "do himself justice" when called upon to speak. Even if he is never called upon, he will have the comfortable feeling of knowing he is ready when the occasion arises. It's like money in the bank.

Here's a suggestion, therefore. Every time you attend a meeting at which speeches or discussions are in order, give yourself a treatment. As you enter the room, or as you unfold your napkin at the table, say to yourself: "Suppose I were suddenly called upon to say something to this crowd. What could I say that would be worthwhile, or that would at least not sound imbecilic?"

"That's silly," you may reply. "There is absolutely no reason why I should be called on to do anything but listen to some dull speeches."

Opportunities Abound

But it is just barely possible that the chairman might have a brainstorm and call on you to report for the committee on elimination of traffic hazards at the intersection of Hogan's Alley and Rocky Road. You are a member of the committee, which has done nothing so far. How would you talk yourself out of a rebuke for being a do-nothing?

Or a discussion might come up on a proposal to increase club membership dues, a proposal to which you are strongly opposed. Will you keep silent, reserving your comments until you get outside the room? Will you let the others go ahead and adopt an unwise course just because you think you can't talk?

A Speaker in Spite of Yourself

Actually, you don't have to mount a platform and address a large audience in ringing tones to be a speaker. You are making speeches every time you engage in conversation.

448

Since you are a speaker in spite of yourself, you ought to try to be as good a speaker as you are capable of being—for the good of those with whom you converse. It is just as wrong to bore people in conversation as it is to bore them with dull utterances from the platform.

Thus you can see how favored you are in having a wonderful chance to become a competent speaker, painlessly and practically, through training yourself in your daily conversation. Your best conversational style may be your best style for public address, for most of the public speaking we hear is essentially "amplified conversation." This being so, you can practice your speaking whenever you talk.

Every conversation is a public speech. The size of the audience does not matter, whether it be one person or a hundred, so long as the speaker has something to say. Of course, when one addresses a large group, the voice must be raised so as to be heard at a greater distance, but the words and the sentences should be well chosen and well arranged in either case.

You are a public speaker, therefore, whether you realize it or not. You must communicate your ideas, your thoughts, or they get nowhere. For your own sake, you must learn to communicate *well*. In a word, you must learn to speak for yourself. If you can't or won't, you are going to lose out on many an occasion.

Upset by Stage Fright?

Stage fright is a common malady. But what are you afraid of? You can face an individual and talk without fear or nervousness. You can talk with two or three persons free from embarrassment. At just what point does your course fail? Try a case study on yourself.

Do you get stage fright when the group around you increases to six, or to eight, or to ten? If you are not keeping count or telling yourself that you are making a speech, probably the presence of 15 or 20 people listening to how you caught the big fish, how you made a hole in one, or how you landed a big contract with a reluctant customer will not raise your blood pressure by so much as a nickel's worth.

This may serve to show you how foolish and unnecessary it is to become disturbed when you face an audience of any size. A crowd is made up of individuals. You could talk to any one of them, or any half dozen of them, without fear. Talk to them, then, as individuals. If you can face one man and win an argument, you can just as well face a hundred and come out victorious.

Having ideas in your mind is like having money in your pocket. It is good in itself, and it has potential value when shared; but money buys nothing so long as it is kept in isolation. Only when it is put into circulation, offered in exchange for something, does cash prove its worth.

It is exactly the same with your thoughts. They become really worthwhile when they are shared, exchanged with others.

The idea is well expressed in the old, familiar analogy: If I have a dollar, and you have a dollar, and we trade dollars, each of us still has a dollar; but if I have an idea, and you have an idea, and we trade our ideas, then each of us has two ideas instead of just one.

If you are a normal human being, then, living in normal surroundings, you must be a talker. That is inescapable.

Since you must talk, you will want to do it as well as you can. Your improvement in speaking depends largely upon your understanding of, and use of, a few fundamental facts. Therefore, I think our best approach is to list some of the various occasions on which you may expect to be called upon to "say something" and briefly discuss each of these in turn. Most of them will permit you sufficient notice for some preparation, but a few of them may come without warning. Your only safety lies, once again, in being prepared.

The Speech of Introduction

This is something which may "happen" to any man or woman in these days of multiplied organization. You may be serving as chairman or member of a program committee, or you may be a friend of the speaker; there are all kinds of circumstances that might lead to your being asked to make an introduction.

Introducing someone, however, is not always such an easy matter if you are to do it properly and effectively. You have seen many a speaker handicapped by an inept introduction. Nothing of that sort must happen when you are performing. And nothing of the kind *need* happen if you will take the trouble to prepare yourself to a reasonable extent. Now is the time to prepare, before the fatal moment arrives.

The speech of introduction should be short. Rarely should it last more than one or two minutes. The introducer is not expected to make the speech of the day, and if he carries on for

*   *   *

I think I know something about what an American audience will listen to, and how they want it said. And there is nothing whatever about it that a man worthy to bear important business responsibility cannot learn to do if he will. Practice is all that is required, starting with small occasions, and building up to large, always assuming of course that the man in question has something to say. There is really only one trick to the trade and that is to be yourself at all times and let the amplifier do the rest.

—Clarence B. Randall

*   *   *

three or four minutes, the audience may easily become restive, and someone may call out, "Say, when are you going to turn the speaker loose?"

The more important and better known the speaker, the shorter should be the introductory remarks. Thus, when the President is presented to make a speech, all you hear is, "Ladies and Gentlemen, the President of the United States." If you are introducing some really big shot, one whose name is a household word, you need not give him a buildup. His name and reputation will do more than all your words of introduction.

In framing an introductory speech, ask yourself what the audience really needs or wants to know about the speaker and the speech. What would *you*, as a listener, want to know?

First, what he is going to talk about. Second, we would like to know why he is to talk on that particular subject. Third, who is he, and how does he happen to be talking about this topic?

These three items are essential. We do not especially care to know where he was born, where he attended school or college, whether he is married and how many children he has unless these points of information are directly related to the subject and the occasion.

If he were to talk on youth problems, or juvenile delinquency, or on our educational system, it might be worthwhile to mention that he is the father of several young children; but if he is lecturing on some business subject, it would be more in order to mention that he has had years of experience in that field or specialty.

When you plan the introduction, list the things you might say if you had 10 minutes for your talk. Then eliminate everything that is not essential, and condense that which must be said to cover the three points listed above. You will be amazed to find how little wordage really is necessary.

Avoid stilted forms and routines. Don't start out, as one man did, by saying, "It gives me great pleasure to have the pleasure of introducing our distinguished speaker of the day this evening . . ."

The audience is not interested in your pleasure or privilege. The listeners want to know what the chap on the platform with you is going to talk about, why he is qualified to talk on that subject, and what his name is and occupation or connection. When you have told them this, speaking clearly and distinctly so that all may hear, you will have done your duty.

Besides striving for brevity, be sure of two things. Be very certain that you know how to pronounce the speaker's name, and that you have his subject clearly in mind.

There is an old story about William Jennings Bryan, dating back to his young manhood, when he was not so widely known.

The chairman spoke in glowing terms about this brilliant young man who was to entertain them, and then, when he came to the critical moment, he hesitated, and leaned over to Mr. Bryan to say, "Excuse me, please, but do you talk, or sing?"

I had a similar experience some years ago, when the man who introduced me suddenly forgot my name, of all things. It *does* happen.

There is also the introducer who starts out with, "Our speaker is so well known that he needs no introduction," and then talks on for five minutes, giving the speaker just what he does not need—a lengthy buildup.

One rather inspired chairman turned the tables on speaker and audience by introducing the audience. He explained that the speaker was well known to all those present because of his notable work and because of the wide publicity he had received, but that the audience was quite unknown to the speaker. Therefore he claimed the privilege of presenting the audience to the learned speaker.

Somehow, his introduction seemed to put both speaker and listeners on a friendly footing.

And so it appears that the speech of introduction offers a wide range of choice for the chairman. There are few binding rules for him to observe, except the rules of brevity and good taste, and of clearness in making the announcement.

Here is the accepted formula: Answer the three basic questions *What, Why, Who?*

Announce the speaker's name and the title of his speech in your last sentence. Then step back from the speaking position and remain standing while the speaker takes his place. When he says, "Mister Chairman," acknowledge his words with a slight bow or gesture and take your seat. Do not sit down until the speaker is in position, and do not get in his way as he steps forward. Be courteous.

It is just as well to avoid the expression "I give you Mr. . . ." It smacks too much of the professional master of ceremonies. And someone in the crowd might be tempted to respond, "We don't want him!"

The Speech of Welcome

The whole purpose of this kind of speech is to give the guests a feeling of being welcome, and to help them get into the business of their meeting without loss of time or interest.

Probably the time limit for your speech will be set for you. Then it is your obligation to adhere to this limit. If no exact limit is mentioned, you can make yourself popular by setting your own limits for brevity. Plan to speak on some definite point and to be enthusiastic in your delivery.

Speak of the good work being done by the organization or group you are welcoming. When you close, add further assurances of welcome, good wishes for the success of the meeting, and so forth.

Just be a bit careful of the way you word your pleasant sentiments. Do not get into the predicament of the old lady who had considerable company in for what she had hoped would be a short visit. She welcomed them by saying, "Well, we folks are all at home, and we wish you were, too."

The Response

This is a formality frequently observed at the convention or convocation. The response to the words of welcome is given by a member of the visiting organization, who expresses the thanks of his group for whatever pleasant things have been said by the welcomer.

It may well begin with a reference to what has been said, and it may include something about the purpose of the meeting. Whatever the exact content, it should be brief and sincere.

The Speech of Presentation

There are some very important points to be borne in mind when one makes a presentation. This really is a simple and easy kind of speech, provided one knows how to handle it properly.

As a rule, you are informed well in advance that you are "to do the honors." This gives you the opportunity to find out who is to receive the gift, why he gets it, and whether there is some interesting background to be noted. For example, it might be an annual scholarship, awarded to a student because of some achievement. In this case, a sentence or two about the history of the award may be in order, but that is not always required. Of it might be any of a hundred other types of presentations. At any rate here are the points to always keep in mind:

Be sure you know the nature of the presentation and the nature of the award, and make very certain that you know the name of the recipient.

When you speak, explain quickly and in plain terms just how or why the honored one came to merit this gift. If he is being favored because he is retiring from his position after

* * *

All those who undertake public speaking know the feeling well. None who are effective ever fully recover from the butterfly in the stomach just before the introduction, or the tremendous surge of relief when it is all over.
—Clarence B. Randall

* * *

many years of faithful service, this fact indicates the approach you should take. If he has performed some noble and heroic feat, you will take a different line. If he is a student winning a scholarship or other reward for good work in his school, it will obviously require still another approach.

In any case, tell the reason for the presentation.

Then pay attention to the object to be given. You may display it, so that all may see it, if it is large enough to be seen. If it carries an inscription, you may read that. If the object in itself has any special significance, mention this also.

In this connection, it is wise to assure yourself in advance that the gift is at hand, and know just where it is located. You should have it in a place where you can pick it up when the time comes. Don't risk having to walk around a table to get hold of it.

Present the gift directly to the recipient. Speak his name clearly. As you speak, hand it to him, perhaps shaking his hand in congratulations. Then step back and stop talking. He may have something to say in reply.

Especially—and emphatically—do not prolong your speech, and *do not* call on the audience to "give this little fellow a big hand" unless you are deliberately trying to burlesque the proceedings.

All you need do is convey the gift to the recipient, with only so much talking as will explain to the audience what is being given and why, and will express the friendliness and good will accompanying the presentation.

Once more, be sure you know *what* and *why* and *who*.

It is easy to forget the name of the person being honored. As a measure of safety, have his name written on a card which you can hold in your hand, or have it inscribed on the package you hand to him.

Sometimes it may be in order for the recipient of the gift to say a simple "Thank you" and sit down. Frequently he must say more than that.

The natural beginning for such a speech is with an expression of gratitude. Whatever the honor or the gift may be, let the audience know that you appreciate it. Then it is in order to speak of the beauty, appropriateness, usefulness, or significance of the award, and you may very well add words of praise for any person or persons whose thoughtfulness or cooperation helped you to qualify for the gift.

You may properly speak of your determination to carry on with whatever meritorious conduct or work it may be that has led to this happy occasion for you.

Conclude with a grateful repetition of your thanks and then sit down. The entire performance should require not more than a minute or two if you speak well and without hesitation.

Whenever you attend a meeting at which such a presentation is made, watch the speakers involved and try to see how they could improve, or how you could improve on what they say.

456

When your turn comes, be ready at least to say "Thank you" in a sincere manner. That will suffice if you can't think of anything else to say.

Accepting an Office

A similar situation exists when you are elected to an office or when you accept a nomination. Very little needs to be said in most cases, but if something must be said, make it brief and let it be words of appreciation or thanks, with a promise to do your best.

If the occasion is your installation as an officer, there may be need for a little longer, more formal utterance, in the form of an inaugural speech. This may involve a very brief review of the purposes or ideals of the group or organization, or a preview of activities which you believe should be undertaken under your leadership, together with your promise to act with this purpose in mind.

You may outline an inaugural address in three parts, or perhaps four: First, your thanks for the honor and responsibility; second, an outline of the work to be done; third, a promise to do your best to uphold the purposes and traditions of the organization; and perhaps, fourth, an appeal to all the members to join with you "in making the coming year the best, most productive, most useful period that our group (or association) has ever known."

But whatever you say, once again, make it brief. Don't become long-winded.

Approximately the same suggestions apply when responding to a nomination. Fortunately, this does not happen too often, but once in a while it does. If it should ever happen to you, follow this formula: Be appreciative, be gracious, be brief.

Announcements and Reports

Almost anyone can find himself in a position in which there are reports and announcements to be made.

In any organization, all it takes to be appointed to a committee is a willingness to work, and when one is on a committee, reports are a matter of course. Generally speaking, reports and announcements are dull and boring. Yet they need not be.

When an announcement has to be made, it can be made clearly and concisely. Those who hear it are primarily concerned about *what, where, why, who,* and *how.* They don't want to listen to a long speech, and any display of your own cleverness should be quite incidental. Your business is to inform them of the facts. For example:

"The meeting which was scheduled for next Friday evening at the Community Center has been changed to next Monday evening, the 15th, because conflicting engagements made it impossible to secure a proper meeting place or the attendance of many of our members at the Friday evening time and place. You are requested to be on hand at 7:30 next Monday, ready to take part in the discussion of . . . ."

That covers it, and there is no room for doubt in the minds of those who listen. Answer the five questions indicated, and when you have given the answers, plainly stated, stop talking.

The report on whatever work may be involved is given in similar fashion. It may take more words and more explanation than is required in the announcement.

In this case, state the purpose for which the committee was appointed, or if it is a standing committee, tell what task was assigned to it. Then say that the work has been done, or is in process, and that the conclusions of the committee are ". . . . ." (whatever they are). You may need to include something as to the reasons for reaching the decision or making the recommendations involved.

If it is necessary to have arguments presented in favor of the course that is recommended, it is well to have some other member of the committee do this. If there is a division in the committee's opinions, a minority report may be offered. Indeed, you might be making the report for the minority yourself. In this case, present the arguments on the matter in question, speaking clearly and concisely.

Here, as in all speaking, try to be *clear, definite, easily understood,* and *brief.*

The Complimentary Speech

This may be a eulogy or a farewell, or some other form of praising a person.

The purpose is to pay tribute to some person who is to be honored for some accomplishment or service. Usually, it is a tribute to someone who is dead, but often it deals with some member of an organization or a business to whom honor is due.

One very important consideration is that the speaker should not overdo in an effort to be complimentary. Probably every member of the group or of the business staff knows "good old Joe" well enough to appraise his worth, and if the speaker allows himself to be carried away by his own eloquence, the tribute may turn into a joke. You may recall the old story about the funeral at which the minister was extremely complimentary in his remarks about the man who had passed away.

The wife listened in amazement to the fine things said about her late husband, and then said to her son, "Go up there, Jimmy, and look in the coffin. That doesn't sound like your pa that he is talking about."

Remember that the man being honored, whether living or dead, is a man, after all, and do not attempt to lift him to a place among the demigods. Effusive praise is offensive to the listener. Sincerity is essential, even in a eulogy.

It is a good plan to relate some anecdotes about the one who is honored, always choosing those which will reflect his good qualities and not embarrass him or any members of the audience. All stories must be selected only after careful thought.

Fortunately for all of us, formal eulogies, valedictories, and other definitely complimentary speeches are infrequent, so that we are spared the difficulty of giving such a talk more than two or three times in a lifetime. We may be grateful for this, for it is a difficult speech to do well.

But we may practice complimentary talking in our daily contacts with others. It is a good way to win favor and to inspire others to greater efforts. Show appreciation to all who deserve it.

If you listen to a public speaker who gives you something to remember—information, entertainment, inspiration, or whatever it may be—take time to tell him afterward that you enjoyed his talk, and perhaps you can add an explanation of what you especially liked about it. This will help him, and it will make you feel good at the same time.

The After-Dinner Speech

Most of our speeches nowadays are after-dinner speeches, in that they follow a meal. It may be breakfast, luncheon, or dinner, depending on the group you are addressing, but the type of speech is much the same, whatever the time of day.

This speech may be in a serious or light vein, but the speaker must keep in mind that the audience, having satisfied their hunger, are ready to welcome some pleasant mental stimulation, but may be resentful toward anything which will seriously disturb them.

It has been said that an after-dinner speech is supposed to be "a popular diversion, principally entertaining, so that it requires a joke, a quotation, and a platitude or two." That definition was more timely a generation ago than it is today, however, when so many service clubs and other groups of busy men meet at noon or evening to eat and listen. The after-dinner speech of today may be educational, inspirational, or even controversial, therefore, depending upon the circumstances.

The distinguishing marks of a speech in this category are (a) simplicity, (b) geniality, (c) humorous effects, (d) and, again, that time-honored quality—brevity. The material should, as a rule, be of a popular nature, easy to follow, nontechnical, and informally presented. It is not an oration. It need not make the welkin ring or include oratorical flag-waving. It is best done in the "amplified conversational" style.

CHAPTER 33

REMEMBERING NAMES AND FACES

By Bruno Furst

There is an old proverb that says: "It is not what you eat, but what you digest, that makes you strong. It is not what you earn, but what you save, that makes you rich. It is not what you learn, but what you *remember*, that makes you wise."

Memory is the basis of all knowledge. We know only what we remember. Yet more than 80 percent of all the information we receive by way of our five senses is lost because we are unable to retain it. Think how much wiser we would all be if we were able to retain just 10 percent of the knowledge we lose.

Never sell yourself short on the value or importance of a good memory—or a trained memory. In fact, no aspect of memory is more spectacular and rewarding than the ability to remember people's names and faces. It is hardly a coincidence that those who have acquired this power to an exceptional degree are usually celebrated for it.

Napoleon Bonaparte, for instance, knew every officer of his army by name. He tried to compensate for his unimpressive stature by using showmanship whenever there was an opportunity. He liked to wander through his camp, meet an officer, greet him by name, and talk about a battle or maneuver in which he knew this officer had been involved. He never missed an opportunity to inquire about a soldier's home town, wife, and family; it always amazed the man to see how much detailed personal information about him his Emperor was able to store in his memory.

Since every officer felt Napoleon's personal interest in him

461

—proved by his statements and questions—it is easy to understand the devotion they all felt for him.

In more recent times, as you know, Franklin Delano Roosevelt, James Farley, and many others have based their success in vote-getting partly on their ability to call thousands of voters by their first as well as last name. Farley is said to have been able to recognize as many as 20,000 people and call them by name during political campaigns.

A memory for names and faces is obviously of enormous value to politicians. But it is equally important for the businessman. Ninety percent of his work, whether in his office or outside his actual place of business, has to do with people. And what better way for him to impress people; to win their good will and business; to persuade, influence, and sell them his ideas than to be able to recall their names and faces without more than a second's hesitation? The point hardly needs belaboring.

Some people have a natural gift for remembering names and faces. But such a gift is just as rare as a voice like Caruso's or the painting skill of a Michelangelo. Most of us don't have an innate talent like this. But we may console ourselves with the fact that we can develop a strong memory for anything we put our mind to consistently enough—whether it be for facts, numbers, words, anecdotes, or names and faces.

If you are the least bit skeptical—and many people are—about your ability to improve your own memory, let me cite the cases of thousands of businessmen, lawyers, scientists, housewives, and students who have attended my classes or taken my home-study course and found it possible to improve their memory by several hundred percent.

"I developed my memory to a greater degree than I had ever thought possible," wrote one of my students; and the same idea is repeated in countless letters we have on file. There is no secret to it. All that is required is determination, conscientious work, and mastery of the proper principles of memory retention.

Let's take a look at how you and I can go about this. First of all, we must realize that a person's inability to remember people may be due to one of two entirely different reasons. There is, for example, the man you met three months ago at Brown's cocktail party; later you meet him at Smith's office. His failure to address you by name may be due to either of these reasons:

He may not recall that he ever saw you before; this means a faulty memory for faces.

Or he may recall that he met you, may even remember that it was at Brown's cocktail party, but your name has slipped his mind. This means he has a bad memory for names.

These two types of deficiency are entirely different; it is obvious that their remedies must also be different.

How to Remember Faces

In recognizing faces, it is obvious that accurate observation is of the essence. Whenever we meet a person for the first time, we must observe his face and his entire appearance very closely, noticing especially his eyes, nose, mouth and hair. Skip every feature which is just average or normal and regard those which are outstanding.

My advice is that you sit down with a friend and observe what types of features you see in his face. Look at him and ask yourself: Is his nose straight, arched, or snubbed? Is his mouth large or small; are his lips full, narrow, or protruding?

After doing this several times with the people you see daily, you will form a valuable habit; you will be apt to observe a new face and apply clues like this automatically whenever you meet a stranger.

There are over 20 points to observe in every face; you can't very well take note of that many, however, and fortunately it is not necessary. It is enough if you remember two or three outstanding points.

The main purpose of this practice is not only to sharpen your observation of faces but also to make you aware of *what* to observe. The principal reason for your bad memory for faces (if you have one) is that all faces look too much alike to you; you don't see the distinctive marks, and therefore you have difficulty.

You must learn to pick out the prominent features, such as a cartoonist seizes upon and exaggerates. A chubby face, a bald, domelike head, and a long cigar identify Sir Winston Churchill for all the world.

As we all know very well, there are no two faces exactly alike with the single exception of identical twins. Therefore your task is to observe the principal characteristics and remember them. You will not find this too difficult if you use the chart. It will soon become second nature, and after a short time you will observe the distinctive marks without even thinking of the chart.

Observation alone is not enough. You must cultivate the ability to describe a person in his absence. Start by describing somebody you know very well; then recall the appearance of a person you have met several times. Finally try to describe someone who has just been introduced to you.

Don't be satisfied with generalities, such as "a bearded old man of 70," or "a young girl with brown hair." Recall as many details as you can.

When you feel sure that you can describe persons adequately, do so immediately in everyday life. Whenever you are introduced to somebody, use a quiet moment and try to draw a picture of him while he is not present.

If you are artistically inclined, use your pencil and draw an actual picture. If you are not gifted this way, be satisfied with a mental picture—that is, "visualize" the outstanding characteristics of a new acquaintance in his absence. Either way, think more of a cartoon than a true-to-life picture. Exaggerate those features that distinguish him from others. Remember, you aren't going to have to reveal your "cartoon" to the person in question.

As soon as you see him again, compare your drawing—the actual or the mental picture—with his appearance, correct your mistakes mentally, and repeat your drawing in his absence. You will soon discover that your ability to construct a picture increases with continued efforts.

When you are able to find the outstanding and distinguishing features in the faces of new acquaintances, you have taken a long step toward your goal. But it is only one step. Your goal is still ahead. You must remember the *name* that belongs to this face.

How to Remember Names

Most of us find we have more difficulty with names than with faces, and the reasons are easy to understand. If we meet Joe Smith for the first time, we see his face but we hear his name, and we know that the impressions we receive through our eyes last longer than those we receive through our ears.

That is the principal reason a face remains longer in our memory than a name. However, there is another explanation, equally easy to understand. Let's assume you meet Joe Smith for the first time, and have a five-minute conversation with him. During the five minutes you are talking with him, you are looking continuously at his face.

Therefore, the impression of his face is constantly repeated and sinks deeper and deeper into your memory. But Joe Smith's name was mentioned to you only once, when he was introduced. You have had a constant repetition of the face, but no repetition of the name at all—another good reason Joe Smith's face remains much longer in your memory than his name.

Fortunately I can again give you six steps for strengthening the impression a newcomer's name makes upon your memory:

1. *Get the name clearly.*
2. *Repeat the name immediately after the introduction.*
3. *See whether or not the name has a meaning in itself.*
4. *If it has no meaning, find an appropriate substitute.*
5. *Repeat the name several times.*
6. *Write the name down.*

CHAPTER 34

POLITICAL PARTICIPATION

By William Harrison Fetridge

What's happened to the American businessman and politics?

Why is it that out of 500 men in the national Congress only a handful identify themselves as businessmen?

Why is it a rarity that a Romney is elected governor of a state? Or a Charles Percy wins a Senate seat?

Why is it that so few businessmen are mayors of our great cities?

Why is it that so few businessmen are active in party councils—and so few even willing to help support able candidates with time, effort or money?

These are questions that have puzzled observers of the political scene for many years, and there are some who still feel there is no satisfactory answer to them.

On this point I disagree, for out of a background of three decades of active political effort, I have become convinced that there are three fundamental reasons for this attitude.

First, businessmen are afraid of politics.

Second, businessmen are just not interested in politics.

Third, businessmen are too preoccupied with their own business to permit their participation in politics.

Let's take a closer look at these three statements.

Is the average American businessman really afraid of politics? My answer can only be *yes,* for I have heard many of them voice concern over what might happen if they really got active in political affairs. They speak mysteriously of threats of building or fire inspections, of tax investigations, of failure to get needed government business, or of other punitive actions that might be taken by politicians they would oppose.

Pure Fantasy

This, of course, is nothing but hogwash. It just doesn't work that way except in remote instances. In fact, just the reverse is true.

The businessman who takes a stand in politics is usually held in considerable respect by political leaders even of the opposite party. Professional politicians may sound like the bitterest of enemies to judge by their political pronouncements, but they are frequently the very best of friends.

At the height of the 1962 political campaign, President Kennedy campaigned in Illinois against Senator Dirksen— yet a few hours afterwards invited him to the White House for the Cuban crisis talks. And you will recall that Mr. Dirksen showed no umbrage at Mr. Kennedy's campaign comments. They were to be expected, he indicated, because that's how politics is played.

In my own case, I have frequently opposed Mayor Daley of Chicago, and he has made some unkind statements about me, just as have I about him. But he has always been gracious and cordial to me personally, and the same holds true for the governor of our state.

Is there something shallow about this? I don't believe so. I disagree, for instance, with my wife on certain matters— sometimes rather eloquently—but I say here and now that I love, respect, and cherish her—even though she is invariably wrong in these instances!

To be specific, I have never seen evidences of any political retaliations against my company or me for my political efforts. On the contrary, I think and hope my company has benefited substantially from my activity. The only case I can recall when anyone tried to use my political efforts against me in a business way fell flat on its face.

The company I headed at the time was bidding on some municipal truck business in a suburb of Chicago that had a Democratic administration. One of our competitor's salesmen introduced the fact that the executive vice-president of Diamond T Motor Truck Company was that arch-Republican W. H. Fetridge. The Democratic leaders of that suburb's administration were so disgusted by this maneuver that they threw the competitor's bid out and bought Diamond T trucks.

Charles Percy, former board chairman of Bell & Howell and the Republican candidate for governor of Illinois in 1964, asserts that he has never seen any evidence of retribution against his company because of his political activities. Bell & Howell equipment is bought regularly in Chicago schools and in other areas dominated by the Democratic party. Percy states that this age-old fear is vastly overemphasized.

Stature Actually Increases

Actually, there is nothing a businessman needs to fear if he becomes active in politics. His business will not suffer—it will probably benefit. There will be no retaliation by the opposition. On the contrary, there will be a new regard for the man and his company—and the man, in turn, will find himself stimulated by the challenge of politics, and he will, no doubt, do a far better job for his company than he has ever done before.

I said also that businessmen are not interested in politics. This is true. I don't mean they fail to read the political news—especially that which has to do with their own industry. And I don't mean they do not have strong opinions on politics and political leaders. Businessmen are among the most articulate and opinionated persons in the world on what is wrong with our political life. But try to get them to do something more than talk!

Will they stand for public office? Heaven forbid!

Will they work a precinct during the next election? They'd love to, but they've a trip coming up, and besides, this is the busy season of the year.

Will they help, then, by contributing to the campaign fund? Well, maybe, but how about a little while to think it over?

Do you think I am overdoing it with these comments? Listen to what Governor William Scranton of Pennsylvania has to say on this subject.

Of 22 people from the business world he had considered for his cabinet, he was shocked to learn that "eleven of them had not voted in the previous primary election; eight of them did not vote when Scranton was a candidate for governor; and five did not vote for President in 1960."

Believe me, it is a wearying task to get businessmen to do anything in politics. Very, very few will ever run for public office. Very, very few will ever work to help elect candidates who will run for office.

And far too few contribute far too little so that their party can run the type of campaign needed for victory.

Sam Witwer, who ran against Senator Douglas of Illinois in 1960, told me a typical story highlighting the abysmal lack of interest of businessmen in politics. One fall, Roy Ingersoll, the great industrialist who headed Borg-Warner for so many years, invited 86 business leaders to talk politics. Fifty of the invitees didn't even have the graciousness to reply; 32 said, "Sorry, can't make it"; only four accepted this distinguished citizen's invitation.

The luncheon had to be canceled for lack of interest.

Only a Few Willing

The truth of the matter is that only a small band of stalwarts can be depended upon. For years and years, I've seen the same people stepping in to do the jobs that must be done.

The rest? Too busy—or maybe, just too uninterested.

Perhaps the answer to all this is the third reason—that businessmen are too preoccupied with their own business to participate in politics. Certainly a prevalent attitude is, "Let George do it—I've got problems of my own."

There is much justification for this attitude of course. It's a wonder, in fact, that we have time to do anything but our own demanding work. Your days are filled, I am sure, as are mine with seemingly unrelenting pressures, tensions, and demands. There are problems always to be solved, work always unfinished. And, no doubt, many of you are required, as I am, to travel extensively, which makes the days at the office even more demanding.

But we not only have responsibilities to our companies. We have responsibilities to our families—yes, and to the communities in which we live, and to this beloved country of ours. Therefore, we must find time for the chores of citizenship in spite of the demands of our jobs.

Professional management groups now recognize this. Thus, managements are now judged not only by their managerial achievements but also by their contributions to civic, political, and charitable activities. The managers who are so immersed in their own businesses that they have no time for their communities are no longer regarded as well-rounded, socially adjusted, or properly oriented for industrial leadership today.

And who is better qualified for leadership in governmental and political affairs?

I think I heard the answer one year at the National Automobile Show Industry dinner of the Automobile Manufacturers Association in Cobo Hall, Detroit. There 2,000 of America's top automobile and truck men sat at a black-tie banquet, a truly distinguished industrial group. One of my tablemates said: "Here are 2,000 highly successful men. I bet 95 percent began their careers without a cent in their pockets."

He was probably right. And men like these, who, by their intelligence, integrity, ambition, and hard work, scaled the heights of industrial leadership in a rough, tough industry are precisely the type who could, I believe, win similar success in politics, and thereby make contributions of lasting significance to this country of ours.

Well, what's the answer?

I think I know. It's simply this: It's up to everyone in top management to stimulate a sense of political responsibility in his people.

470

Encourage Participation

Employees should be encouraged to get into politics—at any level and for the party of their own choice.

Employees should be encouraged to be election judges and clerks—and honored for such service.

Employees should be asked to serve as poll watchers to guarantee honest elections.

Employees who want to run for public office should be given the blessing and needed support to make the race.

Employees should be made to feel that performance in civic affairs is one of the standards by which their future in the company will be judged.

Finally, we in top management must, by example, lead the way by demonstrating our own sincere, active interest in the political welfare of our city, our state and nation.

I think our future is bright, but I believe America's business leaders can make it even brighter by stepping in, rolling up their sleeves and going to work in the political life of our country.

CHAPTER 35

ABOUT AUTOMATION
By Eugene J. Benge

The ingenuity of man has, throughout the ages, sought ways to organize his thought processes or to harness natural forces. On Roman chariots, for example, each turn of the wheels caused a marble to drop through a hole; a count of marbles at the end of a trip made possible a computation of the distance traveled.

We find an almost perfect example of automation as early as 1789. Oliver Evans, a versatile inventor, of Philadelphia, used water power to operate belts, buckets and screw conveyors to process grain into finished flour without human intervention.

In 1804, when Joseph Jacquard of Lyons, France, developed a punched-card-controlled loom, he was mobbed by angry textile workers, and his looms were burned. But the city of Lyons so prospered from his invention that by 1840 a repentant people erected a monument to Jacquard's memory at the very spot of the one-time burning.

During the first half of the present century, thousands of scientific inventions and ingenious applications paved the way for the methods which we have come to call *automation*.

Much Misunderstood Term

Automation is changing the industrial scene so rapidly that you, as an executive, need to learn all you can about it. High degrees of automation have already been reached in the automotive, chemical, petroleum refining, telephone, and utility

472

industries. Automation is also being adopted on a large scale in brewing, cigarettes, coal mining, concrete, electrical manufacturing, food processing, glass making, light bulbs, machine tools, pulp and paper, radio tubes, railroading, roller bearings, textiles, tin cans, toys, and in office practice.

At the moment, it is primarily a tool of survival rather than of greatly increased profits. It means higher wages for those who are employed and lower costs to the consumer—but so far, at least, lower return on invested capital.

Some Features of Automation

Automation, whether in manufacturing or in data processing, includes these four characteristics:

1. Input—of materials, information or energy.
2. Storage—of inputs; or of automatic controls for directing the equipment.
3. Processing—of materials. A machine positions, shapes, assembles, treats, transports, and so forth
   —of information. A machine computes, rearranges or applies logic to basic data.
4. Output—altered materials, information or energy, emerging as products or services; feedback to change processing, if necessary.

Mechanization in the past has lifted muscular drudgery from the backs of men; electronic computers are lifting mental drudgery from their brains. Developments in automation are replacing the hands and senses of the worker, freeing him for what one authority calls "the human use of human beings."

In addition to the much-touted savings of labor, automation offers these important advantages:

1. *Great improvement of quality.*
2. *Shortening of lead time between receipt of an order and shipment of the product.*
3. *Better control of the entire production process.*

There are, however, certain disadvantages:

1. Higher capital investment required.

2. Loss of flexibility in product specifications.

3. A compelling necessity for large sales volume of standardized products.

Authorities in the new field of automation are making fantastic predictions about it. John I. Snyder, Jr., president of U.S. Industries, says, "There is absolutely no doubt that automation will change the world." John Diebold, a specialist on automation, states, "At the end of the automation revolution, probably not 50 years from now, life may be radically different altogether."

Already researchers have pointed out that:

1. The production of goods and services is increasing more rapidly than the number of people at work.

2. The labor force is growing more rapidly than jobs are being created—it may reach 85 million by 1973.

3. As a consequence, the percentage of unemployed in the labor force is slowly rising. It seems that technological change multiplies itself: New machines require more machines rather than more people. Service industries continue to grow, absorbing some—but not all—of the unemployed. Past experience suggests that a severe depression could readily double the number of persons unemployed.

The Electronic Computer

The electronic computer is less than two decades old, but already more than 20,000 have been installed, nearly half of them in business concerns. In this brief period, two generations of computers have been developed, predicated on the vacuum tube and the transistor. Currently we are on the threshold of a fabulous third generation.

We use the term *computer* here to mean any combination of data input, storage, processing and output equipment that uses electronic pulses in some part of the system. Here are some of the things an electronic computer can do:

1. Read a punched card, paper tape, or magnetic tape to take off—or to reject—the information on it.

2. Perform the usual arithmetic operations of addition, subtraction, multiplication or division.

3. By use of a numeric code, combine digits to create letters, and hence words.

4. Store both numeric and alphabetic data, including programming instructions, and recall these data as needed.

5. Compare two numbers as to equality, or reject the lower of two numbers.

6. Merge data from two sources, as from cards and magnetic tape.

7. Signal the operator when there are impossibilities in data, or machine failures, or sometimes when there are errors.

8. Yield various types of output.

Eight Computer Benefits

The principal benefits from electronic data processing are:

1. *High accuracy.*

2. *Rapid data processing.*

3. *Better customer servicing.*

4. *Sometimes a saving in clerical payroll.* For example, the Burroughs Visual Record Computer, with one operator, can do the work of 31 bank clerks.

5. *Information selection for top-management decisions.* For example, a company that has a problem of investing large funds, such as an insurance company, can secure magnetic tape or punched cards that contain significant investment data on over a thousand companies.

6. *Forecasting.*

7. *Management controls.*

8. *Analysis of complex data or formulas.*

Dr. Elmer E. Engstrom, president of R.C.A., asserts that "Barely one-fourth of the practical uses of the electronic computer have been found so far."

A large electronic computer is not a single piece of equipment but is rather an assemblage of various mechanical and electronic units into an integrated system.

Computers are of various sizes, with rentals ranging from one to a hundred thousand dollars a month, depending on the volume and complexity of work to be done. Most companies find that after they have used a computer for a year or two, they are ready to move to a higher level of installation. Hence you should make certain at the beginning that you are undertaking an expandable course of action. Some of the simpler systems do not permit this expansibility.

If you are manager of a small business, you may believe that electronic computing is for large businesses only. Your impression is not necessarily correct, because small- and medium-sized companies can use a computer service bureau, thus getting the advantage of "giant brains" without making large capital investments or hiring additional personnel. Since 387,000 small firms go out of business annually, the survivors must use all facilities at their command to stay in the race.

Some Business Applications

Some typical uses of an electric computer are as follows:

1. *In the office*—payroll, time and material costing, distribution, billing, accounts payable, inventory control, and sales analysis.

2. *In manufacturing*—production scheduling, shop orders, economic lot sizes, standardization, procurement, optimum utilization of production facilities, control of machines on repetitive manufacturing processes.

3. *In transportation*—location of warehouses, routing of trucks, shipping routes, and costs.

4. *In marketing*—market research, sales forecasting, prices, product mix, sales expense, new products, direct costing, location of new sales offices.

5. *In management*—location of a new plant; whether to make or buy manufacturing components; comparing

possible sources of new capital; evaluating possible acquisitions or mergers; analyses of economic data; return on investment; management controls; studies of factual, nonfinancial data.

The next generation of computers will provide man with virtually unlimited information and thinking power. Stored information (including programs) will be 50 to 100 times as great as at present. Because computer operations are performed in millionths (sometimes billionths) of a second, the computer is largely idle when handling one program only. Hence, in the future, a number of programs will be processed virtually simultaneously. This approach is known as "time sharing."

INDEX

INDEX